Microsoft

Microsoft® Windows® Small Business Server 2003 Administrator's Companion

Charlie Russel

Sharon Crawford

Jason Gerend

PUBLISHED BY
Microsoft Press
A Division of Microsoft Corporation
One Microsoft Way
Redmond, Washington 98052-6399

Library of Congress Cataloging-in-Publication Data
Russel, Charlie
    Microsoft Windows Small Business Server 2003 : Administrator's Companion / Charlie Russel, Sharon Crawford, Jason Gerend.
        p. cm.
    Includes index.
    ISBN 0-7356-2020-2
    1. Client/server computing.   2. Microsoft Small Business Server.   I. Crawford, Sharon.   II. Gerend, Jason.   III. Microsoft Corporation.   IV. Title.

QA76.9.C55R866   2004
005.7'1376--dc22   2003071053

Printed and bound in the United States of America.

1 2 3 4 5 6 7 8 9   QWT   8 7 6 5 4

Distributed in Canada by H.B. Fenn and Company Ltd.

A CIP catalogue record for this book is available from the British Library.

Microsoft Press books are available through booksellers and distributors worldwide. For further information about international editions, contact your local Microsoft Corporation office or contact Microsoft Press International directly at fax (425) 936-7329. Visit our Web site at www.microsoft.com/learning. Send comments to *mspinput@microsoft.com*.

Acquisitions Editor: Martin DelRe
Project Editor: Karen Szall
Technical Editor: Nick Cavalancia
Indexer: Seth Maislin

Body Part No. X10-42288

Contents at a Glance

Table of Contents

Part III
Performing the Basic Tasks

Part IV
Performing Advanced Tasks

Part V
Administering Server Components

Part VII
Appendixes

Acknowledgments

We sincerely want to thank the indefatigable Windows Small Business Server MVPs who provided much help and insight—especially Susan Bradley, who made it her business to find answers for us. Thanks also to John Buscher, the Microsoft MVP Lead for Windows Small Business Server.

Jason Gerend would like to thank Ray Fong and David Copeland at Microsoft Windows Small Business Server Product Support Services for their incredible technical acumen and tireless help, especially with 802.1X authentication and L2TP VPN configuration. Thanks also to Liem Nguyen at Dell for generously providing the use of a Dell PowerEdge 1600SC server. Also Amy Martin at Proxim and Anna-Marie Claassen at D-Link Systems for providing WiFi hardware for 802.1X authentication testing.

And all three of us appreciate the great work done by the folks at Microsoft Press, especially Project Editor Karen Szall and Product Planner Martin DelRe, who contributed so much to the pleasures of writing this book and added nothing to the grief level. There is no higher tribute.

Many thanks to Robert Lyon, Technical Editor; Victoria Thulman, Copyeditor; Seth Maislin, Indexer; and to the fine production people who helped produce this book.

As always, we thank past collaborators Rudolph S. Langer and David J. Clark, both gentlemen and scholars.

Introduction

The first time you noticed Microsoft Windows Small Business Server 2003, it might have been because it's such a remarkable bargain. For no more than the price of a mid-level desktop copier, you get Microsoft Windows Server 2003, Windows SharePoint Services, Exchange Server 2003, Routing and Remote Access firewall technology, and five client access licenses. And that's just the Standard Edition.

In the Premium Edition, you get all that plus Microsoft SQL Server 2000, Internet Security and Acceleration Server 2000, and Microsoft Office FrontPage 2003. In both editions, the technologies are optimized to work as a package for the small business user.

But then again, Windows Small Business Server through versions 4.5 and 2000 has always been a bargain. It's unlikely that the price ever stayed anyone's hand from adopting it. However, back in 1999 when we wrote the first book about the first version of Windows Small Business Server, we were obliged to mention its "foibles and blemishes." We even went so far as to describe that first version of Windows Small Business Server as

..[A] product that must be handled with care.... For example, precise attention to hardware requirements is essential and set up must be done "just so" in order to complete successfully. Network faxing and modem sharing are completely new services and ..afflicted with the occasional Version 1.0 eccentricity.

Fortunately, all these reservations have vanished with the appearance of Windows Small Business Server 2003. Although one still has to pay the usual attention to the Hardware Compatibility List, Windows Small Business Server is no longer stressful to install or to use.

The various applications are better integrated than ever before. New tools have centralized and simplified server management, and dozens of wizards are available to help with just about every conceivable task. Best of all, Windows Small Business Server allows companies with as few as three or as many as 75 computers to have an affordable, real client/server network with all the security and efficiencies that implies.

How to Use this Book

Microsoft Windows Small Business Server 2003 Administrator's Companion is a handy reference and assistant for the busy network administrator, whether the administrator is on the scene or accessing the network from another location.

Even though Windows Small Business Server 2003 has automated many, many of the tasks associated with configuring and securing a network, this book is required when you want to do something slightly out of the ordinary—or when you need additional understanding of what a wizard is doing.

Look for book elements such as these:

Under the Hood

Because wizards are so efficient at what they do, it can be very difficult to know what's going on in the background. Sidebars titled "Under the Hood" describe the technical operations being performed by the wizard. These sidebars also include methodological information to help you understand Windows Small Business Server.

Real World

Everyone benefits from the experiences of others. "Real World" sidebars contain elaboration on a particular theme or background based on the adventures of other users of Windows Small Business Server.

Note Notes generally represent alternate ways to perform a task or some information that needs to be highlighted.

Tip Tips are ways of performing tasks more quickly or in a not-so-obvious manner.

Security Alert Nothing is more important than security when it comes to a computer network. Security elements should be carefully noted and acted on.

Caution Don't skip over Caution boxes because they contain important warnings about the subject at hand—often critical information about the safety of your system.

Planning As we stress throughout the book, proper planning is fundamental to the smooth operation of any network. These boxes contain specific and useful hints to make that process go smoothly.

What's in This Book

Microsoft Windows Small Business Server 2003 Administrator's Companion is divided into seven parts. The first six roughly correspond to the developmental phases of a Windows Small Business Server network. The last part has appendixes with helpful information.

- **Part I: Preparation and Planning** Planning and preparation are the *sine qua non* for any kind of network. It comes down to the old saying, "If you don't have the time to do it right, how will you find the time to do it over?" Chapters 1 through 3 are all about doing it right the first time.

- **Part II: Installation and Setup** Chapters 4 through 8 take you through the process of installing or upgrading Windows Small Business Server and performing initial configurations. Also covered are completing the To Do List (a great new feature in Windows Small Business Server) and disk management.

- **Part III: Performing the Basic Tasks** In this part are chapters that cover the day-to-day tasks in running a network: setting up user accounts, arranging the sharing of information among users, adding and removing computers and printers, and backing up and restoring data.

- **Part IV: Performing Advanced Tasks** Chapters 14 through 16 provide insight and information about using Exchange Server, connectivity technologies, and Internet Security and Acceleration Server (Premium Edition).

- **Part V: Administering Server Components** In this part, you'll find chapters about setting up and managing an intranet; plus the basics of Microsoft SQL Server (Premium Edition), the scalable, fast, and versatile data management software.

- **Part VI: Tuning and Troubleshooting** Chapter 20 covers the extensive library of monitoring tools available in Windows Small Business Server, and Chapter 21 is all about how you save your business, your network, and yourself in the face of the many varieties of disaster that can afflict networks.

- **Part VII: Appendixes** At the end of the book are two appendixes. The first is on automating installation and the second is about installing the SQL Server and Internet Security and Acceleration Server components that are part of the Premium Edition of Windows Small Business Server 2003.

There's also a Glossary of networking and SBS-specific terms.

Talk to Us

We've done our best to make this book as accurate and complete as a single-volume reference can be. However, Windows Small Business Server 2003 is large and we are mere humans, so we're sure that alert readers will find omissions and even errors (though we fervently hope not too many of those). If you have suggestions, corrections, or tips, please write and let us know at SBS2003@scribes.com.

We really do appreciate hearing from you.

Part I
Preparation and Planning

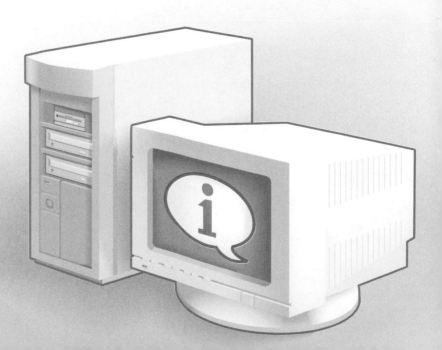

Chapter 1
Looking at the Big Picture

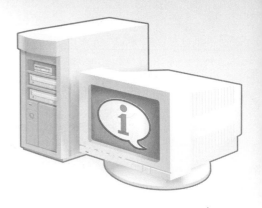

Owners of small businesses say key factors for producing fiscal growth include acquiring new customers, minimizing customer turnover, marketing products and services, and keeping ahead of competitors. You need technology to realize all those factors, but technology is not your business—your business is making a product, selling a product, or providing a service. Every minute that you have to spend doing something else is time taken away from the real business of your business. Plus, the desire to be competitive frequently runs up against the fact of real-world budgets. You need to do more with less—less money, less time, and fewer resources.

Microsoft Windows Small Business Server 2003 is a solution that is comprehensive, easy-to-use, and inexpensive. Microsoft has taken all the components necessary to run a business and combined them into a single, integrated, made-to-work-together package. Easy to set up and even easier to manage, Windows Small Business Server allows you to concentrate more time on what you went into business for.

Windows Small Business Server is available in two versions, so you don't have to pay for what you don't need. Since both versions include Microsoft products that, bought individually, would be considerably more expensive, you get a fully developed business solution that's a bargain to boot.

Windows Small Business Server 2003, Standard Edition, includes Microsoft Windows Server 2003, Standard Edition; Microsoft Windows SharePoint Services; Microsoft Exchange Server 2003; and Microsoft Shared Fax Service. These products give you a fully developed business solution that includes all the essentials: e-mail, Internet connectivity, a preconfigured internal Web site, a shared fax service, services for remote users and mobile users, and wizards to make configuration easy.

Windows Small Business Server 2003, Premium Edition, includes all the preceding features plus Microsoft Internet Security and Acceleration (ISA) Server 2000 for firewall and Web caching services, Microsoft SQL Server 2000 to handle databases, and Microsoft Office FrontPage 2003.

Features of Windows Small Business Server

Although a list of components is impressive—especially when considering the package price—it doesn't really convey the full extent of Windows Small Business Server capabilities. The next sections describe those capabilities and what's special about their use in Windows Small Business Server 2003.

Internet and E-Mail Made Easy

Everyone needs e-mail today and a business without Internet connectivity is viewed as absolutely antiquated. Unfortunately, under normal circumstances, setting up e-mail and an Internet connection is just about as daunting as it ever was. Windows Small Business Server changes all that with tools to make both processes quite painless. For example, the Configure E-mail and Internet Connection Wizard allows you to easily configure the network, set up a shared Internet broadband or dial-up connection, configure firewall services, and customize Exchange Server for e-mail. Use Exchange Server 2003 with Microsoft Office Outlook 2003 and add numerous features including the ability to schedule meetings and hold online conferences.

Chapter 6, "Completing the To Do List and Other Post-Installation Tasks," covers the use of the Configure E-mail and Internet Connection Wizard for the initial set up of e-mail. Details on Exchange Server are provided in Chapter 14, "Using Exchange Server."

Ready-Made Intranet

Most businesspeople know the value of an intranet as a centralized location for users to collaborate and share documents, providing a friendly and easy-to-use framework for teamwork. However, many of those same people have been forced to retreat when faced with the costs of building and maintaining an internal Web site. This particular problem vanishes when Windows Small Business Server is deployed because the product includes a pre-built internal Web site based on Windows SharePoint Services.

The internal Web site comes with preconfigured document and picture libraries, shared lists, and sample content. The site can easily be set up so that users can share documents, read announcements, respond to surveys, make a request to the Help desk, and view the vacation calendar. If the preconfigured elements don't meet your needs, you can remove them or add new ones.

More Info   Chapter 17, "Customizing a SharePoint Web Site," and Chapter 18, "Managing an Intranet Web Server," are all about customizing and maintaining an intranet site for your business.

Quickly Add Users and Computers to the Network

The Add User Wizard in Windows Small Business Server allows you to add a single user or multiple users. The wizard sets up everything a user will need: a mailbox in Exchange; access to shared printers, files, and folders; access to the intranet; a home folder on the server; and a user account in Active Directory. Use a predefined template to add multiple users with settings in common, or create your own template with the Add Template Wizard.

> **More Info**   Adding users with and without a template is covered in Chapter 9, "Users, Groups, and Security."

Client computers can be added to the network simply by browsing to a Web site that contains all the tools for configuring network settings. Client applications included with Windows Small Business Server are installed with the Set Up Computer Wizard, and other software can be set up to deploy to client computers using the Set Up Client Applications Wizard.

> **More Info**   The Setup Computer Wizard is described in Chapter 6 and configuring client software is covered in Chapter 12, "Managing Computers on the Network."

Effortless Remote Access

The number of workers who telecommute—at least part of the time—continues to grow. Whether an organization has a few or many remote users, the mechanisms for access have to be reliable, secure, and easy to use. Unfortunately, this is honored more in the breach than in the observance. In many places, problems with remote access make up the largest single category of calls to the Help desk.

To improve this situation, Windows Small Business Server provides the Remote Web Workplace. Using any device that can connect to the Internet, authorized users can access this dynamically created Web site using a simple Internet address. These users can then read their e-mail, access the company intranet, and connect to their own computers' desktops. Users can download Connection Manager, which automates the process of connecting their remote computers to the company's network, making the whole process quite easy.

> **More Info**   See Chapter 6 for information on configuring remote access. Chapter 15, "Managing Connectivity," discusses remote access administration.

Services for Mobile Devices

Client computers are added to the network using the Setup Computer Wizard. This wizard also configures client computers to support mobile devices. Users of Windows Small Business Server just connect a mobile device to the client computer to access their e-mail, schedule, and task information. See Chapter 6 for more information.

Simple Administration and Management

All the most common network management tasks are made simpler than ever before. As a result, you can spend more time on what you do best (your business) and much less time managing your network.

Set up automatic backups with the Backup Configuration Wizard. This tool and Volume Shadow Copy are powerful ways to protect your data's integrity. You create a backup strategy and Windows Small Business Server takes it from there—on any computer, back up to tape, a network hard drive, or a shared folder. The program will report the success or failure of each backup and even remind the appropriate person when a hard drive is full or it's time to change the tape.

More Info   See Chapter 13, "Backing Up and Restoring Data," for the essentials of backing up and restoring data.

Monitoring and usage tools are easy to set up and reports are easy to read. The Monitoring Configuration Wizard sets up alert notifications, performance reports, and usage updates. You choose when reports are sent and to whom. Authorized recipients can receive notices in e-mail or on a secure Web page on your intranet.

More Info   Chapter 20, "Monitoring and Fine-Tuning Performance," covers monitoring and fine-tuning your network.

You can grant to power users rights and privileges ranging from the very specific to the very general. These users can then take over management chores such as backing up the server, adding new users, or monitoring network performance, or they can perform any other task you want to get out of your hair.

More Info   Chapter 9, "Users, Groups, and Security," is all about granting and restricting rights.

Fax with Fewer Phone Lines

Windows Small Business Server includes a shared fax service that allows faxing from the users' desktops. Faxes can be delivered through e-mail, Windows SharePoint Services, or to a printer. No matter how many or how few faxes your business receives, the ability to share phone lines will reduce the total number of lines needed.

More Info   See Chapter 6 for information about fax services.

Enhanced Security

Of course you want your network to be secure—everyone knows about the menace of hackers, viruses, worms, and other vermin. But how to go about it? Windows Small Business Server includes an internal firewall to protect your network and supports external firewalls as well. The Premium Edition includes Internet Security and Acceleration (ISA) Server, which provides improved security and ease of use beyond that of traditional firewalls. ISA Server includes built-in intelligent filtering of HTTP, FTP, Simple Mail Transport Protocol (SMTP), streaming media, and remote procedure calls. Third-party programs can add the ability to scan for malicious viruses, detect intrusions in real time, improve ISA Server caching, and use additional user authentication methods.

Group Policy allows you to restrict unauthorized software installations, require strong passwords, and ensure that users receive access only to resources they need.

More Info   Chapter 3, "Designing a Network," includes information about planning for security. Chapter 6 has details about adjusting security policies.

Manage Data Effectively

If you have a lot of business information to manage, such as inventory, e-commerce, and data warehousing, you need a way to organize the data to make it useful. The Premium Edition of Windows Small Business Server comes with Microsoft SQL Server, a database that's fast, very reliable, and grows with your business.

Manipulate your data in simple ways, for example, by conducting full-text searches. You can search not only plaintext data stored in relational tables but also formatted documents such as Office and HTML (HyperText Markup Language) documents. Do more complex operations such as developing profiles of your most valued customers and what those customers want. Analyze data, construct business models, and get personalized, real-time reports that can be delivered anywhere, anytime, on any device.

SQL Server will fit your business now and, more importantly, can be scaled up to whatever your future needs might be.

More Info   Chapter 19, "Using SQL Server," covers this topic.

Create Advanced Web Pages

Microsoft FrontPage has long been the preferred application for easy Web page creation. It has been offered as a standalone application and as part of Microsoft Office, adding ever more sophisticated capabilities with each version. Microsoft Office FrontPage 2003 is included in the Premium Edition of Windows Small Business Server.

The delight of FrontPage is that it can be and is used by everyone from true beginners to professional Web developers. Use the pre-made templates and the scripting features in FrontPage 2003 to quickly implement a site with simple interactivity. Create your own templates, each containing multiple content regions, and apply these to pages in your Web site. In fact, you can build, update, and maintain a whole site—even an e-commerce one—without knowing a word of HTML, DHTML (Dynamic HyperText Markup Language), or XML (Extensible Markup Language).

On the other hand, a developer accustomed to writing HTML code will feel equally at home using FrontPage. Complicated, interactive Web sites with precise layouts, imported graphics, scripts, dynamic updating, and other features are cost-effectively constructed using FrontPage. Integration with Windows SharePoint Services and SQL Server makes editing and presenting live data possible—it even allows users to post to the Web using just their browsers.

More Info   Chapter 17 covers using FrontPage 2003.

Online Licensing

Both versions of Windows Small Business Server include five client licenses. If you have more than five client computers, you must purchase additional licenses. You'll receive a paper license from Microsoft (instead of a floppy disk as in the past), and licenses can be activated over the Internet.

Client access licenses can be device-based (one license for each computer) or user-based (one license for each user). The two types of licenses are priced the same. You can even have a mixture of license types, but it's best to choose one type and stick with it to make tracking easier. Chapter 6 covers how to add client access licenses.

Growth Is Good

If you intend to expand your business by leaps and bounds, you might be wondering what happens to Windows Small Business Server when you're no longer a Small Business. In this context, a small business is one with fewer than 50 PCs or fewer than 100 employees.

If it turns out that Windows Small Business Server can't keep pace with the growth of your business, you'll be able to convert to Windows Server 2003 without incurring either major expense or business disruption.

Because Windows Server 2003 is the underlying operating system in Windows Small Business Server, all files, records, and configurations are migrated without change. You lose nothing and gain all the abilities of a Windows Server 2003 domain.

Restrictions on Windows Small Business Server

Because Windows Small Business Server is designed for smaller organizations—and because of its bargain price—you will face specific limits when working with the package. These limits are not recommendations; they're boundaries that can't be transcended.

A Single Domain Controller

All the components of Windows Small Business Server must be loaded on a single machine, the domain controller. You can have other servers such as file servers and print servers, but none of the components of Windows Small Business Server can be run on a computer other than the domain controller.

Under the Hood   The Backup Domain Controller

Only one Windows Small Business Server installation is allowed per domain, but it is technically possible to have a backup domain controller (BDC) on a Windows Small Business Server network. A BDC running Windows Server 2003 provides load balancing and logon capability when the Windows Small Business Server machine is out of service.

You cannot transfer any of the Operation Master roles to the BDC.

Because the server does so much work, you'll need a powerful computer with lots of capacity on which to install Windows Small Business Server.

More Info Chapter 3 provides information about choosing suitable hardware for your network.

Tip If you must have a component of Windows Small Business Server on a separate computer, you can purchase a license for, say, Exchange Server or SQL Server, and install it on a computer other than the domain controller. It will still integrate smoothly with Windows Small Business Server.

A Single Domain

Windows Small Business Server and its clients constitute a single domain. The domain is based on Active Directory, much like a Windows Server 2003 or Microsoft Windows 2000 Server domain, except that it cannot form trust relationships.

Client Limit

Windows Small Business Server comes with five client access licenses (CALs). You can purchase additional licenses up to a maximum of 75, though Windows Small Business Server is designed to work best with no more than 50 users/devices.

The client limit shouldn't restrict you except in the sense that 50 or more clients working off a single server is limiting. You are likely to want to change to a Windows Server 2003 network because of its ability to have multiple domain controllers long before you reach the client limit.

Summary

To be competitive in today's world of commerce, you need the power of technology. You need to find and retain customers, market and sell to those customers, and do all of it better than anyone else. Small businesses have big needs but small budgets.

Windows Small Business Server 2003 integrates e-mail, shared Internet access, fax services, database, remote access, security, Web development and collaboration, and other features into a single package that is easy to deploy and easy to maintain.

The next two chapters provide an overview of networks and specifics on how to design a network that will work for you.

Chapter 2
Networks and Windows Server 2003

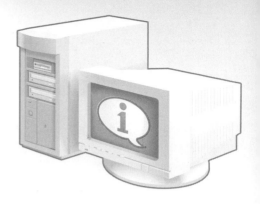

The underlying operating system for Microsoft Windows Small Business Server 2003 is Microsoft Windows Server 2003, the latest version of Microsoft's mission-critical enterprise operating system and an appropriate choice for a small business suite of server products. Your business might be small compared with, say, Microsoft, but that doesn't make it any less mission critical to you and your employees.

In this chapter, we provide some general information about servers, clients, and networks to give you the background you'll need for later chapters.

How Does a Network Work?

If you've ever made a phone call or used a bank ATM, you've already experienced using a network. After all, a *network* is simply a collection of computers and peripheral devices that can share files and other resources. The connection can be a cable, a telephone line, or even a wireless channel. The Internet itself is a network—a global network made up of all the computers, hardware, and peripherals connected to it.

Your bank's ATM consists of hardware and software connected to central computers that know, among other things, how much money you have in your account. When you call cross-country or just across town, telephone company software makes the connection from your phone to the phone you're calling through multiple switching devices. It's something we do every day without thinking about the complicated processes behind the scenes.

Both the telephone and the ATM networks are maintained by technicians and engineers who plan, set up, and maintain all the software and hardware; however, the assumption underlying Windows Small Business Server is that there isn't anyone dedicated to maintaining the network and its operating system full time. Instead, Windows Small Business Server provides the Manage Your Server interface—a unified administrative interface designed to meet the needs of small businesses and simplify your choices.

Servers

A *server* is a computer that provides services. It's really just that simple. The difficulty comes when people confuse the physical box that's providing the service with the actual service. Any computer or device on a network can be a server for a particular service. A server doesn't even need to be a computer in the traditional sense. For example, you might have a "print server" that is nothing more complicated than a device that's connected to the network on one side and to a printer on the other. The device has a tiny little brain with just enough intelligence to understand when a particular network packet is intended for it, and to translate those packets into something that the printer can understand.

In Windows Small Business Server, a single computer acts as the physical server box, but that box provides a variety of services to the network beyond the usual file and print services. These services meet your core business needs, including authentication and security; e-mail and collaboration; an Internet connection; sharing; faxing; and, in the Windows Small Business Server 2003, Premium Edition, database services and a full featured firewall.

Clients

A *client* is anything on the network that avails itself of a server's services. Clients are usually the other computers on the network. The client machines typically print to network printers, read e-mail, work on shared documents, connect to the Internet, and generally use services that aren't available on their local machines. Clients aren't usually as powerful as servers, but they're perfectly capable computers on their own.

Media Connecting Servers and Clients

Another portion of a network is the actual network media that connects the various servers and clients to each other. This media includes both the network cards that are part of the server or client and the physical wire (or wireless connection) between them, and the various other components involved, such as hubs, routers, and switches. When all these media components work as they should, we pretty much forget about this portion of the network and take it for granted. But when a failure of one component of the network media occurs, we face troubleshooting and repairs that can be both frustrating and expensive—a good reason to buy only high-quality network components from vendors and dealers who support their products.

Network Operating Systems

On an ordinary PC, the role of the operating system is to manage the file system, handle the running of applications, manage the computer's memory, and control the input and output to attached devices such as cameras, printers, and scanners. A network operating system (NOS) expands that role, managing the following:

- Remote file systems

- Running of shared applications

- Input and output to shared network devices

- CPU scheduling of networked processes

When the network operating system is distributed among all the connected computers, as shown in Figure 2-1, the result is called a *peer-to-peer network*. Microsoft Windows 98 and Microsoft Windows Me, operating on their own, have this kind of a network.

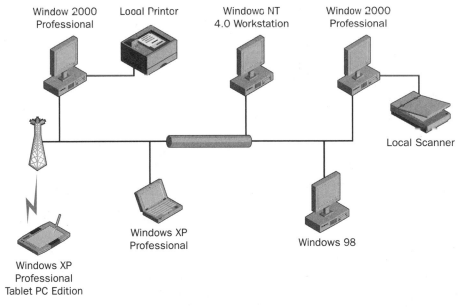

Figure 2-1.   *A peer-to-peer network, which has no central server or management.*

Windows Small Business Server, as shown in Figure 2-2, is a *client/server-based network*—a single, centralized server and multiple clients. The server is the central computer on which most of the network operating system runs, and the client comprises the computers that use the resources managed by the server.

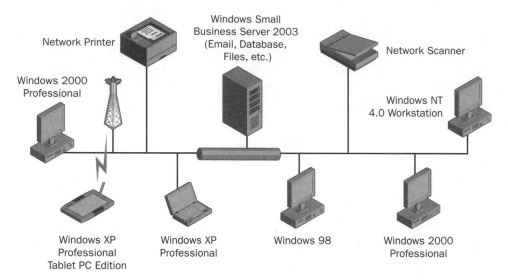

Figure 2-2. *A client/server network, which has a central management and resource server.*

Differences Between Servers and Clients

Even though the underlying hardware for clients and servers in a Windows Small Business Server network is similar, the operating systems they run and the roles they must play are quite different.

Servers Use Network Operating Systems

Because the Windows Small Business Server has to supply services to as many as 75 users, and you're depending on it to run your business, a high-powered, robust operating system and highly reliable hardware are essential. When your users are relying on a server to get their work done and keep your business running, you certainly don't want frequent failures—you don't even want to have to reboot!

In addition to supplying print, file, or other services, the network operating system has to provide network security. Different businesses and organizations have varying security needs but *all* must have some level of data protection, so the system must offer a range of configurable security levels, from the relatively non-intrusive to the very stringent.

Clients Use Workstation Operating Systems

Like other computers, client machines on a network need an operating system. However, a client operating system doesn't need to be as sturdy as the operating system running on a server. Rebooting a workstation can be a pain for the user but doesn't usually disrupt anyone else's work.

A client machine also doesn't require as robust a built-in security system as a server because security is provided by the network operating system and managed by the server. However, the more advanced the client operating system is, the better it is at "cooperating" with the network operating system in areas of security and sharing over the network.

On a Windows Small Business Server network, clients can run Microsoft Windows 95, Windows 98, Windows Me, Windows NT Workstation, Microsoft Windows 2000 Professional, and Microsoft Windows XP Professional as their supported operating systems.

Features of the Windows Operating System

The Windows Server 2003 operating system that underlies Windows Small Business Server is a proven, reliable, and secure operating system with the features to run a business of virtually any size. With Windows Small Business Server, the operating system and server components have been specifically tuned to support from 5 through 75 users in a small business environment, with all the server functions residing on a single machine.

Some of the features that make Windows Server 2003 ideal for a small business server include:

- Easy installation that is almost fully automated in Windows Small Business Server
- A robust yet easy-to-administer security model using Active Directory
- The NTFS file system that fully supports long filenames, dynamic error recovery, shadow copies, user space limitations, and security
- Support for a broad range of hardware and software

Domains and Workgroups

Microsoft provides for two different networking models in their operating systems: workgroups and domains. Windows Small Business Server supports only the domain model of Microsoft networking, but it's worthwhile to go over why this decision makes sense, even in a very small business.

Do Workgroups Work?

Microsoft introduced the concept of the workgroup with Microsoft Windows for Workgroups. The *workgroup* is a logical grouping of several computers whose work or users are connected and who want to share their resources with each other. Usually, all the computers in a workgroup are equal, which is why such setups are referred to as peer-to-peer networks.

Workgroup networks are appealing because they're easy to set up and maintain. Individual users manage the sharing of their resources by determining what will be shared and who will have access. A user can allow other users to use a printer, a CD-ROM drive, an entire hard drive, or only certain files. The difficulty arises when it's necessary to give different levels of access to different users. Passwords can be used for this purpose in a limited way, but as the network gets larger, passwords proliferate and the situation becomes increasingly complicated. Users who are required to have numerous passwords start using the same one over and over or choose passwords that are easy to remember and therefore easy to guess, and there is no way to enforce a minimum password quality level. If someone leaves the company to work for your biggest competitor, passwords have to be changed and everyone in the workgroup has to be notified of the new passwords. Security, such as it is, falls apart.

Another problem that occurs when a workgroup becomes too large is that users have difficulty locating the resources they need. The informal nature of workgroups also means that centralized administration or control is nonexistent. Everything has to be configured computer by computer. This lack of central administration and control, along with the limited security, makes the workgroup model a bad choice for all but the home network.

Defining Domains

To provide a secure and easy-to-manage environment that takes full advantage of Active Directory and the collaborative features of Microsoft Exchange 2003 and the other components of Windows Small Business Server, Microsoft made the decision to use a full, domain networking environment. Management is simplified and centralized on the server, reducing the complexity and security problems caused by having to manage users, resources, and passwords across multiple clients.

A *domain* is really just a type of workgroup that includes a server. It is a logical grouping of users who are connected by more than the cables between their computers. The goal of a domain is to let users share resources within the group and to make it easier for the group to work. However, the key difference is the existence of a server for the group that provides a single point of administration and control.

> **Note**   The Microsoft Active Directory domain isn't the same as an Internet domain. In this book, we use "domain" only in the Microsoft networking sense of the word. We'll let you know when we're talking about an Internet domain name.

Additional Users

When adding a new user to the domain, you won't need to go around to each computer and enter all the information. As the administrator, you can simply connect to the server and add the new user, using the Server Management application. You can create the user's mailbox, set up their home folder, add them to security and distribution groups, configure their Share Point access, set up disk quotas, and even configure a client computer for them—all with only a few clicks and the entering of the user name and password. The change will be immediately seen across the entire domain.

All users, including the newest, can get at their resources, no matter which machine is being used. Permission to access resources is granted to individual users (or a group of users), not to individual computers. And when you need to restrict access to a sensitive document or directory, you need to log on to only a single workstation to make the change across the entire domain. You can easily and quickly grant or restrict access by individual user or by groups of users.

Access Control

In a workgroup, there are limitations on sharing your machine's resources with the rest of the workgroup. At the simplest level, you can either share the resource or not share it. Beyond that, you can require a password for a particular level of access to the resource. This enables only a very limited ability to control access to the resource. And virtually none if your machine is physically accessible to anyone but yourself.

Windows Small Business Server provides *discretionary access control*, which allows, for example, some users to create a document or make changes to an existing one while other users can only read the document and still other users can't even *see* it. You can set access for:

- An individual file or files within a directory
- The entire directory

Windows Small Business Server lets you make selection as fine or as coarse as needed and makes the administration of security easy to manage.

Domain Components

A Windows Small Business Server domain has at least two main components and an optional third component:

- Domain controller
- Member server (optional)
- Workstations or clients

Let's take a look at these components.

Domain Controller

The main computer in the Windows Small Business Server domain is the *domain controller*. In most Windows Small Business Server domains, the domain controller will be the only server. It hosts Active Directory and all components of Windows Small Business Server, as well as acts as the file and print server for the domain. All computers in the domain must authenticate to the domain controller, and all domain security is controlled by it.

Member Servers

In some larger domains, additional Windows Server 2003 computers might be in the domain. These computers can be used to spread some of the network's resource load around so that the domain controller doesn't carry the whole load, and they can even be the Exchange or SQL Server host if you buy separate, stand-alone versions of these products. Unfortunately, the bundling and licensing of Windows Small Business Server 2003 allows the installation of the Windows Small Business Server CD versions on only the main Windows Small Business Server computer.

Workstations or Clients

All the clients of a Windows Small Business Server network must be running Windows 95 or later, but in most networks they will be running Windows XP Professional. For this book, we assume that Windows XP Professional is the client operating system. If we need to talk about earlier versions of Windows, we'll clarify that for you.

 Note Windows Small Business Server does not support the use of Windows XP Home Edition as a client. All Windows XP clients on the network must be running the Professional edition or Windows XP Tablet PC Edition, which is a superset of Windows XP Professional.

Summary

In this chapter, we covered the basic components of networks and how they work, and we discussed the different types of Windows networks. We also described the roles that computers on a Windows Small Business Server 2003 network play. In the next chapter, we'll cover designing your Windows Small Business Server network.

Chapter 3
Designing a Network

Before installing Microsoft Windows Small Business Server 2003, you should work out the design of the network. This chapter starts with establishing the infrastructure, proceeds to designing naming conventions, and finishes with a discussion of security issues that need scrutiny prior to installation.

Planning the Network Infrastructure

The first tasks in designing a network for your company are to evaluate the computing needs of the organization, choose an Internet connection method and local network type, and select network devices. You also need to choose server hardware as well as client hardware and software.

Determining Your Needs

Before designing a network, you need to determine which of the following network capabilities to implement; doing so helps ensure that the network design is dictated by business needs instead of fancy technology:

- Centralized user account management
- Web and e-mail access for employees
- File sharing and centralized file storage
- Database storage using Microsoft SQL Server
- Printer sharing
- Centralized backup
- Centralized fax server
- Remote access to the internal network via the Internet
- Facilitation of group projects via a Windows SharePoint Services intranet or "team" Web site

You also must decide how important the following factors are as well as what resources (money, personnel) are available to support your network choices:

- Performance
- Reliability
- Security

Planning Get a thorough idea of what kind of work will be done on the network, when and where it will be done, and by whom. For example, your organization might need to do payroll every other Friday, during which time the file server and printers are under heavy load.

Choosing an Internet Connection

To choose an Internet connection method, you must balance an organization's bandwidth needs and budget against the available Internet connection methods. The following sections discuss how to do this, as well as how to choose an Internet Service Provider (ISP).

Determining Bandwidth Needs

First, determine the baseline level of bandwidth you require. You can then balance this against the organization's budget and performance goals. Allow for 50 Kbps of download bandwidth and 25 Kbps of upload bandwidth for each simultaneous user of e-mail and the Web. If remote access via Virtual Private Network (VPN) is important, allow for a minimum of 50 Kbps of upload bandwidth for each simultaneous remote access user. Table 3-1 lists a number of Internet connection speeds and the number of users supported for each speed, assuming that users will be browsing the Web and using e-mail; this table does not include requirements for VPN connections.

Caution Running an Internet-accessible Web server on your network requires at least 50 Kbps of upload bandwidth or more per simultaneous visitor depending on the size of images or files. This can quickly swamp your Internet connection, which is why most small businesses pay for Web hosting.

Table 3-1. Bandwidth requirements for Web browsing and e-mail

Download/Upload Speed	Number of Users
256/128 Kbps	1–10
512/256 Kbps	10–20
768/384 Kbps	15–30
1024/512 Kbps	20–40
1536/768 Kbps	30–60

Tip   Users of Windows Small Business Server 2003, Premium Edition, can wring extra Web browsing performance out of their connection by using Microsoft ISA Server, which is discussed in Chapter 16, "Using ISA Server 2000." Similarly, using Microsoft Exchange Server for company e-mail enhances e-mail performance without requiring a faster connection.

Bits and Bytes

Network speeds are measured in either kilobits per second (Kbps) or megabits per second (Mbps), whereas download speed and hard disks are rated in kilobytes or megabytes per second. For example, a 640 Kbps DSL connection might download files at 60 kilobytes (KBps) from a fast Web site, but a 1.5 Mbps cable Internet connection might download at 180 KBps from the same site (some of the bandwidth is used by transmission overhead and inefficiencies).

Types of Internet Connections

To choose an Internet connection method, you need to know which methods are available as well as their performance characteristics. Table 3-2 lists the most common connection methods and their speeds.

Table 3-2.   Internet connection types

Type of Connection	Download Speed	Upload Speed	Notes
Dial-Up	28.8–53 Kbps	28.8–40 Kbps	Analog telephone line. Sometimes referred to as Plain Old Telephone Service (POTS).
ISDN (Integrated Services Digital Network)	64–128 Kbps (one channel or two)	64–128 Kbps (one channel or two)	Must be within 50,000 feet of a telephone company Central Office (CO). Connection is dial-up (not persistent).
ADSL (Asynchronous Digital Subscriber Line)	256 Kbps–8 Mbps	128 Kbps–1 Mbps	Must be within 18,000 feet of a CO.
IDSL (ISDN over DSL)	128–144 Kbps	128–144 Kbps	Works at greater distances from a CO than other DSL variants.
SDSL (Synchronous DSL)	128 Kbps–2.3 Mbps	128 Kbps–2.3 Mbps	Must be within 20,000 feet of a CO.
Cable	128 Kbps–8 Mbps	128 Kbps–1 Mbps	Must have access to broadband cable service; speed can fluctuate.
Microwave Wireless	256 Kbps–10+ Mbps	256 Kbps–10+ Mbps	Must be in line of sight to ISP's antenna; maximum distance 10 miles.

Table 3-2. **Internet connection types**

Type of Connection	Download Speed	Upload Speed	Notes
Frame Relay/T1	56 Kbps–1.54 Mbps	56 Kbps–1.54 Mbps	Good availability; very reliable; consistent throughput; expensive.
802.11b (WiFi)	11 Mbps	11 Mbps	Must be within 1800 feet of an access point, can be unreliable.
Geosynchronous Satellite	150 Kbps–3 Mbps	33.6 Kbps–128 Kbps	Requires line of sight to satellite (southern sky in North America). Unsuitable for real-time multi-media due to high latency.
Ethernet	10 or 100 Mbps	10 or 100 Mbps	Limited availability. Backbone connection might be DSL or T1, limiting actual bandwidth.

Choosing ISPs

After determining the preferred connection type and bandwidth, it's time to actually find ISPs. Three Web sites to check are *http://www.cnet.com/internet/*, *http://www.dslreports.com*, and *http://www.isp.com*. In addition to speed and cost, look for the following features:

- **Static IP address**   To host any kind of Internet accessible service such as e-mail, Microsoft Outlook Web Access, VPNs, or Web sites, you need a static IP address or an ISP that supports the Dynamic DNS service.

- **Transfer limitations**   If the ISP has a monthly data transfer limit, make sure that limit isn't lower than your anticipated usage—charges for going beyond the limit can be significant.

- **Web hosting**   If you want the ISP to host the organization's Internet Web site, look for virtual hosting (so that your organization can use its own domain name) with enough disk space on the ISP's Web servers. If the organization uses FrontPage, look for FrontPage Server Extensions support.

- **Backup Internet connection**   If your business is dependent on always being connected to the Internet, choose a secondary Internet connection with sufficient bandwidth to allow you to limp along in case the primary Internet connection fails.

Choosing a Network Type

The next step in designing a network is to choose a network type (see Table 3-3). Start by looking at where your computers are physically located. If you can easily run cable between all computers, the choices are simple: Gigabit Ethernet or Fast Ethernet. Choose Gigabit Ethernet if the price is right and the network needs extremely high performance file sharing; otherwise, stick to Fast Ethernet.

If the computers are widely scattered or mobile, consider including some *wireless access points* (AP), which are network devices that permit wireless clients access to a wired network. Fast Ethernet is more than twice as fast as the current wireless standards, more reliable, more secure, and cheaper as well. For these reasons, use wireless networks to supplement wired networks, not to replace them.

More Info   For more information about wireless access points, see the section "Choosing a Wireless Standard: 802.11a/b/g" later in this chapter.

Caution   All wireless technologies introduce significant security risks. When using wireless networking, always use some sort of security measures, such as 802.11i, Wireless Protected Access (WPA), 802.1x, or a VPN. For more information, see the section titled "Planning for Security" later in this chapter.

Table 3-3.   Common network types

Technology	Speed	Speed (Real World)	Cabling	Maximum Distance	Other Hardware Requirements
Fast Ethernet	100 Mbps	94 Mbps	Cat 5, Cat 5e, Cat 6	328 feet from hub or switch	Fast Ethernet hub or switch
Gigabit Ethernet	1000 Mbps	327 Mbps	Cat 5, Cat 5e, or Cat 6	328 feet from hub or switch	Gigabit hub or switch
802.11b (WiFi)	11 Mbps	4.5 Mbps	Wireless	1800 feet (60–150 feet typical indoors)	802.11b or 802.11g access point (AP), 32 users per AP
802.11a (WiFi5)	54 Mbps	19 Mbps	Wireless	1650 feet (50–100 feet typical indoors)	802.11a AP, 64 users per AP
802.11g	54 Mbps	13 Mbps	Wireless	1800 feet (60–150 feet typical indoors)	802.11g AP, 32 users per AP

Tip   Avoid the consumer-focused HomePNA and HomePlug network types. They're more expensive, slower, less secure, and less reliable than Ethernet or a properly configured 802.11a/b/g wireless network.

Choosing the Right Network Cable

Choosing the right cable for a wired Fast Ethernet (100 Mbps) network is easy—Cat 5 cable. However, there are exceptions to this rule pertaining to existing installations and new construction.

Cables in an existing network might not be usable. In general, Token Ring equipment should be replaced or phased out, although 10 megabit Ethernet equipment can be used until convenient to replace or until the utilization of the network segment becomes too high (but don't wait until the segment is saturated). Coaxial (thinnet) Ethernet and Cat 3 Unshielded Twisted Pair (UTP) cables are unreliable and slow, and should be replaced or phased out.

New construction should run several strands of Cat 5e or, ideally, Cat 6. Although Cat 5 cable supports Gigabit Ethernet, Cat 5e and Cat 6 cables are more reliable and provide headroom for possible 10 Gigabit Ethernet standards. Cables should converge at a reasonably clean, centrally located wiring closet with adequate power, ventilation, and security for all servers and network devices. (Be sure to leave room for future growth.)

Shielded Cat 5, Cat 5e, and Cat 6 cables are available for situations that potentially involve high levels of electromagnetic interference (such as antennas). Plenum grade cable should be used any time wiring is placed in a drop ceiling. (Before running cable in a drop ceiling, talk to the building manager.)

Choosing a Wireless Standard: 802.11a/b/g

Currently you can choose from three wireless standards: 802.11b, 802.11a, and 802.11g. Here's what you need to know about each (also see Table 3-3):

- **802.11b**   802.11b is the most widely deployed standard, though the speed is limited (11 Mbps theoretical, 5 Mbps real-world). 802.11b supports a maximum of 32 users per AP, and a maximum of 3 simultaneous channels in use in the same location. *Channels* separate wireless networks, with each channel providing 11 Mbps of bandwidth.

- **802.11g**   802.11g is faster than 802.11b (54 Mbps theoretical, 13 Mbps real-world), backward-compatible with 802.11b, and is only marginally more expensive, making it the best choice for most organizations. 802.11g supports a maximum of 32 users per AP, and a maximum of 3 simultaneous channels in use in the same location.

- **802.11a**   802.11a is the fastest standard (54 Mbps theoretical, 19 Mbps real-world) and is more tolerant of microwave interference and network congestion. 802.11a supports a maximum of 64 users per AP, and a maximum of 8 channels in use simultaneously in the same location. Early versions of 802.11a hardware suffered from compatibility problems between different vendors, though newer second- and third-generation devices have improved compatibility and better range. 802.11a is not compatible with either 802.11b or 802.11g.

  If you decide to use 802.11a network devices, stick with devices from the same vendor and consider a tri-mode 802.11a/b/g device that will allow other devices such as laptops with built-in 802.11b connectivity to work on the wireless network. (This also permits the highest network density, with 11 channels available simultaneously for wireless networks).

Choosing Network Devices

After selecting a network type and Internet connection method, create a network diagram to visually show what network devices are needed, and then select the necessary devices for the network, such as switches, wireless access points, firewalls, and network adapters.

> **Tip**   Choose a single brand of network hardware, if possible. This ensures greater hardware compatibility, simplifies administration, and makes obtaining vendor support easier.

> **More Info**   For reviews and information about specific network devices, go to *PC Magazine Online (http://www.pcmag.com)*.

Diagramming the Network

Creating a diagram of the network can quickly show which devices you need and where they should be located, as shown in Figures 3-1 and 3-2.

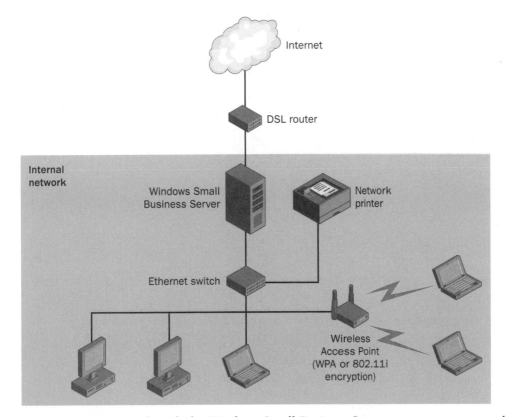

Figure 3-1.   *A network with the Windows Small Business Server computer connected directly to the Internet.*

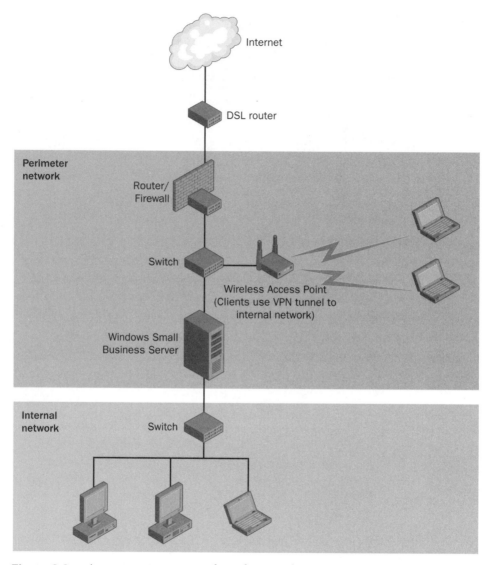

Figure 3-2. *A more secure network with a wireless access point placed outside the internal network.*

Use the following list as a guide when creating the network diagram:

- **Internet connection** The Internet connection usually comes in the form of a telephone or coaxial cable that connects to a DSL or cable router. It is traditionally represented by a cloud at the top of the drawing and a line that connects to the router or firewall.

- **DSL router or cable modem** The Internet usually enters the organization in the form of a telephone or cable line that plugs into a DSL router or cable modem.

- **Firewall**   The DSL router or cable modem is then plugged into the firewall, which can either be the Windows Small Business Server computer, or a standalone firewall or router.

- **Perimeter network**   This is an optional area of the network between the external firewall (if present) and the Windows Small Business Server computer where low-security devices such as wireless access points can be placed. You can also create a perimeter network (also known as DMZ or demilitarized zone) using Windows Small Business Server and three network cards.

- **Internal network**   The Windows Small Business Server computer's second network card connects to the internal network via an Ethernet switch. This is where all other computers and other network devices are located.

Planning   Networks with a small number of wireless clients (1–10) should place their access points on the internal network and use 802.11i or WPA encryption, or place the access points in the perimeter network and use 128-bit WEP keys in combination with VPN connections to the Windows Small Business Server. Access points should also be placed in the perimeter network when you want to provide Internet access to the general public (such as in a coffee shop or lobby).

Larger networks should place access points on the internal network and use 802.1x authentication, as described in Chapter 15.

Choosing a Network Switch

Ethernet networks use the *star* (also known as *hub and spoke*) network topology, which means that all network devices must be plugged into a central hub or switch. Choosing the right switch requires evaluating the following factors:

- **Switch or hub**   Don't buy a hub—get a switch instead. Switches are inexpensive, provide additional performance, and facilitate mixing 10 Mbps, 100 Mbps, and 1 Gbps devices on the same network segment.

- **Number of ports**   Make sure that the switch provides more than enough ports for all computers, access points, network printers, and Network Attached Storage (NAS) devices on the network.

- **Speed**   Fast Ethernet (100/10 Mbps) switches offer plenty of performance for most small businesses, but Gigabit (1000/100/10 Mbps) switches are dropping in price and provide extra bandwidth for heavily used file servers and high-quality streaming video.

- **Management**   Managed switches provide the ability to view the status of attached devices from a remote connection, which can be useful for off-site technicians. In general, save the cash and stick with an unmanaged switch unless the cost difference is slight or the organization uses an off-site consultant who wants the ability to remotely administer switches.

Choosing Wireless Access Points

As you learned earlier in the chapter, wireless access points permit clients to wirelessly connect to a wired network. Access points are often integrated into routers, but they are also available as standalone devices that must be plugged into a switch like any other network device.

Tip   Business-grade access points are more expensive than consumer-oriented access points and routers with integrated access points; however, they are usually more reliable and full-featured.

When choosing an access point, evaluate the following features:

- Routers with built-in access points are often no more expensive than stand-alone access points and can provide an extra layer of security for a network by facilitating the creation of a perimeter network.

- Access points should support 802.11i or WPA encryption. 128 bit WEP is the minimum and appropriate only when used in conjunction with 802.1x authentication or when the access point is located in a perimeter network.

- Access points should support 802.1x (RADIUS) authentication if you want to provide the highest level of security and ease-of-use to a wireless network. This is the best method of authenticating wireless clients, though it does require setting up a RADIUS server, as discussed in Chapter 15.

Caution   Don't bother disabling SSID broadcasting and enabling Media Access Control (MAC) address filtering—they provide an added administrative burden and a hacker with a port scanner can easily defeat them anyway. Always use some type of encryption, and consider placing the access point outside the firewall and using VPN tunnels to gain access to the internal network.

- Some access points have two antennas that can be adjusted for better coverage; others have external antennas that can be mounted on a wall for better placement.

- Typical of many access points is 30 watts, though some offer up to 100 watts for more range. The best access points allow you to adjust the wattage, and by extension, the range. This is useful either to reduce wireless coverage outside the premises, or to permit a higher number of access points to be placed in the same area, increasing the number of wireless clients that can operate in the same area.

- Standalone wireless bridges (often referred to as wireless Ethernet bridges) and some access points provide the ability to wirelessly bridge (connect) two wired networks that can't be connected via cables. There are a number of different types of bridging modes, including Point-to-Point, which uses two wireless bridges to link two wired networks; and AP Client, which uses an AP on the main network (to which wireless clients can connect) and a wireless bridge in AP Client mode on the remote network segment, acting as a wireless client.

  Clients on the other side of a wireless bridge will experience slower performance to the main network segment because of the shared wireless link, so use wireless bridges with discretion, and always use bridges and APs made by the same manufacturer.

- Don't include "turbo" or other high-speed modes offered by some manufacturers in your buying criteria. They provide little performance gain, if any, in the real world.

Placing Access Points for the Best Coverage

Wireless access points have a limited range, especially in the environment of a typical office. The indoor range of 802.11b, 802.11g, and tri-mode 802.11a access points is usually around 60–100 feet at the highest connection speed, and 25–75 feet for first generation single-mode 802.11a access points. With that said, 2.4 GHz cordless phones, microwave ovens, and Bluetooth devices can cause serious interference with 802.11b and 802.11g networks (but not with 802.11a networks) when they are turned on. Fluorescent lights, metal walls, computer equipment, furniture, and standing too close to the access point can also reduce the range of wireless networks. Unfortunately, there is no reliable way to quantify these variables, leaving trial and error as the best way to position access points. However, you can follow some guidelines when selecting access point locations:

- Place the access point and wireless network card antennas as high as possible to get them above objects that might attenuate the signal.

- If you place access points in the plenum (the space between a drop ceiling or raised floor), make sure you obtain access points or enclosures certified for plenum installation.

- Place the access point in the center of the desired coverage area to provide the best coverage while also reducing the publicly exposed "surface area" of the network.

(continued)

- Use multiple access points as necessary to cover multiple floors or large offices, or to service a large number of clients simultaneously. Twenty clients per 802.11b or 802.11g AP is a reasonable maximum, with an average of no more than 2–4 simultaneously active users per AP yielding the best network performance.

- Wireless bridges can be used to place another Ethernet network segment (or another wireless access point) in a location unreachable by cables. Wired clients on this segment communicate with other wired devices on this segment at the speed of the wired network (1000/100/10 Mbps); however, communication with the main network segment takes place at the speed of the wireless network (4–20 Mbps real-world bandwidth).

- When selecting channels for access points, *sniff* for (use a wireless client to look for) the presence of other networks and then choose an unused channel, preferably one that is four channels or more separated from other channels in use. For example, channels 1, 6, and 11 can all be used without interference.

Choosing a Firewall Device or Router

Windows Small Business Server 2003 is designed to connect directly to the Internet and act as a router and firewall for internal clients. However, many companies don't want to expose such a critical server directly to Internet-based attacks and prefer to place the Windows Small Business Server behind its own firewall. This location provides an extra layer of security and can also create a perimeter network in which wireless access points can be placed.

Note The firewall included in Windows Small Business Server contains the same basic features as small office/home office (SOHO) firewall devices or routers, and provides a roughly equivalent level of security to clients (although data stored on the Windows Small Business Server computer is exposed to greater risk). However, Internet Security and Acceleration (ISA) Server, included in Windows Small Business Server, Premium Edition, provides industrial-strength, ICSA-certified firewall capabilities rivaled only by enterprise-level dedicated firewall devices.

If you decide to use an external firewall device (or a router serving this function) as a first layer of protection, evaluate the following features:

- **Packet filtering** Firewalls should support inbound packet filtering and Stateful Packet Inspection (SPI).

- **Protection from specific attacks**   Firewalls should support protection from the denial-of-service (DoS) attack and other common attacks such as Ping of Death, SYN Flood, LAND Attack, and IP Spoofing.

- **Network Address Translation (NAT)**   NAT is the backbone of most firewall devices, providing basic security and Internet connectivity to internal clients.

- **VPN pass-through**   To permit properly authenticated Internet users to establish Virtual Private Network (VPN) connections with a Windows Small Business Server computer behind a firewall, the firewall must support VPN pass-through of the desired VPN protocol (PPTP, L2TP, and/or IPSec).

- **VPN tunnels**   Some firewall devices themselves support establishing VPN connections. Although there are many fans of this approach, it doesn't work well when the Windows Small Business Server computer is acting as a second-layer firewall, because clients still need to tunnel through the Windows Small Business Server computer. If you do choose to use a firewall device to establish VPN connections with clients and servers in remote offices, make sure the firewall supports the necessary number of simultaneous VPN tunnels.

- **UPnP support**   Windows Small Business Server can automatically configure firewalls that support UPnP to work with Windows Small Business Server services such as Exchange Server and remote access (by opening the necessary ports on the firewall). UPnP support can be found in most consumer firewall devices as well as in some business firewalls.

Note   Enabling UPnP on a dedicated firewall device makes configuring the device to work with Windows Small Business Server easy and doesn't significantly increase the security risk to the Windows Small Business Server computer or clients behind it. Although pre-SP1 Windows XP clients do have a significant UPnP vulnerability, placing them behind a firewall device (including a Windows Small Business Server computer) eliminates this vulnerability, as does installing Windows XP Service Pack 1 or later. For more information on this vulnerability, see Microsoft Security Bulletin MS01-059, available at *http://www.microsoft.com/technet/security/bulletin/MS01-059.asp*.

- **Dual-WAN support**   Some firewalls come with support for two WAN connections to increase speed and reliability, which is a great solution for networks looking for a reliable Internet connection. Other firewalls provide a serial port so that an external dial-up modem can be used as a backup connection, but this connection is much slower.

- **Content filtering** Most firewalls make blocking certain Web sites or Web sites containing specified keywords possible. Many businesses use this feature to reduce the employees' ability to visit objectionable Web sites, although most content filters are largely ineffective.

- **ICSA certification** ICSA Labs (*http://www.icsalabs.com*), a division of the private security corporation TruSecure, certifies computer security products that meet its stringent security standards. Firewalls with ICSA certification are known to be secure; others might or might not be. ISA Server 2000, included in Windows Small Business Server 2003, is ICSA certified.

- **Built-in wireless access point** Firewalls with built-in access points save money and make administration easier but might result in non-optimal placement of the access point. Also, built-in access points are stuck in the perimeter network, which won't work if you want wireless clients to have direct access to the internal network (they'll instead need to use a VPN connection).

- **Built-in Ethernet switch** This feature makes it easy to add wireless access points or other network devices to the perimeter network in between the external firewall device and the Windows Small Business Server computer (which acts as a second-layer firewall in this configuration). Otherwise, add an Ethernet switch when the need arises.

Choosing Server Hardware

If you have a server that can meet the capacity needs of the network or can be upgraded to do so while allowing for future growth, by all means use this server, particularly if it happens to be your existing Small Business Server 2000 computer.

More Info See Chapter 5, "Upgrading or Migrating to Windows Small Business Server 2003," for more information about upgrading and migrating to Windows Small Business Server 2003.

Tip For the highest level of compatibility with Windows Small Business Server 2003, make sure that the server and all devices are listed in the Windows Server Catalog (formerly known as the Hardware Compatibility List), which you can access at *http://www.microsoft.com/windows/catalog/server*.

When evaluating server hardware, refer to Table 3-4, which lists the minimum configurations necessary for adequate performance at different load levels.

More Info The sidebar titled "Determining Server Load," appearing later in this chapter, provides more information about configuration and performance.

Table 3-4. Minimum server configurations for different load levels

Component	Light Load	Medium Load	Heavy Load
CPU	Pentium III 500 MHz or dual Pentium II 300 MHz	Pentium III 600 MHz or dual Pentium II 400 MHz	Xeon 2 GHz or dual Xeon 1.4 GHz
Memory	512 MB	1 GB	1.5 GB
Storage	2 or more hard drives with 8 GB available for Windows Small Business Server 2003	3 drive hardware-based RAID using SATA or SCSI drives	5 or more drive hardware-based SCSI RAID
WAN Network Adapter (for Internet access)	100/10 Mbps PCI card	100/10 Mbps PCI card	100/10 Mbps PCI card
LAN Network Adapter	100/10 Mbps card	100/10 Mbps card	Gigabit LAN or 100/10 Mbps card

More Info   See Chapter 8, "Storage Management," for more information about choosing the appropriate storage solution and Chapter 13, "Backing Up and Restoring Data," for more information about creating a backup strategy and choosing backup devices.

Note   Although Windows Small Business Server 2003 runs on servers using the 64-bit AMD Opteron and AMD Athlon 64 processors, Windows Small Business Server 2003 is a 32-bit operating system and can't take advantage of any 64-bit features such as large memory support. However, fence sitters can run Windows Small Business Server 2003 on an Opteron-based server and upgrade to the AMD64 version of Windows Server 2003, Enterprise Edition.

Determining Server Load

The appropriate hardware for a Windows Small Business Server 2003 server depends on the load under which it will be placed. Load can be thought of as equal to the number of requests per unit of time multiplied by the difficulty of fulfilling each request.

The easiest way to determine load is to sample the performance of the existing server over a range of conditions. Of course, this is tricky when you're constructing a new network or restructuring an existing network. In these cases, evaluate the extent to which the following factors will play a role on the network:

- **The usage pattern over time (number of requests per unit of time)**
  A server that handles an average load can easily become swamped at key times, such as at the beginning and end of a work day when many users simultaneously log on or log off; during lunch when users might browse the Internet for personal use; or around deadlines when many users are making heavy use of file, e-mail, or database services.

(continued)

- **The kinds of user requests (the complexity of each request)**
  This determines what server subsystems are stressed most heavily. Database serving stresses storage, memory, and possibly CPU; file serving stresses mostly storage; Internet access places some load on storage and memory (if using ISA Server); Exchange Server stresses storage, memory, and to some extent CPU.

Choosing Client Hardware and Software

When selecting client computers for use on a network, choose systems that are fast enough to perform adequately with Windows 2000 Professional or Windows XP Professional (see Table 3-5 for recommended configurations). Other operating systems such as Windows 98, Mac OS X, and Linux can be made to work on a Windows Small Business Server 2003 network; however, they won't provide full support for such features as automatic application and service pack installations, shared fax and modem services, and Outlook 2003.

Table 3-5. Recommended client computer configurations

Component	Minimum Configuration	Better Configuration
Operating System	Windows 2000 Professional	Windows XP Professional
CPU	Pentium II 300 MHz or faster	Pentium III 1 GHz or faster
RAM	128 MB	512 MB
Hard drive	2 GB	20 GB
Network Adapter	Ethernet or 802.11b	Fast Ethernet, 802.11g, or second-generation 802.11a
Display	15" monitor running at 800×600 resolution	17" monitor running at 1024×768

Under the Hood Terminal Server

Computers too slow to adequately run a Windows XP or Windows 2000 operating system can be put to use as Terminal Server clients. In this configuration, users connect to a separate Windows Server 2003 computer running Terminal Server (a Windows Server 2003 component that was previously known as Terminal Services in Application Server mode), which displays a standard Windows desktop in which users can run any installed program. The server cannot be the Windows Small Business Server computer. All processing is done on the server, and the display is sent back to the client machine, which could be running Windows 98, Windows NT 4.0, or even Mac OS X.

This approach can make more efficient use of resources, and make central management easier, although it's inappropriate for graphics-intensive applications. For more information on Terminal Server, see *Microsoft Windows Server 2003 Administrator's Companion* (Microsoft Press) or *Microsoft Windows Server 2003 Terminal Services* (Microsoft Press).

Choosing Naming Conventions

Creating naming conventions makes choosing names for computers, shared folders, and users easier and lends consistency to the network. This consistency results in a more user-friendly network. The following sections discuss choosing a domain name for the network as well as creating a naming convention for computer names.

More Info   For help with naming users, see Chapter 9, "Users, Groups, and Security." For help with naming shared folders, see Chapter 10, "Shares, Permissions, and Group Policy."

Choosing a Domain Name for the Network

The domain name is the most important and politically sensitive name on the network. When deciding on a domain name, use the following guidelines:

- The name is easy to remember and makes sense for the company. This could be the company name in its most common form or an abbreviation.

- The name should be 15 characters or fewer, consisting only of letters, numbers, the underscore, and a hyphen. This strategy ensures DNS and NetBIOS compatibility.

- The name shouldn't be already in use as an Internet domain name for another company.

- If the company already has an Internet Web site, consider using that domain name with the .local, .lan, or .office top-level domains. For example, if the company uses www.example.com for its Internet Web site, use example.local for the domain name.

Tip   Avoid the .local top-level domain if you want to allow Mac OS X clients to use the network—it conflicts with the Mac OS X Rendezvous automatic network configuration standard.

- Once you choose a domain name, register it (preferably with .com, .net, or .org) on the Internet so that another company can't purchase it.

Caution   Changing a domain name is difficult and can cause numerous problems on a network, so picking a name that will last is important.

Naming Computers

It's easy for *you* to keep a map of what the different clients and servers are and where they are on the network, but if you make life hard on users, you pay in the long run. So naming all the computers after Shakespearean characters or Norse gods might make sense to you, but it isn't going to help users figure out that "Puck" is the Windows Small Business Server and "Hermes" is the desktop used for payroll. On the other hand, using "SRV1" for the Windows Small Business Server server tells everyone immediately which machine it is. When naming computers, use a consistent convention and sensible names such as the following:

- SRV1 or SBSSRV for the Windows Small Business Server 2003 computer

- FrontDesk for the receptionist's computer

Planning for Security

Before planning the security of a network, take a few moments to consider the following list of potential security risks relevant to the network. Then use the sections that follow to address these threats, as well as to learn what to do when the network is successfully hacked.

- **Internet hackers**   All computers and devices attached directly to the Internet are subject to random attacks by hackers. According to the Cooperative Association for Internet Data Analysis (CAIDA), during a random 3-week time period in 2001 there were more than 12,000 DoS attacks: 1200–2400 were against home machines and the rest were against businesses. If your organization has a high profile, it might also be subject to targeted attack by hackers who don't like your organization or who are engaging in corporate espionage.

  For more information about securing a network against Internet hackers, see the "Securing Internet Firewalls" section of this chapter. Also review the "Updating Windows Small Business Server" section of Chapter 6, "Completing the To Do List and Other Post-Installation Tasks."

- **Wireless hackers and theft of service**   Wireless access points are exposed to the general public looking for free Internet access (some are willing to crack WEP encryption) and to mobile hackers. To reduce this risk, refer to the "Securing Wireless Networks" section in this chapter.

- **Viruses and worms**   Networks are subject to virus exposure from e-mail attachments, infected documents, and worms such as CodeRed and Blaster that automatically attack vulnerable servers (and clients that sit directly on the Internet). Look at the "Securing Client Computers" section of this chapter along with the "Updating Windows Small Business Server" section of Chapter 6 for help with this.

- **Nosy or disgruntled employees and former employees**   Internal users and former users might try to attack or steal information using valid accounts. To help prevent this, refer to the "Ensuring Physical Security" section of this chapter as well as Chapter 6.

Ensuring Physical Security

Although security is not something that can be achieved in absolute terms, it should be a clearly defined goal. The most secure operating system and network in the world is defenseless against someone with physical access to a computer. Evaluate your own environment and security requirements to determine what additional steps, such as biometric or smart card controls, might be appropriate. At a minimum, you should take the following precautions (additional measures are covered in Chapter 6):

- Place servers in a locked server room.
- Use case locks on your servers and don't leave the keys in them.
- Place network hubs, routers, and switches in a locked cable room or wiring closet.
- Install case locks on client systems or publicly accessible systems.
- Use laptop locks when using laptops in public.

Securing Client Computers

Even a highly secure network can be quickly compromised by a poorly secured client computer—for example, a laptop running Windows 98 with sensitive data stored on the hard drive. To maximize the security of client computers, use the following guidelines (refer to Chapter 6 and Chapter 12, "Managing Computers on the Network," for more security procedures):

- **Use a secure operating system**   Use Windows 2000 Professional or Windows XP Professional on all client computers (particularly laptops).

- **Use NTFS, file permissions, and possibly EFS**   Use NTFS for all hard drives, and apply appropriate file permissions so that only valid users can read sensitive data. Encrypt sensitive files on laptop computers using Encrypting File System (EFS).

- **Keep clients updated** Use the Automatic Updates feature of Windows XP and Windows 2000 Professional Service Pack 3 or later to keep client systems updated automatically, or use Windows Update. Ideally you should install Software Update Services (SUS) so that you can centrally control which updates are installed, as described in Chapter 12.

- **Use MBSA to check clients for security problems** The Microsoft Baseline Security Analyzer (MBSA) makes it easy to check all computers running Windows Server 2003 (including Windows Small Business Server 2003), Windows XP, Windows 2000, and Windows NT 4.0 for missing service packs, hot fixes, security updates, and other security problems. See Chapter 6 for more information.

- **Enable password policies** Password policies is a feature of Windows Small Business Server 2003 that requires user passwords to meet certain complexity, length, and uniqueness requirements, ensuring that users choose passwords that aren't trivial to crack.

More Info For more information about enabling the password policies feature during the initial Windows Small Business Server 2003 server setup process, see Chapter 6.

Note Remembering passwords has become an increasingly difficult prospect, leading to the resurgence of the yellow-sticky note method of recalling them. It's important to discourage this practice.

- **Install antivirus software** Antivirus software should be installed on the Windows Small Business Server 2003 server as well as all clients. The best way to do this is to purchase a small-business antivirus package that includes client, server, and Exchange Server virus scanning. This package is often no more expensive than purchasing consumer antivirus software for each client, and it provides additional scanning and management capabilities. Companies that provide these solutions include Sophos (*http://www.sophos.com*), Symantec (*http://www.symantec.com*), and McAfee (*http://www.mcafee.com*).

- **Sign and encrypt e-mail** Companies with the need to send secure e-mail should set up users to send digitally signed and possibly encrypted e-mail. If a small number of users need this capability, purchase digital IDs from an Internet Certificate Authority such as Verisign (*http://www.verisign.com*) or Thawte (*http://www.thawte.com*). If a large number of users require this ability, consider installing Certificate Services (included in Windows Small Business Server 2003) and creating your own digital IDs.

- **Keep Web browsers secure**   Web browsers often have security holes in them that allow nefarious Web sites to do such things as read the contents of the Clipboard or access files on the hard drive. To remedy this situation, keep Web browsers patched with the latest security updates, and consider testing a few clients for security issues using a free browser checkup Web site such as the one provided by Qualys at *http://browsercheck.qualys.com.*

Securing Wireless Networks

Wireless networks using the 802.11b, 802.11a, and 802.11g standards are very convenient but also introduce significant security vulnerabilities if not properly secured. To properly secure wireless networks, follow these recommendations:

- Enable 802.11i or WPA encryption on the access points.

- If the access points don't support 802.11i or WPA, either use WEP with 802.1x authentication, or place all access points in a perimeter network, with the Windows Small Business Server 2003 computer acting as a firewall between the perimeter network (and the access points) and the internal network. To reach the internal network, wireless clients must establish a secure VPN connection with the Windows Small Business Server 2003 server.

- If you're relying on the easily cracked WEP encryption method, change WEP keys monthly at a minimum (weekly is better).

Note   WPA provides two methods of authentication: an "Enterprise" method that makes use of a RADIUS server, and a "SOHO" method known as WPA-PSK (Pre-Shared Key), that makes use of an 8–63 character network key, similar to WEP. Using a network key is easier to set up and provides adequate security for most small networks. Some WPA devices also provide the option of using the stronger, hardware-accelerated (and thus faster) AES encryption method used by the 802.11i standard.

- Companies with a lot of wireless clients might want to investigate installing Internet Authentication Services (IAS) and Certificate Services on the Windows Small Business Server 2003 server and using 802.1x Authentication (using IAS as a RADIUS server). This procedure is discussed in Chapter 15.

- Change the SSID from the default. For maximum security, pick a name that doesn't reveal the name or location of your network.

- Use "warchalking" symbols to notify potential wireless users that the network is closed to public users or open to the public for Internet access. To do so, type () before the SSID to indicate a closed node, or type)(to indicate an open node. For example, ()closed1 would be a good SSID for a private network.

- Disable the ability to administer access points from across the wireless network.

- Change the default password of all access points.

Securing Internet Firewalls

Most external firewall devices are secure by default, but you can take some additional steps to maximize the security of a firewall:

- Disable remote administration, or limit it to responding to a single IP address (that of your network consultant).

- Disable the firewall from responding to Internet pings.

- Enable Stateful Packet Inspection (SPI) and protection from specific attacks such as the Ping of Death, Smurf, and IP Spoofing.

- Change the default password for the firewall device.

- Leave all ports on the firewall closed except those needed by the Windows Small Business Server 2003 server. Alternatively, enable UPnP so that Windows Small Business Server 2003 can automatically configure ports as needed.

- Check for open ports using the free Shields Up and Port Scan services at *http://grc.com*.

- Keep the firewall updated with the latest firmware versions, available for download from the manufacturer's Web site.

Summary

The first two chapters of this book introduced you to Windows Small Business Server 2003 and explained how networks work. This chapter discussed how to design or update a network in anticipation of installing Windows Small Business Server. It also covered choosing naming conventions and how to plan for adequate network security. The next chapter starts the coverage of installation and initial setup by showing how to install Windows Small Business Server 2003 on a blank server, including automated installation procedures for network consultants.

Part II
Installation and Setup

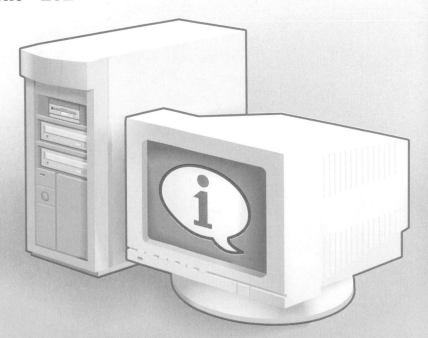

Chapter 4
Installing Windows Small Business Server 2003

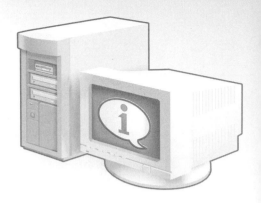

This chapter discusses performing a clean install of Microsoft Windows Small Business Server 2003. Performing a clean install provides the best performance and stability; however, it wipes out any existing data and settings on the server.

More Info If you have a server with Windows Small Business Server preinstalled, you're not in the clear yet—skip ahead to the "Using the Windows Small Business Server Setup Wizard" section of this chapter for more information.

More Info If you already have a server running a previous version of Windows Small Business Server or Windows Server and want to maintain existing settings and data, see Chapter 5, "Upgrading or Migrating to Windows Small Business Server 2003," for more information.

Planning Partitions

It's a good idea to decide how you want your server storage to look *before* you start installing Windows Small Business Server. You're not required to create partitions on your hard disks during the installation phase beyond the disk where Windows Small Business Server is installed, but you certainly can. And by creating all the partitions ahead of time, you have additional options for where some of the components of Small Business Server are placed. To create your initial storage during installation, follow these recommendations:

- Create a partition during the initial text installation screens for the operating system and log files that is at *least* 4 GB in size (8 GB is a more realistic minimum).

- Optionally, create the other partitions you'll be using.

- If you're using hardware-based RAID, you must create the volume for the operating system using the manufacturer's tools *before* you start the installation of Windows Small Business Server. Also, it's a good idea to create any other volumes you'll be using, even if you don't put partitions on them yet.

- If you'll be using software RAID for some or all of your drives, create these after Setup completes processing.

Note For more detailed information about planning a storage solution, see Chapter 8, "Storage Management."

Under the Hood   Dividing Storage

While you can have one, single, large partition and put everything on it, there are compelling reasons to divide hard-drive space into at least three different partitions, even if you are using hardware RAID. The three partitions are:

- The primary operating system partition.

- A partition for static storage, such as programs.

- A partition for data, logs, and other volatile information. This will be the most active partition and should have a storage technology optimized accordingly.

Dividing your storage space into logical partitions in this way makes backups and disaster recovery easier and allows you to focus your efforts on the critical data partition.

Preparing the Server

After planning partitions and gathering network information, perform the following preparations before launching Setup:

- Make sure the server is sized appropriately for the load under which you plan to place it. For more information on server sizing, see Chapter 3, "Designing a Network."

- If installing on an existing server, back up all data and record any important settings.

- Remove the Uninterruptible Power Supply (UPS) management cable from the server (even if it's USB).

- Upgrade the system BIOS to the latest version available.

- Set the boot order in the BIOS to boot from the CD-ROM before the hard disk.

- Locate any mass storage drivers or custom hardware abstraction layer (HAL) files necessary for the system.

- Disconnect the server from the Internet (unless protected by a firewall).

Under the Hood   Active Directory and Domain Name System

As part of installation, Setup installs Active Directory and promotes the computer to a domain controller, creating a domain. Active Directory is a requirement for several Windows Small Business Server components.

The Windows Small Business Server network is TCP/IP-based, so a Domain Name System (DNS) server provides name resolution. Although Active Directory works with any DNS server that complies with the appropriate standards, stick with the DNS server provided with Windows Small Business Server—it works great and is configured automatically by Windows Small Business Server.

During Setup, the DNS service is configured to listen only to DNS queries from the local network. In addition, the DNS server is unbound from the external network adapter so that your internal DNS information is not available to outsiders.

If you need to host your own Internet-accessible DNS server (to host the DNS records for your company Web site and e-mail server), do so on a separate server from the Windows Small Business Server computer, and place this server in a perimeter network (see Chapter 3, "Designing a Network," for more information). Trying to host both an Internet DNS server and an internal DNS server on the same computer results in a security vulnerability and will probably break DNS resolution for client computers. Most small businesses are better off letting their ISP host their DNS records as well as their primary Internet Web site.

Note   See Appendix A for details about automating the operating system portion of the installation using the answer file.

Installing Windows Small Business Server

The Windows Small Business Server 2003 installation process takes place in two phases. The first phase installs a slightly modified version of Windows Server 2003, Standard Edition. The second phase occurs after Windows Server 2003 is installed. In this phase, the Windows Small Business Server Setup Wizard installs Active Directory and other server applications.

If you purchased a server with Windows Small Business Server 2003 prein-stalled, skip ahead to the "Using the Windows Small Business Server Setup Wizard" section; otherwise, read on.

Under the Hood **Text-Mode and Graphical Setup**

The installation of the operating system has two major phases of its own: text-mode setup and Graphical User Interface (GUI)–based setup. Text-mode setup begins after booting from the Windows Small Business Server 2003 Disk 1. You select the partition on which to install Windows. Setup then copies a minimal version of Windows to the hard drive and boots into GUI-based setup, which is home to the familiar Windows Setup Wizard. Setup then detects and installs devices, configures the network, and finishes installing files to the computer.

Finally, the computer restarts a second time, booting into Windows Server 2003. After logging on, you then launch the Windows Small Business Server 2003 Setup Wizard to begin the final phase of Windows Small Business Server setup process.

Installing the Operating System

To install Windows Small Business Server on a server that didn't ship with Windows Small Business Server 2003 preinstalled, you must start by installing the underlying operating system of Windows Small Business Server 2003—a modified version of Window Server 2003, Standard Edition. (This process can be automated, as discussed in Appendix A.)

Under the Hood **NTFS System Drive**

Windows Small Business Server 2003 requires that the system drive be for-matted as the NTFS file system. NTFS is required for Active Directory and Microsoft Exchange Server 2003, among other components. For better security and file management, format *all* drives with NTFS—there is simply no reason to use FAT or FAT32 anymore.

During Setup, disk quotas are applied. By default, each user can use up to one gigabyte of space. A disk quota is not set for administrators. For infor-mation on changing disk quotas, see Chapter 8.

To install the underlying operating system, complete the following steps:

1. Insert Windows Small Business Server 2003 Disk 1 into the CD-ROM drive of the server and turn on or restart the computer. When

prompted, press the Any key (just teasing—press any key you want!) to boot from the CD.

Tip   If you can't boot from the Windows Small Business Server 2003 Disk 1 CD, you need to boot from a Microsoft Windows 98 Startup floppy disk that contains Smartdrv.exe (you might have to add it) and choose the CD-ROM support option. Run Smartdrv.exe so that installation files will copy faster. Insert Windows Small Business Server 2003 Disk 1 and run I386\Winnt.exe to begin the installation. When Setup is started manually this way, all installation files are copied to the hard drive and an additional reboot will occur before the Welcome To Setup screen appears.

2. To use a hard-drive controller for which Windows Small Business Server 2003 has no built-in support, press F6 when prompted. To use a HAL provided by the server manufacturer, press F5.

3. When the Welcome To Setup screen (Figure 4-1) appears, press Enter.

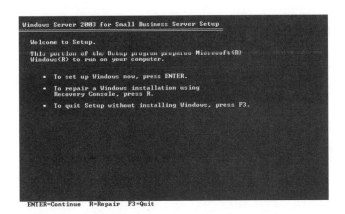

Figure 4-1.   *The beginning of the operating system installation.*

4. Read the licensing agreement and, if you agree, press F8.

5. On the next screen (Figure 4-2), select a disk partition. If no suitable disk partition for Windows Small Business Server 2003 exists, create one:

   • To delete a partition, select it using the arrow keys and then press D. Deleting a partition permanently erases all information on that partition.

   • To create a new partition, select some free space, press C, specify how large to make the partition, and then press Enter.

Caution   If the first partition on the disk is under 50 MB in size, it's probably a utility partition. Leave it alone. The system might not boot or function properly without it.

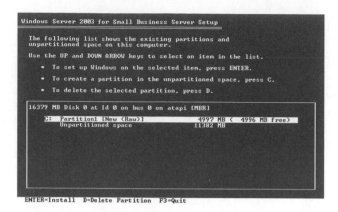

Figure 4-2. *Choosing a disk partition.*

6. Select the partition or free space in which you want to install Windows Small Business Server and then press Enter.

7. If you selected free space or a new partition, choose a formatting option on the next screen. NTFS Quick Format is the fastest way to format, but NTFS Full Format ensures that any bad sectors are properly marked and also wipes out the information on the disk, which is useful if that disk once contained sensitive data. If the selected partition is already formatted as FAT32, choose to convert the partition to NTFS.

8. Press Enter after making your formatting choice and if necessary, press C on the next screen to confirm that you want to convert to NTFS. Setup copies files, which will take several minutes, and then reboots the server. (If Setup needs to convert the hard drive partition to NTFS, an additional reboot will be required.) After the reboot, GUI-based Setup runs and the installation continues for several minutes.

9. When the Regional And Language Options page appears (Figure 4-3), change the regional and language options, if necessary, and then click Next. You can use the Regional And Language Options tool in Control Panel to change regional settings after you install Windows Small Business Server, so you probably don't need to linger here.

10. On the Personalize Your Software page, type the name and organization under which the computer should be registered.

11. On the Your Product Key page, type the product key from the Windows Small Business Server 2003 packaging, and then click Next.

12. On the Computer Name And Administrator Password page, type the name for the computer in the Computer Name text box.

More Info See Chapter 3 for help with naming computers.

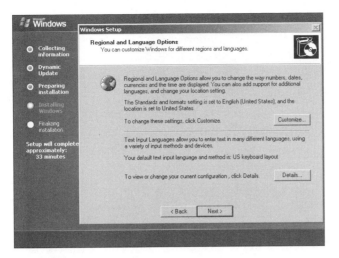

Figure 4-3. *Specifying regional options.*

13. Type an administrator account password in the Administrator Password text box, and type it again in the Confirm Password text box. Click Next.

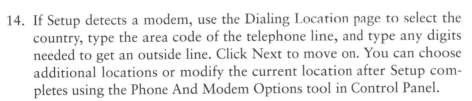

Security Alert As a best practice for security, use passwords that are at least seven characters long and a mixture of uppercase and lowercase letters, numbers, and special characters. Use acronyms for phrases that are meaningful to you, easy to remember, and unlikely to be meaningful or memorable to anyone else, such as Uk,Ur?Ue! (You know, you are what you eat!)

14. If Setup detects a modem, use the Dialing Location page to select the country, type the area code of the telephone line, and type any digits needed to get an outside line. Click Next to move on. You can choose additional locations or modify the current location after Setup completes using the Phone And Modem Options tool in Control Panel.

15. On the Date And Time Settings page, review the date, time, and time zone information; make any necessary corrections, and then click Next. After several minutes, Setup finishes the installation and then reboots. After you log in, the Windows Small Business Server Setup Wizard launches, as discussed in the next section.

Using the Windows Small Business Server Setup Wizard

The second major phase of the Windows Small Business Server 2003 setup process is the Windows Small Business Server Setup Wizard. During this phase, Active Directory, Exchange Server, and the rest of the server applications are installed. If you purchased a server with Windows Small Business Server 2003 preinstalled, this is the only phase of Setup you'll see, and it will probably be a few steps shorter than the procedure listed below, so don't be alarmed.

Note Copies of Windows Small Business Server 2003 purchased before February 1, 2004 contain a bug on Windows Small Business 2003 CD 3 that causes an error during setup. To resolve the issue, use a newer version of the CD (available free of charge from Microsoft at *http://go.microsoft.com /fwlink/?LinkId=21682*) or install Windows Server 2003 Hotfix Q832880 from Windows Update after completing setup. See Microsoft Knowledge Base Article 832880 for more information.

Under the Hood **Configuring Network Settings**

During Setup, all network cards on the server are disabled except the one identified as connecting to your internal network. Settings on the disabled adapters are retained.

During installation, network cards are enabled and configured to use Transmission Control Protocol/Internet Protocol (TCP/IP). As part of installation, you select the network adapter that connects to your local network (also called your private or internal network) and Setup prompts you to supply a static IP address (Setup provides a default value of 192.168.16.2). Several network functions performed by the server require an unchanging TCP/IP address.

The Windows Small Business Server Setup Wizard launches automatically the first time you log into Windows Small Business Server after the underlying operating system is installed. To use this wizard, follow these steps:

1. Make sure that all network adapters have the correct drivers installed and are functioning properly (but plug in the external Internet-connected network adapter). Also, plug in any UPS devices that you unplugged during the first phase of Setup. When you're ready, click Next on the first page of the Windows Small Business Server 2003 Setup Wizard (Figure 4-4).

2. If the requirements for Setup are not met, a Setup Requirements page appears. Review the requirements and, if necessary, take further action to correct.

3. On the Company Information page, provide the phone, fax, and address for your company or organization and then click Next. Setup uses this information to configure server tools.

4. On the Internal Domain Information page, optionally change the default DNS and NetBIOS names provided by Setup to the domain name you decided upon in Chapter 3, and then click Next.

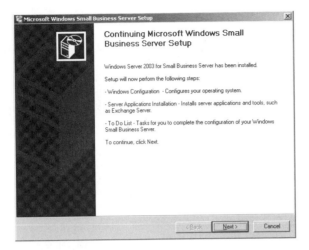

Figure 4-4. *The Windows Small Business Server Setup Wizard lists what remains to be done.*

Security Alert   To be as secure as possible, your internal domain must be kept isolated from the Internet. Using a top-level domain such as *.local* or *.office* that isn't in use on the Internet is an important way of doing that. (Don't use .local if you want to allow Mac OS X clients to use the network.)

The NetBIOS name is used for backward compatibility and to create the organization name for Exchange Server.

5. If there are two or more network adapters in your Windows Small Business Server computer, specify which one connects to the local network and then click Next.

6. If Setup detects an existing DHCP server on the network, click Yes in the dialog box that appears (see Figure 4-5) to use the Windows Small Business Server DHCP Server service, ensuring the correct setup of DHCP on the network. You should then manually disable the existing DHCP server, which is most likely in a firewall or wireless access point. (See the Under the Hood sidebar, "DHCP," for more information.)

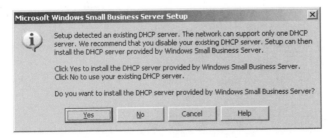

Figure 4-5. *What happens when an existing DHCP server is detected.*

7. On the Local Network Adapter Configuration page, confirm or change the default settings for the internal network adapter card and then click Next.

8. During the remaining parts of Setup, the computer will reboot several times. To save time logging on, provide your password on the Logon Information page. This saves your password only until Setup is completed.

9. Follow the screen prompts as the operating system is configured, the system reboots, and components are loaded. This process will take several minutes (see Figure 4-6).

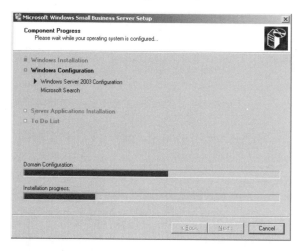

Figure 4-6. *The Component Progress page.*

10. The next page is Component Selection (see Figure 4-7). By default all components are selected. Click the arrows to select items not to install and then click Next.

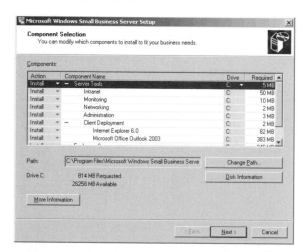

Figure 4-7. *The Component Selection page.*

11. The Data Folders page displays components and the folders in which they'll be placed. To make changes, select the item and click Change Folder. Click Next to continue.

12. The Component Summary page provides an opportunity to review your choices and modify them.

From this point on, the installation requires no further input except the changing of CDs. Any errors are reported on a Component Messages page. After the final reboot, you see the To Do List. To tackle the chores on the list, go directly to Chapter 6, "Completing the To Do List and Other Post-Installation Tasks."

Under the Hood DHCP

Dynamic Host Configuration Protocol (DHCP) is a method of assigning dynamic IP addresses to devices on a network. With dynamic addressing, clients boot up and automatically receive an IP address and other TCP/IP settings such as DNS servers, WINS servers, and the default gateway.

Although you can assign static IP address settings to your client computers rather than use a DHCP service, it's not a good idea. With DHCP, the network automatically allocates and keeps track of IP addresses, ensuring that there are no conflicts. With static addresses, the administrator becomes the keeper of the list, resulting in more management overhead and room for error. Also, without DHCP you won't be able to use the network Setup to configure clients running Windows 2000 Professional or Windows XP Professional automatically.

Setup can configure DHCP server settings on devices that support Universal Plug and Play (UPnP), but some devices can't take advantage of all the settings that Setup can configure.

Summary

This chapter discussed how to prepare and perform a clean installation of Windows Small Business Server 2003. After installation, a few elements must be configured to fit your unique situation. Details are in Chapter 6.

Chapter 5, the next chapter, describes how to upgrade a computer running Windows Small Business Server 2000 and how to migrate from Windows 2000 Server or Windows Server 2003.

Chapter 5
Upgrading or Migrating to Windows Small Business Server 2003

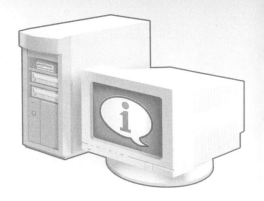

Upgrading to Microsoft Windows Small Business Server 2003 preserves data and settings that might otherwise be lost performing a clean installation. So if you have an existing network with a server, upgrading is the best approach.

Choosing Between Upgrading and Migrating

First decide whether you want to upgrade an existing server or migrate to a new server. Upgrading an existing server is relatively easy and causes the least disruption to the network. It requires the least expense for hardware and consulting, even when you must upgrade the server hardware to reach an acceptable performance level.

Migrating to a new server is a complex process that requires a new domain (hosted by the new server) and moving all data and accounts. When you migrate, the new server is unencumbered by old programs, unused accounts, and incorrect settings. Combined with the opportunity to choose a more powerful server platform, migrating to a new server provides the highest level of performance and stability possible while preserving the existing network. Migration is also the only practical option when the current server is too slow or isn't running Microsoft Windows Small Business Server 2000, Windows 2000 Server, or Windows Server 2003. (If the server is not running one of these operating systems, you'd have to upgrade to one of them and then upgrade to Windows Small Business Server 2003. It's very nearly as much work as migrating.)

> **Tip** You can enhance the performance of a current server by upgrading the RAM to 1 GB or more, adding a SCSI-based RAID, and even upgrading the processor. You can also offload some tasks to another server on the network—file sharing, printer sharing, and hosting the SharePoint intranet site are several good candidates. However, the Windows Small Business Server 2003 computer must host Microsoft Exchange Server 2003, Active Directory, and the Premium Technologies components (ISA Server 2000 and SQL Server 2000).

Planning   You can back up the existing server and restore the software to a new server that shares the same motherboard chipset, number of processors, and mass storage controller. However, minuscule hardware differences often lead to large problems, and you should restore a backup set to a different server only when the original server can't be repaired—not because you want to migrate to a faster server. For additional information, see Chapter 13, "Backing Up and Restoring Data," and the Restrdoc.htm file on the Windows Small Business Server 2003 CD 1.

Preparing for a Migration

Migration is better documented and automated on Windows Small Business Server 2003 than it was on Small Business Server 2000, though there are potential bumps on the road:

- Exchange Mailbox rules, the Administrator account mailbox, and public folders aren't migrated and must be manually exported using the Exchange Mailbox Merge Wizard (ExMerge.exe).

- Custom settings such as DHCP scope options and Exchange server SMTP connector settings aren't migrated.

- Group Policy Objects (GPOs) aren't migrated, and must be manually exported from the existing domain using the Group Policy Management Console in Windows Small Business Server 2003.

- Custom Web sites aren't automatically migrated—copy the Web site files to the new server and recreate the site in Microsoft Internet Information Services (IIS), or use the IIS 6.0 Migration Tool.

- References to the original server break during the migration (shortcuts, mapped drives, and so forth).

The following steps provide an overview of the migration process:

1. Disable the DHCP Server service on the source server (the existing server).

2. Install Windows Small Business Server 2003 on the destination computer (creating the new domain) and perform the tasks on the To Do List.

3. Disconnect the destination server from the Internet and disable real-time antivirus software on both servers.

4. Prepare client computers for migration by removing unnecessary software and deleting any shortcuts to the existing server.

5. Use the Active Directory Migration Tool (ADMT) on the destination server to migrate users, groups, and computer accounts to the new domain.

6. Use the Exchange Migration Wizard in Windows Small Business Server 2003 to migrate Exchange mailboxes to the new server.

7. Use ExMerge on the Windows Small Business Server 2003 computer to export Exchange public folders and the Administrator account mailbox from the existing server. ExMerge is available for download at *http://www.microsoft.com/exchange*.

8. Move shared folders and application data to the destination server.

9. Migrate any SQL Server databases to the destination server, as discussed in Microsoft Knowledge Base article 314546 "HOW TO: Move Databases Between Computers That Are Running SQL Server."

10. Assign migrated user accounts to Windows Small Business Server 2003 templates and assign applications to client computers.

11. Import Exchange server public folders; and configure Exchange distribution lists, custom recipient policies, and the Microsoft Connector for POP3 Mailboxes.

12. Connect client computers to the new domain. (See Chapter 12, "Managing Computers on the Network.")

13. Remove permissions used for migration, uninstall ADMT, and then retire the source server.

More Info   For in-depth information about migrating to Windows Small Business Server 2003, see the migration white papers on the CD included with this book: "Migrating from Small Business Server 4.5 or Windows NT Server 4.0 to Windows Small Business Server 2003" and "Migrating from Small Business Server 2000 or Windows 2000 Server to Windows Small Business Server 2003." Also visit the Microsoft Small Business Server Web site at *http://www.microsoft.com/sbserver* for updated information and migration tools.

Preparing for an Upgrade

Start preparing for an upgrade by checking for compatibility issues, creating a disaster recovery plan, and updating the server and clients. Complete final preparations the day before the upgrade. Perform the actual upgrade outside of business hours and with a realistic deadline that minimizes disruption to the business. (In other words, calculate how long the process will take and then double it.)

Checking for Compatibility Issues

Windows Small Business Server 2003 seldom exhibits compatibility problems, though it's nonetheless a good idea to check the following areas for potential trouble:

- **System requirements**   To complete the upgrade, the existing server must be running Small Business Server 2000, Windows 2000 Server, or Windows Server 2003; have a minimum of 2 GB of free disk space; and meet all the system requirements listed in Chapter 3, "Designing a Network."

- **Third-party applications**   Some third-party applications are incompatible with Windows Server 2003, most notably antivirus programs and some Web applications. Read the updated release notes on the Windows Small Business Server Web site (*http://www.microsoft.com /windowsserver2003/sbs*), and verify with the developers of third-party software that their software is compatible.

- **Device drivers**   Some older network cards and other devices aren't supported by Windows Small Business Server 2003 and must be replaced. Visit the Microsoft Windows Catalog at *http://www.microsoft.com /windows/catalog/server* for a listing of certified devices.

- **Client computers**   Computers running Microsoft Windows 95 or older operating systems should be upgraded or replaced. (If you can't upgrade Windows 95 clients, install the Active Directory client extensions, as discussed in Chapter 12.)

- **Language**   The Windows Small Business Server 2003 upgrade software must be the same language edition as the existing operating system.

Tip   Server applications that aren't compatible with Windows Small Business Server 2003 can be run in a virtual machine using Microsoft Virtual Server, or moved to another server on the network.

Preparing for the Worst

Windows Small Business Server is the virtual brain of a small business network, and even when other domain controllers are on the network, the failure of the Windows Small Business Server computer constitutes a disaster. Users lose access to the Internet, Exchange Server e-mail, fax services, and any resources shared by the Windows Small Business Server computer, such as shared folders and printers.

Therefore, it's extremely important to have a fallback plan if the upgrade doesn't go smoothly. Start by planning how you can restore from a current backup set and estimating how much time is required. (A major failure during the upgrade could require a basic installation of Windows to access backup sets.)

The upgrade meets an acceptable level of functionality when users can:

- Log on successfully
- Access their Exchange server accounts
- Browse the Internet
- Access their usual resources (files and printers)
- Access vital business applications

You might have additional criteria to add to this list.

If the network doesn't meet the minimum level of functionality by the deadline you've set, implement the recovery plan, restore the existing server from backup, and verify proper server functioning. Then evaluate the problems and redesign the upgrade plan to compensate for them (and possibly allow more time to deal with unanticipated issues).

More Info   For more information about disaster preparation an d recovery, see Chapter 21, "Disaster Planning and Fault Tolerance."

Preparing the Server

To prepare a server for upgrading to Windows Small Business Server 2003, fix any current problems, install required service packs, remove unnecessary software, and check the items in this list:

- **Check Event Viewer**   Fix problems reported in Event Viewer *before* the upgrade.

- **Collect Internet setup information**   Although Internet settings are preserved during an upgrade, you should have the following information available: the server's Internet IP address and subnet mask, the host name, the default gateway, DNS server addresses, any PPP Over Ethernet (PPPoE) user name and passwords, and external mail server addresses used by your company.

- **Uninstall unnecessary software**   Unless you need a software package on the server, uninstall it. This is especially applicable for end user applications such as Microsoft Office—these have no place on a server.

- **Remove Windows 2000 Administration Tools**   These tools are incompatible with Windows Small Business Server 2003 and must be uninstalled before upgrading.

- **Install the latest system BIOS**   This reduces the likelihood of device errors or BIOS issues causing stability problems in Windows.

Note You should also update the firmware on your firewall device (especially if it supports UPnP) and any wireless access points (especially if you plan on using WPA or 802.1X authentication).

- **Install all necessary service packs and updates** Install the service packs that are relevant to the existing server:

  - Small Business Server 2000 Service Pack 1

  - Windows 2000 Service Pack 4 (included in Small Business Server Service Pack 1a)

  - Exchange 2000 Service Pack 3 (included in Small Business Server Service Pack 1)

  - ISA Server 2000 Service Pack 1

  - ISA Server 2000 Required Updates For Windows Server 2003 (see Microsoft Knowledge Base article 331062 "Running ISA Server on Windows Server 2003")

  - SQL Server 2000 Service Pack 3a

- **Remove discontinued Exchange components** In the Add Or Remove Programs tool, select Microsoft Small Business Server 2000, click Change/Remove, and then use the Microsoft Small Business Server 2000 Setup Wizard to remove the following Exchange components (if installed):

  - Microsoft Exchange MSMail Connector

  - Microsoft Exchange Connector for Lotus cc:Mail

  - Microsoft Exchange Instant Messaging Service

  - Microsoft Exchange Chat Service

  - Microsoft Exchange Key Management Service

More Info Microsoft Exchange Instant Messaging Service and Microsoft Exchange Chat Service have been replaced by Microsoft Live Communications Server 2003. See *http://office.microsoft.com* for more information.

- **Remove Remote Storage** If you're using the Remote Storage service, use the Windows Components Wizard (available from the Add Or Remove Programs tool) to remove it before upgrading.

- **Remove any trust relationships** Windows Small Business Server supports only a single domain, so if you have any trust relationships established with other domains, disable them before upgrading.

- **Remove CALs** If you're running Windows 2000 Server or Windows Server 2003, reset the number of installed CALs to five. After installing

Windows Small Business Server 2003, you can install additional Windows Small Business Server CALs.

- **Remove the Windows Server 2003 POP3 service**   If the Windows Server 2003 POP3 service is installed, you must remove it using the Windows Components Wizard, available from the Add Or Remove Programs tool.

- **Make sure that all domain controllers are online**   Windows Small Business Server can't install if it can't contact all domain controllers in the domain, so don't take any domain controllers offline during the upgrade.

- **Assign all operations master roles to the Small Business Server computer**   If you have multiple domain controllers, make sure that the Small Business Server computer is the schema master, domain master, relative identifier (RID) master, primary domain controller (PDC) emulator, and infrastructure master.

More Info   For information about transferring operations master roles, see the "Transferring Operations Master Roles" page in Windows Help.

- **Upgrade or retire any Windows NT 4.0 BDCs**   Windows NT 4.0 backup domain controllers (BDCs) cause the upgrade to halt at the end of the operating system installation phase because Windows Small Business Server 2003 needs to convert the domain to Windows 2000 native functional level. To avert this, upgrade any BDCs to Windows 2000 with SP3 or later, or retire them.

Real World   Upgrading Remote Domain Controllers

To reduce the amount of replication traffic generated when upgrading or deploying a new domain controller in a remote office, back up the system state information from the Windows Small Business Server 2003 computer and physically ship the backup media to the remote site. Next, upgrade the remote domain controller to Windows Server 2003, or perform a clean install, and restore the system state files to a local hard drive *before* running the Active Directory Installation Wizard (by specifying Restore Files To: Alternate Location in Backup). Then run the Active Directory Installation Wizard (Dcpromo.exe) with the */adv* switch and specify the location of the restored files. This seeds the new or upgraded domain controller with slightly out-of-date Active Directory data, which is updated during the first replication. This first replication is significantly faster than transferring the entire Active Directory.

Preparing Client Computers

Windows 95 and Windows NT 4.0 computers must be updated before they can communicate with a Windows Small Business Server 2003 computer, as described in the following list. (Windows XP and Windows 2000 computers require no prior preparation.)

- **Upgrade or retire any Windows 95 clients** Windows 95 (and older) clients can't communicate on a Windows Small Business Server 2003 network without some additional work (as discussed in Chapter 12, "Managing Computers on the Network"), so you should replace the computers, or upgrade them to a newer version of Windows. If that's not possible, install the Active Directory Client Extensions (included on the companion CD with this book, Small Business Server 2000 CD 1, and the Windows 2000 Server CD).

- **Update Windows NT 4.0 computers** Install Windows NT 4.0 Service Pack 6a and Internet Explorer 6 on Windows NT 4.0 computers before upgrading the Small Business Server computer so that these computers can continue communicating on the network.

Planning Besides preparing client computers, you must also prepare users as far ahead of time as possible. Tell users when the upgrade will occur, how long the network will be down, and how the upgrade will benefit them.

More Info Outlook 2003 can only be installed on Windows XP and Windows 2000 clients. For more information about the limitations of earlier clients, see Chapter 12.

Final Preparation

The day before you upgrade to Windows Small Business Server 2003, perform the following tasks:

1. Check all hard drives for errors using **chkdsk** *c:* at a command prompt (where **c** is the drive letter you want to check). If any errors are detected, run **chkdsk** *c:* **/f** to correct the errors.

2. Use the Disk Cleanup Wizard to find and delete unnecessary files.

3. Defragment the system drive.

4. Update virus definitions and perform a complete virus scan. Then uninstall the antivirus program. If you know that the program works under Windows Server 2003 without modification, you can simply disable it.

Caution   Don't back up or scan the Exchange M: drive for viruses. Doing so can lead to Exchange database corruption.

5. Locate all drivers and operating system CD-ROMs.

6. Reboot into Safe Mode (unless you're running Windows Server 2003) and then perform a full backup including the system state. Test the backup set by restoring some randomly selected files to an alternate location and comparing the files with the originals. If you don't have a satisfactory backup solution, implement one before performing the upgrade.

Note   In a normal backup, many files aren't backed up because the system is using them. Backing up the system in Safe Mode increases the number of files that are backed up because fewer are in use. Windows Server 2003 systems allow backing up open files using shadow copies, making a Safe Mode reboot unnecessary.

7. Stop and disable third-party services that are using the Local System account. Open Services in the Administrative Tools folder, double-click third-party services that show Local System in the Log On As column, stop the service, write down the startup types so that you can restore the settings after the upgrade is complete, and then change the startup type to Disabled. Repeat until all third-party services are disabled. (There's no easy way to identify third-party services—you'll just have to read their names and descriptions.)

Performing the Upgrade

When all preparations are complete, use the following steps outside of normal business hours to upgrade a server running Small Business Server 2000, Windows 2000 Server or Windows Server 2003 to Windows Small Business Server 2003:

1. Disable disk utilities such as backup programs and antivirus programs.

2. Disconnect any uninterruptible power supply (UPS) devices, including USB models.

3. Notify users that the server will be upgraded by typing the following command at a command prompt (change the text as desired):

   Net send * *The server will be unavailable in five minutes. Please save your work and disconnect from the server.*

4. Unless you have a hardware firewall, disconnect the Internet connection device from the Internet.

5. Log on using an Administrator account and insert the Windows Small Business Server 2003 DVD or CD 1. The Microsoft Windows Small Business Server Setup window appears automatically.

6. Click Set Up Windows Small Business Server.

7. On the first page of the Microsoft Windows Small Business Server Setup Wizard, click Next, review the upgrade information, and then click Next again.

8. On the Setup Requirements page, review any warnings, select the I Acknowledge All Warnings check box, and then click Next.

9. On the License Agreement page, review the license agreement, choose I Agree, and then click Next.

10. On the Product Key page, type the product key from the Windows Small Business Server 2003 packaging, and then click Next.

11. On the Required Components page, click Next. Setup installs Windows Small Business Server 2003 and reboots the computer several times.

12. Log on using an Administrator account and then click Next on the first page of the Microsoft Windows Small Business Server Setup Wizard. (Double-click the Continue Setup icon on the desktop if the wizard doesn't appear automatically.)

13. If the Setup Requirements page appears, address any requirements and then click Next.

14. On the Company Information page, type the phone, fax, and address for your company or organization, and then click Next. This information is used by Setup to configure server tools.

15. If the Internal Domain Information page appears, enter the DNS domain name, NetBIOS domain name, and computer name, and then click Next.

16. On the Local Network Adapter Information page (Figure 5-1), select the network adapter connected to the local network and then click Next.

17. If the Local Network Adapter Configuration page appears, specify the IP address and subnet mask for the network adapter that connects to the local network and then click Next.

18. During the remaining parts of Setup, the computer reboots several times. To save time logging on, provide your password on the Logon Information page and then click Next. (This saves your password only until Setup is complete.) Click Next again to continue Setup.

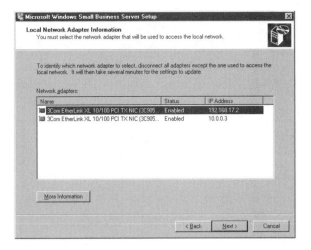

Figure 5-1. *The Local Network Adapter Information page of the Microsoft Windows Small Business Server Setup Wizard.*

19. On the Component Selection page (Figure 5-2), all components are selected by default. Click the arrowheads to select items you do not want to install and then click Next.

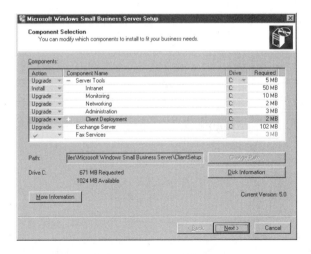

Figure 5-2. *The Component Selection page.*

20. The Data Folders page displays components and the folders in which they'll be placed. To make changes, select the item and click Change Folder. Click Next to continue.

21. The Component Summary page provides an opportunity to review your choices and modify them. Click Next to continue. Windows installs the specified components and then reboots the computer.

From this point on, the installation requires no further input except the changing of CDs. Errors are reported on a Component Messages page. After the final reboot, you see the To Do List, covered in Chapter 6, "Completing the To Do List and Other Post-Installation Tasks." However, there's one more task to complete—migrating user permissions. Users of Windows Small Business Server 2003, Premium Edition, who upgraded from Windows 2000 Server or Windows Server 2003 and aren't currently running SQL Server 2000 and ISA Server 2000 should also install these applications from the Premium Technologies CD, as discussed in Appendix B.

Caution   After upgrading from Windows Server 2003, reinstall the service packs and hotfixes that were on the original server.

Migrating User Permissions

After upgrading to Windows Small Business Server 2003, run the Change User Permissions Wizard to apply appropriate permissions to existing user accounts. This ensures that users can access domain resources, use the Internet, and connect to the internal network from across the Internet using the Remote Web Workplace and VPN connections (if you apply the Mobile Users template to the users). The wizard also configures disk quotas and creates Exchange mailboxes and home folders for users that don't already have them.

To use the Change User Permissions Wizard, complete the following steps:

1. In the To Do List, click Migrate Users to launch the Change User Permissions Wizard, and then click Next.

2. On the Template Selection page (Figure 5-3), select the user template to apply to a group of existing users and choose whether to replace existing permissions, which provides the most consistent results, or to add to existing permissions. Click Next to continue.

Note   To apply different permissions to groups of users, run the Change User Permissions Wizard multiple times, each time choosing a different template and group of users.

3. On the User Selection page, select the users whose permissions you want to change, click Add, and then click Next.

4. Review the settings and then click Finish to apply the new permissions.

Note   Existing permissions applied directly to user accounts are preserved—only group permissions are changed.

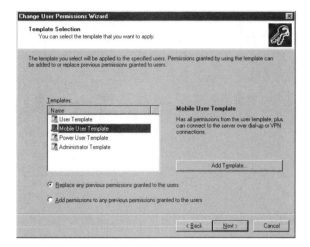

Figure 5-3.   *The Template Selection page of the Change User Permissions Wizard.*

Summary

Upgrading an existing server to Windows Small Business Server 2003 is the easiest way to install Windows Small Business Server while preserving existing settings and data, though when the server is incompatible with Windows Small Business Server 2003 or too slow, you must instead perform the more complex migration process. Once you've decided between upgrading and migrating, it's important to adequately prepare the server and clients for the upgrade, which is straightforward.

The next chapter covers how to complete the To Do List and Windows Small Business Server 2003 configuration.

Chapter 6

Completing the To Do List and Other Post-Installation Tasks

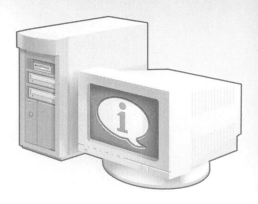

When installation of Microsoft Windows Small Business Server 2003 is complete, you need to tweak several components to fit your unique situation. The To Do List and an assortment of helpful wizards make these chores considerably easier. This chapter covers the settings needed to make your system work properly.

After installation of Windows Small Business Server, the first thing you see when you log on is the Windows Small Business Server To Do List. If the To Do List is not displayed, select Server Management from the Start menu. In the Server Management console, click To Do List, as shown in Figure 6-1.

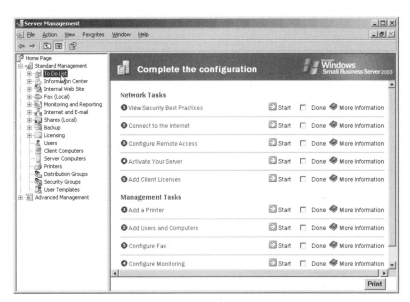

Figure 6-1. *The To Do List, which you can summon easily.*

Security Best Practices

It's best to tackle the items on the To Do List in the order they're listed, and the very first is View Security Best Practices. This is not mere happenstance. Implementing and maintaining the best security practices are the most crucial tasks on a network. Click Start next to View Security Best Practices to open Security Best Practices help.

Security strategies are of three types:

- Protecting your network against external assault in the form of hackers and malicious code.

- Protecting against internal threats. Internal threats are more likely the result of accidents than malice, but it's necessary to protect from both kinds.

- Monitoring the network for security issues and keeping current on security information.

Completing the To Do List configures some of all three elements.

Connecting to the Internet

The first action item on the To Do List is Connect To The Internet. Click Start next to Connect To The Internet to launch the Configure E-Mail and Internet Connection Wizard. On the first page, click the link for Required Information For Connecting To The Internet. This link connects to a help file (Figure 6-2) that tells you what you need for your network.

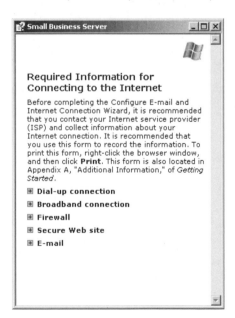

Figure 6-2. *The help file that determines what information you'll need for your connection to the Internet.*

> **Tip**   Determining the information you need to connect to the Internet can be one of the more complicated tasks required by Windows Small Business Server, so you might want to print this help file. To print this help file, right-click inside the help window and select Print.
>
> Determine what details you need and note the answers on the printed form. And don't hesitate to press your Internet Service Provider (ISP) for all the assistance you can get.

The information you collect depends on your Internet connection type. Windows Small Business Server supports four Internet connection types:

- Broadband connection with a local router
- Direct broadband connection
- Broadband connection with user authentication (PPPoE)
- Dial-up connection

To complete the Configure E-Mail and Internet Connection Wizard, select one of these Internet connection types. The following sections describe setting up each connection type.

Real World   Internet Connection Choices

Many options are available for connecting to the Internet. Not all of them will be available in every location, but wherever you are, balancing budget restrictions with performance needs will be the thorniest issue. Before making a decision, do your research. Contact the local telephone company, cable company, and ISPs to determine the availability of different connections and the costs and hardware requirements associated with each. Some of the usual types of connections are described here.

Dial-Up

A dial-up connection uses a standard analog modem over regular telephone lines. Dial-up connections are easy to configure, though data transmission speed depends on the quality of the line. Most dial-up connections provide bandwidth of 56 kilobits per second (Kbps) or less. Dial-up connections are the slowest and (usually) least expensive way to connect to the Internet.

Integrated Services Digital Network

Integrated Services Digital Network (ISDN) is a telephone company technology that provides digital service typically in increments of 64 Kbps. An ISDN line is similar to an analog telephone line except that it connects faster and transmits data much faster. Basic Rate ISDN can be more than twice as fast as an ordinary dial-up connection, with two 64-Kbps channels and a total bandwidth of 128 Kbps. Primary Rate ISDN, with 23 B-channels and one D-channel (U.S.) or 30 B-channels and one D-channel (Europe) can rival the 1.544 megabits per second (Mbps) speed of a T1 line.

In the United States, ISDN calls are frequently charged by the minute, even for local calls. This varies from state to state, but if your ISDN provider uses this method, charging by the minute will make a very large difference in the cost of your connection.

ISDN has been largely eclipsed by other broadband technologies, but it's a viable option in areas where DSL or other fast connections aren't available.

Digital Subscriber Line

A Digital Subscriber Line (DSL) is similar to ISDN inasmuch as both operate over existing copper telephone lines and both require short runs to a central telephone office (usually fewer than 20,000 feet). However, DSL speeds start at about 128 Kbps and go up to 1.5 Mbps, and some connections can go as fast as 50 Mbps depending on the equipment used, distance to the telephone office, cabling quality, and other factors.

DSL is available only in some areas and is often available in one part of a city but not in others. (Nevertheless, the availability of DSL is spreading rapidly.) DSL is an always-on connection and as such is fast and convenient to use.

Cable Modem

A cable modem connection is a fast connection in which your cable company is your ISP. Cable modems are primarily used by home customers, but many cable companies offer businesses transmission speeds up to 10 Mbps, though speeds up to 3.5 Mbps download and 384 Kbps upload are more typical. Cable connections to the Internet can be a viable alternative for a small business but are sometimes expensive depending on the locality.

T1

A full T1 (E1 is the European near equivalent) line supports up to 1.544 Mbps of total bandwidth. T1/E1 cabling requirements are more rigorous than those for DSL and the setup costs are correspondingly high. T1 is a more expensive option than DSL or cable modems but the service level for T1 lines is typically superior.

Fractional T1

The T1 bandwidth of 1.544 Mbps actually consists of 24 separate 64-Kbps channels. A fractional T1 line lets you purchase as many of these channels as you need. For example, if you need 512 Kbps of total bandwidth, you can make a cost comparison between eight channels of a fractional T1 and a 512-Kbps DSL line.

Setting Up a Broadband Connection with a Local Router

A broadband connection using a local router can be set up with either one or two network adapters in the server. Figure 6-3 shows the arrangement when you have two network adapters. In this setup, your server is the default gateway and default firewall.

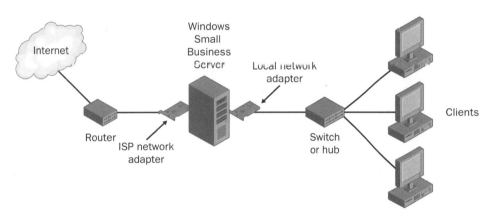

Figure 6-3. *How the network is connected using two network adapters on your Windows Small Business Server.*

> **Tip** Using one network adapter, the router becomes the default gateway and the Windows Small Business Server firewall can't be configured. If you don't have an existing firewall device, install a second network adapter. It's much cheaper than having your network invaded.

To set up a broadband connection to the Internet using a local router, complete the following steps:

1. On the To Do List, click Start next to Connect To The Internet.

2. On the Connection Type page, select Broadband and click Next.

3. On the Broadband Connection page, select A Local Router Device With An IP Address from the drop-down list and click Next.

4. On the Router Connection page, type the DNS server addresses and the IP address for the router. Clear the check box for using a single network connection and click Next.

Note If you are already running Microsoft Internet Security and Acceleration Server (ISA), the wizard will automatically configure ISA to work with Windows Small Business Server.

---

5. If the adapter obtains an IP address using DHCP, select that option on the Network Connection page. Otherwise, select Use The Following ISP Address and provide the addresses. When you click Next, the ISP network configuration is completed.

6. On the second Network Connection page, verify that the ISP network connection and the server local connection are correct and click Next.

7. Follow the steps in the "Configuring the Firewall" section (appearing later in this chapter) to complete the Configure E-Mail and Internet Connection Wizard.

Setting Up a Direct Broadband Connection

A connection to the Internet made through a DSL modem or cable modem is a *direct broadband connection*. Figure 6-4 shows the arrangement for a direct broadband connection.

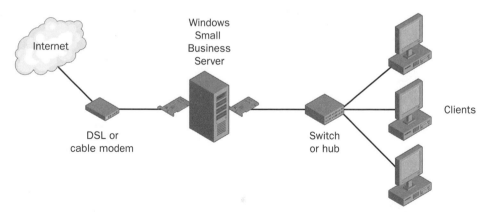

Figure 6-4. *Hardware arranged for a direct broadband connection.*

To set up a direct broadband connection, complete the following steps:

1. On the To Do List, click Start next to Connect To The Internet. Click the link for Required Information For Connecting To The Internet. When you're ready to proceed, click Next.

2. On the Connection Type page, select Broadband and click Next.

3. On the Broadband Connection page, select A Direct Broadband Connection from the drop-down list and click Next.

4. On the Network Connection page, verify that the ISP network connection and the local network connection are correct and click Next.

5. On the Direct Broadband Connection page, supply the IP addresses for the default gateway and DNS servers. (Your ISP provides these addresses.) Click Next.

6. Follow the steps in the "Configuring the Firewall" section (appearing later in this chapter) to complete the Configure E-Mail and Internet Connection Wizard.

Setting Up a Broadband Connection with User Authentication (PPPoE)

If your broadband connection requires user authentication and uses a device such as a DSL or cable modem, you need two network adapters in the Windows Small Business Server, and the firewall is configured on the server. To set up a Point to Point Protocol over Ethernet (PPPoE) connection, complete the following steps:

1. Click Start next to Connect To The Internet on the To Do List. Click the link for Required Information For Connecting To The Internet. When you're ready to proceed, click Next.

2. On the Connection Type page, select Broadband and click Next.

3. On the Broadband Connection page, select A Connection That Requires A User Name And Password (PPPoE) from the drop-down list and click Next.

4. On the PPPoE Connection page, select the PPPoE connection from the drop-down list. (If the connection isn't listed, click the New button and type the name for the connection and the service name.)

5. Type the ISP user name and password (that is, the user name and password that the ISP associates with your connection). If your ISP has assigned a static IP address to the connection, select that check box and supply that IP address and the IP addresses for the DNS servers for name resolution. Click Next.

6. On the Local Network Connection page, select the local connection and verify the IP address and click Next.

7. Follow the steps in the "Configuring the Firewall" section (appearing later in this chapter) to complete the Configure E-Mail and Internet Connection Wizard.

Setting Up a Dial-Up Connection

To set up a connection to the Internet using a modem or an ISDN (Integrated Services Digital Network) adapter, complete the following steps:

1. On the To Do List, click Start next to Connect To The Internet. Click the link for Required Information for Connecting to the Internet. When you're ready to proceed, click Next.

2. On the Connection Type page, select Dial-up and click Next.

3. On the Dial-Up Connection page, select the dial-up connection. If the connection hasn't been configured, click New and provide a name for the connection and the telephone number for connecting to your ISP.

4. Type the ISP user name and password (that is, the user name and password that the ISP associates with your connection), as shown in Figure 6-5. If your ISP has assigned a static IP address to the connection, select that check box and supply the IP address and the IP addresses for the DNS servers on the Internet for name resolution. Click Next.

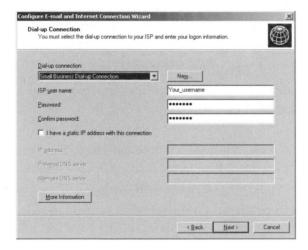

Figure 6-5. *Providing the logon information for your dial-up connection.*

5. On the Local Network Connection page, select the local connection and verify the IP address and click Next.

6. Follow the steps in the "Configuring the Firewall" section to complete the Configure E-Mail and Internet Connection Wizard.

Under the Hood   E-Mail Delivery and Retrieval

When you have a choice, always use DNS for delivering your e-mail. When you use DNS, you are responsible for deciding where e-mail goes. The e-mail headers are correct and you're actually being a good Internet citizen. When you forward e-mail to what's called a "smart host," the headers will show that the e-mail was forwarded or relayed, and in today's world when people are being swamped with spam, that alone is enough to get your e-mail blocked from many servers.

E-mail is retrieved either directly from POP3 (Post Office Protocol 3) mailboxes and then routed to Exchange, or the e-mail is delivered directly to Exchange. POP3 mailboxes are the easiest to manage. They will have addresses such as user@YourISP.com. Many ISPs include 5 or 10 free POP3 e-mail accounts with their service.

How your ISP handles incoming e-mail determines the configuration of e-mail delivered directly to Exchange. Either it's delivered to Exchange as soon as received, or it's held until your server sends a signal to the ISP. Two types of signal are in use:

- ETRN, which requires that you use a static IP address supplied by the ISP.

- TURN After Authentication, which allows the ISP to deliver to a dynamic IP address. If you choose this option, the TURN Authentication Information page of the wizard will prompt for the user name and password used to authenticate your server to the ISP.

Your ISP will tell you which signal to use.

Configuring the Firewall

Unless you have another firewall (hardware or ISA), you must use the Windows Small Business Server firewall or your network will be completely vulnerable to attack from the Internet. When running the Configure E-Mail and Internet Connection Wizard, you are prompted to enable the firewall and then configure the services. Complete the following steps:

1. On the Firewall page, click Enable Firewall and then click Next.

2. On the Services Configuration page (Figure 6-6), select the services that you'll need and then click Next.

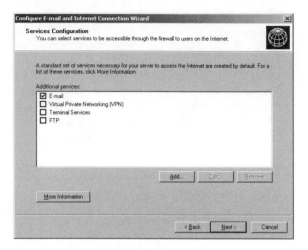

Figure 6-6. *Selecting the services to pass through the firewall.*

Tip   If you select Virtual Private Networking (VPN), the system will warn that your server isn't configured for remote access. Click OK. Remote access is enabled in the next To Do List item.

3. On the Web Services Configuration page (Figure 6-7), select the Web services you want available to users connecting from the Internet.

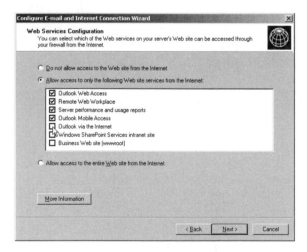

Figure 6-7. *Selecting the Web services to pass through the firewall.*

If you don't allow any access, you'll have maximum security but you won't be able to use some of the best features of Windows Small Business Server, including Remote Web Workplace and Outlook Mobile Access. On the other hand, allowing access to the entire Web site will allow users to access all the Web site directories. So it's advisable to pick and choose specific services:

- Outlook Web Access is a component of the Web-based messaging client in Microsoft Exchange Server that gives users secure access to their e-mail, a personal calendar, and group scheduling from any browser.

- Remote Web Workplace allows authorized users to connect through an Internet address to Outlook Web Access, your Share-Point Services intranet site, and their own desktop. If you select this option, you must also select Outlook Web Access, SharePoint Services, and Server Performance And Usage Reports if you want users to be able to use these services.

- Server Performance And Usage Reports allows authorized users to receive scheduled performance and usage statistics and to receive immediate alerts when an issue arises on the server.

- Outlook Mobile Access allows users to read and send e-mail from a mobile device.

- Outlook Via The Internet allows a user with an Outlook profile on the server to access e-mail from a computer on the Internet without creating a Virtual Private Network (VPN) connection. The client computer must be running Microsoft Windows XP Professional with the latest Service Pack and Microsoft Office Outlook 2003 or later.

- Windows SharePoint Services Intranet Site allows users to make use of the intranet site from the Internet.

- Business Web Site permits user to access your Internet Web site from the Internet.

4. Click Next.

Tip If your network adapter for the Internet has a dynamically assigned IP address via DHCP, a warning message will appear. If your server is assigned a new IP address, your Internet domain name might not be resolved properly causing your Web services to be inaccessible from the Internet. If your IP address is dynamically assigned, ensure your ISP supports dynamic DNS or consider getting a static IP address.

5. If you choose to allow access to some or all of your Web site, the Web Server Certificate page appears prompting you to specify a Web certificate, which is necessary to configure Secure Sockets Layer (SSL).

Security Alert   A Web certificate is a security tool for ensuring safe communications on the Web. A site certificate ensures that the server is the one it claims to be, not an imposter, and that data sent to the server will not be intercepted.

A self-signed certificate will work perfectly well, but customers and visitors accessing your Internet site—if their browser security settings are what they should be—are notified that the site certificate is not signed by a third-party Certification Authority.

A commercial certificate can cost from $200 to $900 per year but is a good investment in security for your customers and visitors. VeriSign (*http://www.verisign.com*), Thawte (*http://www.thawte.com*), and GeoTrust (*http://www.geotrust.com*) are the best known of the commercial providers. Although some providers sell 40-bit as well as 128-bit encryption, 40 bits is too weak to offer adequate protection.

For information about the SSL Certificate technology and the Certification Authorities who issue 128-bit SSL Certificates, see the SSLreview (*http://www.sslreview.com*).

6. On the Internet E-Mail page, select Enable Internet E-Mail to use Exchange for Internet e-mail and click Next.

7. On the E-Mail Delivery Method page, select how to deliver your Internet e-mail and click Next.

8. On the E-Mail Retrieval Method page, specify how e-mail is retrieved from the Internet. Select Use The Microsoft Connector For POP3 Mailboxes if your organization's e-mail accounts are at your ISP. If you are using Exchange, select Use Exchange and specify how the e-mail is delivered to Exchange and click Next. For more information about e-mail delivery and retrieval, see the Under the Hood sidebar, "E-Mail Delivery and Retrieval," earlier in this chapter.

9. On the E-Mail Domain Name page, enter your e-mail domain name. This must be a registered Internet domain. Click Next.

10. If you selected to retrieve e-mail using POP3, the POP3 Mailbox Accounts page appears where you can configure your POP3 mailbox accounts and how e-mail is routed to your Exchange server. Since you probably haven't created user accounts yet, you won't be able to specify Exchange accounts where the e-mail should be routed to. E-mail configuration is discussed in Chapter 14, "Using Exchange Server," so you can leave this till later.

11. If you selected to retrieve e-mail using POP3, the Mail Schedule page appears. Select a frequency for how often to send and receive e-mail.

12. On the Remove E-Mail Attachments page, you can specify the e-mail attachments you want Exchange to remove automatically (Figure 6-8).

If you want, you can save attachments in a folder—preferably one available to administrators only. Click Next.

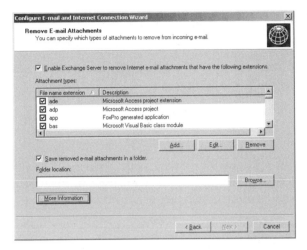

Figure 6-8. *Configuring the automatic removal of e-mail attachments.*

Note   Attachments sent with internal e-mail on the local network aren't affected by these settings.

13. The final page of the Configure E-Mail and Internet Connection Wizard summarizes all that has gone before, beginning with the type of connection selected and ending with the settings for e-mail attachments. Click the link at the bottom of the page for detailed information. Save, print, or e-mail the details for your records (Figure 6-9).

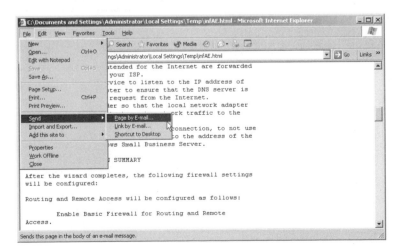

Figure 6-9. *Save the details of your e-mail and Internet configuration.*

After the wizard has completed, you're prompted to enable password policies. You can do this now or later. You will also be connected to the Windows Update

Web site to obtain any critical updates. Keeping Windows Small Business Server up to date is discussed in the "Updating Windows Small Business Server" section.

More Info See Chapter 9, "Users, Groups, and Security," for details about establishing strong passwords.

Configuring Remote Access

The next item on the To Do List is Configure Remote Access. With remote access, users—on the road, at home, just about anywhere—can connect to the local network and use the resources as if they were physically present in the office. A mobile user can connect a laptop to the local network, and then take it on the road and connect remotely. The user experience will be the same in either scenario. Remote access can be configured in two ways: virtual private networking or dial-up.

Under the Hood **Virtual Private Networking**

Private networks are geographically isolated from remote users and other private networks by insecure communication lines like the Internet. VPN emulates a private connection between two separate networks. Both requestor and authenticator perceive the connection as a private dedicated line. Before passing the data through insecure extranets and intranets, the data is encrypted. Because encryption protects the data packet, any in-transit interception results in unreadable data.

Before you can establish a VPN connection, VPN authorization must be confirmed for the client. The policies established in Configure Remote Access, the user's group membership, and the client computer's settings determine authorization.

Once the client establishes a VPN connection, the user appears to be accessing the private network directly, as shown in the following illustration.

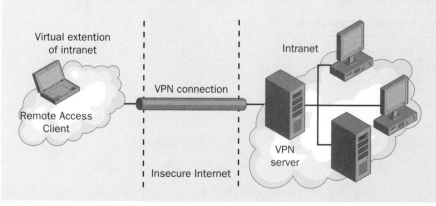

Remote Access via Virtual Private Networking

To configure remote access via virtual private networking, complete the following steps:

1. Click Start next to Configure Remote Access on the To Do List to launch the Remote Access Wizard. Click Next on the Welcome page.

2. On the Remote Access Method page, select Enable Remote Access and VPN (Virtual Private Networking) access. (See the Under the Hood sidebar, "Virtual Private Networking," later in this chapter for additional information.) Click Next.

3. If the Client Addressing page appears, specify that the DHCP server assigns IP addresses to remote clients, or designate a range of addresses. Click Next.

Caution   If you assign a specific range of IP addresses, make sure the number of addresses is large enough to provide connections for the number of clients likely to connect at any given time plus one for the server. If all the IP addresses in the range are in use, any additional remote clients will not be able to connect.

4. On the VPN Server Name page, supply the full Internet name for your VPN server. This is the name of your server with your registered Internet domain name (Figure 6-10). Click Next.

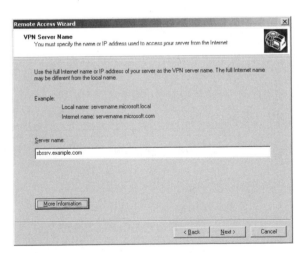

Figure 6-10.   *Supplying the full name of the VPN server.*

5. The last page of the Configure Remote Access Wizard displays a summary of the settings you've made. Click the link at the bottom of the page to save, print, or e-mail the details for your records.

Remote Access via Dial-Up

To configure dial-up remote access, complete the following steps:

1. Click Start next to Configure Remote Access on the To Do List to launch the Remote Access Wizard.

2. On the Remote Access Method page, select Enable Remote Access and Dial-in Access and click Next.

3. If the Client Addressing page appears, specify that the DHCP server assigns IP addresses to remote clients, or designate a range of addresses. Click Next.

Caution If you assign a specific range of IP addresses, make sure the number of addresses is large enough to provide connections for the number of clients likely to connect at any given time plus one for the server. If all the IP addresses or all the modems are in use, any additional remote clients will not be able to connect.

4. On the Modem Selection page, select the modems designated for remote users. As with the range of IP addresses, make sure there are enough for the number of remote users that will connect at one time. Click Next.

5. On the Dial-Up Phone Numbers page, type the primary and alternate telephone numbers that remote users will dial to connect to the server and click Next.

6. The last page of the Configure Remote Access Wizard displays a summary of the settings you've made. Click the link at the bottom of the page to save, print, or e-mail the details for your records.

7. After the wizard has completed, you're prompted to enable password policies. You can do this now or later.

More Info See Chapter 9, "Users, Groups, and Security," for details about establishing strong passwords.

The big issue with remote access isn't configuring the server. As you've seen, doing that is relatively simple. The difficulty arises when users in the field attempt to connect to the server. To help in this process, Windows Small Business Server includes Connection Manager.

More Info See Chapter 12, "Managing Computers on the Network," for details about installing Connection Manager on networked and remote computers.

Activating Your Server

The Activate Your Server item on the To Do List is refreshingly easy to take care of. Click Start next to Activate Your Server to open the Let's Activate Windows page shown in Figure 6-11. Select the first option to activate over the Internet (there's no reason to put it off) and click Next.

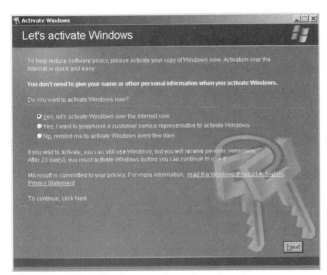

Figure 6-11. *Activating your server.*

Choose to register (or not) at the same time as activation, and click Next again. The system connects using the method you configured while completing the Connect To The Internet item on the To Do List.

Adding Client Access Licenses

The next task on the To Do List is to activate new licenses for the network's client computers or reissue existing licenses after reinstalling Windows Small Business Server. To perform this task, complete the following steps:

1. Click Start next to Add Client Licenses to launch the Add License Wizard and click Next on the Welcome page.

2. On the License Agreement page, review the license agreement, and if you agree, select I Agree and click Next.

3. On the Contact Method page, select the Internet or telephone as a method of connecting. Click Next.

4. On the License Code Information page, type the license codes that were provided when you purchased Windows Small Business Server or the license codes you purchased later.

Note To transfer licenses from one computer to another, use the Transfer License Wizard. Launch Server Management from the Start menu, click Licensing, and then click Transfer Licenses in the details pane.

5. Check that each code is correct and then click Next.

6. If you're connecting through the Internet, the wizard will continue and the license codes will be activated. If connecting by telephone, call the number the wizard provides and provide the Installation IDs from the Telephone Information page. Write down the confirmation IDs and type them in when requested.

Adding Printers

The Add A Printer item on the To Do List allows you to set up a local or network printer.

More Info For more than you ever wanted to know about installing, configuring, or sharing every sort of printer, see Chapter 11, "Installing and Managing Printers."

Adding Users and Computers

The Add User Wizard is available from the To Do List, or you can launch Server Management from the Start menu, click Users, and click Add A User or Add Multiple Users in the details pane.

More Info See Chapter 9 for all the details about adding and configuring user accounts, managing groups, and user profiles. Managing client computers is the subject of Chapter 12.

Configuring Fax Services

Every organization has to cope with faxes—but you no longer have to cope with a fax *machine* and the daily stack of junk faxes (what we used to complain about before we complained about spam). Windows Small Business Server will send, receive, and route faxes. Faxes can be printed, sent to an e-mail address, stored in a folder (shared or not), or stored in a document library on your intranet Web site. Or you can install multiple modems and set routing differently on each one.

To set up the fax service, complete the following steps:

1. Click Start next to Configure Fax on the To Do List to launch the Fax Configuration Wizard. Click Next on the Welcome page.

2. The Provide Company Information page should show the name, the telephone and fax numbers, and the address that you provided during installation of Windows Small Business Server. Enter any missing information and click Next.

3. The Outbound Fax Device page lists the fax modems installed on the server. If you have more than one, use the arrows to set the order in which the devices are used. Click Next.

4. On the Inbound Fax Device page, select which modems will receive faxes. Check the option for all devices using the same routing information, or choose to have each device route independently.

5. On the Inbound Fax Routing page, select the routing methods. As you check an option, a Configure link prompts you for the e-mail address, folder, document library, or printer to use (Figure 6-12).

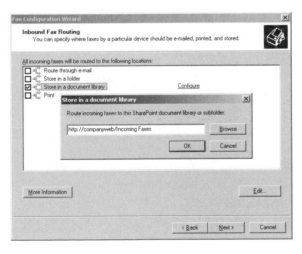

Figure 6-12.   *Selecting methods of fax routing.*

6. On the final page of the wizard is a summary of all the settings made. Click the link at the bottom of the page to save this information.

More Info   For information about connecting to the Shared Fax Service from client systems, see Chapter 12.

Planning   Windows Small Business Server 2003 supports up to four fax modems to increase the number of simultaneous faxes the server can send and receive.

Changing Fax Sending and Receiving

To change how faxes are sent and received, complete the following steps:

1. In the Server Management console, expand the Fax container, expand Devices And Providers, and then select Devices to view a list of fax modems installed on your system.

2. To change the attributes for a device, right-click the device and choose Properties from the shortcut menu. Use the Properties dialog box to configure the device's send and receive settings:

   - Select the Send Faxes and Receive Faxes check boxes to enable the device to send and receive faxes.

   - If you chose to enable the receipt of faxes, choose how many rings to allow before the fax modem answers the line and attempts to receive the fax.

   - Type the sender ID text (usually your company name and telephone number) that you want to appear on outgoing faxes in the Transmitting Subscriber ID (TSID) box.

   - Type the ID text you want to provide to callers who send you faxes in the Called Subscriber ID (CSID) box (this is usually the same text).

3. Select Outgoing Routing in the console tree and then use the Groups and Rules containers to optionally route outgoing faxes to different fax devices based on the recipient's fax number. (This can be useful to send all international faxes using a specific telephone line, for example.)

4. To work with cover pages, select Cover Pages in the console tree. Double-click a cover sheet to edit it in the Fax Cover Page Editor.

Setting Fax Service Properties

To change fax service properties such as delivery receipts, archiving, permissions, and logging, right-click Fax in the Server Management console, choose Properties from the shortcut menu, and then use the Fax Properties dialog box to change the server settings:

- Select the Receipts tab to specify how to notify clients when faxes are sent successfully.

- The Event Reports and Activity Logging tabs control what will be reported in Event Viewer.

- Select the Outbox tab (Figure 6-13) to make settings for the outgoing fax queue.

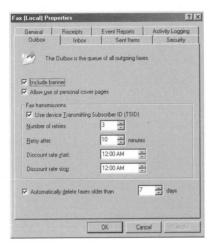

Figure 6-13.   *The Outbox tab of the Fax Properties dialog box.*

- Use the Inbox and Sent Items tabs to control how faxes are archived (archiving is done separately from the normal delivery of faxes).

- Select the Security tab to set fax server management permissions so that only the users and groups you select can send faxes, manage the fax service, or manage fax documents. (If you're going to mess about with default fax permissions, do so either here or in the Printers And Faxes folder in Control Panel—not in both places). Click OK when you're finished.

Configuring Monitoring

Monitoring the performance and usage of the network is an important component of security. Click Start next to Configure Monitoring on the To Do List to launch (what else?) the Monitoring Configuration Wizard. Chapter 20, "Monitoring and Fine-Tuning Performance," covers what to monitor, what alerts to set up, and what to do with the information after you get it.

Configuring Backup

Regular backups are essential, which is why this item is on the To Do List. Launch the Backup Configuration Wizard from here, but first read Chapter 13, "Backing Up and Restoring Data," to develop the optimal backup strategy.

Security Basics

Before leaving the To Do List, be sure that security basics are taken care of. This includes configuring automatic updates and setting up a method to regularly scan the network for security flaws.

Updating Windows Small Business Server

A key part of security is keeping your Windows Small Business Server current on updates. When vulnerabilities are exposed, Microsoft makes fixes available almost instantly. And "almost instantly" is none too soon for your network. Click the globe icon in the notification areas of the Taskbar to start the Automatic Updates Setup Wizard.

On the Notification Settings page, select the updating method you want. Essentially, the three methods are:

- Don't do anything without telling me.
- Download updates but don't install automatically.
- Download and install. Don't bother me with the details.

The first option lends itself too much to delay. The third option is a bit aggressive for many users because some updates require a reboot and with this option the reboot occurs no matter what the server is doing or who is using it. The second option is an effective choice. Updates are downloaded when they become available but you can choose when to install them—important when a server reboot is required to complete the installation.

Updating Client Computers

Automatically updating your server with Windows Automatic Updates is easy enough, but what about client machines? You can't count on users consistently updating their own machines nor do you want to have to deal with it manually. The solution is to use the Automatic Updates client on Windows XP, Windows 2000, and Windows Server 2003 systems to automatically download and install updates daily or weekly. (See the "Using Group Policy to Set Clients to Update Automatically" section in Chapter 10 for Group Policy settings that make this happen.)

Note   The Automatic Updates client is available only on Windows 2000, Windows XP, and Windows Server 2003 systems. Computers running other operating systems must be updated manually.

Centralizing Updates

Software Update Services (SUS) is a free tool from Microsoft that provides a seamless patch, scanning, and installation service. SUS scans the machines on your network, lets you know which patches are needed, connects to Windows Update, downloads needed patches, and then applies your local policy for automatic distribution of patches.

SUS is a good solution for networks large enough to require centralized control over patch management (and the centralized downloading of updates), but it takes some time to set up and configure and requires a monthly commitment to reviewing patches.

Installing Software Update Services

To install Software Update Services, complete the following these steps:

1. Launch the Software Update Services installation program (available from the Microsoft Download Center at *http://www.microsoft.com/downloads/*).

2. Read and accept the terms of the Licensing Agreement, and then click Next.

3. For type of installation, click Typical and then click Install to install SUS, or click Custom to do a custom installation.

Caution   You can change most settings after installation; however, the only time you can easily change where SUS stores downloaded updates is during a Custom setup.

4. If you chose to perform a custom installation, click the first Browse button on the Choose File Locations page (Figure 6-14) to specify in which folder the Software Update Services Web site files should be installed.

Figure 6-14.   *Choosing where to store update files.*

5. To download all updates to the Windows Small Business Server and host them locally, select the Save The Updates To This Local Folder option and click Browse to specify in which folder updates should be stored; otherwise, select Keep The Updates On A Microsoft Windows Update Server, To Which I Will Direct Clients. Click Next to continue.

6. On the Language Settings page, select which languages are supported on the network and then click Next.

7. On the Handling New Versions Of Previously Approved Updates page, specify whether new versions of updates that you previously approved should be automatically approved, click Next, and then click Install.

 Planning Hosting all updates on the Windows Small Business Server 2003 computer provides the fastest update experience for clients (all updates are installed from the local server), and can conserve bandwidth. However, the fact that updates are downloaded only once can be somewhat offset by the fact that SUS downloads all patches instead of just the ones that you decide to install. If you do want to host updates locally, make sure that you have at least 6 GB of free disk space on the server.

Setting Options

After setup is complete, the Software Update Services administration Web site (*http://localhost/SUSAdmin*) opens automatically. This site is accessible only to users who are members of the SUS computer's Local Administrators group and requires Internet Explorer 5.5 or later.

To set options, complete the following steps:

1. Click Set Options and then specify the proxy server settings, as shown in Figure 6-15. For Windows Small Business Server 2003, Standard Edition, select Do Not Use A Proxy Server To Access The Internet. For Windows Small Business Server 2003, Premium Edition, select Use A Proxy Server To Access The Internet, choose Use The Following Proxy Server To Access The Internet, type the Windows Small Business Server computer name and ISA server port number (usually 8080), and provide appropriate user credentials in the form of *DOMAIN\USER*.

 Planning Users of Windows Small Business Server 2003, Premium Edition, must host updates locally for clients to successfully download updates, unless ISA Server is configured not to require authentication. Additionally, users should either administer Software Update Services from the local computer (by logging on locally or via Remote Desktop) or configure Software Update Services to use SSL encryption. (Click the About Software Update Services hyperlink in the Software Update Services administration Web site for help with this.)

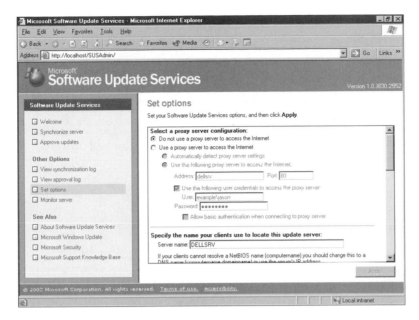

Figure 6-15. *Setting options on the Software Update Services administration Web site.*

2. If Windows 2000 and Windows XP clients have NetBIOS Over TCP/IP disabled (this setting is located in the Advanced TCP/IP Settings dialog box on the client), type the SUS computer's DNS name or IP address in the Server Name box.

3. In the Select How You Want To Handle New Versions Of Previous Approved Updates section of the page, specify whether new versions of updates that you previously approved should be automatically approved.

4. To download all updates to the Windows Small Business Server and host them locally, select the Save The Updates To A Local Folder option in the Select Where You Want To Store Updates section of the page; otherwise, select Maintain The Updates On A Microsoft Windows Update Server.

5. Select which languages are supported on your network, and then click Apply.

Setting a Synchronization Schedule

Software Update Services must synchronize with a Microsoft Windows Update server (or another SUS server) to provide updates to clients. This process can be time-consuming the first time when you're hosting updates locally (SUS downloads around 600 MB and can be larger depending on your language choices), and when new service packs are released. For this reason, schedule Software Update Services to synchronize automatically during off-hours.

To synchronize Software Update Services and create a new schedule, complete the following steps:

1. On the Software Update Services administration Web site, click the Synchronize Server link.

2. Click Synchronize Now to perform an immediate synchronization, or click Synchronization Schedule to schedule synchronizations.

3. In the Schedule Synchronization dialog box, select Synchronize Using This Schedule, specify the time and days on which to synchronize, and specify how many times SUS should retry a failed synchronization (with a 30-minute retry interval).

Approving Updates

Software Update Services differs from Automatic Updates in that it allows administrators to select which updates to deploy to clients. You should plan on performing this process monthly, shortly after the regular release of the Microsoft Security Bulletin on the second Tuesday of the month. (View the bulletin at *http://www.microsoft.com/security.*) Install critical patches as they are released. (Subscribe to the Microsoft Security Update or Microsoft Security Notification Service at *http://www.microsoft.com/security/security_bulletins /alerts.asp* to ensure that you receive notification of these patches.)

To approve patches for deployment, complete the following steps:

1. On the Software Update Services administration Web site, click the Approve Updates link. This displays a list of available updates, as shown in Figure 6-16.

2. Click the Details link next to an update. In the Update Details dialog box, click the page icon in the Info column to view details about the update, or click the update's file name to save the update to another location for testing. Click Close to return to the Approve Updates page.

Tip If you want to save an update and then assign it to a computer for testing before you approve it for all clients, take note of the Setup Parameters listed in the Update Details dialog box and make sure to include them in the path when adding the update to the list of applications.

3. Select the check box next to an update to approve it for installation on client systems.

4. Click Approve when you're finished. Click Yes to overwrite the previous list of approved updates, click Accept to accept the licensing agreement for the updates, and finally click OK. The Approve Updates page then shows that the specified updates are approved.

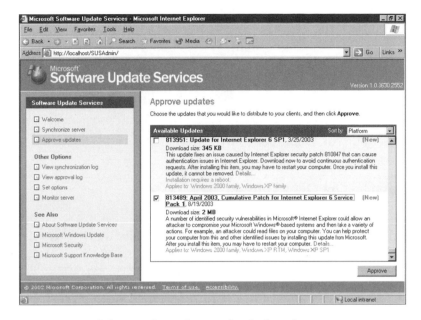

Figure 6-16. *Selecting the updates to be deployed.*

Configuring Client Systems

Computers on the network must be configured to take advantage of SUS. This is most conveniently done by creating a new Group Policy Object (GPO) with the appropriate settings. (See "Using Group Policy to Set Clients to Update Automatically" in Chapter 10.)

Summary

When you finish this chapter, the basic installation and configuration of Windows Small Business Server is complete. Of course, there's more you can do to polish your Windows Small Business Server network to a high gloss. In the next chapters, you'll find information on disk management and storage alternatives.

Chapter 7
Disk Management

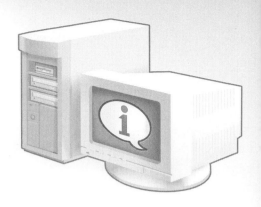

Arguably the single most important function that a server provides to the rest of the network is to be a central, secure, managed file storage area. By centralizing file storage on a server, it becomes an order of magnitude easier to ensure the safety, integrity, recoverability, and availability of the core files of your business. Instead of having files spread all across the network on individual client computers, you have them in a single place—easier to share among collaborators, easier to back up, easier to recover in the event of a disaster, and easier to secure so that only those people who *should* have access to a file, do. The downside to having all your important files in a single location is the potential for a single point of failure and the need for high availability of the files, since your business depends on them. This makes it imperative that you carefully manage the underlying disks that support your file storage and that those disks be both redundant and thoroughly backed up.

In this chapter, we'll cover the underlying disk management that makes it possible to store your files and protect against loss, corruption, or disaster. In Chapter 8, "Storage Management," we'll cover some of the new features of Microsoft Windows Small Business Server 2003 that enable you to manage storage, protect critical files, and provide versioning of shared files to protect against corruption or misadventure. Additional backup and recovery details are covered in Chapter 13, "Backing Up and Restoring Data."

The Search for Disaster Protection

Traditionally, large businesses have used a variety of techniques to ensure that files stored on a server were both secure and safe. These solutions tend to be expensive, but, when spread across all the supported workstations and buried in a large MIS budget, they are feasible. The same solutions would *not* be feasible or acceptable in most small businesses, but that doesn't change the very real need of those small businesses to protect themselves from disaster. Fortunately, there are both hardware and software solutions that can provide a very high level of security and safety. However, before we can talk about those solutions, let's make sure we all understand the terminology of disk management.

Understanding Disk Terminology

Before going into the details of managing disks and storage, let's review some definitions.

- **Physical drive** The actual hard disk itself, including the case, electronics, platters, and all that stuff. Not terribly important to the disk administrator.

- **Partition** A portion of the hard disk. In many cases, this will be the entire hard disk space, but it needn't be.

- **Allocation unit** The smallest unit of managed disk space on a hard disk or logical volume. Also called a *cluster*.

- **Primary partition** A portion of the hard disk that's been marked as a potentially bootable logical drive by an operating system. MS-DOS can support only a single primary partition, but Microsoft Windows NT, Windows 2000, Windows XP, and Windows Server 2003 can support multiple ones. Only four primary partitions can be on any hard disk.

- **Extended partition** A non-bootable portion of the hard disk that can be subdivided into logical drives. There can be only a single extended partition per hard disk, but this partition can be divided into multiple logical drives.

- **Extended volume** Similar to, and sometimes synonymous with, a spanned volume, this is any dynamic volume that has been extended to make it larger than its original size. When it uses portions of more than one physical disk, it is more properly referred to as a spanned volume.

- **Logical drive** A section or partition of a hard disk that acts as a single unit. An extended partition can be divided, for example, into multiple logical drives.

- **Logical volume** Another name for a logical drive.

- **Basic disk** A traditional disk drive that is divided into one or more partitions, with a logical drive in the primary partition, if present, and one or more logical drives in any extended partitions. Basic disks do not support the more advanced functions of Disk Management, but they can be converted to dynamic disks in many cases.

- **Dynamic disk** A managed hard disk that can be used to create various volumes.

- **Volume**   A unit of disk space composed of one or more sections of one or more dynamic disks.

- **Simple volume**   The Disk Management equivalent of a partition. A portion of a single dynamic disk, it can be assigned either a single drive letter or no drive letter and can be attached (mounted) on zero or more mount points.

- **RAID (redundant array of independent [formerly "inexpensive"] disks)**   The use of multiple hard disks in an array to provide for larger volume size, fault tolerance, and increased performance. RAID comes in different levels, such as RAID-0, RAID-1, and RAID-5. Higher numbers don't necessarily indicate greater performance or fault tolerance, just different methods of doing the job.

- **Spanned volume**   A collection of portions of hard disks combined into a single addressable unit. A spanned volume is formatted like a single drive and can have a drive letter assigned to it, but it will span multiple physical drives. A spanned volume—occasionally referred to as an extended volume—provides no fault tolerance and increases your exposure to failure but does permit you to make more efficient use of the available hard disk space.

- **Striped volume**   Like a spanned volume, a striped volume combines multiple hard disk portions into a single entity. A striped volume uses special formatting to write to each of the portions equally in a stripe to increase performance. A striped volume provides no fault tolerance and actually increases your exposure to failure, but it is faster than either a spanned volume or a single drive. A stripe set is often referred to as RAID-0, although this is a misnomer because plain striping includes no redundancy.

- **Mirror volume**   A pair of dynamic volumes that contain identical data and appear to the world as a single entity. Disk mirroring can use two drives on the same hard disk controller or use separate controllers, in which case it is sometimes referred to as *duplexing*. In case of failure on the part of either drive, the other hard disk can be split off so that it continues to provide complete access to the data stored on the drive, providing a high degree of fault tolerance. This technique is called RAID-1.

- **RAID-5 volume**   Like a striped volume, this combines portions of multiple hard disks into a single entity with data written across all portions equally. However, it also writes parity information for each stripe onto a different portion, providing the ability to recover in the case of a single drive failure. A RAID-5 volume provides excellent throughput for read operations but is substantially slower than all other available options for write operations.

- **SLED (single large expensive disk)** Now rarely used, this strategy is the opposite of the RAID strategy. Rather than using several inexpensive hard disks and providing fault tolerance through redundancy, you buy the best hard disk you can and bet your entire network on it. If this doesn't sound like a good idea to you, you're right. It's not.

Choosing the Storage Solution for Your Network

The first decision you need to make when planning your storage solution for Windows Small Business Server is really made when you specify your main server. If your budget can afford it, you should definitely consider choosing a hardware RAID solution that lets you add disks "on the fly" and reconfigure the array without powering down the server or rebooting. This is absolutely the best and most flexible storage solution for protecting your data, and could take the form of hot-swappable SCSI hard drives, or even a Storage Area Network (SAN). None of the possible solutions comes cheap, and in most cases you need to make at least some portion of the decision as part of the original server purchase.

Real World   Network Attached Storage

Although most hardware storage solutions require you to make decisions very early in the buying process, a growing number of Network Attached Storage (NAS) solutions can provide a cost effective way to increase the storage flexibility of your Windows Small Business Server network. When these NAS solutions are based on Microsoft Windows Storage Server 2003, they support all the features of Windows Small Business Server and will easily integrate into your Windows Small Business Server network. For more on Windows Storage Server 2003 powered NAS servers, see *http://www.microsoft.com/windowsserversystem/wss2003*.

Once the server is actually in place and is being used, you can't really make a change to the underlying hardware that would allow you to use a hardware RAID solution—at least not easily. But you *can* use the built-in facilities of Windows Small Business Server to make your existing disk subsystem more fault-tolerant by using dynamic disks and the software RAID of Windows Small Business Server as described in "RAID-5 Volumes" later in the chapter.

Storage Connection Technologies

If you're reading this chapter before you buy your server, congratulations on being a thorough person. If not, some of these decisions have already been made, but you may well find that you will have to add storage. If you do, you'll want to focus on storage solutions designed and optimized for servers—a very different set of needs from the typical workstation. Your choices are:

- **Integrated Device Electronics (IDE)** Primarily a client solution. Inexpensive, but not really best on a server.

- **Serial Advanced Technology Attachment (ATA)** A way to take IDE to the server level. Very promising, but still very new and relatively more expensive.

- **Small Computer System Interface (SCSI)** Perfect for servers and high-end workstations, but significantly more expensive than IDE. Ability to have up to 13 drives per SCSI channel.

- **Internet SCSI (iSCSI)** The next wave, but not there yet.

- **FireWire** Hot-pluggable, fast, and appropriate for a lower-end server. But still more expensive than IDE.

- **Universal Serial Bus (USB)** Only appropriate if you use USB 2.0. Good for CD and DVD drives. Hot pluggable. Not really a server product for storage.

- **Fiber Channel** Great if you have large amounts of money to spend.

- **Network Attached Storage (NAS)** A good way to provide large amounts of storage that can be flexible to meet your needs. Specify Windows Storage Server 2003–based NAS for the greatest flexibility and compatibility.

- **Storage Area Networks (SAN)** Faster and more robust than the typical NAS, but also much more expensive and difficult to configure.

Managing Disks

There are two different kinds of disks in Windows Small Business Server: basic disks and dynamic disks. *Basic disks* are the conventional disks we're used to. *Dynamic disks* were introduced in Windows 2000 Server, and support additional management and agglomeration options.

Basic disks support two different kinds of partitions: primary and extended. They cannot be used with the advanced disk management techniques that are supported by Windows Small Business Server. They can, however, be seen by other operating systems if you have your Small Business Server machine configured for dual booting.

Dynamic disks use volumes instead of partitions, and support the additional management, redundancy, and agglomeration features of Windows Small Business Server, including Spanned Volumes, Stripped Volumes (RAID-0), Mirrored Volumes (RAID-1), and RAID-5.

Using Disk Management

The primary method for managing disks on Windows Small Business Server is the Disk Management snap-in. This can be used as a stand-alone, from the Computer Management console, or from the Server Management console, as shown in Figure 7-1.

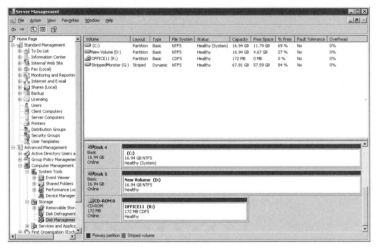

Figure 7-1. *The Disk Management snap-in from inside the Server Management console.*

The Disk Management snap-in is divided into two panes. The top pane shows the drive letters (volumes) associated with the local disks and gives their properties and status; the bottom pane has a graphical representation organized by physical drive.

Real World **Hardware RAID**

Although Disk Management provides an excellent software RAID solution, hardware RAID is also now widely available, from either the original server vendor or from third parties, and it provides substantial advantages over software RAID. Hardware RAID solutions range from a simple RAID controller to fully integrated, stand-alone subsystems. Their features vary, as does their cost, but all claim to provide superior performance and reliability over a simple software RAID solution such as that included in

Windows Small Business Server. In general, they do. Some of the advantages they can offer include:

- Hot-swap and hot-spare drives, allowing for virtually instantaneous replacement of failed drives

- Integrated disk caching for improved disk performance

- A separate, dedicated system that handles all processing, for improved overall performance

- Increased flexibility and additional RAID levels, such as RAID-10 (also called RAID 0+1), which is a combination of striping (RAID-0) and mirroring (RAID-1) that provides for fast read and write disk access with full redundancy

Single Server

Although not all hardware RAID systems provide all the possible features, they all have the potential to improve the overall reliability and performance of your hard disk subsystem. With Windows Small Business Server being an essentially single server environment, you have your entire business running on that single server. This makes hardware RAID a particularly sound investment for your Windows Small Business Server machine.

NAS and SAN

Many NAS systems are built on hardware RAID, providing an easy and cost-effective way to expand your original server storage in a highly fault-tolerant way. However, it pays to look closely at exactly what you are buying—some are built on RAID-0, which is *not* fault tolerant at all and actually increases your risk.

We only briefly mentioned Storage Area Networks (SANs) earlier, and we won't mention them again. Although they are excellent, fast, flexible, and highly fault tolerant, they are only for those with really large IT budgets at this point. Plus they can be rather tricky to implement and configure. Given the strong advances in NAS, we think it provides a better solution for those running on realistic budgets.

Dynamic Disks

Windows Small Business Server supports dynamic disks. A basic disk can be converted to a dynamic disk, allowing you to use Disk Management to manage it in new ways, *without requiring a reboot* in most cases. You can extend a disk volume, span a volume across multiple physical disks, stripe the volume for improved performance, mirror it, or add it to a RAID-5 array—all from the Server Management console and all without a reboot, after the disk is converted to a dynamic disk. The initial creation or conversion of the first of your basic disks to a dynamic disk requires a reboot, unfortunately, but when you get over that hurdle, you'll breeze through the remaining tasks. Dynamic disks give the system administrator powerful tools for managing the type and configuration of hard disk storage across the enterprise.

Under the Hood **Command Line**

Windows Small Business Server adds to the system administrator's toolkit a complete command-line interface for managing disks—Diskpart.exe. This command-line utility is scriptable or it can be used interactively. Here is a simple script to create a volume on an existing dynamic disk and assign it to the next available drive letter:

```
REM Filename: MakeVol.txt
REM
REM This is a DiskPart.exe Script. Run from the command line
REM or from another script, using the syntax:
REM
REM    diskpart /s MakeVol.txt > logfile.log
REM
REM to run this script and dump the results out to a log file.
REM
REM This script creates a simple volume of 28 Gb on disk #3, and then
REM assigns a drive letter to it. Note that this does NOT format
REM the volume -- that requires using the format command, not part
REM of diskpart.exe

REM First, list out our disks. Not required for scripting, but useful
REM to show the overall environment if we need to troubleshoot problems
list disk

REM Next, select which disk will have the simple volume created on it.
select disk 3

REM Now, create the volume...
create volume simple size=28672

REM Assign without parameters will choose the next available HD letter.
Assign
```

Adding a Partition or Volume

Adding a new drive or partition to Windows Small Business Server is straightforward. First, obviously, you need to physically install and connect the drive. If you have a hot-swappable backplane and array, you don't even have to shut the system down to accomplish this task. If you're using conventional drives, however, you need to shut down and power off the system.

After the drive is installed and the system is powered up again, Windows Small Business Server automatically recognizes the new hardware and makes it available. If the disk is a basic disk that is already partitioned and formatted, you're able to use it immediately. If it's a brand new disk that has never been partitioned or formatted, you need to prepare it first. If it's a dynamic disk or disks, but from another machine, you can use it as soon as you import it. If the disk is a basic disk that has already been formatted, you don't get prompted to upgrade it to a dynamic disk, but do so anyway. If the disk has never been used before, the Initialize and Convert Disk Wizard prompts you.

Adding a New Disk Using the Initialize and Convert Disk Wizard

When you install a new hard drive, the drive is automatically recognized, and the Initialize and Convert Disk Wizard starts automatically when you open Disk Management. To add a new disk, complete the following steps:

1. Open the Server Management console.

2. In the console tree, expand Advanced Management, Computer Management, Storage, and then click Disk Management. If the disk is new, you see the first page of the Initialize and Convert Disk Wizard, shown in Figure 7-2. This wizard allows you to upgrade the new disk to a dynamic disk. Click Next.

Figure 7-2. *The first page of the Initialize and Convert Disk Wizard.*

On the Select Disks To Initialize page, you see a confirmation of the disk (or disks, if you added more than one) that can be selected for initializing, as shown in Figure 7-3.

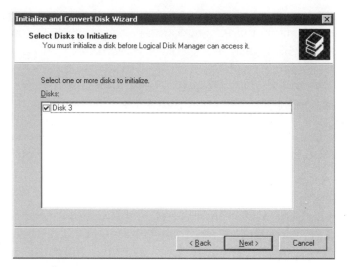

Figure 7-3. *The Select Disks To Initialize page of the Initialize and Convert Disk Wizard.*

3. Make sure a check mark appears to the left of the disk or disks to be upgraded, and then click Next again.

4. On the Select Disks To Convert page, select from the list the disks you want to convert to dynamic disks, as shown in Figure 7-4, and then click Next.

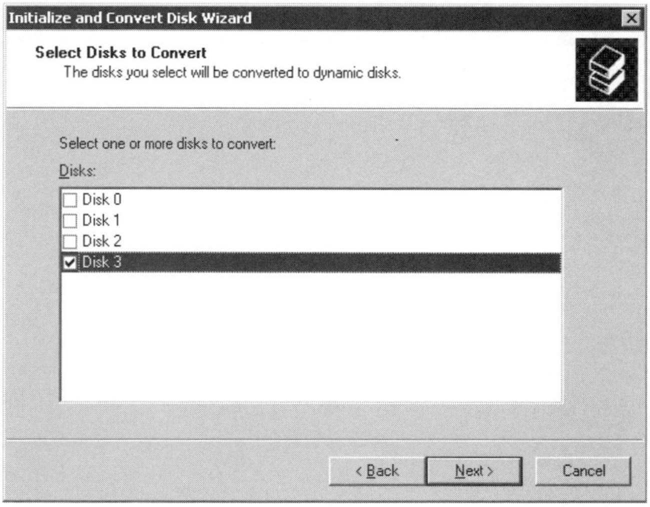

Figure 7-4. *The Select Disks To Convert page of the Initialize and Convert Disk Wizard.*

5. You get a confirmation message. If all the options are correct, click Finish. The disk is initialized and converted to a dynamic disk.

When the wizard finishes, you're at the main Disk Management console, shown in Figure 7-5. Notice that the disk is still not formatted or allocated and is highlighted in black (if you haven't changed the default color settings for the Disk Management console).

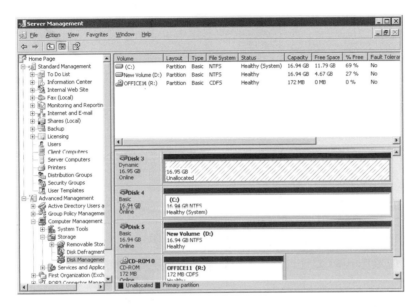

Figure 7-5. *The main Disk Management console, showing the new disk (Disk 3).*

Creating a Volume

To create a new volume (the dynamic disk equivalent of a partition), complete the following steps:

1. In the Disk Management console, right-click the unallocated disk and choose New Volume from the shortcut menu. The New Volume Wizard opens to guide you through the process of creating the new volume on the dynamic disk. Click Next.

2. On the Select Volume Type page, select the type of volume you'll be creating (Figure 7-6). Depending on the number of available unallocated volumes, you see one or more options for the type of volume. These options include Simple, Spanned, Striped (RAID-0), Mirrored (RAID-1), and RAID-5. Click Next.

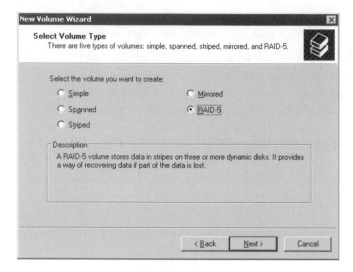

Figure 7-6. *Select the type of dynamic volume you want to create.*

3. On the Select Disks page, select the dynamic disks to use for the new volume. The choices available and the selections you need to make depend on the type of volume you're creating and the number of available unallocated disks. Figure 7-7 shows a RAID-5 volume being created.

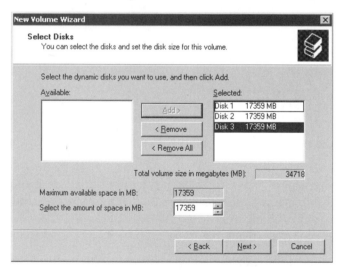

Figure 7-7. *Select the dynamic disks that will be part of this volume.*

4. On the same page, adjust the size of the new volume. By default, the new volume will use the maximum available space from each of the selected disks. For spanned volumes, this will be the sum of the free space on the selected disks; for other types of volumes, it will be the number of disks multiplied by the available space on the smallest

of the selected disks multiplied by the factor for the type of volume. Mirror is 50 percent of the smallest volume; RAID-5 is n-1 multiplied by the size of the smallest volume in the group. All others are 100 percent of the size of the smallest volume multiplied by the number of disks in the group. Click Next.

5. On the Assign Drive Letter Or Path page, select either a drive letter or a mount point for the new volume (Figure 7-8), or opt not to assign a drive letter or path at this time. With Windows Small Business Server, you can mount a volume on an empty subdirectory, minimizing the number of drive letters and reducing the complexity of the storage that is displayed to the user. If you want to take advantage of this feature, click Browse to locate the directory where you will mount the new volume. Click Next.

More Info   For more information about mounting a volume, see the Real World sidebar "Mounted Volumes" later in this chapter.

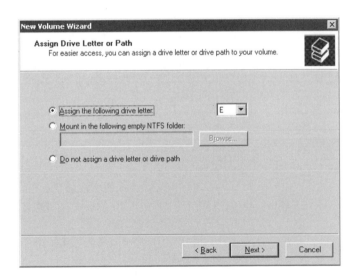

Figure 7-8.   *Select a drive letter or mount point for the new volume.*

6. On the Format Volume page, select the formatting options you want (Figure 7-9). Even when mounting the volume rather than creating a new drive, you can choose your format type without regard to the underlying format of the mount point. Click Next.

7. You see a confirmation page. If all the options are correct, click Finish to create and format the volume, which will take a few minutes depending on the size of the disk. You return to the Disk Management console, where you see the new volume (Figure 7-10).

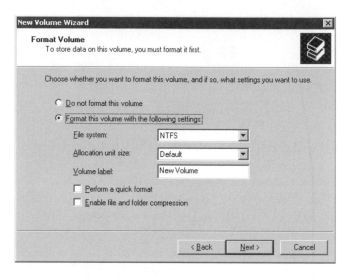

Figure 7-9. *Set the formatting options for the new volume.*

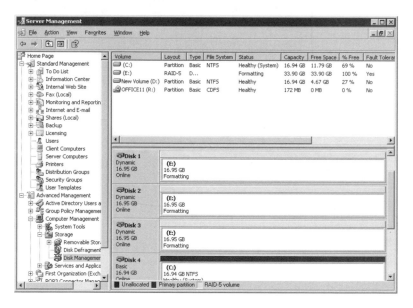

Figure 7-10. *The new RAID volume being generated and formatted.*

Real World   Mounted Volumes

Windows Small Business Server borrows a concept from the UNIX world by adding the ability to mount a volume or partition on a subfolder of an existing drive letter. A mounted volume can also have a drive letter associated with it, although it does not need to, and it can be mounted at more than one point, giving multiple entry points into the same storage.

A volume must be mounted on an empty subfolder of an existing NTFS volume or drive. FAT and FAT32 drives do not support mounted volumes. You can, however, mount a FAT or FAT32 volume at any mount point, though with Windows Small Business Server, the use of FAT and FAT32 file systems is strongly discouraged (and not supported for the system drive). You can mount only a single volume at a given mount point, but you can then mount further volumes on top of an existing mounted volume, with the same rules and restrictions as any other mount. An important caution, however—the properties of a drive do not show all the available disk space for that drive, because they do not reflect any volumes mounted on the drive. Further, mounted volumes are not supported with Windows Services for UNIX on shared Network File System (NFS) exports.

Mounted volumes can be used to provide a mix of redundant and non-redundant storage in a logical structure that meets the business needs of the business while hiding the complexities of the physical structure from the users.

Creating a Partition

You can create partitions only on basic disks, not on dynamic disks. To create a new partition, complete the following steps:

1. In the Disk Management console, right-click the unallocated basic disk and select New Partition. The New Partition Wizard, shown in Figure 7-11, opens to guide you through the process of creating the new partition on the basic disk. Click Next.

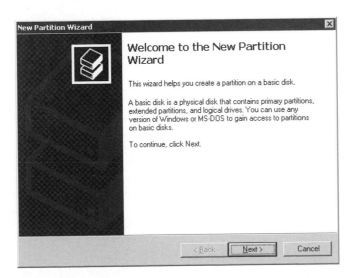

Figure 7-11. *The first page of the New Partition Wizard.*

2. On the Select Partition Type page, select the type of partition you'll be creating (Figure 7-12). If this is a removable drive, you see only an option for a primary partition, but if this is a non-removable disk, you're able to choose either a primary or an extended partition. A basic disk can hold up to four primary partitions or three primary partitions and one extended partition. Click Next.

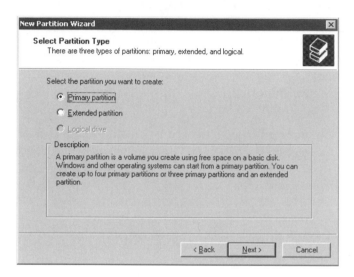

Figure 7-12. *Select the type of partition you want to create.*

3. On the Specify Partition Size page, specify how much of the available space on the disk you want to use for this partition (Figure 7-13). Click Next.

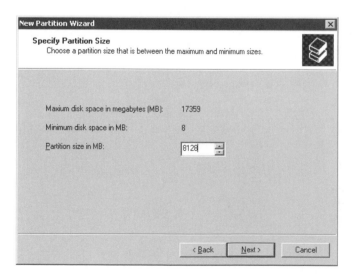

Figure 7-13. *Specify how much of the disk will be used by this partition.*

4. If you're creating an extended partition, continue with Step 6. If you're creating a primary partition, the Assign Drive Letter Or Path page appears. Select either a drive letter, as shown in Figure 7-14, or a mount point for the new partition. You can also choose to defer giving the new partition a mount point or drive letter until later. However, this partition is unavailable to your users until you do. Click Next.

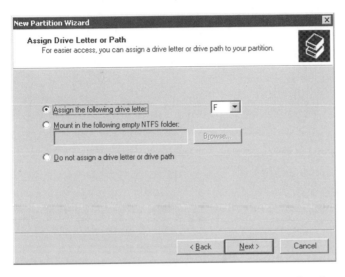

Figure 7-14. *Select a drive letter or a mount point for the new partition.*

5. On the Format Partition pages, select the formatting options you want, or opt to defer formatting until later. Click Next.

6. You see a confirmation page. If all the options are correct, click Finish to create the partition. If it is a primary partition, it will be formatted and the drive letter or mount point assigned. If it is an extended partition, you'll need to format it and choose the drive letters and mount points for it, as discussed in the next section, "Creating Logical Drives in an Extended Partition."

Under the Hood Formatting Options

Windows Small Business Server can recognize hard drives that are formatted in any of the three file system formats: FAT, FAT32, and NTFS. However, only NTFS is supported by Windows Small Business Server because it is required for the more advanced features of Windows Small Business Server.

You can choose to quick-format a drive to make it available more quickly, but this option simply removes the file entries from the disk and does no checking for bad sectors. Select to quick-format a drive only when recycling a disk that has already been formatted and when you are confident it hasn't been damaged.

On an NTFS volume or partition, you can specify the allocation unit size. This option lets you tune the disk for a particular purpose, depending on the disk's size and intended function. A database storage volume that will contain large database files managed by the database program might lend itself to large allocation units (also called *clusters*), whereas a disk that must hold many small files is a candidate for smaller clusters. However, the default sizes are an excellent compromise for most situations—modify them only with caution and with a clear understanding of the consequences for your environment.

You can also choose to enable disk and folder compression on NTFS volumes and partitions. This causes all files and folders on the volume (as opposed to individual files or folders you select) to be compressed. Compression can minimize the amount of hard disk space used by files but can have a negative impact on performance. Given the cost of hard drive space today, it hardly seems worth it and is certainly not a good idea for frequently updated data.

Creating Logical Drives in an Extended Partition

If you created a new extended partition, the next step is to create logical drives in the partition. You can assign one or more logical drives in an extended partition, and each of those logical drives can be assigned a drive letter and one or more mount points. Each of the logical drives can be formatted with any of the supported file systems, regardless of the format of other logical drives. To create a logical drive, complete the following steps:

1. In the Disk Management console, right-click the Free Space portion of the extended partition and select New Logical Drive from the shortcut menu to open the New Partition Wizard (shown earlier in Figure 7-11). Click Next.

2. On the Select Partition Type page, shown in Figure 7-15, you see the Logical Drive option selected and the only choice active. Click Next.

3. On the Specify Partition Size page (Figure 7-16), specify the size of the logical drive you'll be creating. You can specify the entire partition for

a single drive, or you can divide the partition into multiple logical drives. Click Next.

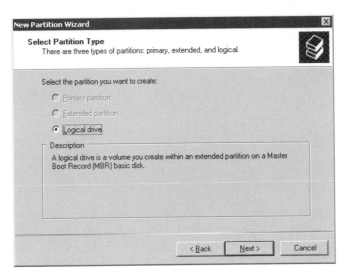

Figure 7-15. *The Select Partition Type page of the New Partition Wizard.*

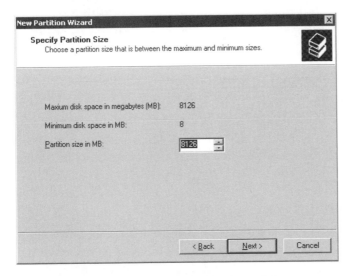

Figure 7-16. *Adjusting the size of the logical drive.*

4. On the Assign Drive Letter Or Path page, select the drive letter or mount point for the new logical drive, as shown in Figure 7-17. You can also choose not to assign a letter or mount point at this time. Click Next.

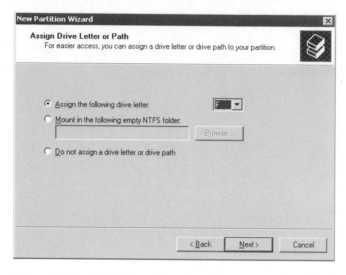

Figure 7-17. *Assigning a drive letter or mount point for the logical drive.*

5. On the Format Partition page, select the formatting options you want. Click Next, and you see the final confirmation page. If all the options are correct, click Finish to create and format the new logical drive. If you need to create additional logical drives on the partition, you can repeat these steps as many times as required to create the number of logical drives desired.

Deleting a Partition, Volume, or Logical Drive

Deleting a partition, deleting a logical drive, and deleting a volume are essentially the same task, with one important exception. When you delete a logical drive, you end up with free space in the partition, but other logical drives in the partition are untouched. When you delete a partition or volume, the entire volume or partition is deleted. You cannot, however, delete an extended partition until all the logical drives in the partition have first been deleted. You can directly delete a primary partition or a volume.

In all cases, when you delete a volume, logical drive, or partition, you end up with free or unallocated space and no data on the volume, drive, or partition when you're done, so make sure you have a good backup if there's a chance you might later need any of the data. To delete a partition, logical drive, or volume, follow these steps:

1. Right-click the partition, logical drive, or volume and choose Delete Partition, Delete Logical Drive, or Delete Volume.

2. If you're deleting a volume or partition, you see a warning message similar to the one shown in Figure 7-18. Deleting an extended partition involves extra steps, because you must first delete the logical drives in the partition before you can delete the partition itself.

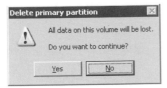

Figure 7-18. *Confirmation message for deleting a partition.*

When the volume or partition is completely deleted, the space it occupied will be unallocated. Space that is unallocated on dynamic disks can be used to create mirrors, extend an existing volume, create a RAID array, or otherwise manage the storage on your server. Space that is unallocated on basic disks can be partitioned.

Converting a Disk to a Dynamic Disk

The advantages of dynamic disks are substantial. Even if you use hardware RAID controllers and hot-swappable disks to manage your hard disks, you'll probably find it a good idea to use dynamic disks. There is a caveat, however. Because you can't boot from or even see a dynamic disk from any other operating system released prior to Windows 2000 Server, you might want to consider leaving at least your boot drive as a basic drive. Doing so makes working with it somewhat easier. If you need to provide for redundancy on that drive, and if hardware RAID is an option, use RAID level 1 to make recovery from a failed hard disk or other disaster as painless as possible. To convert a basic disk to a dynamic disk, complete the following steps:

1. Right-click the disk's icon on the left side of the Disk Management console, and choose Convert To Dynamic Disk from the shortcut menu.

2. You see a Convert To Dynamic Disk dialog box like the one shown in Figure 7-19, listing the available basic disks on your machine. The disk you clicked is checked, and you can select other disks to upgrade at the same time. Click OK to continue with the upgrade.

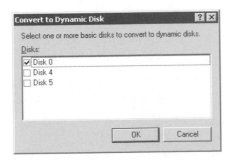

Figure 7-19. *You can select more than one disk to convert.*

3. You see a Disks To Convert dialog box that shows the disks that will be converted. Click Convert if all is correct.

4. You get a warning message stating that no other version of Windows can use these disks. Click Yes to continue.

5. If there are no file systems on the disks you chose to upgrade, that's all there is to it. However, if there are file systems on any of the disks, you get a warning message stating that the file systems will be dismounted. Click Yes and the upgrade proceeds. Existing partitions will be converted into Simple volumes. You can now manage the disks dynamically, and they can be part of mirrors, RAID-5 arrays, or other enhanced disk configurations that aren't supported by basic disks.

Caution If there are any open files on the disk to be upgraded, you might experience data loss. Perform disk upgrades only during quiet times when no users are logged on to or using the server.

Extending a Volume

You can add space to a volume without having to back up, reboot, and restore your files if the volume is on a dynamic disk and if it is a simple volume or a spanned volume. You do this by converting the volume to a spanned or extended volume that incorporates unallocated space on any dynamic disk. Unfortunately, you can't increase the size of a RAID-5 or RAID-0 (striped) volume simply by adding disks to the array, unless you're using a version of hardware RAID that supports this functionality. To extend a volume, complete the following steps:

1. In the Disk Management console, right-click the volume you want to extend. Choose Extend Volume from the shortcut menu to open the Extend Volume Wizard. Click Next.

2. On the Select Disks page, select one or more disks from the list of dynamic disks that are available and have unallocated space. Click Add to add the selected disk or disks, and indicate the amount of space you want to add (Figure 7-20). Click Next.

3. The Extend Volume Wizard displays a final confirmation page before extending the volume. Click Finish to extend the volume, or click Cancel if you change your mind.

> **Caution**   A spanned (extended) volume is actually less reliable than a simple disk. Unlike a mirror or RAID-5 volume, in which there is built-in redundancy, a spanned or striped volume will be broken and all its data lost if any disk in the volume fails.

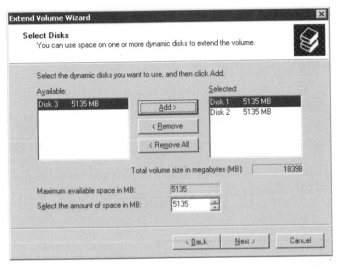

Figure 7-20.   *Selecting the disks to use to extend the volume.*

Real World   Extending—Friend or Foe?

Most people responsible for supporting a busy server have wished at some point that they could simply increase the space of a particular volume or drive on the fly when it got low on space—preferably without having to bring the system offline for several hours while the entire volume is backed up and reformatted to add the additional hard disks, the backup is restored, and the share points are recreated. Fun? Hardly. Risky? Certainly. And definitely a job that means coming in on the weekend or staying late at night—in other words, something to be avoided if at all possible.

All this makes Windows Small Business Server's ability to create additional space on a volume without the need to back up the volume, reformat the disks, and recreate the volume a seductive feature. However, unless you're running hardware RAID, you should think twice before jumping in. Only spanned or stripped volumes allow you to add additional storage on the fly, and because neither is redundant, using them exposes your users to the risks of a failed drive. Yes, you have a backup, but even under the best of circumstances, you'll lose some data if you need to restore a backup. Further, using spanned volumes actually *increases* your risk of a hard disk failure. If any disk used as part of the spanned volume fails, the entire volume is toast and will need to be restored from backup.

Why, then, would anyone use spanning? Because they have hardware RAID to provide the redundancy. This combination offers the best of both worlds—redundancy provided by the hardware RAID controller and flexibility to expand volumes as needed, using Windows Small Business Server Disk Management. Yet another compelling argument for hardware RAID, as if you needed any more.

Note Windows Small Business Server uses the terms "extended" and "spanned" nearly interchangeably when describing volumes. Technically, however, a spanned volume must include more than one physical disk, whereas an extended volume can also refer to a volume that has had additional space added to the original simple volume on the same disk.

Adding a Mirror

When your data is mission-critical and you want to make sure that the data is protected and always available no matter what happens to one of your hard disks, consider mirroring the data onto a second drive. Windows Small Business Server can mirror a dynamic disk onto a second dynamic disk so that the failure of either disk does not result in loss of data. To mirror a volume, you can either select a mirrored volume when you create the volume or you can add a mirror to an existing volume. To add a mirror to an existing volume, complete the following steps:

1. In the Disk Management console, right-click the volume you want to mirror. If a potential mirror is available, the shortcut menu lists the Add Mirror command.

2. Choose Add Mirror to display the Add Mirror dialog box, shown in Figure 7-21, where you can select the disk to be used for the mirror.

3. Select the disk that will be the mirror, and click Add Mirror. The mirror is created immediately and starts duplicating the data from the original disk to the second half of the mirror, as shown in Figure 7-22. This process is called *regeneration*, or sometimes *resynching*. (The process of regeneration is also used to distribute data across the disks when a RAID-5 volume is created.)

Note   Regeneration is both CPU-intensive and disk-intensive. When possible, create mirrors during slack times or during normally scheduled downtime. Balance this goal, however, by the equally important goal of providing redundancy and failure protection as expeditiously as possible.

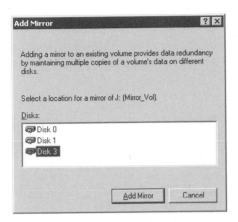

Figure 7-21.   *The Add Mirror dialog box.*

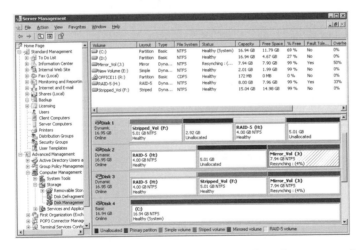

Figure 7-22.   *A newly created mirrored disk in the process of regeneration.*

Tip   To improve your overall data security and reliability, mirror your volumes onto disks that use separate controllers whenever possible. This process is known as *duplexing*, as mentioned earlier in the chapter, and it eliminates the disk controller as a single point of failure for the mirror while actually speeding up both reading and writing to the mirror, because the controller and bus are no longer potential bottlenecks.

Drive Failure in a Mirrored Volume

If one of the disks in a mirrored volume fails, you continue to have full access to all your data without loss. Windows Small Business Server marks the failed disk as missing and takes it offline, as shown in Figure 7-23, while sending alerts to the alert log and popping up a balloon on the server console, as shown in Figure 7-24. It continues, however, to read and write from the other half of the mirrored volume as though nothing had happened. Be warned, however. You no longer have any fault tolerance on that volume, and any additional failure will result in catastrophic data loss.

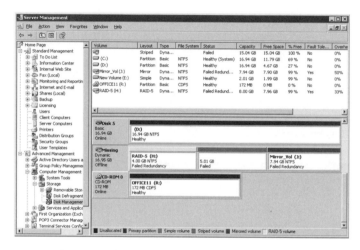

Figure 7-23. *Failed disk in mirror shown as missing and offline.*

Figure 7-24. *Balloon opens on the console to warn of a failed drive in a fault tolerant volume.*

After you replace the failed disk or correct the problem and reactivate it, the mirror automatically starts regenerating. If the problem can be solved without powering down the system, you can regenerate the mirror on the fly. To reactivate the failed disk, complete the following steps:

1. Right-click the icon for the failed disk on the left of the Disk Management console, shown in Figure 7-25.

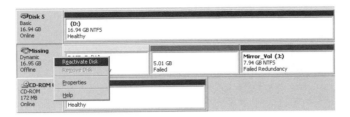

Figure 7-25. *Reactivating a failed disk that's part of a mirrored volume.*

2. Choose Reactivate Disk. Windows Small Business Server warns you about running Chkdsk on any affected volumes, and then brings the disk back online and starts regenerating the failed mirror, as shown in Figure 7-26. When the mirror has been regenerated, the disk status changes from Regenerating to Healthy.

Figure 7-26. *Data being regenerated on a reactivated mirrored disk.*

Removing a Mirror

If you need to make additional disk space available on your system and you have no additional disks available, you can remove the mirror from a mirrored volume. When you remove a mirror, the data on one of the disks is untouched, but the other disk becomes unallocated space. Of course, you will have lost all redundancy and protection for the data, so you need to take steps to restore the mirror as soon as possible. Until then you might want to modify your backup schedule for the remaining disk. To remove a mirror, complete the following steps:

1. In the Disk Management console, right-click either half of the mirror. Choose Remove Mirror from the shortcut menu, and the Remove Mirror dialog box opens, shown in Figure 7-27.

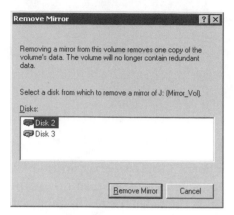

Figure 7-27.   *The Remove Mirror dialog box.*

2. Select the disk you want to remove from the mirror. Click Remove Mirror. You get one last chance to change your mind. Click OK, and the disk you highlighted becomes unallocated space.

Breaking a Mirror

If a disk fails and you can't replace it with an identical one, break the mirror until a replacement becomes available. Breaking a mirror severs the connection between the two disks, allowing the remaining disk to continue to function normally until a replacement disk becomes available. Once the replacement disk is available, the mirror can be re-created.

You might also find it useful to break a mirror even when both disks are still functioning, because you then end up with two identical copies of the same data. One half of the broken mirror continues to have the same drive letter or mount point, while the second half of the broken mirror is assigned the next available drive letter. To break a mirror, complete the following steps:

1. In the Disk Management console, right-click either disk of the mirrored volume.

2. Choose Break Mirror from the shortcut menu. You're asked to confirm that you really want to break it.

3. Click Yes, and the mirror is broken. You'll have two volumes. One retains the drive letter or mount point of the original mirror, and the other is assigned the next available drive letter. They will both contain exact duplicates of the data at the instant of the break but will immediately start to diverge as they are modified.

RAID-5 Volumes

Windows Small Business Server 2003 supports a software implementation of RAID-5 that allows you to have a redundant file system without the 50 percent capacity overhead of using mirrored volumes. The overhead on a RAID-5 volume decreases for each additional disk you add to the volume, making this the most space efficient method of providing redundancy in Windows Small Business Server.

Unfortunately, this efficiency doesn't come without some costs. RAID-5 arrays are inherently slower at write operations than even a plain old stand-alone drive. You also don't have the flexibility that you have with mirrored volumes in Windows Small Business Server. You can't simply remove a drive from a RAID-5 volume, nor can you break a failed drive out of the volume, allowing the remaining drives to regenerate. Further, when a disk fails on a RAID-5 volume, not only is the volume no longer redundant, but it also gets a lot slower because both read and write operations must calculate the correct value for every byte read or written.

Some of the tasks you do with a mirror also apply to a RAID-5 volume. You can:

- Create the RAID-5 volume.
- Assign a mount point or drive letter to the RAID-5 volume.
- Format the RAID-5 volume.
- Continue to use the RAID-5 volume after the failure of one of the disks in the volume.

What you can't do is add or remove disks from the RAID-5 volume once you have created it, except for replacing a failed disk. To be able to dynamically add and remove disks from a RAID-5 array, the array needs to be a hardware RAID array that supports dynamic reconfiguration.

Real World   **Assigning Volume Names**

The name you assign to a volume, partition, or drive should tell you something about it rather than simply mimicking the drive letter. A volume name like "Big70GBSCSI" tells you pretty conclusively that it's that big new SCSI drive you just bought, unless, of course, you already have a half dozen of them on your server, in which case you're going to need to come up with a more effective name. On the other hand, a volume name of "C_DRIVE" is just about useless, because the drive letter is available from anywhere that the volume name is. A common scheme is to assign volume names based on the primary use of the volume, so "UserHome" or "DB_STORE" make it pretty clear which volume it is from a logical (but not necessarily physical) view.

Mounting a Volume

Windows Small Business Server allows you to mount a dynamic volume—or any partition or logical drive in an extended partition—on an empty directory of a non-removable NTFS drive. The volume being mounted appears to users as a simple directory. This feature makes it possible to create larger file systems that use multiple hard disks without the inherent risks of using spanned volumes, because the failure of any one of the mounted volumes affects only the directories that were part of that volume. You can also easily support multiple formats from a single drive letter. To mount a volume, complete the following steps:

1. From the Disk Management console, right-click a volume or partition. Choose Change Drive Letter And Paths from the shortcut menu. The Change Drive Letter And Paths dialog box opens.

2. Click Add. The Add Drive Letter Or Path dialog box (Figure 7-28) opens.

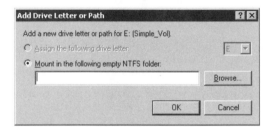

Figure 7-28. *The Add Drive Letter Or Path dialog box, used to mount a volume.*

3. You can type the mount point or click Browse to select or create a mount point. Any empty directory that resides on a non-removable NTFS volume or drive can be the mount point.

4. After you select or type the mount point, click OK, and the volume or partition is mounted.

Caution It's actually easy to get yourself into trouble with this new feature. Disk Management lets you make multiple levels of mounted volumes, including ones that are recursive. You're well advised to mount volumes *only* at the root level of a drive. Trying to mount below that point can lead to confusion and make management and documentation difficult.

Summary

In this chapter, we covered the details of how to manage the hard disks on your Windows Small Business Server machine, and how to configure them for data integrity and redundancy. In the next chapter, we'll cover the configuration and management of file storage on your Windows Small Business Server.

Chapter 8
Storage Management

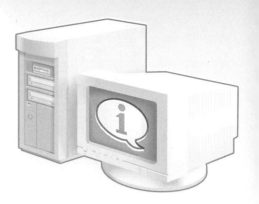

Whereas disk management is all about the mechanics of configuring disks, storage management is where you actually get to use those disks for something. In this chapter we'll cover some of the features of Microsoft Windows Small Business Server 2003 that enable you to manage storage, protect critical files, and provide versioning of shared files to protect against corruption or misadventure. Additional backup and recovery details are covered in Chapter 13, "Backing Up and Restoring Data." But first, a word about file systems and why we care.

Under the Hood   NTFS

The underlying file system format for Windows Small Business Server is the Microsoft Windows NT File System, or NTFS. Originally introduced with the first version of Windows NT and essentially unchanged until Microsoft Windows 2000, NTFS was substantially enhanced for Windows 2000 and then again for Microsoft Windows Server 2003. Although it is technically possible to use the old File Access Table (FAT or FAT32) file system for some of your storage with Windows Small Business Server 2003, by attaching or installing disks that have already been formatted with FAT, NTFS is the only supported file system and is necessary to support disk quotas, shadow copies, and encryption.

Disk Quotas

Windows Small Business Server uses *disk quotas* to limit the amount of disk space individual users can have for file storage on the server. By default, all non-administrative users are limited to the amount of disk space they are allowed to use on the drive that contains the Users shared folder. This is a good thing and allows the Windows Small Business Server administrator to take advantage of some of the special features of Windows Small Business Server such as My Documents Redirection (more on that in just a moment) without having to worry about any one user grabbing all the storage space on the server to store all their home videos.

What happens when users reach their quota limit? As they get close, they will reach the warning level and get reminded that they're close to using up all their allocated space on the drive. If you've chosen to use *"hard" disk quotas*, that is, to deny disk space to users who exceed their limits, they get an error message that their disk is full. And for them, it is. Other users or groups of users who have not exceeded their quota will continue to be able to use the volume for storage, but any users who are over their quota will get a "disk full" message until they delete enough files to get below the limit. Note also that just like with any other disk operation, files in the Recycle Bin count just as much as regular files, so users not only have to delete files to get below the limit, but they also need to remove them from the Recycle Bin.

An alternative to the default hard disk quotas are soft quotas. These aren't really quotas at all—just warnings. A user subject to *soft quotas* can continue to store files on a drive until the entire drive is full, at which point no one can store any more files on the drive. The user will get some annoying messages about reaching their limits, but nothing will actually stop them. Generally, we think soft quotas don't make much sense.

Enabling Disk Quotas

By default, disk quotas are turned off for all partitions and volumes except the volume that includes the Users shared folder. You must enable disk quotas for each additional volume on which you want a quota. Quotas are available only for volumes that are assigned a drive letter. You can set different quotas for individual users or for groups of users, or you can set them the same for all users. To enable quotas on each volume where you want them, complete the following steps:

1. Right-click the drive letter in Microsoft Windows Explorer and choose Properties.

2. Click the Quota tab (Figure 8-1).

3. Select the Enable Quota Management option.

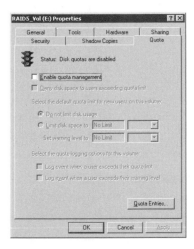

Figure 8-1.   *The Quota tab of the Properties window for a logical drive.*

4. Define the limits on disk usage for this drive letter. The available choices are:

   - **Deny Disk Space To Users Exceeding Quota Limit**   When this option is selected, the quotas are enforced for all disk usage. When it is cleared, the limits are advisory only—that is, soft quotas.

   - **Limit Disk Space To**   Here you can specify the limits of disk space usage for new users on the volume.

   - **Set Warning Level To**   This option indicates the limit at which users will receive a warning message.

   - **Logging Options**   You can choose to log when users exceed their warning level or their usage limit, or you can leave these options blank when you don't want logging.

5. You see a confirmation message. If everything is correct, click OK to scan the drive and enable quotas.

Setting Quota Entries for Users

There's one catch with quotas that are enabled as described in the previous procedure: they apply only to users. Administrators slip by without having quotas enforced unless you explicitly set them in a separate quota entry. To set quotas for administrators, or to tweak the quotas for individual users, you need to perform these additional steps:

1. In Windows Explorer, right-click the drive you want to set quota entries for and choose Properties. Click the Quota tab to display the dialog box shown previously in Figure 8-1.

2. Click Quota Entries to display the quota entries for the volume. You see the window shown in Figure 8-2. This window contains entries for everyone who has ever stored files on the volume, unless you have explicitly removed the entries for users who no longer store files there.

Status	Name	Logon Name	Amount Used	Quota Limit	Warning Level	Percent Used
OK		BUILTIN\Administrators	9.18 GB	No Limit	No Limit	N/A
OK		NT AUTHORITY\SYSTEM	0 bytes	No Limit	No Limit	N/A
OK		NT AUTHORITY\LOCA...	0 bytes	No Limit	No Limit	N/A
OK		NT AUTHORITY\NET...	0 bytes	No Limit	No Limit	N/A
OK	Mobile User Template	EXAMPLE\Mobile User...	0 bytes	1 GB	900 MB	0
OK	User Template	EXAMPLE\User Tmpl	0 bytes	1 GB	900 MB	0
OK	Power User Template	EXAMPLE\Power User...	0 bytes	1 GB	900 MB	0
OK	Administrator Template	EXAMPLE\Administrat...	0 bytes	No Limit	No Limit	N/A
OK	William	Wally@example.local	48.53 MB	1 GB	900 MB	4
OK	Charlie Russel	Charlie@example.local	15 KB	No Limit	No Limit	N/A
OK	Jason Gerend	Jason@example.local	0 bytes	No Limit	No Limit	N/A
OK	Sharon Crawford	Sharon@example.local	1 KB	No Limit	No Limit	N/A

12 total item(s), 1 selected.

Figure 8-2. *The Quota Entries window.*

3. You can change the properties for any entry by double-clicking the entry, which displays the dialog box shown in Figure 8-3. The figure shows a user whose quota has been lowered so that he is now exceeding his disk space limit. He will be unable to store any additional data on the volume until he is below the limit.

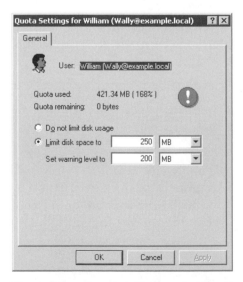

Figure 8-3. *Quota settings and status for a user.*

The Quota Entries window lets you sort by any of the columns to make it easy to quickly identify problem areas or to locate an individual entry. You can also use the Find function to locate a specific entry.

Real World **Avoid Individual Quotas**

Resist the temptation to fine-tune a disk's quotas for each individual. Giving in will lead to an administrative nightmare, especially because you then cannot manage quotas for the all-users audience, only for individual users. Make changes to the quotas for an individual only when there is a compelling reason to do so, and then keep careful records so that all administrators have ready access to the information.

Exporting and Importing Quotas

If you have a complicated quota system set up so that some users get more space than others, implementing that system on a new volume can be a pain. But Windows Small Business Server lets you export the quotas from one volume to another. If there isn't an entry for a user on the new volume yet, one will be created. If a user already has a quota entry, you're asked whether you want to overwrite it with the imported quota entry for that user, as shown in Figure 8-4.

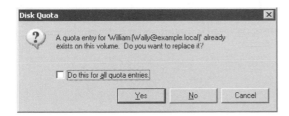

Figure 8-4. *Confirmation message for overwriting a quota entry with an imported entry.*

Avoid importing quota settings to an existing drive unless you're changing your overall quotas across the entire server. Any customizations you made on the current drive could be lost, and having to acknowledge each change that affects an existing user lends itself to mistakes. Or worse, you could check the Do This For All Quota Entries check box, now overwriting the current quota settings with no warning or confirmation at all. Finally, any special limits set for specific users on the source volume will be applied to the target volume.

There are two ways to import quotas from one volume to another. You can open the Quota Entries window for the source volume, click Quota and choose Export to save the entry to a file, and then open the Quota Entries window for the target volume and choose Import from the Quota menu. Or you can simply open both Quota Entries windows and drag the entries you want to import from the source window to the target one.

Creating Quota Reports

You can use the Quota Entries window to create reports about disk usage. Select the accounts you want to include in the report and drag them into the reporting tool you'll be using. The supported formats include Rich Text Format, Comma Separated Value, CF_UNICODETEXT, and CF_TEXT. If you drag the entries into Microsoft Excel, for example, you get not only the entries but also the column headings. This makes whipping out a disk usage report pretty trivial.

Encrypting Files

Windows Small Business Server includes the ability to encrypt individual files or entire subdirectories in a totally transparent way. To their creator, encrypted files look exactly like regular files—they can be opened, read, modified, or deleted just like any other file. No changes to applications are required to use them. However, to anyone except the creator/encryptor, the files are unavailable, and even if someone did manage to gain access to them, the files would be gibberish because they're stored in encrypted form. In this section, we'll cover the basics about how to enable encryption on a folder or file.

More Info For more details about encryption, including how to share encrypted files and how to un-encrypt files in the event an employee leaves, see Chapter 10, "Shares, Permissions, and Group Policy."

Encryption is simply an advanced attribute of the file, just as compression is. However, a file cannot be both compressed and encrypted at the same time—the attributes are mutually exclusive. Encrypted files are available only to the encryptor or to those individuals who are explicitly granted access, but the files can be recovered by the domain recovery agent if necessary. Encrypted files can be backed up by normal Windows Small Business Server backup procedures, and the files remain encrypted. Restoring encrypted files retains their encryption.

By default, no user except the actual creator of an encrypted file has access to the file. Even a change of ownership does not remove the encryption. This prevents sensitive data, such as payroll and annual reviews, from being accessed by the wrong users, even if those users have administrative rights. The catch is that encryption is enabled for an individual user, not for a group of users, which limits its effectiveness. Although you can add individual users with the appropriate certificates to the list of users who can access a file, you can't add groups of users to the list. On our wish list for the Encrypting File System (EFS) is the ability to make the encryption transparent to either a group of users or any user with a specific key, smartcard, or other security identifier or combination of security identifiers.

Note Encryption is available only on NTFS and only on versions of NTFS beginning with Windows 2000. If the owner/encryptor of an encrypted file copies it to a disk or to another computer that doesn't support encryption, the encryption will be removed.

Enabling Encryption

When you encrypt a folder, all new files created in that folder are encrypted from that point forward. You can also elect to encrypt the current contents when you perform the encryption. Be warned, however: If you choose to encrypt the contents of a folder when it already contains files or subfolders, those files and subfolders are encrypted *for the user performing the encryption only*. This means that even files that are owned by another user are encrypted and are thus available for your use only—the owner of the files will no longer be able to access them. Of course, if you don't have the Modify privilege on the file owned by someone else, you won't be able to encrypt it.

When new files are created in an encrypted folder, the files are encrypted for use by the creator of the file, not the user who first enabled encryption on the folder. Unencrypted files in an encrypted folder can be used by all users who have security rights to use files in that folder, and the encryption status of the files does not change unless the file names themselves are changed. Users can read, modify, and save the files without converting them to encrypted files, but any changes in the name of the files triggers an encryption, and the encryption makes the files available only to the person who triggers the encryption.

To encrypt a file or folder, complete the following steps:

1. In Windows Explorer, right-click the folder or files you want to encrypt, and choose Properties from the shortcut menu.

2. Click Advanced on the General tab to open the Advanced Attributes dialog box shown in Figure 8-5.

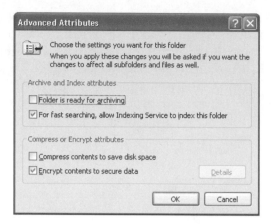

Figure 8-5. *The Advanced Attributes dialog box.*

3. Select the Encrypt Contents To Secure Data option, and click OK to return to the main Properties window for the folder or file. Click OK or Apply to enable the encryption. If any files or subfolders are already in the folder, you're presented with the dialog box shown in Figure 8-6.

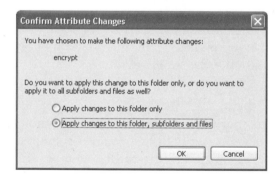

Figure 8-6. *Choosing whether to encrypt the files already in a folder or just new files.*

4. If you choose Apply Changes To This Folder Only, all the current files and subfolders in the folder remain unencrypted, but any new files and folders are encrypted by the creator as they are created. If you choose Apply Changes To This Folder, Subfolders, And Files, all the files and folders below this folder are encrypted so that only you can use them, regardless of the original creator or owner of the file.

5. Click OK and the encryption occurs.

Users can choose to have files that are encrypted appear in a different color in Windows Explorer. When they do, the file will appear in green text as shown in Figure 8-7 for the file Encrypted.txt. Notice that even though all new files in this folder are encrypted, the files that were already in the folder have not been encrypted.

Figure 8-7. *Encrypted file is shown in green.*

Shadow Copies of Shared Folders

Windows Small Business Server includes the ability to create shadow copies of shared folders. This allows you to create backup snapshots of the files in shared folders. These snapshots are created automatically on a schedule you control, enabling easy fallback to older versions of a particular file in the event of corruption, deletion, or inadvertent and undesired changes. And, considering that a file deletion from a network share would otherwise be both immediate and permanent, with no intervening Recycle Bin, shadow copies are highly recommended. But even when you're not dealing with the deletion of a file, shadow copies are a really useful tool. How many times have you inadvertently saved the wrong version of a file? With shadow copies, you can retrieve an earlier version and recover it quickly without having to restore from a backup tape.

Configuring Shadow Copies

Shadow copies provide a sort of "network Recycle Bin" by taking snapshots of shared folders at a set interval. This allows you to go back and look at earlier versions of files stored in network shares, even if a user deleted the original files or modified them. This permits you to recover deleted or overwritten files, or compare modified files to earlier versions (up to 64 versions can be kept). You'll still need to perform regular backups, but shadow copies can be a great way to supplement your backup strategy.

Enabling Shadow Copies

Shadow copies are enabled by default on Windows Small Business Server on the volume that houses the Users shared folder, so you don't need to do anything at all to enable them. However, you do need to think about your overall strategy for shadow copies and how you want to use them. You should consider the total amount of storage you'll use for shadow copies, where the shadow copy storage will reside, how often automatic shadow copies will be made and how many versions you're going to keep.

If you want to enable shadow copies on other volumes, you will need to manually enable them, as described in this section.

Caution If you're storing shadow copies on a different volume from the source files, you should make any disk changes to that volume before you enable it for storage. If you convert from a basic disk to a dynamic disk, you might lose the shadow copy data.

If the source volume is a dynamic disk, you can get around this problem by first taking the source volume offline, and then converting the volume storing the shadow copies to a dynamic disk and bringing the source volume back online. (This must be performed in fewer than 20 minutes to preserve the existing shadow copies.) But much better to configure all your disks first.

To enable shadow copies, complete the following steps:

1. In Windows Explorer, right-click the volume on which you want to enable shadow copies and select Properties.

2. Click the Tools tab, and click the Defragment Now button to open the Disk Defragmenter tool and defragment the volume.

3. When defragmentation is done, return to the main volume Properties page and click the Shadow Copies tab.

4. Select a volume on which to enable shadow copies, as shown in Figure 8-8.

5. Click Settings.

6. If you're going to store your shadow copies on a separate volume, select the target volume from the Located On This Volume drop-down list.

7. Type in the maximum amount of storage to allocate in the Use Limit box, as shown in Figure 8-9.

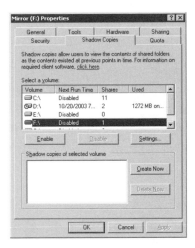

Figure 8-8. *Enabling shadow copies on a volume.*

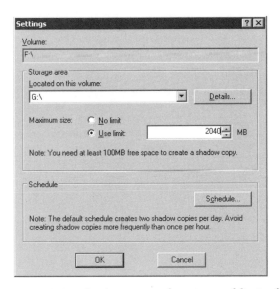

Figure 8-9. *Setting storage location and limits for shadow copies.*

8. Click Schedule and specify the schedule for shadow copy creation. The default is twice a day.

9. Click OK in the Settings dialog box to return to the Shadow Copies tab.

10. Click Enable to display the Enable Shadow Copies dialog box, shown in Figure 8-10. Even though it says that Windows will use the default settings, the settings you just made will actually be used.

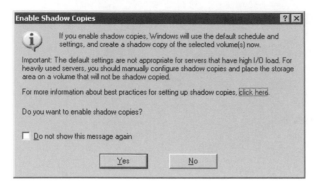

Figure 8-10. *The Enable Shadow Copies dialog box.*

11. Configure any additional volumes and click OK when you're finished.

Setting Up Clients to Use Shadow Copies

To access stored shadow copies, clients need to have the Previous Versions Client software installed. The Previous Versions Client software is automatically installed on Windows 2000 (SP3 or later) and Microsoft Windows XP clients when you configure a new client computer in Windows Small Business Server. The software is located in the ClientApps\ShadowCopy folder on the server. For Microsoft Windows 98 Second Edition and Windows Me, the client must be installed manually, as discussed in Chapter 12, "Managing Computers on the Network."

Accessing Shadow Copies

To access shadow copies from a client using the Previous Versions Client software, complete the following steps:

1. In Windows Explorer, right-click the network share and choose Properties from the shortcut menu.

2. Click the Previous Versions tab, shown in Figure 8-11.

Tip For the Previous Versions tab to show up, at least one shadow copy on the server must be created. To create a shadow copy on the server immediately, open the Properties dialog box for the volume, click the Shadow Copies tab, and click Create Now.

3. Select the folder version and then click the button corresponding to the action you want to perform:

   • **View** Opens the shadow copy in Windows Explorer. You can then open or copy the files just like in a normal folder (although you can't delete anything or save to these folders).

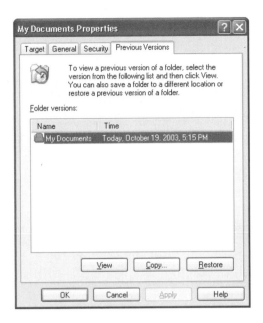

Figure 8-11.   *Accessing previous versions of a file.*

- **Copy**   Copies the shadow copy to the location you specify.
- **Restore**   Rolls back the shared folder to its state as of the snapshot image you selected.

Tip   To access shadow copies from the server, connect to the shared folder using its UNC path (for example, \\sbssrv\Users\Wally) instead of using a local path.

Disabling Shadow Copies

To disable shadow copies on a volume, complete the following steps:

1. In Windows Explorer, right-click the volume you want to disable shadow copies on and select Properties.

2. Select the Shadow Copies tab.

3. Select the volume to disable and click Disable.

4. Click Yes to confirm that Windows will delete all previous shadow copies on the volume.

Caution   Disabling Shadow copies on a volume deletes all previously saved shadow copies (snapshots) for that volume.

Tip If you want to delete a volume on which shadow copies is enabled, first disable shadow copies for the volume. If you don't first disable shadow copies, the event log will fill up with errors.

Under the Hood **Command Line**

To administer shadow copies from a command line, use the following command:

```
vssadmin [Add ShadowStorage] [Create Shadow] [Delete Shadows] [Delete
   ShadowStorage] [List Providers] [List Shadows] [List ShadowStorage]
   [List Volumes] [List Writers] [Resize ShadowStorage]
```

The available parameters for vssadmin are:

- **Add ShadowStorage** Specifies on what volume shadow copies should be stored for the specified source volume

- **Create Shadow** Manually creates a shadow copy

- **Delete Shadows** Deletes all shadow copies for the specified source volume

- **Delete ShadowStorage** Deletes the association between a source volume and the volume on which the shadow copies are stored

- **List Providers** Displays the installed shadow copy providers (Windows Server 2003 ships with only one)

- **List Shadows** Displays the complete list of stored shadow copies

- **List ShadowStorage** Displays all associations between source volumes and the volumes on which shadow copies are stored

- **List Volumes** Displays all volumes on which shadow copies can be enabled

- **List Writers** Displays a list of all applications that make use of shadow copies

- **Resize ShadowStorage** Changes the maximum size allocated to storing shadow copies

For additional help with individual parameters, type:

```
vssadmin <parameter> /?
```

Summary

In this chapter, we covered the features of Windows Small Business Server 2003 that give it a flexible, robust, and recoverable storage system. With a pure NTFS file system as a requirement, Windows Small Business Server uses volume shadow copies, disk quotas, and file and folder encryption—the tools for handling the storage needs of your business.

In the next chapter, we'll cover users, groups, and managing the security and accounts of your Windows Small Business Server.

Part III
Performing the Basic Tasks

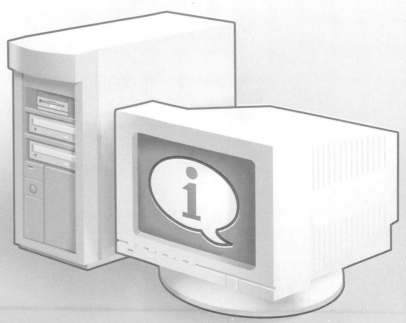

Chapter 9
Users, Groups, and Security

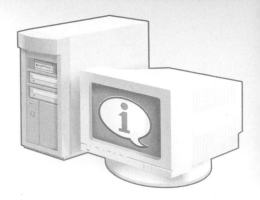

The whole purpose behind a network is to provide users with everything they need and clear away the clutter that hampers their progress. What they need includes access to the files, folders, applications, printers, and Internet connections required to do their jobs. What they don't need is any trouble getting at what they *do* need.

The person in charge of the network has his or her own needs, such as shielding need-to-know material from those who don't need to know and protecting the users from themselves. The key to all these needs is the configuration of groups and users—the topic of this chapter.

> **More Info** See Chapter 10, "Shares, Permissions, and Group Policy," for information about Group Policy.

Understanding Groups

By definition, Microsoft Windows Small Business Server groups are Active Directory directory service or local computer objects that can contain users, contacts, computers, or other groups. In practice, though, a *group* is usually a collection of user accounts. The point of groups is to simplify administration by allowing the network administrator to assign rights and permissions to groups rather than individual users.

Windows Small Business Server allows two group types: security and distribution. Almost all groups are security groups because they're the only groups through which permissions can be assigned. Each security group is also assigned a *group scope*, which defines how permissions are assigned to the group's members. Programs that can search Active Directory can use security groups for nonsecurity purposes, such as sending e-mail to a group of users. Distribution groups are not security-enabled and can be used *only* with e-mail applications to send e-mail to sets of users.

User rights are assigned to security groups to establish what members of the group can or cannot do. Some rights are automatically assigned to some groups—for example, a user who is a member of the Print Operators group has the ability to administer the printers in the domain.

> **Tip** Permissions and user rights are different. *Permissions* determine what resources members of a group can access. *User rights* determine what members of a group can or cannot do. See the Under the Hood sidebar "Rights and Permissions" later in this chapter for additional information.

Why Use Groups at All?

Groups are an effective way of simplifying administration. If you have only a handful of users, you don't need to do much to change the built-in groups and memberships. One Administrator account handles everything related to administration, and the other few users all belong to the Users group and all have the same rights and permissions. But when the total number of users gets to 20 or more, groups are the way to organize permissions. For example, when you have a number of people who travel or telecommute, you don't need to keep track of which users have permission to log on remotely if you add them all to the Mobile Users group.

Under the Hood   About Group Scopes

All groups, whether built-in or created later, are assigned a group scope that defines how permissions are assigned. When you create a new group, by default, the new group is configured as a security group with universal scope.

Built-in local groups cannot be members of other groups. Universal groups, on the other hand, can be members of any other groups. Universal groups can have the following as members:

- Other universal groups
- Global groups
- Individual accounts

Global groups are best used for directory objects that require frequent maintenance, such as user and computer accounts. Global groups can be members of other groups, and they can have other global groups and individual user accounts as members.

Managing Built-in Groups

Because Microsoft Windows Server 2003 is the underlying operating system for Windows Small Business Server 2003, all the built-in security groups integral to Windows Server 2003 still exist. However, many of these groups are focused on a much larger, multidomain network, so the designers of Windows Small Business Server created a subset of organizational units to simplify administration.

To view a list of groups (Figure 9-1), select Server Management from the Start menu and then click Security Groups in the console tree.

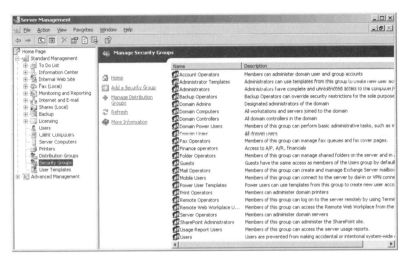

Figure 9-1.   *The security groups built in to Windows Small Business Server.*

Note   Some groups, such as DHCP Administrators and DHCP Users, are listed in Active Directory Users and Computers.

Built-in Universal Groups

All the built-in universal groups, which are described in Table 9-1, are specific to Windows Small Business Server. With few exceptions, these are the groups that all users belong to and that are used to make templates. Templates are discussed in more detail later in the chapter.

Table 9-1.   Universal groups in Windows Small Business Server

Universal Group	Description
Administrator Templates	Members of this group are the templates that an Administrator can use to create new user accounts. The built-in user templates are default members.
Domain Power Users	Members can create and modify user accounts and install programs on the local computer but cannot view other users' files. This group is a default member of Fax Operators, Folder Operators, Mail Operators, Remote Operators, and SharePoint Administrators—all other built-in universal groups. Domain Power Users is also a member of Account Operators and Print Operators, which are built-in local groups.
Fax Operators	Members of this group can manage fax cover pages and queues. The Domain Power Users group is a member by default.
Folder Operators	Members can manage shared folders in the domain. The Domain Power Users group is a member by default.
Mail Operators	Members can create and manage Microsoft Exchange Server mailboxes. The Domain Power Users group is a member by default.
Mobile Users	Members can connect to the server remotely. Default members are the Administrator account, Administrator Template, Mobile User Template, and Power User Template.
Power User Templates	Members of this group are the templates that power users utilize to create new user accounts. Default members are the built-in Mobile User Template and the User Template.
Remote Operators	Members can log on to the server remotely but not locally. The Domain Power Users group is a member by default.
Remote Web Workplace Users	Members can access the Remote Web Workplace from the Internet. The built-in templates are default members.
SharePoint Administrators	Members can administer the SharePoint Web site. Default members are the Domain Power Users group and the STS Worker account (used by the Windows Small Business Server to route faxes).
Usage Report Users	Members can view server usage reports. The Domain Admins group is a member by default.

Built-in Local Groups

Built-in local groups are created when Windows Small Business Server is installed. These groups can't be members of other groups and their group scope can't be changed. Table 9-2 shows the built-in local groups.

Table 9-2.   Built-in local groups in Windows Small Business Server

Group	Description
Account Operators	Members can add, change, or delete user and group accounts. The Domain Power Users group is a member of this group.
Administrators	Members can perform all administrative tasks on the computer. The built-in Administrator account that's created when the operating system is installed is a member of the group. When a member server or a client running Microsoft Windows XP Professional or Microsoft Windows 2000 Professional joins a domain, the Domain Admins group (see Table 9-4) is made part of this group.
Backup Operators	Members can log on to the computer, back up and restore the computer's data, and shut down the computer. Members cannot change security settings but can override them for purposes of backup and restore.
Guests	Members have the same access as members of the Users group. The Guest account has fewer rights and is a default member of this group.
Print Operators	Members can manage printers and print queues on domain printers. The Domain Power Users group is an automatic member.
Server Operators	Members can administer servers. No default members.
Users	Members of this group can log on to the computer, access the network, save documents, and shut down the computer. Members cannot install programs or make system changes. When a member server, Windows 2000 Professional, or Windows XP Professional machine joins a domain, the Domain Users group is added to this group.

If you don't want members of the Domain Users group to have access to a particular workstation or member server, remove Domain Users from that computer's local Users group. Similarly, if you don't want the members of Domain Admins to administer a particular workstation or member server, remove Domain Admins from the local Administrators group.

Built-in Domain Local Groups

The built-in domain local groups provide users with rights and permissions to perform tasks on domain controllers and in Active Directory. The domain local groups have predefined rights and permissions that are granted to users and global groups that you add as members. DHCP Users and DHCP Administrators groups are listed in Active Directory Users and Computers. Table 9-3 shows the built-in domain local groups used in Windows Small Business Server.

Table 9-3. Domain local groups used in Windows Small Business Server 2003

Domain Local Group	Description
DHCP Users (installed with DHCP Server service)	Members of this group can read DHCP information stored at a specific server for troubleshooting purposes. No default members.
DHCP Administrators	Members of this group can administer DHCP Server service but do not have access to other parts of the server.

Security Alert On Microsoft Windows NT Server networks, all domain users are members of the Everyone group. This group is controlled by the operating system and appears on any network with Windows NT servers. In Windows Small Business Server 2003, all domain users are members of the Authenticated Users group. Unlike Everyone, Authenticated Users contains no anonymous users or guests. The Everyone group survives as a *special identity*. You don't see it when you administer groups, and it cannot be placed in a group. When a user logs on to the network, the user is automatically added to Everyone. You can't see or change the membership of the special identities, which also includes the Network and Interactive groups.

Built-in Global Groups

Built-in global groups are created to encompass common types of accounts. By default, these groups do not have inherent rights; an administrator must assign all rights to the group. However, some members are added to these groups automatically, and you can add more members based on the rights and permissions you assign to the groups. Rights can be assigned directly to the groups or by adding the built-in global groups to domain local groups. Table 9-4 describes the built-in global groups that are commonly used.

Table 9-4. Commonly used built-in global groups

Global Group	Description
Domain Admins	This group is automatically a member of the built-in local Administrators group, so members of Domain Admins can perform administrative tasks on any computer in the domain. The Administrator account is a member of this group by default.
Domain Computers	All servers and workstations in the domain are members.
Domain Controllers	The Windows Small Business Server.
Domain Users	All domain users are members. The Domain Users group is automatically a member of the built-in local Users group.

Creating Security Groups

The security groups built in to Windows Small Business Server 2003 are sufficient for most operations. Changing the options for the built-in templates can cover a lot of variation among companies. One conspicuous lack is a security group granting access to personnel and financial information. Every company has confidential information that must be accessed by only a limited number of people. To handle needs of this type, create a new security group by following these steps:

1. Select Server Management from the Start menu. Click Security Groups and then click Add A Security Group to launch the Add Security Group Wizard.

2. On the Security Group Information page, provide a name and description for the group.

3. On the Group Membership page, select members. You can add individual users or another security group. You can also make a template (see "Managing User Templates" later in this chapter) to create user accounts specific to the new group.

4. On the final page of the wizard, the settings are summarized. Click the link at the bottom of the page to save the summary.

Creating Distribution Groups

Distribution groups are mechanisms for managing the delivery of information. Windows Small Business Server creates a default distribution group that includes all users of the network. Messages sent to the distribution group's e-mail address go to all members of the group.

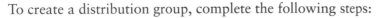

> **Tip**   Multiple distribution groups are useful when you don't maintain an internal Web site, which is a more efficient and manageable method of delivering information to users.

To create a distribution group, complete the following steps:

1. Launch Server Management from the Start Menu. Click Distribution Groups in the console tree then click Add A Distribution Group to launch the Add Distribution Group Wizard.

2. On the Distribution Group Information page, provide a name, description, and e-mail alias for the distribution group. (See Chapter 14, "Using Exchange Server," for more information about creating e-mail aliases.)

3. On the Group Membership page, select members.

4. On the Group Manager page, you can specify a group manager from the distribution group. The group manager can change the membership of the group using Microsoft Office Outlook 2003.

5. On the Group Options page, select the group options to enable (Figure 9-2).

- **Create A Public Folder To Archive E-Mail Messages Sent To This Group.** Depending on the nature of the distribution group, you might want all messages sent to the group saved in an Exchange public folder. Select this option and a public folder named Distribution_Group_Name Archive will be added as a member of this group.

- **Enable This Group To Receive E-Mail Messages From Users Outside Of Your Network.** Select this option when part of this distribution group's role is communicating with people outside the network. If the group is strictly internal, clear this check box.

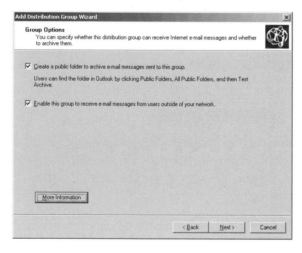

Figure 9-2. *Selecting options for a new distribution group.*

6. On the final page of the wizard, the settings are summarized. Click the link at the bottom of the page to save the summary.

Understanding User Accounts

Gaining access to the network requires a domain user account, which authenticates the identity of the person making the connection and controls what resources a user has a right to access.

Windows Small Business Server creates two predefined accounts: the Administrator account, which is granted all rights and permissions, and the Guest account, which has limited rights and is disabled by default. All other accounts are created by an administrator and are either domain accounts (valid throughout the domain by default) or local accounts (usable only on the machine where they are created).

Configuring Password Policy

Passwords are a critical line of defense in the security wars. Passwords must be sufficiently complex and changed often. Before adding new user accounts, open Server Management from the Start menu, click Users in the console tree, and then click Configure Password Policies to open the Configure Password Policies dialog box (Figure 9-3).

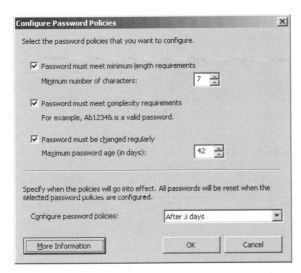

Figure 9-3. *Setting password requirements.*

Set the minimum password length (at least seven characters). Select the second check box to require that the password be of sufficient complexity—that is, it meets three of the following four conditions:

- It includes at least one capital letter.

- It includes at least one lowercase letter.

- It includes at least one numeral.

- It includes at least one nonalphanumeric character (such as +, *, ^, $, and @).

Select the third check box to set the number of days that a password can be used before the system requires a change. The default setting is 42 days. Resist the temptation to make the number smaller. If users are required to change passwords too often, it won't be long before passwords start appearing on sticky notes in desk drawers or attached to monitors.

At the bottom of the dialog box, you specify when these password policies go into effect. If your Windows Small Business Server is new, postpone activating strong passwords until after you configure the clients but before users log on the first time.

Under the Hood Rules for Good Passwords

A good password has the following characteristics:

- It is not a rotation of the characters in a logon name.

- It contains at least two alphabetic characters and one nonalphabetic character.

- It is at least seven characters long.

- It isn't the user's name or initials, the initials of his or her children or significant other, or any of these items combined with other commonly available personal data such as a birth date, telephone number, or license plate number.

- It isn't the name of a pet or a favorite sport, drink, television show, or any other personal term that could be easily guessed.

Among the best passwords are alphanumeric acronyms of phrases that have a meaning to the user but are not likely to be known to others. This makes the password easy for the user to remember while at the same time making it hard for an outsider to guess. For example, you could use a catch phrase such as "too good to be true" and change it into the password *Twogood2bTru*. Or "forever and a day" could be transformed into the password *4ever+24*. It just takes a little imagination.

Security Alert   It pays to educate your users about passwords and password privacy, but most of all, it pays to heed your own advice: make sure the password you select for administration is a good password, and change it frequently. Doing so will help you avoid the consequences of having somebody break into your system and wreak havoc in your own kingdom.

Administrators should have two accounts on the system: one administrative account and one normal user account. Use the normal user account unless you are performing administrative tasks. Because administrative accounts have virtually unlimited privileges, they are a prime target for intruders.

Creating User Accounts

Adding user accounts could scarcely be easier than it is in Windows Small Business Server. Using the templates provided or templates of your own devising, you can add all users at once, in bunches, or one at a time.

Under the Hood   Naming User Accounts

In Active Directory, each user account has a *principal name*. This name consists of two parts, the *security principal name*, and the *principal name suffix*. For Windows Small Business Server user accounts, the administrator assigns the security principal name. The principal name suffix is the DNS name of the root domain in the domain tree. So Active Directory sees CharlieR@example.local as the user's principal name. The security principal name is CharlieR and the principal name suffix is example.local.

Assign the security principal name using a consistent naming convention so that you and your users can remember user names and find them in lists. The Add User Wizard proposes these:

- Entire name without spaces
- Last name followed by first name
- First initial plus last name
- First name plus last initial

You can overrule the wizard and type in your own choice for a logon and e-mail name. In a smaller organization, there's no need for long names. Users type their logon names and e-mail addresses every day. The simpler you can make it, the happier everyone will be. (Save the complexity for passwords.)

Adding a Single User

To add a user account to the network, complete the following steps:

1. Select Server Management from the Start menu, click Users in the console tree, and click Add A User to launch the Add User Wizard.

2. On the User Account Information page, add the user information. As you type in the user's name, the Add User Wizard automatically proposes a corresponding logon name and e-mail alias. Logon name variations are available in the drop-down list (Figure 9-4).

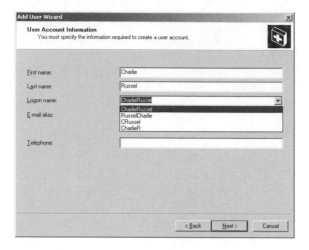

Figure 9-4. *Choosing a logon name variation for a user account.*

3. On the User Password page, provide a password. This is a temporary password that the user will be required to change when logging on for the first time and at whatever intervals you've specified in password policies.

4. On the Template Selection page, choose a template to define user rights. (Fore more information about templates, see "Managing User Templates" later in this chapter.) Select the check box to display the template's default settings.

Tip Use templates whenever possible. Without a template, you must configure all the user's groups and other rights manually. It's very easy to slip up while doing this and create problems that are very difficult to trace.

5. On the Security Groups page, the default group memberships assigned by the template (in this case, the Mobile User template) are listed (Figure 9-5). As shown, these memberships allow the user to log on to the domain locally, log on to the domain from a remote location, and use the Remote Web Workplace. Add other group memberships if they are required.

6. On the Distribution Groups page, you can make the user a member of any other distribution groups that you've created. All users are members of the default distribution group. (See "Creating Distribution Groups," earlier in this chapter.)

Figure 9-5. *Mobile users are members of three groups by default.*

7. On the SharePoint Access page, specify the user's roles on your Share-Point site.

8. On the Address Information page, supply address information.

9. On the Disk Quotas page, set a limit of hard drive space that the user can fill on the Windows Small Business Server. (See Chapter 8, "Storage Management," for more about the pros and cons of disk quotas.)

10. On the Set Up Client Computer page, specify whether to set up a client computer for the user. The wizard creates a computer account with the user's name plus a number—though you can type in a different name. (If you choose not to set up a computer, the configuration of the user account is summarized and the wizard is complete.)

11. On the Client Applications page, select the applications you want installed on the client computer. (See Chapter 12, "Managing Computers on the Network," for details about assigning applications to client computers.)

12. On the Mobile Client And Offline Use page (Figure 9-6), select the options to install on this client. If the client computer is going to travel, install Connection Manager so that the user can connect to the Windows Small Business Server remotely. Install ActiveSync to allow devices such as Microsoft Pocket PC Phone Edition to synchronize with the client computer and with the Windows Small Business Server.

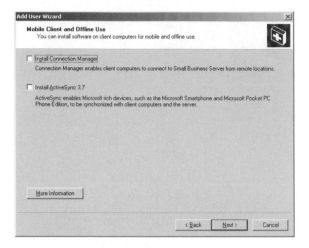

Figure 9-6. *Options for mobile clients.*

13. The final page of the Add User Wizard summarizes all your settings. Click the link at the bottom of the page to save the information.

Adding Multiple Users

The ability to add several user accounts at once is a new and highly helpful feature in Windows Small Business Server 2003. The process works much like adding a single user. To add multiple user accounts, complete the following steps:

1. Select Server Management from the Start menu, click Users in the console tree, and click Add Multiple Users to launch the Add User Wizard.

2. On the Template Selection page, choose a template that will define the users' rights. (For more information about templates, see "Managing User Templates" later in this chapter.)

3. On the User Information page, click the Add button. Specify the first user's information. As you type in the user's name, the Add User Wizard automatically proposes a corresponding logon name and e-mail alias. Logon name variations are available in the drop-down list. Click OK after each user. When the User Information page is complete (Figure 9-7), click Next.

4. On the Set Up Client Computers page, if you want to set up client computers for these users, select the Set Up Computers Now option, specify computer names on the Client Computer Names page, and follow Steps 11 through 13 in the preceding section, "Adding a Single User."

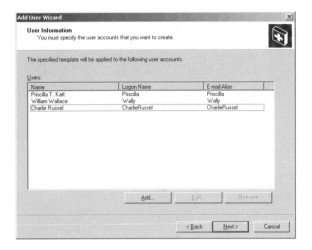

Figure 9-7.   *Creating multiple user accounts.*

Managing User Templates

User rights, privileges, permissions, and shares are some of the mechanisms that make Windows Server 2003 quite daunting to many. Windows Small Business Server can shield you from these details with user templates. When you create or modify user accounts, you can apply templates to the accounts. By using templates, many of the account properties and permissions will already be specified, making account management easier.

Creating a New User Template

Most organizations can use the supplied user templates with or without modification. However, it's a simple matter to make your own templates when you follow these steps:

1. Select Server Management from the Start Menu. Click User Templates in the console tree and then Add A Template to launch the Add Template Wizard.

2. On the Template Account Information page, provide a name for the template and specify whether it is to be the default template for the Add User Wizard and whether power users will be able to use it.

3. On the Security Groups page, select the security group memberships for user accounts created with this template.

4. On the Distribution Groups page, select the distribution groups for user accounts created with this template.

5. On the SharePoint Access page, specify the roles user accounts created with this template will have on your SharePoint site.

6. On the Address Information page, type in address information that will be applied to all the users created with this template. When address information will be different for different user accounts, leave the fields empty and click Next.

7. On the Disk Quotas page, specify disk quotas if they are to be applied to the user accounts.

8. On the final page of the wizard, the settings you made for this template are summarized. Click the link at the bottom of the page to print, save, or e-mail the summary.

Applying a Template to Existing Users

When you create a new template, modify an existing one, or just want to make changes to users' permissions, you can apply a template to one or more user accounts.

1. Select Server Management from the Start menu then click Users in the console tree. Click Change User Permissions to launch the Change User Permissions Wizard.

2. On the Template Selection page, select the template to apply (Figure 9-8).

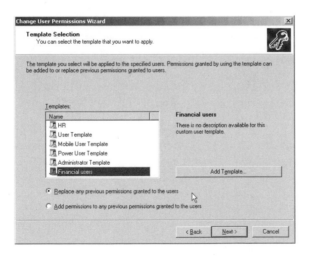

Figure 9-8. *Choosing a template to apply to existing user accounts.*

3. Select the option to replace existing permissions or to add this template's permissions to the existing ones.

4. On the User Selection page, select the users to whom this template will apply. (Note that you can use this template to change other templates.)

5. The final page of the Change User Permissions Wizard displays a summary of the operations the wizard will complete. Click the link at the bottom of the page to select a method of saving this information.

Tip   Previous group memberships will be replaced by group memberships in the new template. But permissions previously granted directly to a user account remain unchanged after applying the template.

Under the Hood   **Rights and Permissions**

What users can and cannot do depends on the rights and permissions that have been granted to them. *Rights* generally apply to the system as a whole. The ability to back up files or to log on to a server, for example, is a right that the administrator can assign or remove. Rights can be assigned individually, but most often they are characteristics of groups, and a user is assigned to a particular group on the basis of the rights that the user needs.

Permissions indicate the access that a user (or group) has to specific objects such as files, directories, and printers. For example, a user's ability to read a particular directory or access a network printer is a permission.

Rights, in turn, are divided into two types: privileges and logon rights. *Privileges* include such things as the ability to run security audits or force shutdown from a remote system—obviously not things that are handled by most users. *Logon rights* are self-explanatory; they involve the ability to connect to a computer in specific ways. Rights are automatically assigned to the built-in groups in Windows Small Business Server, although they can be assigned to individual users as well as groups. Assignment by group is preferred, so whenever possible, you should assign rights by group membership to keep administration simple. When membership in groups defines rights, rights can be removed from a user by simply removing the user from the group.

Managing User Accounts

Disabling, enabling, deleting, and renaming user accounts are tasks easily done from the Manage Users taskpad. Launch Server Management and click Users in the console tree. Select a user account to expand the options, as shown in Figure 9-9.

Click the task you want to perform. Most of these are completely self-explanatory but a few require more explanation.

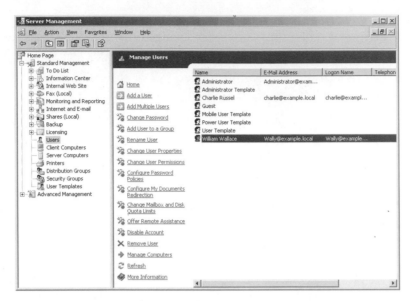

Figure 9-9. *Using the Manage Users taskpad to make changes to user accounts.*

For documents to be safest, they should be stored on the Windows Small Business Server, but users are not always conscientious about storing important files on the local hard drive.

Redirecting My Documents to the Default Server Folder

Windows Server 2003 has the capacity to redirect users' folders by applying Group Policy. Windows Small Business Server, however, has a single setting that implements the redirection of each user's My Documents folder to the server.

> **Tip** Redirecting all My Documents folders to the server will take up a lot of disk space. Make sure you have sufficient room. The partition on which the Users Shared Folder is created has default disk quotas of 1 GB per new user.

To redirect all My Documents folders, complete the following steps:

1. Select Server Management from the Start menu and click Users. Click Configure My Documents Redirection. The Client Document Redirection dialog box appears.

2. Select the option to Redirect All My Documents Folders To The Default Shared Folder For Users On The Small Business Server. This option will automatically send all the documents saved to users' My Documents folders to Users Shared Folder, a built-in shared folder on the server.

3. Click OK.

> **Tip**   A copy of the My Documents folder remains on the user's computer. When a user logs on or logs off the network, the copy on the client computer synchronizes with the copy on the server.

Redirecting My Documents to a Network Folder

Although redirecting the My Documents folder to the default server folder is the simplest approach, you might want to use a shared folder at a different location. This requires setting several types of permissions on the shared folder to be sure that the user's My Documents folder is accessible to the user but not to the world at large. To redirect all users' My Documents folder to a network folder, complete the following steps:

1. In Windows Explorer, create the folder you want to use and give it a descriptive name.

2. Right-click the folder and select Sharing And Security from the shortcut menu. The Properties dialog box appears.

3. On the Sharing tab, select Share This Folder, and then click the Permissions button.

4. Click the Add button and add the groups Domain Users, Domain Admins, and Folder Operators. Assign all three groups Full Control. (Remove the Everyone group.) Click OK.

5. On the Security tab, click the Advanced button, and clear the check box for Allow Inheritable Permissions. A security prompt appears asking how to assign permissions. Click Remove.

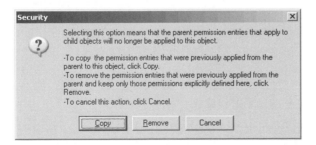

6. Click the Add button and add the Creator Owner group. In the Permission Entry dialog box, select This Folder Only from the Apply Onto drop-down list. Then select the options to allow List Folder/Read Data, Read Attributes, and Create Folders/Append Data. Click OK.

7. Repeat Step 6, adding Domain Admins, Folder Operators, and SYSTEM. When finished, close the open dialog boxes.

8. Launch System Management and click Users in the console tree. Click Configure My Documents Redirection. The Client Document Redirection dialog box appears.

9. Select the option to redirect to a network folder, and type in or browse to the network folder you created (Figure 9-10). Click OK.

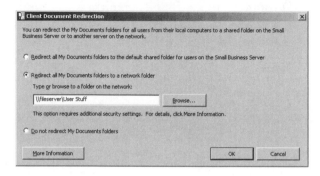

Figure 9-10. *Redirecting the My Documents folder to a shared folder on the network.*

When completed, all the My Documents folders are redirected to the new folder. Admittedly, this is a tedious process, but fortunately it has to be done only once.

Tip To stop redirecting folders, select Server Management from the Start menu and click Users. Click Configure My Documents Redirection and select the option Do Not Redirect My Documents Folders.

Tip In addition to My Documents, other special folders are Application Data, Desktop, and Start Menu on Windows 2000 or later systems. These folders can also be redirected either to a single location or to locations based on group membership. To configure this form of redirection, see "Redirecting Special Folders Using Group Policy" in Chapter 10.

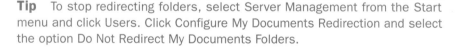

Maintaining User Profiles

A *profile* is an environment specifically customized for a user. The profile contains the desktop and program settings for the user. Every user has a profile, whether the administrator configures one or not, because a default profile is automatically created for each user who logs on to a computer. Profiles offer a number of advantages:

- Multiple users can use the same computer, with the settings for each user restored at logon time to the same state as when he or she logged off.

- Desktop changes made by one user do not affect any other user.

- If user profiles are stored on a server, they can follow users to any computer on the network running Windows Server 2003, Windows XP Professional, Windows 2000, or Windows NT 4.0.

Administrators can also set up *mandatory* profiles that allow a user to make changes to the desktop while logged on but not to save any of the changes. A mandatory profile always looks exactly the same every time a user logs on. There are three types of profiles:

- **Local profiles**   Profiles created on a computer when a user logs on. The profile is specific to a user, local to that computer, and stored on the local computer's hard disk.

- **Roaming profiles**   Profiles created by an administrator and stored on a server. These profiles follow a user to any computer on the network running Windows Server 2003, Windows XP Professional, Windows 2000, or Windows NT 4.0.

- **Mandatory profiles**   Roaming profiles that can be changed only by an administrator.

Real World   **What's Stored in a Profile?**

All profiles start out as a copy of the Default User profile that is installed on every computer running Windows Server 2003, Windows XP Professional, Windows 2000, and Windows NT 4.0. Registry data for Default User is in the Ntuser.dat file contained in the Default User profile. Profiles contain some or all of the following folders:

- **Application Data**   Program specific settings determined by the program manufacturer plus specific user security settings

- **Cookies**   Messages sent to a Web browser by a Web server and stored locally to track user information and preferences (not in Windows NT 4.0)

- **Desktop**   Desktop files, folders, shortcuts, and the desktop appearance

- **Favorites**   Shortcuts to favorite locations, particularly Web sites

- **Local Settings**   Application data, History, and Temporary files (not in Windows NT 4.0)

- **My Documents**   User documents and My Pictures, which contains user graphics files (not in Windows NT 4.0)

- **NetHood**   Shortcuts to My Network Places

- **PrintHood**   Shortcuts to items in the Printers folder
- **My Recent Documents**   Shortcuts to the most recently accessed folders and files
- **SendTo**   Items on the Send To menu
- **Start Menu**   Items on the user's Start menu
- **Templates**   Application templates

By default, only the Cookies, Desktop, Favorites, My Documents, and Start Menu folders are visible in Microsoft Windows Explorer. The other folders are hidden; to see them, in Windows Explorer, click the Tool menu, click Folder Options, click the View tab, and select Show Hidden Files And Folders.

Local Profiles

Local profiles are created on computers when individual users log on. On a computer with a new installation of Windows Server 2003, Windows XP Professional, or Windows 2000, the user profile is in the Documents And Settings folder.

The first time a user logs on to a computer, a profile folder is generated for the user, and the contents of the Default User folder are copied into it. Any changes made to the desktop by the user are saved in that user's profile when he or she logs off.

If a user has a local account on the computer as well as a domain account and logs on at different times using both accounts, the user will have two profile folders on the local computer: one for when the user logs on to the domain using the domain user account, and one for when the user logs on locally to the computer. The local profile is shown with the logon name. The domain profile is also shown with the logon name but has the domain name appended to it.

Roaming Profiles

Roaming profiles are a great advantage for users who frequently use more than one computer. A *roaming profile* is stored on a server and, after the user's logon attempt is authenticated in the directory service, is copied to the local computer. This allows a user to have the same desktop, application configuration, and local settings at any machine running Windows Server 2003, Windows XP Professional, Windows 2000, or Windows NT 4.0.

Here's how it works. You assign a location on a server for user profiles and create a folder shared with users who are to have roaming profiles. You type a path to that folder on the Profile page of the user's account properties. The next time the user logs on to a computer, the profile from the server is downloaded to the local computer. When the user logs off, the profile is saved both locally and in the user profile path location. Specifying the user profile path is all it takes to turn a local profile into a roaming profile, available anywhere in the domain.

When the user logs on again, the profile on the server is compared to the copy on the local computer, and the more recent copy is loaded for the user. If the server isn't available, the local copy is used. If the server isn't available and this is the first time the user has logged on to the computer, a user profile is created locally using the Default User profile. When a profile isn't downloaded to a local computer because of server problems, the roaming profile is not updated when the user logs off.

Setting Up Roaming Profiles

To set up a roaming profile, you assign a location on a server and complete the following steps:

1. In Windows Explorer, create a shared folder for the profiles on the server.

2. In Server Management, open the Properties dialog box for a user account.

3. On the Profile tab, provide a path to the shared folder, such as *SBS_server_name**shared_profile_folder*\%*username*%.

Figure 9-11 shows an example of a path for a roaming profile. When you use the variable %*username*%, the operating system automatically replaces the variable with the user account name.

After you create a shared profile folder on a server and supply a profile path in the user account, a roaming profile is enabled. The user's configuration of his or her desktop is copied and stored on the server and is available to the user from any computer. Most of the time, though, you don't want to send your users off to fend for themselves. Life is easier for them, and for you, when users are assigned a customized profile that is already set up with appropriate shortcuts, network connections, and Start menu items. For this, you need to set up customized profiles.

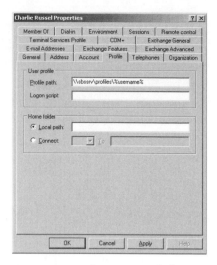

Figure 9-11. *Setting a path for a roaming profile.*

Creating Customized Roaming Profiles

Creating customized roaming profiles is a simple—albeit multistep—process:

1. Create a user account that will be used to develop the roaming profile. This is a "dummy" account that will be used just for this purpose.

2. Log on to the server using the dummy account and create the desktop settings you want, including applications, shortcuts, appearance, network connections, and printers.

3. Log off the account. Windows Small Business Server creates a user profile on the system root drive in the Documents And Settings folder.

4. Log on again using an administrator account. Find the accounts that are going to have this customized roaming profile.

5. Open the Properties dialog box for each account, click the Profile tab, and in the Profile Path box, type *SBS_server_name**profile_folder* **%username%**. Click OK.

6. In Control Panel, open System.

7. Click the Advanced tab, and then in the User Profiles section, click Settings. Select the dummy account and click Copy To.

8. In the Copy To dialog box, type the path of the profiles folder on the server, *SBS_server_name**profile_folder**username*. Note that this time you must use the actual name of the roaming profile or the profile will be stored under the name of whoever is logged on.

9. In the Permitted To Use area, click Change. Give the appropriate permissions for the user to use the profile. Click OK to copy the template profile.

Under the Hood   On Mandatory Profiles

If you're going to all the trouble of assigning customized profiles, perhaps you'd like to make the profiles mandatory. To change a profile into a mandatory profile, you need only rename the hidden file Ntuser.dat to Ntuser.man.

If you don't see the Ntuser file in the individual's profiles folder, choose Folder Options from the Tools menu and click the View tab. In Advanced Settings, select Show Hidden Files And Folders.

Mandatory profiles allow the user to change the desktop, but the changes aren't saved when the user logs off.

Tip   Don't create a mandatory user profile for a group of users unless all the users use computers with the same video hardware, because the profiles won't work consistently when the hardware isn't consistent.

Assigning a Logon Script to a User Profile

Logon scripts can be assigned by profile or through Group Policy. (Group Policy is covered in Chapter 10.) The following steps describe how to assign a script to a profile:

1. Select Server Management from the Start menu.

2. In the console tree, click Users. Right-click the user account and choose Properties.

3. Click the Profile tab and type the name of the logon script in the Logon Script box.

4. Click OK when you're finished.

Windows Small Business Server always looks for logon scripts in the same place—on the server at *%SystemRoot%*\SYSVOL\sysvol*domain_name*\scripts. Scripts in this folder can be typed in the Logon Script path by name only. If you use folders inside the Scripts folder, you must show that part of the path in the Logon Script path. Table 9-5 shows some of the environment variables that can be used when creating logon scripts. Logon scripts can also be created in VBScript and JScript.

Table 9-5.   Logon script variables

Variable	Description
%homedrive%	Letter of the drive containing the user's home directory on the user's local workstation
%homepath%	Full path of the user's home directory

Table 9-5. Logon script variables

Variable	Description
%os%	User's operating system
%processor_architecture%	Processor type on the user's workstation
%processor_level%	Processor level of the user's workstation
%userdomain%	Domain where the user's account is defined
%username%	Account user name

Using the Run As Command

Recommended administrative practice dictates that an administrator be logged on to a privileged account (one with administrative rights) only while doing chores that require privileges. For ordinary work, the administrator is supposed to log off from the privileged account and then log on again to an ordinary account. Of course, 10 minutes later a situation again arises requiring use of the privileged account. So then it's necessary to log off from the ordinary account and log back on to the administrator account, with the process reversed again a few minutes later.

After a few days of this, even the most security-conscious person begins to toy with the idea of logging on to the administrator account and staying there. This practice makes Windows Small Business Server systems highly susceptible to Trojan horse attacks. Just running Microsoft Internet Explorer and accessing a non-trusted Web site can be very risky when done from an administrator account. A Web page with Trojan code can be downloaded to the system and executed. The execution, done in the context of administrative privileges, can do considerable mischief, including such things as reformatting a hard disk, deleting all files, or creating a new user with administrative access.

The Run As service allows you to work in a normal, nonprivileged account and launch applications or tools using the credentials of a different account without logging off and then logging back on again.

To use the Run As feature, create an ordinary user account for your own use (if you don't have one already). Make sure that the user account has the right to log on locally at the machine you want to use. Log on using that account. When you need to perform a task requiring administrative privileges, complete the following steps:

1. Hold down the Shift key and right-click the desired program, Control Panel tool, or Administrative Tools icon.

2. Choose Run As from the shortcut menu. The Run As dialog box appears.

> **Note**   After using the Shift key to display the Run As option on the shortcut menu, Run As is permanently available in the shortcut menu for that user.

3. Enter the user name and password of an administrator account to use.

4. Click OK to open the program or tool using the specified account's credentials.

> **Note**   Some administrative tasks, such as setting system parameters, require an interactive logon and do not support Run As.

Making Shortcuts to Run As

Run As is meant to encourage administrators to work outside the administrator's account, and the configuring of useful shortcuts makes this more likely. Create the shortcuts while logged on with an account without administrative rights. Right-click an open area of the desktop, choose New, and then choose Shortcut. Table 9-6 shows examples of useful shortcuts.

Table 9-6.   Useful Run As shortcuts

A Shortcut To	Enter
A command prompt with local administrative privileges	**runas /user:*AdministratorAccountName* cmd**
A command prompt with domain administrative privileges	**runas /user:*DomainAdminAccountName@Domain* cmd**
Active Directory Users and Computers with domain administrative credentials	**runas /user:*DomainAdminAccountName@Domain* "mmc %windir%\system32\dsa.msc"**
Performance Monitor with domain administrative credentials	**runas /user:*DomainAdminAccountName@Domain* "mmc %windir%\system32\perfmon.msc"**
Group Policy Management Console with administrative credentials	**runas /user:*AdministratorAccountName@Domain* "%windir%\system32\gpmc.msc"**

After you open one of the shortcuts in Table 9-6, you're prompted for the administrative account's password. Keep a few of the most used shortcuts on your desktop and you'll find it easier to stay in your less privileged account most of the time.

Summary

This chapter explored the options available to the administrator for configuring groups, group scope, and user accounts in Windows Small Business Server. The next chapter covers shares, permissions, and using Group Policy—additional tools to provide accessibility and security for your network.

Chapter 10
Shares, Permissions, and Group Policy

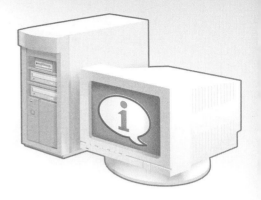

If you think all this talk of shares, permissions, rights, and privileges is confusing—you're right. All the terms appear to be nearly synonymous. However, just as you learned that words like inflammable and sanction can mean completely opposite things depending on context, you can also learn to distinguish among these words.

More Info See Chapter 9, "Users, Groups, and Security," for more information about rights and permissions assigned to users and groups.

Sharing Resources

Shared resources are folders, files, printers, devices, or applications that are available to users over a network. Until a drive or folder is shared over the network, users can't see it or gain access to it. After a folder is shared, everyone on the network has, by default, read access to all files in the folder, and to all subfolders of that folder, and so on. After a drive or folder is shared, restrictions can be added or removed in the form of *share permissions*. These permissions apply only at the drive or folder level—not at the file level—and are limited to allowing or denying Full Control, Read, and Change. Table 10-1 summarizes the three types of access, from most restrictive to least restrictive.

Table 10-1. Types of share permissions

Share Permission	Type of Access
Read	Allows viewing of file and subfolder names, viewing data in files, running programs
Change	Allows the access under Read, plus allows adding files and subdirectories to the shared folder, changing data in files, and deleting files and subdirectories
Full Control	Allows all the access under Change, plus allows changing permissions (NTFS volumes only) and taking ownership (NTFS volumes only)

Folder Sharing

To share a folder, you have only to open Server Management and select Shares (Local) in the console tree, and then complete the following steps:

1. Click Add A Shared Folder to launch the Share a Folder Wizard.

2. On the Folder Path page, type in the path to the folder you want to share. Better yet, click Browse and navigate to the folder, as shown in Figure 10-1.

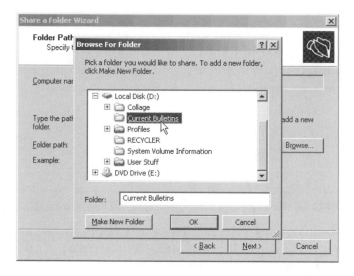

Figure 10-1. *Specifying a folder to be shared.*

Tip You can create a new folder to share in this process. Just click Browse, navigate to the location for the new folder, and click Make New Folder.

3. On the Name, Description, And Settings page, you can change the default settings for the share. For example, if the original name of the folder isn't helpful, type in a more comprehensible Share Name that will appear to users as the name of the folder. You can also add a description (always useful) and change the settings for offline use. (See "Setting Offline File Rules" later in this chapter for more information.)

4. On the Permissions page, you can select one of the three preconfigured settings or click the option to Use Custom Share And Folder Permissions and click Customize. (See "Working with NTFS File and Folder Permissions" later in this chapter for details about setting permissions.)

5. The final page of the wizard shows the details of the share and includes an option to run the wizard again to share another folder.

Removing a Share

To turn a shared folder into an unshared one, open Server Management and select Shares (Local) and find the folder in the details pane. Right-click the folder and select Stop Sharing from the shortcut menu.

Moving or Renaming a Shared Folder

After a folder has been shared, if you move or rename it, it loses its shared status. You need to run the Share a Folder Wizard to make the folder shared again.

Under the Hood   Using Special Shares

In addition to shares created by a user or administrator, the system creates a number of special shares that shouldn't be modified or deleted. The special share you're most likely to see is the ADMIN$ share, which appears as C$, D$, E$, and so on. These shares allow administrators to connect to drives that are otherwise not shared.

Special shares exist as part of the operating system's installation. Depending on the computer's configuration, some or all of the following special shares could be present. (None of them should be modified or deleted.)

- **ADMIN$**   Used during the remote administration of a computer. The path is always the location of the folder in which Windows was installed (that is, the system root).

- *driveletter*$ The root folder of the named drive. Only Administrators, Backup Operators, and Server Operators can connect to these shares on Windows Server 2003 or Windows 2000 Server. On Microsoft Windows XP Professional and Windows 2000 Professional computers, only Administrators and Backup Operators can connect to these shares.

- **IPC$**   Used during remote administration and when viewing shared resources. This share is essential to communication and can't be deleted.

- **NETLOGON, SYSVOL**   Essential to all domain controllers. Do not remove.

- **FsxSrvCp$**   A shared folder used by fax clients while sending a fax. The folder is used to store shared cover pages and to cache files.

- **Resources$**   Contains Event Log files.

- **PRINT$**   A resource that supports shared printers.

To connect to an unshared drive on another computer, you need to be logged on using an account with the necessary rights. Use the address bar in any window and type the address using this syntax:

\\computer_name\[driveletter]$

To connect to the system root folder (the folder in which Windows Small Business Server is installed) on another computer, use this syntax:

\\computer_name\admin$

Other special shares such as IPC$ and PRINT$ are created and used solely by the system. NETLOGON is a special share used while processing domain logon requests. NETLOGON is on Windows Small Business Server, Windows Server 2003, Windows 2000, and Windows NT servers.

Adding a $ character to the end of a share name hides the share from *all* users. To access a hidden share, you need to specify it explicitly; you can't browse the network for the share.

Creating a New Share for a Shared Folder

A single folder might be shared more than once. For example, one share might include Full Control for Administrators and another share for users might be more restricted. To add a new share, complete the following steps:

1. Right-click the Start button and select Explore. Navigate to the shared folder.

2. Right-click the folder and select Sharing And Security from the shortcut menu.

3. On the Sharing tab, click the New Share button.

4. In the New Share dialog box, enter a new Share Name. (Each share must have a unique name.) Set a user limit, if necessary.

5. Click Permissions to set permissions for this new share. As you can see in Figure 10-2, in this new share only Administrators and members of the Finance Operators group can connect to it.

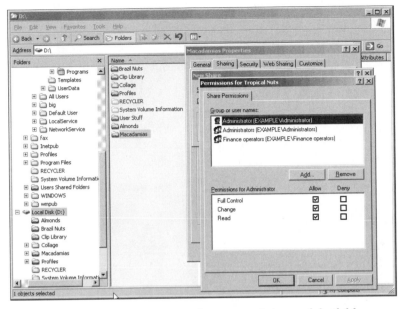

Figure 10-2.   *Setting permissions for a second share of the folder.*

The original share of the Macadamias folder (Hawaiian Nuts) now has an additional share called Tropical Nuts—though both shares access the same folder (Figure 10-3).

Clip Library   D:\Clip Library
Tropical Nuts   D:\Macadamias
Hawaiian Nuts   D:\Macadamias
Profiles   D:\Profiles

Figure 10-3.   *A shared folder can be shared under more than one name.*

Note   A second share can't be added through Shares (Local) in Server Management because the option isn't available. You must find the folder through My Computer or Windows Explorer and add the share directly.

Setting Offline File Rules

When you share a folder in Windows Small Business Server, you can also set rules for accessing the folder when users are offline. The default setting is to allow users to access files that they manually specify. To set offline rules on a folder, complete the following steps:

1. Select Server Management from the Start menu.

2. In the console tree, right-click Shares (Local) and select New Share to launch the Share a Folder Wizard.

3. On the Folder Path page (Figure 10-4), type in the path to the folder or click Browse and select a folder or create a new one.

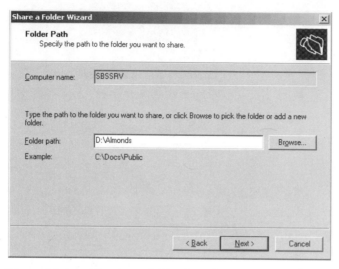

Figure 10-4. *Selecting a folder for which to set offline files.*

4. On the Name, Description, And Settings page, click Change to open the Offline Settings dialog box shown in Figure 10-5.

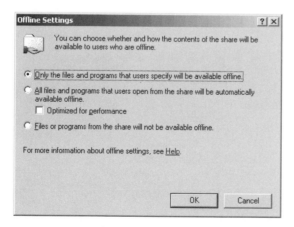

Figure 10-5. *Choosing how offline users can access this share.*

5. Choose the setting you want:

- **Only The Files And Programs That Users Specify Will Be Available Offline**   With this setting, users must identify the shared files that they want to be able to use while offline.

- **All Files And Programs That Users Open From The Share Will Be Automatically Available Offline**   If programs are to be available to run offline, select the Optimized For Performance check box. Programs are cached at the local user's machine to minimize network traffic. If the shared folder contains files that might change, don't use this option unless the files can first be made read-only.

- **Files Or Programs From The Share Are Not Available Offline** With this setting, users cannot use the shared files offline.

6. Click OK and then click Next.

Tip If the folder is already shared, it's easiest to right-click it and select Sharing And Security from the shortcut menu. On the Sharing tab, click Offline Settings and select the option you want.

---

7. On the Permissions page, you can choose from one of the three commonplace permission settings. Or select Use Custom Share And Folder Permissions, then click Customize and set up the permissions you want. When you click Finish, the settings are applied.

Synchronizing Offline Files

Users choose when to synchronize their files. The default settings are to synchronize at log on and log off, so changes made to an offline file are synchronized with the network version when the user first connects to the network and again when the user logs off. In most cases, the default settings are fine, but to make a change, open a folder window, and select Synchronize from the Tools menu to display the Items To Synchronize dialog box (Figure 10-6).

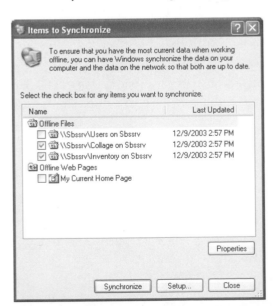

Figure 10-6. *Selecting the items to synchronize.*

In the Items To Synchronize dialog box, select the check boxes next to items that you want to synchronize and clear the others.

Making Shares Available Offline

Users who want to use a shared folder on the server offline just have to right-click the folder and select Make Available Offline from the shortcut menu.

Share Permissions vs. NTFS Permissions

Share permissions determine the maximum access over the network. NTFS permissions can be more restrictive but can't expand beyond the limits established by the share permissions. Share permissions have no effect on a user who logs on locally or to a terminal server user of the computer. Share permissions are the only restrictions available for shares on a FAT volume.

On NTFS volumes (required for Windows Small Business Server), folders have the same share permissions as those on a FAT volume, but another type of permissions—greatly superior to share permissions—is available beyond that. *NTFS permissions* use access control lists (ACLs) to limit access to resources, and can be assigned only to resources on an NTFS volume. NTFS permissions can be assigned to both files and folders and apply over the network and locally.

Microsoft Windows Server 2003 (and therefore Windows Small Business Server) uses the default share permission of Everyone = Read. (Microsoft Windows 2000 and Windows NT uses a default share permission of Everyone = Full Control.) You can change the share permission to Everyone = Full Control or Domain Users = Full Control (for more security) and use NTFS permissions for more granular control.

Whatever your choice, avoid configuring both share permissions *and* NTFS permissions because the result can be unpredictable and hard to troubleshoot.

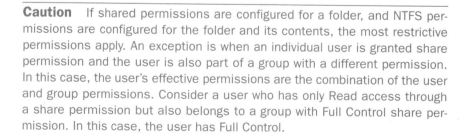

Caution If shared permissions are configured for a folder, and NTFS permissions are configured for the folder and its contents, the most restrictive permissions apply. An exception is when an individual user is granted share permission and the user is also part of a group with a different permission. In this case, the user's effective permissions are the combination of the user and group permissions. Consider a user who has only Read access through a share permission but also belongs to a group with Full Control share permission. In this case, the user has Full Control.

How Permissions Work

If you take no action at all, the files and folders inside a shared folder have the same permissions as the share. Permissions for both directories and files can be assigned to the following:

- Groups and individual users on this domain

- Global groups, universal groups, and individual users from domains that this domain trusts

- Special identities such as Everyone and Authenticated Users

The important rules for permissions can be summarized as follows:

- By default, a folder inherits permissions from its parent folder. Files inherit their permissions from the folder in which they reside.

- Users can access a folder or file only when they are granted permission to do so or they belong to a group that has been granted permission.

- Permissions are cumulative, but the Deny permission trumps all others. For example, if the Sales group has Read access to a folder and the Finance group has Modify permission for the same folder, and Wally is a member of both groups, Wally has the higher level of permission, which is Modify. However, if the Sales group permission is changed to explicitly Deny, Wally is unable to use the folder, despite his membership—and ostensibly higher level of access—in the Finance group.

- The user who creates a file or folder owns the object and can set permissions to control access.

- An administrator can take ownership of any file or folder.

- Members of the Administrators, Backup Operators, and Server Operators built-in security groups can take ownership and reassign ownership.

Working with NTFS File and Folder Permissions

Windows Small Business Server has a set of standard NTFS permissions that are combinations of specific kinds of access. The individual permissions are Full Control, Modify, Read & Execute, List Folder Contents, Read, and Write. Each of these permissions consists of a group of special permissions. Table 10-2 shows what special permissions are included with each standard permission.

Table 10-2. Special permissions for folders

Special Permission	Full Control	Modify	Read & Execute	List Folder Contents	Read	Write
Traverse Folder/Execute File	Yes	Yes	Yes	Yes	No	No
List Folder/Read Data	Yes	Yes	Yes	Yes	Yes	No
Read Attributes	Yes	Yes	Yes	Yes	Yes	No
Read Extended Attributes	Yes	Yes	Yes	Yes	Yes	No
Create Files/Write Data	Yes	Yes	No	No	No	Yes
Create Folders/Append Data	Yes	Yes	No	No	No	Yes
Write Attributes	Yes	Yes	No	No	No	Yes
Write Extended Attributes	Yes	Yes	No	No	No	Yes
Delete Subfolders and Files	Yes	No	No	No	No	No
Delete	Yes	Yes	No	No	No	No
Read Permissions	Yes	Yes	Yes	Yes	Yes	Yes
Change Permissions	Yes	No	No	No	No	No
Take Ownership	Yes	No	No	No	No	No

File permissions include Full Control, Modify, Read & Execute, Read, and Write. As with folders, each of these permissions controls a group of special permissions. Table 10-3 shows the special permissions associated with each standard permission.

Table 10-3. Special permissions for files

Special Permission	Full Control	Modify	Read & Execute	Read	Write
Traverse Folder/Execute File	Yes	Yes	Yes	No	No
List Folder/Read Data	Yes	Yes	Yes	Yes	No
Read Attributes	Yes	Yes	Yes	Yes	No
Read Extended Attributes	Yes	Yes	Yes	Yes	No
Create Files/Write Data	Yes	Yes	No	No	Yes
Create Folders/Append Data	Yes	Yes	No	No	Yes
Write Attributes	Yes	Yes	No	No	Yes
Write Extended Attributes	Yes	Yes	No	No	Yes
Delete Subfolders and Files	Yes	No	No	No	No
Delete	Yes	Yes	No	No	No
Read Permissions	Yes	Yes	Yes	Yes	Yes
Change Permissions	Yes	No	No	No	No
Take Ownership	Yes	No	No	No	No

Caution Any user or group assigned Full Control on a folder can delete files and subfolders no matter what the permissions are on the individual files or subfolders.

Considering Inheritance

Just to complicate matters a bit more, there are two types of permissions: explicit and inherited. *Explicit permissions* are the ones you set on folders you create. *Inherited permissions* are those that flow from a parent object to a child object. By default, when you create a subfolder, it inherits the permissions of the parent folder.

If you don't want the child objects to inherit the permissions of the parent, you can block inheritance at the parent level or at the child level. Where you block inheritance is important. Block at the parent level and no subfolders inherit permissions. Block selectively at the child level and some folders inherit permissions but others do not.

To block a file or folder from inheriting permissions, right-click the folder, select Properties, and then click the Security tab. Click Advanced and clear the check box for Allow Inheritable Permissions From The Parent To Propagate To This Object And All Child Objects.

> **Caution**   An additional check box is shown on the Advanced Security Settings page. It's Replace Permission Entries On All Child Objects With Entries Shown Here That Apply To Child Objects. If you select this option, subfolders and files have their permissions reset to those they inherit from a parent object. Once you select this item and click Apply or OK, you can't go back and undo it.

When the check boxes for permissions appear shaded, it means the permissions are inherited from a parent object. When the check boxes are shaded *and* have a check mark (Figure 10-7), some permissions are inherited and others have been added. There are three ways to change this situation:

- Clear the check box for Allow Inheritable Permissions From the Parent To Propagate To This Object And All Child Objects. When the check box is cleared, you can make changes to the permissions or change the users or groups in the list.

- Change the permissions of the parent folder.

- Select the opposite permission—Allow or Deny—to override the inherited permission.

If neither Allow nor Deny is selected, the users or groups might have acquired the permission through a group membership. Otherwise, failure to explicitly configure Allow effectively denies the permission.

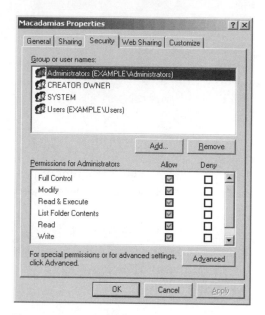

Figure 10-7. *A folder with inherited and noninherited permissions.*

Configuring NTFS Folder Permissions

Before sharing a folder on an NTFS volume, set all the permissions on the folder. When you set folder permissions, you're also setting permissions on all the files and subfolders in the folder. To assign permissions to a folder, right-click the folder in Windows Explorer, choose Properties from the shortcut menu, and then click the Security tab.

- To remove an individual or group from the list, select the name and click Remove.

- To add to the list of those with permissions, click Add. This opens the Select Users, Computers, Or Groups dialog box. Or click Advanced to perform a more sophisticated search, as shown in Figure 10-8. Click OK when you're finished.

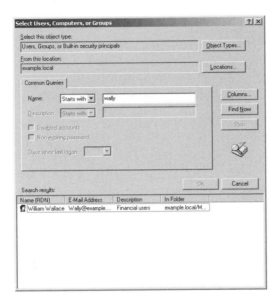

Figure 10-8.   *Selecting users and groups.*

Assigning NTFS Permissions to Files

Permissions for individual files are assigned in the same way as folders. There are, however, some special considerations:

- Remember to grant permissions to groups, rather than to individuals.

- Create universal groups and assign file permissions to them rather than assign permissions directly to local groups.

Caution   Groups or users who have Full Control for a folder can delete files and subfolders, no matter what protective permissions are assigned to the files and folders.

Configuring Special Permissions

In some circumstances, you might find it necessary to set, change, or remove special permissions on either a file or folder. To access special permissions, complete the following steps:

1. Right-click the file or folder and choose Properties from the shortcut menu.

2. Click the Security tab, and then click Advanced.

   - To add a user or group, click Add. Supply the name of the user or group. Click OK to open the Permission Entry dialog box.

- To view or modify existing special permissions, select the name of the user or group and click Edit.

- To remove special permissions, select the name of the user or group and click Remove. If the Remove button is unavailable, clear the check box for Allow Inheritable Permissions From Parent To Propagate To This Object, and skip to Step 6.

3. In the Permission Entry dialog box (Figure 10-9), select where you want the permissions applied in the Apply Onto box. (See Table 10-4 and Table 10-5 for explanations of the choices in this drop-down box.) Apply Onto is available when configuring folders only. You can choose to apply permissions to all the files in the folder, but different settings for different files require configuring each file separately.

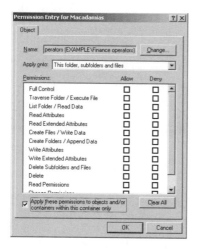

Figure 10-9. *Setting special permissions for a folder.*

4. In Permissions, select Allow or Deny for each permission.

5. To prevent subfolders and files from inheriting these permissions, select Apply These Permissions To Objects And/Or Containers Within This Container Only.

6. Click OK to close the dialog box.

In the Permission Entry dialog box for folders, you can choose how and where the special permissions are applied. Table 10-4 and Table 10-5 demonstrate the application of the special permissions depending on whether Apply These Permissions To Objects And/Or Containers Within This Container Only is selected.

Table 10-4.   Application of special permissions when Apply These Permissions To Objects And/Or Containers Within This Container Only is selected

Selected in Apply Onto	Applies to Current Folder?	Applies to Subfolders in Current Folder?	Applies to Files in Current Folder?	Applies to Subsequent Subfolders?	Applies to Files in Subsequent Subfolders?
This folder only	Yes	No	No	No	No
This folder, subfolders and files	Yes	Yes	Yes	No	No
This folder and subfolders	Yes	Yes	No	No	No
This folder and files	Yes	No	Yes	No	No
Subfolders and files only	No	Yes	Yes	No	No
Subfolders only	No	Yes	No	No	No
Files only	No	No	Yes	No	No

Table 10-5.   Application of special permissions when Apply These Permissions To Objects And/Or Containers Within This Container Only is not selected

Selected in Apply Onto	Applies to Current Folder?	Applies to Subfolders in Current Folder?	Applies to Files in Current Folder?	Applies to Subsequent Subfolders?	Applies to Files in Subsequent Subfolders?
This folder only	Yes	No	No	No	No
This folder, subfolders, and files	Yes	Yes	Yes	Yes	Yes
This folder and subfolders	Yes	Yes	No	Yes	No
This folder and files	Yes	No	Yes	No	Yes
Subfolders and files only	No	Yes	Yes	Yes	Yes
Subfolders only	No	Yes	No	Yes	No
Files only	No	No	Yes	No	Yes

Ownership and How It Works

As you've seen, Administrators and members of a few other select groups are the only ones who can grant and change permissions. The exception is when a user is the owner of the folder or file in question. Every object on an NTFS partition has an owner, and the owner is the person who created the file or folder. The owner controls access to the file or folder and can keep out anyone he or she chooses.

For example, Wally (a user) creates a folder on his computer called My Private Stuff. After creating the folder, he right-clicks the folder, chooses Properties, and then clicks the Security tab (Figure 10-10).

Figure 10-10. *Viewing the NTFS permissions for a new folder.*

Wally sees that the Administrators group has full access to his folder, but because he is the owner of the folder, he can change the permissions so that he has the folder all to himself. He clicks Advanced to open the Advanced Security Settings dialog box and clears the Inherit From Parent check box (Figure 10-11).

Figure 10-11. *Removing inheritance from a permission entry.*

When the Security dialog box appears, Wally clicks Remove to remove the permission entries that were previously applied from the parent. After clicking Remove and accepting the security warning, Wally clicks OK and a Security warning appears indicating that everyone has been denied access to the folder. Wally clicks Yes to continue and returns to the Properties dialog box. He clicks the Add button and adds his user account with Full Control. After this is done, even the administrator receives an Access Denied message when trying to open the folder.

Of course, nothing on the network can be *completely* beyond the reach of administrators, so an administrator can change the ownership by following these steps:

1. Right-click the My Private Stuff folder and choose Properties from the shortcut menu to open the Properties dialog box. Select the Security tab. A Security warning appears indicating that you don't have permissions to the folder but can take ownership. As shown in Figure 10-12, no changes can be made on the Security tab and only the Advanced button is enabled.

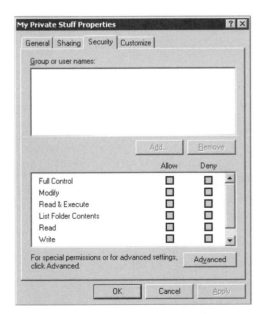

Figure 10-12. *The administrator viewing permissions for a folder owned by a user.*

2. Click Advanced to open the Advanced Security Settings dialog box and then click the Owner tab (Figure 10-13).

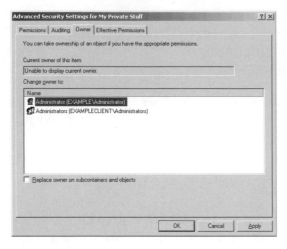

Figure 10-13. *Changing the ownership of a folder.*

3. No matter what the status of the folder is, the administrator can take ownership. Select the new owner and click OK.

4. Close the Properties dialog box. Then right-click the folder again and select Properties and then the Security tab. The Properties dialog box now reveals Wally as the only user with permission to use the folder.

5. Click Advanced and on the Permissions tab, select the check box for Inherit From Parent The Permission Entries That Apply To Child Objects. Click Apply (Figure 10-14), and all the previously removed permissions are reinstated.

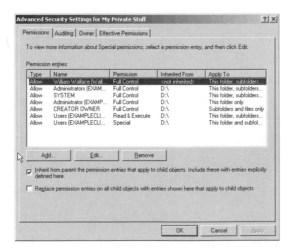

Figure 10-14. *Reinstating the default inherited permissions.*

6. Click OK twice to close the dialog boxes.

When Wally logs on the next time, he still has access to My Private Stuff. If he opens the Properties dialog box, clicks the Security tab, clicks Advanced and then clicks the Owner tab, he sees that he's no longer the only user with Full Control. Changing the ownership of the folder doesn't automatically give administrators access to the contents of the folder, but ownership does grant the ability to read and change permissions. With that, an administrator can change permissions and attain access to the folder contents.

Note The owner of a file or folder can also grant the Take Ownership special permission to others, allowing those users to take ownership at any time.

Tip Windows Small Business Server goes to considerable lengths and offers many tools to simplify the running of a network. However, there are several different ways to turn administration into a tangled mess, and one of them is to get too deeply into setting lots of specific permissions.

Always try to operate with the simplest possible permissions. Set as few restrictions as possible. Assign permissions to groups, not individuals. Don't set file by file permissions unless it is unavoidable. Managing the minutiae of permissions can quickly soak up all your time and much of your life's blood as well, unless you guard against it.

Determining Effective Permissions

What with the complexities of inheritance and the nested nature of groups, it's no small chore to find out exactly what permissions a user or group has. Windows Small Business Server 2003 includes a tool to help determine which permissions are in effect for a given object. Follow these steps:

1. Log on as a member of Domain Administrators.

2. Right-click a file or folder and select Properties from the shortcut menu.

3. Click Security, and then click the Advanced button.

4. In the Advanced Security Settings dialog box, click the Effective Permissions tab.

5. Click Select and locate the user or group you have questions about in the Select User, Computer, Or Group dialog box. Click OK. The effective permissions are displayed (Figure 10-15).

Figure 10-15. *Showing the permissions for Folder Operators on an object.*

Tip The effective permissions result is more an estimation than a precise determination. Included in the calculation of effective permissions are memberships in global and local groups, local permissions, and local privileges.

Not included are share permissions and any permissions based on how the user logs on. If you're viewing effective permissions remotely, membership in local groups and local privileges are not part of the formula for determining effective permissions.

Privileges and Logon Rights

In addition to permissions, Windows Small Business Server includes assignable rights, which are of two types: *privileges* and *logon rights*. Privileges include such things as the ability to run security audits or force shutdown from a remote system—obviously not things that are handled by most users. Logon rights are self-explanatory; they involve the ability to connect to a computer in specific ways. Rights are automatically assigned to the built-in groups in Windows Small Business Server, although they can be assigned to individual users as well as groups. Whenever possible, you should assign rights by group membership to keep administration simple. When membership in groups defines rights, rights can be removed from a user by simply removing the user from the group. Tables 10-6 and 10-7 list the most-used logon rights and privileges and the groups to which they are assigned by default.

Table 10-6.   Logon rights assigned to groups by default

Name	Description	Groups Assigned the Right by Default
Access Windows Small Business Server from the network	Permits connection to the computer through the network	Administrators, Domain Power Users, Everyone.
Log on as a service	Allows logging on as a service using a specific user account and security context	None.
Log on to Windows Small Business Server locally	Permits logon at the computer's keyboard	Administrators, Account Operators, Backup Operators, Print Operators, Server Operators.
Allow Logon through Terminal Services	Permits logon as a Terminal Services client	Administrators on Domain Controllers. Administrators and Remote Desktop Users on workstations and stand-alone servers.

Table 10-7.   Privileges assigned to groups by default

Privilege	Description	Groups Assigned the Privilege by Default
Act as part of the operating system	Allows a process to authenticate as any user. A process that requires this privilege should use the LocalSystem account, which already includes this privilege.	None.
Add workstations to domain	Allows a user to add new workstations to an existing domain.	Authenticated Users on domain controllers.
Backup files and directories	Allows backing up the system; overrides specific file and folder permissions.	Administrators, Backup Operators.
Change the system time	Allows the setting of the computer's internal clock.	Administrators and Service Operators on domain controllers. Administrators, Domain Power Users on workstations and stand-alone servers.
Force shutdown from a remote system	Allows the shutdown of a computer from a remote location on the network.	Administrators and Server Operators on domain controllers. Administrators on workstations and stand-alone servers.
Generate security audits	Sets which accounts can use a process to make entries in a security log.	None.

Table 10-7. Privileges assigned to groups by default

Privilege	Description	Groups Assigned the Privilege by Default
Increase scheduling priority	Allows the use of Task Manager to change the scheduling priority of a process.	Administrators.
Lock pages in memory	Allows a process to keep data in physical memory. This is an obsolete privilege that can have a seriously negative effect on system performance. Avoid assigning it.	None.
Restore files and directories	Allows restoring files and folders to a system; overrules specific file and folder permissions.	Administrators, Backup Operators, and Server Operators on domain controllers. Administrators and Backup Operators on workstations and stand-alone servers.
Take ownership of files or other objects	Allows a user to take ownership of any security object including files and folders, printers, registry keys, and processes. Overrules specified permissions.	Administrators.

Caution Privileges can sometimes override permission settings. For example, a user can create a file and set permissions that deny access to all users, but members of the Backup Operators group can still access the file and back it up, and Administrators (as we saw earlier in this chapter) can take ownership of the file.

Understanding Group Policy

For most users of Windows Small Business Server, the built-in groups and default group policy provide adequate protection against mischief and malice whether it comes from outside or inside the network. However, many networks require a few new policies to address specific needs or at least to tweak existing policies.

Group Policy was introduced in Windows 2000 and is the successor to the System Policy Editor in Windows NT. Like many very powerful tools, Group Policy can be treacherous to work with. It's often difficult to get just the results you want without any odd side effects. So proceed with caution and never make a change without knowing how to undo it.

To add or change a Group Policy Object (GPO), you must have sufficient permissions. You needn't log on as the administrator—instead, use Run As (described in Chapter 9).

> **Tip** Limit who can create and modify GPOs. Ill-considered changes can have far-reaching consequences.

As powerful as Group Policy is, it does not work retroactively. GPOs affect only computers running Windows 2000 or later. You must rely on share permissions for clients using other operating systems.

Under the Hood   **Components of Group Policy**

Group policy is an abstraction that consists of two parts, a Group Policy Container (GPC) and a Group Policy Template (GPT). Both parts are contained in a Group Policy Object (GPO). The GPO is what we work with directly. The GPO contains all the settings that can apply to users and computers, and when those settings are changed, the changes are made to the GPO. The two components of the GPO exist in different places.

The GPC is the Active Directory component of the GPO and includes subcontainers with version information, status information, and a list of which Group Policy extensions are employed in the GPO. It also contains some information used by clients, such as the software installation policy.

The GPT is a set of files in the SYSVOL folder on the server. When you create a GPO, the corresponding GPT folder structure is created automatically. The actual name of the folder for the GPT is the *globally unique identifier* (GUID) for the GPO—a number that is useful to the computer but is otherwise incomprehensible. To see the policy folder, look in %SystemRoot% \SYSVOL\sysvol\domain_name\policies. But *do not* change this folder in any way. Do your work on Group Policy through the Group Policy Management Console (GPMC) or Server Management.

In a GPO, most settings have three states: not configured, enabled, and disabled. Additionally, GPOs have two configuration nodes: Computer Configuration and User Configuration. In case of a conflict, the computer setting overrides the user setting.

Group policies are inherited and cumulative. When you associate a GPO with an Active Directory container, the Group Policy is applied to all computer and user accounts in the container.

Creating a Group Policy Object

The installation of Windows Small Business Server creates an Active Directory domain that comes with a default domain policy, a default Domain Controllers policy, and several policies specifically for Small Business Server. With some judicious adjustments to meet the needs of your own situation, you might never need anything else. When you need to set up a GPO of your own, you can follow these steps:

1. Choose Group Policy Management from the Administrative Tools menu to launch the Group Policy Management Console (GPMC). (GPMC is also under Advanced Management in the Server Management tool.)

2. In the console tree, expand the domain container, right-click Group Policy Objects and select New from the shortcut menu.

3. Type the name of the new GPO and click OK.

4. In the console tree, right-click the new GPO and select Edit to launch the Group Policy Object Editor.

5. Specify settings for the GPO. When you're finished, close the Group Policy Object Editor.

6. In the Group Policy Management Console, right-click the domain name or the organizational unit this GPO is to be associated with and select Link An Existing GPO from the shortcut menu.

7. In the Select GPO dialog box, select the GPO to link and click OK.

   You can also right-click the domain or organizational unit and select Create And Link A GPO Here, to shorten the process by one step.

Tip The fewer GPOs per user and per computer, the better. The processing of GPOs takes time, and too many of them can slow logons and logoffs. The number of settings within a GPO doesn't have a negative impact—it's the number of GPOs.

Tip Avoid making changes to the default GPOs. Instead, create new GPOs that can easily be disabled.

Under the Hood   Inside the Group Policy Object Editor
When you edit a policy in the Group Policy Object Editor, you see that the editor displays two nodes: Computer Configuration and User Configuration. When you expand these nodes, you find that each displays extensions for Software Settings, Windows Settings, and Administrative Templates.

Use the Computer Configuration node to customize policies for computers on the network. These policies go into effect when the computer is turned on and the operating system starts. Settings in these folders apply to any user who logs on to the computer. For example, if you have machines in a training room for which you want to enforce a strict environment, the Computer Configuration node is where you make those settings.

The User Configuration node contains settings for customizing environments or setting policies for users on the network. User Configuration policies come into play when a specific user logs on to the network.

Deleting a Group Policy Object

To delete a Group Policy Object, right-click it in the Group Policy Management Console and select Delete from the shortcut menu. When you delete a GPO, all links to the GPO will also be deleted. Be sure that you are logged on to an account with sufficient permissions. Neither the Default Domain Policy nor the Default Domain Controllers Policy can be deleted.

Order of Inheritance

As a rule, Group Policy settings are passed from parent containers down to child containers. This practice means that a policy that is applied to a parent container applies to all the containers—including users and computers—that are below the parent container in the Active Directory tree hierarchy. However, if you specifically assign a Group Policy for a child container that contradicts the parent container policy, the child container's policy overrides the parent Group Policy.

If policies are not contradictory, both can be implemented. For example, if a parent container policy calls for an application shortcut to be on a user's desktop, and the child container policy calls for another application shortcut, both appear. Policy settings that are disabled are inherited as disabled. Policy settings that are not configured in the parent container are not inherited.

Order of Implementation

Group policies are processed in the following order:

1. Local Group Policy Object
2. GPOs linked to the site, in administratively specified order
3. Domain GPOs, in administratively specified order
4. Organizational unit Group Policy Objects, from largest to smallest organizational unit (parent to child organizational unit)

Exceptions to this order are GPOs with enforced or disabled links, GPOs with disabled user or computer settings, and organizational units (or the whole domain) set to block inheritance.

To see the order of precedence for GPOs for a domain or organizational unit, open Group Policy Management and in the console tree, select the domain name or the organizational unit. In the details pane, click the Group Policy Inheritance tab (Figure 10-16).

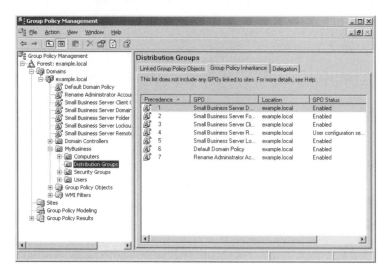

Figure 10-16. *Viewing the order of precedence for the execution of GPOs.*

To change the order of precedence, click the Linked Group Policy Object tab, select the link you want to move, and use the up and down arrow buttons to change the order.

Overriding Inheritance

Two options are available for changing how inheritance is processed. One option is to enforce a link (called No Override on computers without GPMC). When this option is set, child containers cannot override any policy setting set in a higher level GPO. This option is not set by default and must be turned on in each GPO where it's wanted. To set the Enforced option, complete the following steps:

1. Select Group Policy Management from the Administrative Tools menu.

2. In the console tree, navigate to Group Policy Objects and select the GPO for which you want to enforce a link.

3. In the details pane, on the Scope tab, right-click the link to be enforced, and select Enforced from the shortcut menu (Figure 10-17).

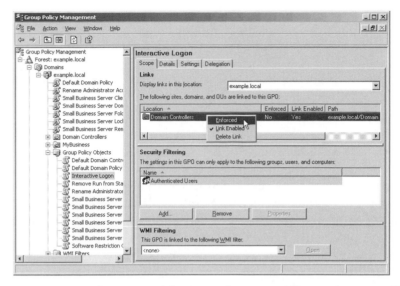

Figure 10-17.   *Preventing inheritance from overriding settings on a GPO.*

A second option is Block Inheritance. When you select this option, the child container does not inherit any policies from parent containers. GPO links set to Enforced can't be blocked. To block inheritance, complete the following steps:

1. Select Group Policy Management from the Administrative Tools menu.

2. Right-click the domain or organizational unit for which you want to block inheritance and select Block Inheritance from the shortcut menu (Figure 10-18).

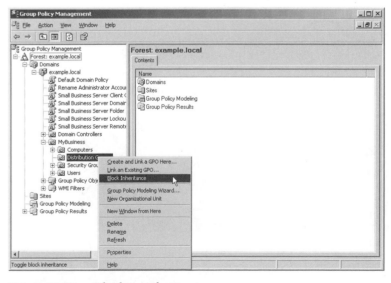

Figure 10-18.   *Blocking inheritance.*

Explicit permissions take precedence over inherited permissions—even an inherited Deny. So if you explicitly grant access to an object, the inherited Deny does not prevent access.

> **Tip** Because these options can have unpredictable results, use Block Inheritance and Enforced sparingly.

Real World Using Group Policy Scripts

A set of scripts addressing everyday tasks is included with Group Policy Management Console. They're located in Program Files\GPMC\Scripts. Although the script names are generally self-explanatory, you must enter *scriptname /?* at a command prompt to see the parameters for using the script. For example, enter **SetGPOCreationPermissions /?** at a command prompt and this dialog box opens:

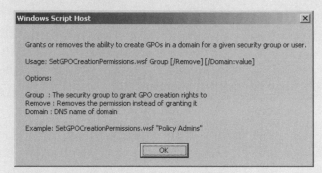

The scripts execute from the command line using Cscript.exe, so to run SetGPOCreationPermissions.wsf and thereby allow a designated group to create GPOs, you type

```
cscript \"program files"\GPMC\Scripts\SetGPOCreationPermissions.wsf
  "Group Name"
```

Press Enter and the command window displays the following output:

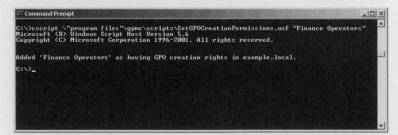

To operate, many of the scripts require the library file Lib_Common-GPMCFunctions.js. If you move or copy scripts to another location, move a copy of this file to the same location.

Enabling and Disabling GPO Links

To check or change the status of a GPO link, complete the following steps:

1. Select Group Policy Management from the Administrative Tools menu.

2. In the console tree, navigate to the Group Policy Objects under your domain name and select the GPO.

3. On the Scope tab, links are listed and the status of the link is shown under Link Enabled. To change the status, right-click the link and select Link Enabled from the shortcut menu (Figure 10-19).

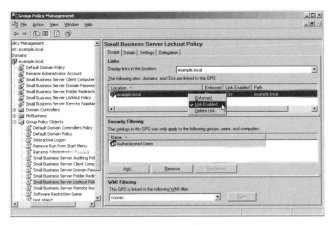

Figure 10-19.   *A check mark shows the link is enabled.*

Finding Group Policy Links

With numerous GPOs on a network, it's important to keep track of GPO links within the domain. To find out what links exist for a particular GPO, complete the following steps:

1. Select Group Policy Management from the Administrative Tools menu.

2. Right-click the domain name in the console tree and select Search from the shortcut menu.

3. In the Search Item drop-down list, select GPO-links.

4. Click Add and then click Search.

5. In the Search Results box (Figure 10-20), double-click a GPO to view its links and other settings.

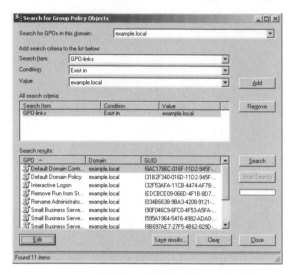

Figure 10-20.   *Finding GPO links.*

Setting the Scope of the GPO

A Group Policy Object applies to all the users and computers in the container with which the GPO is associated. Most GPOs default to applying to Authenticated Users—namely, everyone who can log on to the network. Inevitably, there are GPOs that should apply only to some. To filter the application of a GPO, complete the following steps:

1. Select Group Policy Management from the Administrative Tools menu.

2. Select the Group Policy Object you want to filter and click the Scope tab.

3. On the Scope tab in the Security Filtering section, click Add and locate the groups or users who should have the policy applied to them (Figure 10-21). Make your selection and click OK twice.

4. If Authenticated Users appears in the Security Filtering list on the Scope page, select it and click Remove. This ensures that the GPO is applied only to the groups or users you added.

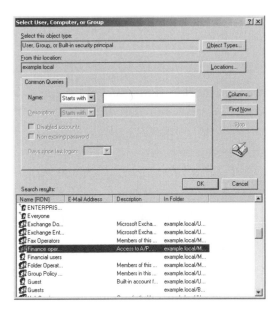

Figure 10-21.   *Selecting the groups or users to which the Group Policy Object applies.*

Disabling a Branch of a GPO

If a GPO has an entire node under User Configuration or Computer Configuration that's not configured, disable the node to avoid processing those settings. This speeds startup and logon events for all users subject to that GPO. To disable a node, complete the following steps:

1. Select Group Policy Management from the Administrative Tools menu. In the console tree, right-click the Group Policy Object you want to change and select Edit from the shortcut menu.

2. In the console tree of the Group Policy Object Editor, right-click the GPO and select Properties.

3. On the General tab, select the check box to disable the User Configuration or Computer Configuration settings for this GPO.

4. Click OK when you're finished.

The settings you disable no longer affect any object to which the GPO is linked.

Refreshing Group Policy

Policy changes are immediate, but they are not instantly propagated to clients. Client computers request policy only when one of the following occurs:

- The computer starts.
- A user logs on.

- An application requests a refresh.
- A user requests a refresh.
- A Group Policy refresh interval is enabled and the interval has elapsed.

By default, Group Policy refreshes in the background every 90 minutes with a random offset of 0 through 30 minutes (so not all computers request a refresh at the same time).

To change the Group Policy refresh interval, complete the following steps:

1. Select Group Policy Management from the Administrative Tools menu.

2. To add the setting to an existing GPO, right-click the GPO and select Edit. To create a new GPO, right-click the domain name or organizational unit and select Create And Link A GPO Here. Supply a name for the new GPO then right-click it in Group Policy Management Console and select Edit.

3. In the console tree, expand Computer Configuration, Administrative Templates, System, and then select Group Policy.

4. In the details pane, double-click Group Policy Refresh Interval For Computers.

5. On the Setting tab, select Enabled then supply the new settings. Click OK when finished.

Don't make the interval very short because of the large amount of network traffic generated by each refresh.

Because policy can be set at several levels, when you look at a policy object, what you see is both local policy and the policy in effect on the system. Local policy and actual policy in effect might not be synonymous if the computer is inheriting settings from domain-level policies. If you make a policy setting and it isn't reflected in effective policy, a policy from the domain is overriding your setting.

More Info For more information, see "Determining Effective Permissions," earlier in this chapter.

It's also possible that the policy change hasn't been refreshed since the change was made. To force a policy refresh for the local computer, open a command window and type:

```
gpupdate [/target:{computer | user}] /force
```

Tip For details about the update parameters, open a command window and type **gpupdate /?**

Backing Up and Restoring Group Policy Objects

It's only prudent to back up your system's Group Policy Objects. They're complicated enough that no one would want to be faced with the task of recreating them. Be sure backed-up GPO files are in a folder that can be accessed only by administrators.

Backing Up Group Policy Objects

Backing up a Group Policy Object saves all the information that is inside the GPO. This includes:

- GPO settings
- The GPO domain and globally unique identifier (GUID)
- WMI filter link but not the actual filter
- Links to any IP Security Policies
- The GPO discretionary access control list
- Any user-supplied description of the GPO

A backup of a GPO does not save the links, any existing WMI filter, or the IP security policy.

To back up a single GPO to a folder, right-click the object in Group Policy Management Console and select Back Up from the shortcut menu. Multiple GPOs can be backed up to the same location. To back up all GPOs, complete the following steps:

1. Select Group Policy Management from the Administrative Tools menu.

2. In the console tree, right-click Group Policy Objects and select Back Up All from the shortcut menu (Figure 10-22).

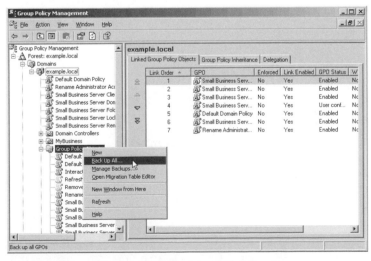

Figure 10-22. *Backing up all GPOs in the domain.*

3. Specify a location and description in the Back Up Group Policy Object dialog box. Click Backup, and the Backup dialog box displays the progress of the backup.

4. Click OK when finished.

Restoring a Backed-Up GPO

When you restore a GPO from a backup, all the existing settings for the GPO are replaced by the settings in the backed-up version. To restore a backed-up GPO, complete the following steps:

1. Select Group Policy Management from the Administrative Tools menu.

2. Right-click the GPO and select Restore From Backup to launch the Restore Group Policy Object Wizard.

3. On the Backup Location page, provide the location of the backed-up GPO. Click Next.

4. On the Source GPO page, you can specify which version of the GPO you want to restore (Figure 10-23). Backups are time and date stamped. Click Next.

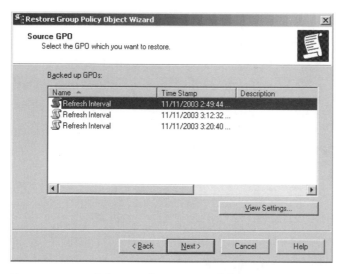

Figure 10-23. *Selecting the version of the GPO to restore.*

5. The final page of the wizard summarizes what is to be restored. To restore the GPO, click Finish.

Importing GPO Settings

GPO settings can be imported from any backed-up GPO. Importing settings for a GPO, unlike restoring, doesn't overwrite links and security filtering. To import settings, complete the following steps:

1. Select Group Policy Management from the Administrative Tools menu.

2. Right-click a GPO and select Import Settings to launch the Import Settings Wizard.

3. On the Backup GPO page, you can choose to do a backup of the existing GPO if you don't have a recent saved version.

4. On the Backup Location page, specify the backup location for the GPO you're importing.

5. On the Source GPO page, select the GPO with the settings you want to import.

6. On the Scanning Backup page, the wizard scans the GPO settings to determine whether there are references to security principals or UNC paths that might need to be imported as well.

7. The final page of the wizard summarizes what is to be imported. To import the GPO settings, click Finish.

Predicting Group Policy Outcomes

Because of the complexity of inheritances, user versus computer configuration, and a host of other variables, foreseeing the outcome of any policy change is usually not possible. Two tools in Windows Small Business Server can help you keep out of deep water—an all-too-common outcome for those who mess about with Group Policy.

Group Policy Modeling

The Group Policy Modeling tool lets you simulate a policy deployment and see the results. (Group Policy Modeling is essentially the same as Resultant Set of Policy planning mode on Windows Server 2003 prior to the release of Group Policy Management Console.)

To use Group Policy Modeling, complete the following steps:

1. Select Group Policy Management from the Administrative Tools menu.

2. Right-click Group Policy Modeling in the console tree and select Group Policy Modeling Wizard.

3. On the Domain Controller Selection page, your Windows Small Business Server is selected.

4. On the User And Computer Selection page, you can select the following combinations:

- A container with user information combined with a computer container

- A container with user information combined with a specific computer

- A single user and a computer container

- A single user and a specific computer

- A computer container alone

- A specific computer alone

- A user container alone

- A specific user alone

5. On the Advanced Simulation Options page, select any advanced simulation options you want to include.

6. On the Alternate Active Directory Paths page, you can simulate changes to the network location.

7. If you specified a user or user container, the User Security Groups page appears showing group membership (Figure 10-24). To see the results of changes to group membership, add or remove groups from the list.

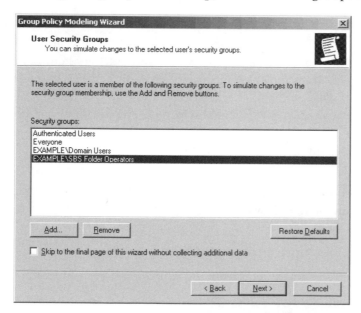

Figure 10-24. *Simulating a change in group membership.*

8. If you specified a computer or computer container, the Computer Security Groups page appears. You can change the security group memberships for the computer or computer container you're modeling.

9. Leave the default settings for the WMI Filters For Users and WMI Filters For Computers pages.

10. Review the settings on the Summary Of Selections page (Figure 10-25). Click Next. When Group Policy Modeling is complete, click Finish.

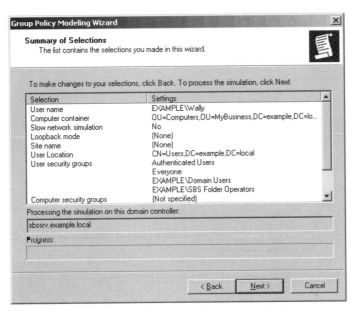

Figure 10-25. *Review the selections for this simulation.*

The report is generated and appears in the console tree under Group Policy Modeling. In the details pane, the Summary tab shows the applied and denied GPOs and the simulated group memberships.

11. Click the Settings tab to review the policies that apply to this simulation, what the settings are, and the GPO that determines each setting. The Query tab summarizes the settings that the report is based on.

12. Right-click the name of the saved report and select Rerun Query to run it again after you've made changes.

Under the Hood   WMI Filters

Windows Management Instrumentation (WMI) allows the dynamic checking of the scope of a GPO. When a GPO linked to a WMI filter is applied on a computer, the filter is evaluated. If the filter evaluates to false, the GPO is not applied. If the filter evaluates to true, the GPO is applied—except on Windows 2000 computers, which ignore the filter altogether and always apply the GPO.

WMI filtering applies only to computers running Windows Server 2003 and Windows XP and is really designed for very large networks, so its use in a Windows Small Business Server environment is akin to using a cannon to ring a doorbell.

If you want to read up on WMI filters, select Help and Support from the Start menu. Search for WMI filters in the Help and Support.

Group Policy Results

Use the Group Policy Results tool to determine current policy settings for a specific user or computer. To use Group Policy Results, complete the following steps:

1. Select Group Policy Management from the Administrative Tools menu.

2. Right-click Group Policy Results in the console tree and select Group Policy Results Wizard.

3. On the Computer Selection page, you must specify the computer to use. But you can select the option to display only the user policy settings and not display the policy settings for the computer (Figure 10-26).

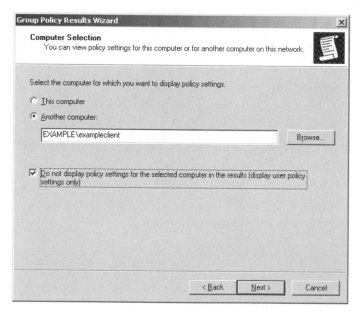

Figure 10-26. *On the Computer Selection page, choose whether you want to view only user policy settings.*

4. On the User Selection page, specify a specific user. On this page, you can select the option to report just the computer settings and not the user policy settings.

5. On the Summary Of Selections page, the summary of your selections is displayed. Click Next and then Finish to generate a Group Policy Results report.

   The report is generated and appears in the console tree under Group Policy Results. In the details pane, the Summary tab shows the applied and denied GPOs and the actual group memberships.

6. Click the Settings tab to review applied policies, what the settings are, and the GPO that determines each setting.

Renaming the Administrator Account Using GPMC

It's always a good practice to rename the Administrator account because any account with that name is a target for hackers and other pests. When renaming the account, avoid obvious names such as admin, boss, or root. Even the dumbest hacker can figure those out in no time.

To rename the Administrator account, complete the following steps:

1. Select Group Policy Management from the Administrative Tools menu.

2. In the console tree, right-click your domain name and select Create And Link A GPO Here from the shortcut menu (Figure 10-27).

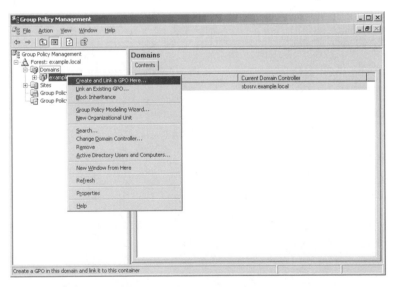

Figure 10-27.   *Creating a new GPO (Group Policy Object).*

3. In the New GPO dialog box, type **Rename Administrator Account**. Click OK.

4. In the console tree, expand the Group Policy Objects container.

5. In the details pane, right-click the new Rename Administrator Account GPO, and select Edit (Figure 10-28) to launch the Group Policy Object Editor.

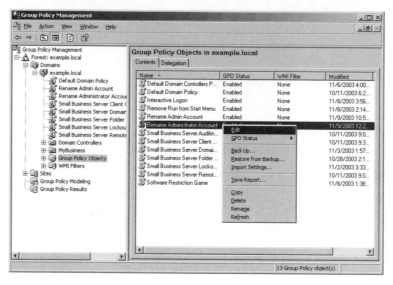

Figure 10-28. *Right-clicking the new policy to edit it.*

6. In the Group Policy Object Editor console tree, expand Computer Configuration, Windows Settings, Security Settings, Local Policies, and then Security Options.

7. In the details pane, double-click Accounts: Rename Administrator Account.

8. In the Security Policy Setting dialog box (Figure 10-29), select the check box to define this policy setting and type the new name for the Administrator account. Click OK.

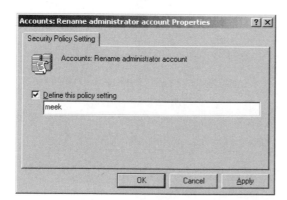

Figure 10-29. *Changing the name of the Administrator account.*

9. Close the Group Policy Object Editor and the Group Policy Management Console. Log off and log back on using the new name for the Administrator account.

To rename the account back to Administrator, don't disable the policy. Just return to the Security Policy Setting dialog box for the Accounts: Rename Administrator Account policy and type **Administrator.**

Using Group Policy to Set Clients to Update Automatically

To take advantage of Software Update Services (see Chapter 6, "Completing the To Do List and Other Post-Installation Tasks," for more information), computers on the network must be configured. This is most conveniently done by creating a new Group Policy Object (GPO) with the appropriate settings and linking it to the desired container using Group Policy, as shown in the following steps:

1. Select Group Policy Management from the Administrative Tools menu.

2. In the console tree under the domain name, right-click MyBusiness and select Create And Link A GPO Here from the shortcut menu.

3. Type in the name for the GPO and click OK.

4. Right-click the new GPO and choose Edit from the shortcut menu to launch the Group Policy Object Editor.

5. Navigate to Computer Configuration, Administrative Templates, Windows Components, and double-click Windows Update.

6. In the details pane, double-click Configure Automatic Updates (Figure 10-30).

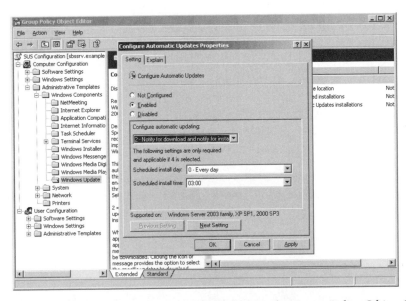

Figure 10-30.   *Configure Automatic Updates in the Group Policy Object Editor.*

7. Select Enabled, and then specify when and how Automatic Updates should run. The options are:

   - **2 – Notify For Downloading And Notify For Install** Presents a local notification message prompting a locally logged-on (or Remote Desktop) administrator to download and install the update.

   - **3 – Auto Download And Notify For Install** Automatically downloads new updates, and presents a local notification message allowing a locally logged-on (or Remote Desktop) administrator to install the update.

   - **4 – Auto Download And Schedule The Install** Automatically downloads new updates and installs them at the specified day and time.

8. Click Next Setting to continue. (Or click OK to finish.)

9. If you want clients to get updates from an intranet site instead of connecting to Windows Update over the Internet, select Enabled in the Specify Intranet Microsoft Update Service Location setting and type the address of the SUS server (**http://sbssrv**) in both boxes, and then click Next Setting.

10. In the Reschedule Automatic Updates Scheduled Installations setting, select Enabled to force clients to retry previously missed scheduled installations and specify how long after the next system startup the system should wait. Click Next Setting to continue.

11. In the No Auto-Restart For Scheduled Automatic Updates Installations setting, select Enabled to disable the automatic restart after an update. This allows the locally logged-on user to decide when to reboot after a scheduled installation that requires a restart. (The default behavior is to notify the user 5 minutes before the restart occurs automatically.)

12. Click OK when you're finished.

Tip Steps 9–11 aren't necessary to configure automatic updates. You must use Step 9 if updates are to be on an intranet, but Steps 10 and 11 are optional.

---

13. Type **gpupdate** at a command prompt to refresh Group Policy.

Redirecting Special Folders Using Group Policy

Windows Small Business Server makes it easy to redirect the path of users' My Documents folder to a new location. (See the redirection sections under "Managing User Accounts" in Chapter 9.) But My Documents is only one of several "special folders" that can be redirected using Group Policy. Other folders in this category are Application Data, Desktop, Start Menu, and, under some conditions, My Pictures.

With redirected folders, the following conditions apply:

- A user can log on to different computers and still have the folders available.

- When employing roaming profiles, only the network path to the redirected folders is part of the profile, not the folders themselves. This makes logging on and off much faster.

- Folders on a network server can be backed up as part of routine maintenance with no action on the part of the user.

Folders can be redirected to one location for everyone in the Active Directory container affected by the Group Policy Object. They can also be redirected to different locations according to security group membership.

By far the most common form of redirection is to send My Documents folders to a single location on a network server but it's also possible to redirect the other special folders as well as redirect folders based on group membership. To redirect special folders using Group Policy, complete the following steps:

1. Select Group Policy Management from the Administrative Tools menu.

2. In the console tree, right-click Group Policy Objects and select New from the shortcut menu. Type in a name for this policy and click OK.

3. Right-click the new policy in the list of Group Policy Objects and select Edit from the shortcut menu.

4. In the Group Policy Object Editor console tree, expand User Configuration, Windows Settings, and then Folder Redirection.

5. Right-click the folder to be redirected and select Properties.

6. On the Target tab, select Basic – Redirect Everyone's Folder To The Same Location or Advanced – Specify Locations For Various User Groups from the Setting drop-down list.

7. If you choose Basic, select a Target Folder Location and type in the Root Path. For Advanced, specify the security group, then the Target Folder Location, and the Root Path. The Target Folder Locations are:

- **Create a folder for each user under the root path** System creates a folder for each user at the specified location. (Not available for the Start Menu.)

- **Redirect to the following location** You specify a UNC address or a local address. A UNC address is in the form \\ServerName\ SharedFolder. Figure 10-31 shows the root path to redirect Application Data folders to the server.

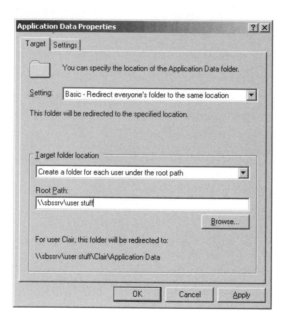

Figure 10-31. *Setting folder redirection.*

Tip If you have roaming profiles, always use UNC paths even for local folders. Local paths are disregarded by roaming profiles.

- **Redirect to the local userprofile location** Returns to default setting, which is the local user profile.

- **Redirect to the user's home directory** Folder is redirected to the user's home folder, created at the time as the user account. (Available only for the My Documents folder.)

8. After the target has been specified, click the Settings tab. The following settings are enabled by default:

- **Grant The User Exclusive Rights To** *SpecialFolderName*   The user and the local system have exclusive rights to the folder. No administrative rights are enabled. If this setting is disabled, the permissions that exist on the folder in its present position remain.

Caution   Start Menu folder redirection doesn't have the option to Grant The User Exclusive Rights. Start Menu redirection should be used only for Terminal Server users so that all users can share the same Start Menu.

- **Move The Contents Of My Documents To The New Location**   The contents of the specified folder are sent to the new location. If this option is disabled, the user has a new, but empty, My Documents folder at the new location.

- **Policy Removal**   The default is to leave the folder in the new location when the policy is removed. If you choose to redirect the folder back to the local user, see the next section, "Removing Redirection."

9. Click OK when you're finished.

Tip   Offline files are set up independently of folder redirection. However, if you redirect Application Data or Start Menu, set offline files to be automatically available. If you redirect the Desktop folder, select automatically available if the desktop is Read Only. See "Setting Offline File Rules" earlier in this chapter for more information.

After creating a GPO, link it to the domain or organizational unit where the policy is to be applied. Open the GPMC, right-click the domain name (or organizational unit), and select Link An Existing GPO from the shortcut menu. In the Select GPO dialog box, select the GPO to be linked, and then click OK.

Removing Redirection

When folders have been redirected and you later remove the policy, the effect on the folders depends on the combination of choices made on the Settings tab in the special folder's Properties dialog box. Table 10-8 shows the various combinations of settings and the outcome when the policy is changed.

Table 10-8. Settings and their outcome when redirection is removed

Policy Removal Option	Move Contents of Folder to New Location	Outcome When Policy Is Removed
Redirect the folder back to the local user profile location when policy is removed.	Enabled	The folder returns to its user profile location; the contents of the folder are copied back to the original location; the contents are not deleted from the redirected location.
Redirect the folder back to the local user profile location when policy is removed.	Disabled	The folder returns to its user profile location; the contents of the folder are not moved or copied back to the original location. Warning: this means the user cannot see the folder contents.
Leave the folder in the new location when policy is removed.	Enabled or Disabled	The folder and its contents remain at the redirected location; the user has access to the contents at the redirected location.

Auditing Events

Auditing is a necessary part of network administration. By reviewing reports and event logs, you can track usage patterns, security problems, and network traffic trends. Beware of the impulse to audit everything, however. The more events you audit, the bigger the logs. Reviewing huge event logs is a painful chore, and eventually no one looks at them anymore. Therefore, it's critical to decide on an auditing policy that protects your network without creating a large administrative burden. Also bear in mind that every audited event results in a small increase in performance overhead.

Pre-Defined Performance and Usage Reports

To set up Windows Small Business Server auditing, complete the following steps:

1. Select Server Management from the Start menu. Select Monitoring and Reporting in the console tree, and then click Set Up Monitoring Reports And Alerts to start the Monitoring Configuration Wizard.

2. On the Reporting Options page, make report choices.

   - **Performance Report** After the wizard completes, the performance report is viewable (by a member of the Domain Admins group) in Server Management. Select the option, and receive a daily report in e-mail as well. Performance reports include information about the server specifications, the processes being run, and any critical errors in critical logs.

   - **Usage Report** The Usage Report includes information about Internet, fax, and e-mail use. You can select just the option to view the report in Server Management, or you can also specify that you want to receive the report in e-mail.

3. If you chose an e-mail option, supply the destination e-mail address (or addresses) on the E-mail Options page.

4. On the Business Owner Usage Report, which is perhaps not the most unambiguous title, you can specify users (other than members of the Domain Admins group) who should receive reports. These users receive an e-mail telling them where to view the reports on the intranet.

5. On the Alerts page, click the option to receive notification of performance alerts by e-mail. Because these alerts warn of system problems that can be serious, someone with an administrative account should receive them. Supply one or more destination e-mail addresses.

6. The final page of the wizard summarizes the choices made. Click Finish to set up the reports.

   The wizard performs the configuration, and a dialog box (Figure 10-32) keeps you apprised of its progress.

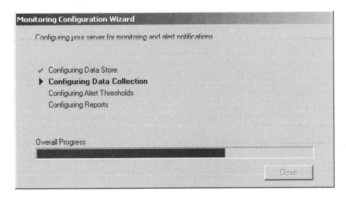

Figure 10-32.   *The Monitoring Configuration Wizard finishes setup.*

Note   Neither Performance nor Usage Reports are available instantly. The first Usage Report can take up to 24 hours to assemble and Performance data is gathered just once per hour.

Customizing Auditing

Every audited event tells you something, but it's not always something you need to know. For example, auditing successful logons and logoffs might reveal the use of a stolen password, or it might just produce countless pages showing that your duly authorized users are logging on and off as expected. Auditing logon failures, however, can definitely be rewarding when someone is trying a random password hack.

Table 10-9 lists the categories of events that can be audited.

Table 10-9. **Auditing categories**

Event Category	Activated When
Account logon events	A domain controller receives a logon request
Account management	A user account or group is created or changed
Directory service access	An Active Directory object is accessed
Logon events	A user logs on or logs off
Object access	An object is accessed
Policy change	A policy affecting security, user rights, or auditing is modified
Privilege use	A user right is used to perform an action
Process tracking	An application executes an action that is being tracked
System events	A computer is rebooted or shut down, or another event occurs that affects security

To change the settings on auditing events, complete the following steps:

1. Select Group Policy Management from the Administrative Tools menu.

2. In the console tree under Group Policy Objects, right-click Default Domain Controllers Policy and select Edit.

3. In the console tree of the Group Policy Object Editor, expand Computer Configuration, Windows Settings, Security Settings, and Local Policies to reach Audit Policy (Figure 10-33).

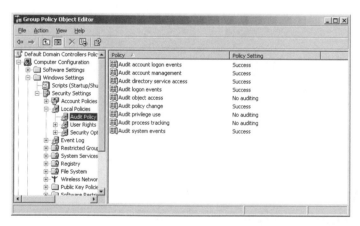

Figure 10-33. *Auditing categories in the GPO for domain controllers.*

4. Double-click an auditing category in the details pane to change a policy definition. Click OK when finished.

Viewing Event Logs

Event logs must be viewed with regularity for auditing to be useful. To view the security log, open Event Viewer from the Administrative Tools folder and then click Security. Double-click any entry to see more information about it. The security entries in Figure 10-34 occurred over a couple of minutes because the object being audited was set to audit successful events. Of course, you'll generally learn more from auditing failed events than from auditing successful ones, but this does demonstrate the need to choose your auditing battles carefully.

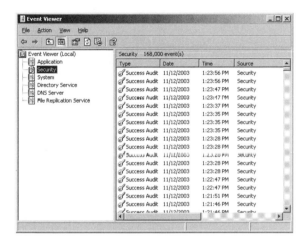

Figure 10-34. *Viewing the security log.*

Searching Event Logs

No matter how selective you are, the event logs mix all sorts of information together, making searches for specific information difficult. To search for a specific type of event, select the log in Event Viewer, and choose Filter from the View menu. In the Properties dialog box, shown in Figure 10-35, select the type or types of events you want returned. Table 10-10 describes the filtering options in the Properties dialog box.

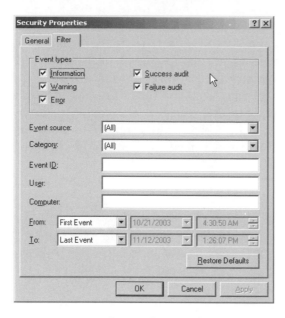

Figure 10-35. *Filtering for specific types of events in a log.*

Table 10-10.   Options for filtering event logs

Option	Use to Search or Filter for
Information	Notification that some major operation has been performed successfully.
Warning	Notification of some problem or potential problem. Warnings might or might not be significant. For example, an "unexpected" reboot of the server with the reason "other" generates a warning.
Error	Notification of an important event. Errors signify a loss of data or a loss of function. For example, failure of a service to start during bootup generates an error.
Success Audit	Events audited for success.
Failure Audit	Events audited for failure.
Event Source	A source for an event, such as a system component or a program.
Category	Events by category, such as logon/logoff, policy change, or process tracking.
Event ID	The specific ID number assigned to each logged event.
User	A specific user.
Computer	A specific computer.
From	Events after a specific date. The default is the first date in the log. You can click the drop-down box to select events on a specific date.
To	Events before a specific date. The default is the last date in the file.

Setting the Size of Event Logs

When an event log is full, a dialog box pops up to notify you. If this happens often, you might want to reduce the number of items being reported or increase the size of the log. To set event log options, complete the following steps:

1. Select Event Viewer from the Administrative Tools menu.

2. Right-click the log you want to configure and choose Properties.

3. On the General tab, select the options you want. Under When Maximum Log Size Is Reached, there are three options:

   - If you don't archive this log, select Overwrite Events As Needed.

   - If you archive this log at regular intervals, you can select the Overwrite Events Older Than option. Fill in the appropriate number of days.

   - Do Not Overwrite Events, the last option, means that the log must be cleared manually. When the maximum log size is reached, new events are simply not recorded.

4. Click OK when you're finished.

Caution   Caution is in order if you primarily log failure attempts. It's possible that users persistently trying to access a resource that they're not authorized to use could produce enough failure audits to fill the log and prevent the server from recording any more audit events.

Encrypting Sensitive Data

It's deceptively simple to encrypt and decrypt files in Windows Small Business Server. Of course, anything that's sensitive enough to be encrypted should be treated very carefully, so take time to plan before implementing file and folder encryption.

Encrypting Folders

Encrypting folders with the Encrypting File System (EFS) is as easy as setting any other folder attribute, such as Hidden or Read-Only. To encrypt a folder, complete the following steps:

1. In Windows Explorer, right-click the folder and choose Properties.

2. On the General tab, click Advanced.

3. Select the Encrypt Contents To Secure Data check box.

Caution Encrypt entire folders only. If you encrypt individual files but not their folders, a program might create a temporary file (which won't be encrypted) and then save the file over the original file, thereby leaving the file decrypted.

Note Remember that system files, compressed files, and files on partitions other than NTFS can't be encrypted using EFS. Further, a drive's root folder cannot be encrypted.

Like other files, encrypted files can be moved and copied with the Edit menu commands Cut, Copy, and Paste. Files moved or copied using drag-and-drop editing do not necessarily retain their encryption. You can also rename encrypted files as you do any other file. Any files or folders subsequently added to an encrypted folder are encrypted as well.

Caution Encrypted files and directories are not immune from deletion. Any user with appropriate rights can delete an encrypted file.

Note To ensure the security of temporary files that have been created by applications, mark your system's Temp folder for encryption.

Real World   Encryption Best Practices

Here are some encryption best practices to consider:

- Encrypt the My Documents folder of sensitive desktops and laptops.

- Encrypt the Temp folders of appropriate user profiles to protect temporary data, or data that was marooned in the Temp folder following a program crash.

- If you use spool files while printing, encrypt the Spool folder.

- Don't tamper with the RSA folder; this is the repository for EFS keys.

Decrypting Files and Folders

EFS allows a user to permanently reverse the encryption process. (*Any* encrypted file is also decrypted whenever a user or application accesses it.)

To decrypt a file or a folder, complete the following steps:

1. In Windows Explorer, right-click the file or folder and choose Properties.

2. Select the General tab and click Advanced.

3. Clear the Encrypt Contents To Secure Data check box.

Summary

Shares, permissions, and group policy are the foundations of security in Windows Small Business Server. This chapter, along with Chapter 9, provides the basic information needed to keep your network safe. In Chapter 11, "Installing and Managing Printers," you'll find the details about installing and configuring both printers and the fax service.

Chapter 11
Installing and Managing Printers

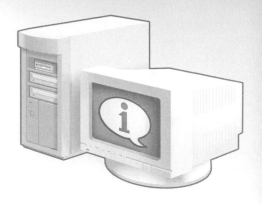

This chapter covers everything you need to know about printer sharing, one of the most important functions of a network. The chapter starts by discussing how print servers work and how to choose a suitable printer. It then launches into a discussion about installing printers, changing printer driver and print server settings, as well as printer troubleshooting.

Understanding Print Servers

Print servers are computers (or sometimes network appliances) that manage the communications between printers and the client computers generating the print jobs.

Generally, there are two approaches to print servers. The Microsoft approach is to use a Windows computer as an "intelligent" print server that handles communication between the printers and the client computers (reducing strain on the clients), and maintains a common print queue for all clients. Microsoft print servers also make it easy to find printers on the network by name (NetBIOS, DNS, or Active Directory), and install the appropriate printer drivers.

> **Planning** Microsoft Windows XP Professional and Microsoft Windows 2000 Professional can be used as print servers; however, they support a maximum of 10 simultaneous users. Additionally, if the shared printer is connected via a USB or parallel interface, the desktop computer acting as a print server can slow to a crawl while clients print, which will have an impact on any user who is logged on locally.

In contrast, other operating systems such as Linux and printers with built-in network interfaces use a relatively "dumb" print server called the Line Printer Daemon (LPD), which acts strictly as an interface between the network and the printer. Each client maintains its own printer queue and performs all pre-print processing, increasing the amount of time the computer is partially or completely unavailable for other tasks.

These two approaches aren't in opposition to each other and, in fact, the best way to connect a printer to a Windows print server is via a network connection to a printer, which usually runs the LPD service. The Windows print server connects to the printer using the traditional Line Printer Remote (LPR) service (the client-side equivalent of LPD) or via the higher-performance standard TCP/IP printer port, and shares the printer on the network. The Windows print server holds the printer queue and sends each print job to LPD, which passes the job to the printer.

Printer Terminology

Although the term "printer" is usually used to refer to both the physical device and its software interface, strictly speaking, a *printer* is a device that does the actual printing, and a *logical printer* is the software interface (printer driver) for the printer. You can have one logical printer associated with a single printer, or you can have several logical printers associated with a single printer. In this second arrangement, the logical printers can be configured at different priority levels so that one logical printer handles normal printing and another handles print jobs that should be printed during off-peak hours. For a printer that supports both PostScript and Printer Control Language (PCL), two logical printers allow users to choose which type of printing to do.

A single logical printer can also be associated with multiple physical printers in a printer pool, as long as all the printers work with the same driver. Printer pools distribute printing load more evenly, increasing performance. Because the physical printers in the pools are interchangeable, printer pools also make it possible for an administrator to add or remove physical printers without affecting the users' configurations.

Choosing Printers

Choosing the right printers for an organization is a lot like choosing the right car. There are certain practical matters to look at such as up-front cost, cost of consumables (gas, ink, or toner), and suitability to the task at hand (for example, hauling lumber or printing brochures). Use Table 11-1 to decide which basic category of printer would work best for your company.

Consumable costs vary widely, especially for inkjet printers, so try to find reviews that list the cost per page for the printer in question. Look for printers with built-in network interfaces because they print faster, require less processing power on the print server, and can be flexibly located anywhere there's a network cable. Printers with a USB connection can be used if print volumes are low (or for backup printers), but steer clear of printers using parallel port connections if possible—they can drastically slow a print server.

Table 11-1.   Printer types and suitability to different print volumes

Document Type	Low Volume (100–500 Pages/Month)	High Volume (500+ Pages/Month)
Black and white text and graphics	Consumer inkjet or laser printer	Black and white laser printer
Color text and graphics	Consumer inkjet printer	Color laser printer
Documents with pictures	Consumer inkjet printer	Business inkjet or color laser printer
Photo prints	Consumer inkjet printer	Inkjet photo printer, business inkjet printer, or high-quality color laser printer

Tip   Having at least two printers online in an organization is a good idea in case one runs into problems at an inopportune moment. One sensible approach is to use a laser printer as the primary printer and an inkjet printer as a backup printer that can also be used for high-quality photo prints.

Installing Printers

Before a Windows print server can share a printer on the network, it must first connect to the printer and install the necessary drivers. The following sections walk you through adding printers that are attached directly to the print server via USB or parallel port interface, as well as connecting to printers with built-in network adapters.

Adding Locally Attached Printers

If you're using a USB or IEEE 1394 (Firewire) connection to the printer, as soon as you plug the printer into the server, Windows automatically detects, installs, and shares the printer on the network, and also publishes it in Active Directory (although you might be prompted for drivers).

To use the Add Printer Wizard to set up a local printer that is physically connected to your system using a legacy parallel port, complete the following steps:

1. Connect the printer to the appropriate port on the server.

2. Click Start, choose Printers And Faxes, and then double-click Add Printer. Alternatively, select Printers from the Standard Management tree in the Server Management console and then click the Add A Printer link.

3. Click Next in the first page to begin using the Add Printer Wizard.

4. On the Local Or Network Printer page, select the Local Printer Attached To This Computer option, select the Automatically Detect And Install My Plug And Play Printer check box (Figure 11-1), and then click Next.

Caution If you're installing a Plug and Play (PnP) printer, always select the Automatically Detect And Install My Plug And Player Printer check box in the Add Printer Wizard. If you don't select this option, Windows detects the printer the next time the system is rebooted and attempts to install the printer a second time.

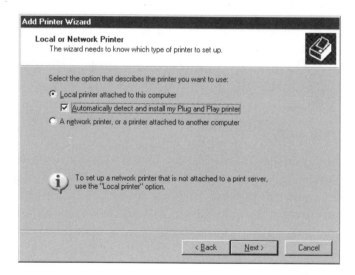

Figure 11-1. *The Local Or Network Printer page of the Add Printer Wizard.*

5. Windows displays the New Hardware Found dialog box when it locates the printer. If Windows has the appropriate drivers for the device, it installs them automatically.

6. If the printer wasn't detected, click Next to set up the printer manually.

7. On the Select A Printer Port page, shown in Figure 11-2, choose the port the printer is attached to, and then click Next.

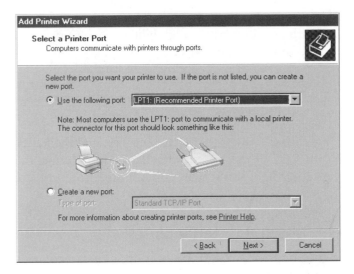

Figure 11-2. *The Select A Printer Port page of the Add Printer Wizard.*

8. On the Install Printer Software page, select the manufacturer and model of the printer from the Install Printer Software page. Click Windows Update to search for drivers online, or click Have Disk to provide the location of updated drivers. When finished, click Next.

Note Microsoft strongly recommends that you use only digitally signed drivers. If the driver isn't digitally signed, Windows warns you, and you should go find a driver that has been certified by Microsoft for use on Microsoft Windows Server 2003 or Windows 2000.

---

9. On the Name Your Printer page, type a name for the printer in the Printer Name text box and click Next. Try to keep the total length of the printer name, including the server's fully qualified domain name (FQDN), to 31 characters or fewer, and don't use spaces or special characters if you want to support Mac OS clients.

10. On the Printer Sharing page, select Share Name and then type a share name for the printer. Windows automatically creates an 8-letter name for optimal compatibility with MS-DOS and Microsoft Windows 3.x clients; don't use spaces when you want to maintain compatibility with Macintosh clients and automated Windows installations. Click Next.

Caution Printers with share names longer than 13 characters are invisible to clients running Microsoft Windows Me, Microsoft Windows 98, and earlier versions of Windows.

---

11. On the Location And Comment page, type the location name for the printer in the Location box, describe the capabilities of the printer in the Comment text box, and then click Next.

Note The Location field was designed for large networks that have the Printer Location Tracking feature enabled; however, on a smaller network, it's still useful for communicating the location of a printer to users.

12. On the Print Test Page, print a test page by clicking Yes, and then click Next to display a summary of the printer installation. To change the installation choices, click Back; otherwise, click Finish to complete the installation.

Adding Printers with Network Interfaces

If you have a printer with a built-in network connection, you can connect to it in two ways: via a standard TCP/IP printer port, or via the slower LPR service if the printer refuses to work with a Standard TCP/IP printer port.

Note You can also connect Windows Small Business Server to printers shared by other Windows servers or clients, and turn around and share these connections using the Add Printer Wizard (choose the Network Printer option).

Adding Printers on a Standard TCP/IP Printer Port

The best solution for connecting to network printers is to use a standard TCP/IP printer port. The standard TCP/IP printer port in Windows Small Business Server 2003 supports network printers that use TCP/IP (most commonly implemented with LPD), as well as printers connected to network devices such as the Hewlett-Packard JetDirect or the Intel NetPort. The standard TCP/IP printer port is easier to set up, provides more printer status information, and is 50 percent faster than an LPR Port Monitor (which is discussed in the next section).

To set up a network-based printer through a standard TCP/IP printer port—which Windows Small Business Server treats as a local port—complete the following steps:

1. Connect the printer to the network and configure the printer with the proper TCP/IP settings for the network. (You might want to disable DHCP so that the printer's IP address doesn't change.)

2. Click Start, choose Printers And Faxes, and then double-click Add Printer. Alternatively, select Printers from the Standard Management tree in the Server Management console, and then click the Add A Printer link.

3. Click Next on the first page to begin using the Add Printer Wizard.

4. On the Local Or Network Printer page, select the Local Printer Attached To This Computer option, clear the Automatically Detect And Install My Plug And Play Printer check box, and then click Next.

5. On the Select A Printer Port page, select Create A New Port, select Standard TCP/IP Port from the drop-down list (Figure 11-3), and then click Next. Windows launches the Add Standard TCP/IP Printer Port Wizard.

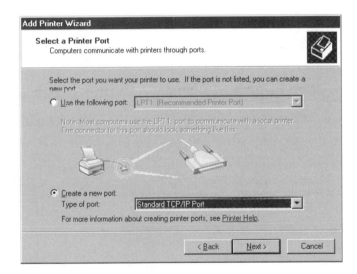

Figure 11-3.   *The Select A Printer Port page of the Add Printer Wizard.*

6. Make sure the printer is turned on and connected to the network, and then click Next on the first page of the Add Standard TCP/IP Printer Port Wizard to begin using the wizard.

7. On the Add Port page, type the printer name or IP address in the first text box, as shown in Figure 11-4.

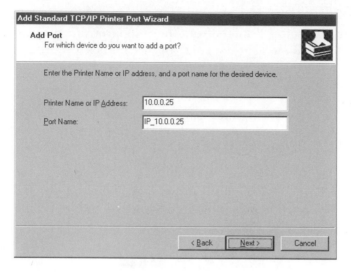

Figure 11-4. *The Add Port page of the Add Standard TCP/IP Printer Port Wizard.*

8. If necessary, modify the TCP/IP port name that Windows automatically fills in and then click Next. Windows attempts to connect to the printer.

9. If Windows can't detect the printer, the Additional Port Information Required page is displayed. Select the printer type from the Standard list (Figure 11-5), click Next, click Finish, and then skip to Step 15. Or select Custom and click Settings to display the Configure Standard TCP/IP Port Monitor dialog box, shown in Figure 11-6 and discussed in the next steps.

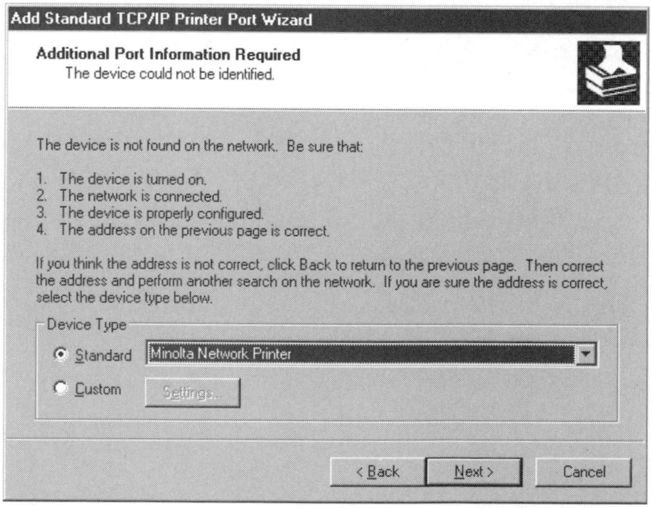

Figure 11-5. *The Additional Port Information Required page.*

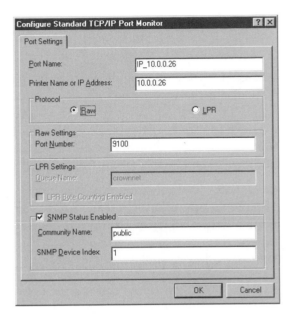

Figure 11-6. *The Configure Standard TCP/IP Port Monitor dialog box.*

10. Choose the protocol the printer uses, either RAW or LPR. Use RAW if possible; it closes the printer port when finished with a print job, reducing the likelihood of hanging the print spooler.

11. Type the port number for the printer if you're using the raw protocol. Use the default port number (9100) unless the printer documentation specifies that you must use a different port.

12. If using the LPR protocol, type the queue name in the box provided.

13. If the printer supports Simple Network Management Protocol (SNMP), select the SNMP Status Enabled check box, and type the Community Name (usually "public") and SNMP Device Index. SNMP allows the printer to communicate status information to the server.

Tip   Select the LPR Byte Counting Enabled check box if you're having problems with incomplete or missing documents. However, be aware that selecting this check box tells the server to count the number of bytes in a document before sending it to the printer, requiring the server to spool the job twice (taking extra time).

14. Click OK when you're finished configuring the TCP/IP port, click Next, and then click Finish.

15. If Windows Small Business Server doesn't detect the printer, the Install Printer Software page is displayed. Choose the manufacturer and printer model and then click Next.

16. On the Name Your Printer page, type a name for the printer in the Printer Name text box. Try to keep the total length of the printer name, including the server's fully qualified domain name (FQDN), to 31 characters or fewer, and don't use spaces or special characters if you want to support Mac OS clients. Specify whether to make the printer the default printer, and then click Next.

17. On the Printer Sharing page, select Share Name and then type a share name for the printer. Windows automatically creates an 8-letter name for optimal compatibility with MS-DOS and Windows 3.x clients; don't use spaces when you want to maintain compatibility with Macintosh clients and automated Windows installations. Click Next.

Caution   Printers with share names longer than 13 characters are invisible to clients running Windows Me, Windows 98, and earlier versions of Windows.

18. On the Location And Comment page, type the location name for the printer in the Location box, describe the capabilities of the printer in the Comment text box, and then click Next.

Note   The Location field was designed for large networks that have the Printer Location Tracking feature enabled; however, on a smaller network, it's still useful for communicating the location of a printer to users.

19. On Print Test Page, print a test page by clicking Yes, and then click Next to display a summary of the printer installation. To change the installation choices, click Back; otherwise, click Finish to complete the installation.

Adding Printers on an LPR Printer Port

If you have an old network printer or print device that won't work using a Standard TCP/IP printer port, you should use an LPR printer port. You'll probably also have to use an LPR printer port if the printer is being shared by a Linux system using the LPD service.

To set up a network-based printer through an LPR port, complete the following steps:

1. Connect the printer to the network and configure the printer with the proper TCP/IP and LPD settings.

2. Install Print Services For Unix: In Control Panel, click Add Or Remove Programs, click Add/Remove Windows Components, select Other Network File And Print Services, click Details, select Print Services For Unix, click OK, and then click Next.

3. Click Start, choose Printers And Faxes, and then double-click Add Printer. Alternatively, select Printers from the Standard Management tree in the Server Management console and then click the Add A Printer link.

4. On the Local Or Network Printer page, select the Local Printer Attached To My Computer option, clear the Automatically Detect And Install My Plug And Play Printer check box, and then click Next.

5. On the Select A Printer Port page, choose Create A New Port, select LPR Port from the drop-down list, and click Next.

6. In the Add LPR Compatible Printer dialog box, type the IP address or DNS name of the printer or print server running LPD in the first text box, shown in Figure 11-7.

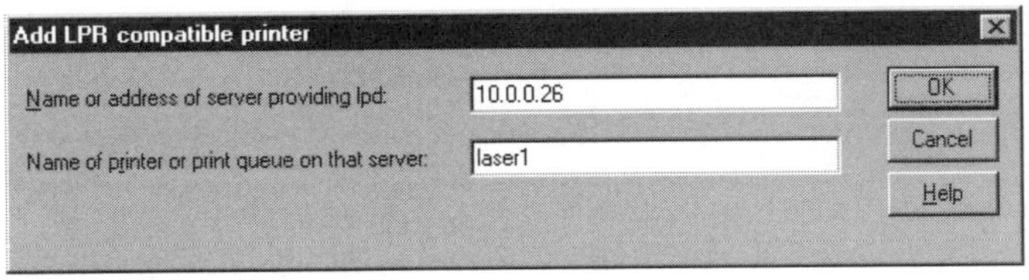

Figure 11-7.   *The Add LPR Compatible Printer dialog box.*

7. In the second text box, type the name of the printer or print queue on the LPD server, and then click OK. Windows adds the port to the list of ports.

8. If Windows doesn't detect the printer, the Install Printer Software page is displayed. Choose the manufacturer and printer model and then click Next.

9. On the Name Your Printer page, type a name for the printer in the Printer Name text box. Try to keep the total length of the printer name, including the server's fully qualified domain name (FQDN), to 31 characters or fewer, and don't use spaces or special characters if you want to support Linux or Mac OS clients. Specify whether to make the printer the default printer, and then click Next.

10. On the Printer Sharing page, select Share Name and then type a share name for the printer. Windows automatically creates an 8-letter name for optimal compatibility with MS-DOS and Windows 3.x clients; don't use spaces when you want to maintain compatibility with Macintosh and Linux clients and automated Windows installations. Click Next.

Caution Printers with share names longer than 13 characters are invisible to clients running Windows Me, Windows 98, and earlier versions of Windows.

11. On the Location And Comment page, type the location name for the printer in the Location box, describe the capabilities of the printer in the Comment text box, and then click Next.

12. On the Print Test Page, print a test page by clicking Yes, and then click Next to display a summary of the printer installation. To change the installation choices, click Back; otherwise, click Finish to complete the installation.

Changing Printer Driver Settings

Windows Small Business Server installs new printers with printer options designed to work for most users, but frequently, you need to change them so that the printer works optimally. Some modifications you might need to make include installing additional client printer drivers, specifying color profiles, changing printer availability, determining group printing priorities, and setting up printer pools. These features might not be available until you actively enable them.

Note Depending on the printer driver you use, the dialog boxes and printer options you have are probably different from those shown here. Printing preferences such as quality and paper types aren't covered here because they are extremely driver-dependant and, for the most part, self-explanatory.

Sharing a Printer and Providing Client Drivers

To change the share name the printer uses on a network, to stop sharing the printer, or to install drivers that client machines can use for the printer, follow these steps:

1. In the Printers And Faxes folder, right-click the printer you want to modify, and then choose Properties from the shortcut menu.

2. Click the Sharing tab, click the Share This Printer option (if not already selected), and type the share name for the printer in the text box provided (Figure 11-8).

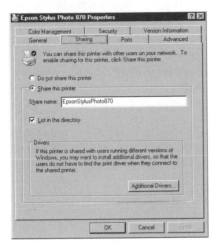

Figure 11-8.   *The Sharing tab of a printer's Properties dialog box.*

3. To publish the printer in Active Directory, select the List In The Directory check box.

4. To add client drivers that are automatically downloaded and installed when a Windows client other than Windows XP, Windows 2000, or Windows Server 2003 connects to the printer, click Additional Drivers.

Tip   Not all drivers reliably download automatically on client systems running Windows 98, Windows Me, or Microsoft Windows NT 4.0, though this is more of a problem for home printers than business printers. If you run across a driver that doesn't download automatically while setting up the printer on a client, simply point the Add Printer Wizard to a network or local path for the driver files.

5. In the Additional Drivers dialog box, select the check box next to any client drivers to be installed, and then click OK. To install additional client drivers, you need access to the installation files for the appropriate driver version, either on CD-ROM or across the network. To reinstall a previously installed driver, see the "Setting Print Server Options" section of this chapter.

Tip   To change the driver that the print server uses for a printer, click the Advanced tab and then choose a driver from the Driver drop-down list, or click New Driver to start the Add Printer Driver Wizard.

Under the Hood   Automatic Printer Driver Installation Behavior

If appropriate client drivers are installed on a print server, Windows clients automatically download the drivers when they are initially connected to the printer. Windows XP, Windows 2000, and Windows NT 4.0 clients automatically check for updated versions of the printer drivers at startup and download newer versions when necessary. Microsoft Windows 95, Windows 98, and Windows Me clients don't automatically check for updated drivers and must be updated manually.

Specifying a Color Profile

Windows Small Business Server 2003 includes the Integrated Color Management (ICM) 2 API for maintaining consistent colors across monitors, color printers, and scanners. When you need to achieve accurate color reproduction, it's useful to set up the printer, as well as the users' monitors and scanners, with an appropriate color profile. To specify a color profile, complete the following steps:

1. In the Printers And Faxes folder, right-click the printer you want to modify and select Properties from the shortcut menu.

2. Click the Color Management tab. Select the Automatic option to have Windows choose the best color profile.

3. To manually select a color profile, choose the Manual option, and then select a profile from the list or click Add to install an additional color profile from the device manufacturer. Click OK.

Tip   Color management in Windows has come a long way, but most graphics professionals still use third-party, hardware-based, color-matching solutions when color accuracy is important. However, ICM provides a good way to attain a reasonable measure of accuracy.

Changing Printer Availability and Priorities

To set up a printer to be available only during certain times—perhaps to discourage after-hours printing—complete the following steps:

1. In the Printers And Faxes folder, right-click the printer you want to modify and select Properties from the shortcut menu.

2. Click the Advanced tab, and then click the Available From option.

3. Select the earliest and latest times the printer is to be available to users, and then click OK.

Determining Group Printer Priorities

To set up user groups to have different priorities on a printer, you need to set up two or more logical printers for the physical printer. Assign each printer a different priority, and give your highest priority groups print permissions to the highest priority logical printer. To do this, follow these steps:

1. In the Printers And Faxes folder, double-click the Add Printer icon and use the Add Printer Wizard to add one or more duplicate logical printers for a physical printer already installed on the print server.

2. Right-click the logical printer for which you want to change the priority, and then select Properties from the shortcut menu. Click the Advanced tab, shown in Figure 11-9.

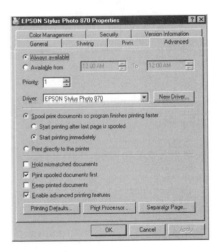

Figure 11-9. *The Advanced tab of a printer's Properties dialog box.*

3. Change the priority to be assigned to the logical printer for the users and groups who use this printer driver by typing a number in the Priority text box. The priority range goes from 1, which is the lowest priority, through 99, which is the highest priority.

4. Click the Security tab and add the users and groups you want to allow to print at this priority level. Remove or deny print permissions to users whose printing should occur at a different priority level. Those users will utilize another printer driver with a different priority level.

5. Click OK, and repeat the process for all other logical printers created for the printer, until you prioritize the user groups.

Setting Up Printer Pools and Changing Port Settings

As you learned earlier in the chapter, in a printer pool, more than one printer shares a single driver and appears as one printer. The advantage of using a printer pool is that clients don't need to find which printer is available; they simply print to the single logical printer (print driver) on the print server, which then sends the print job to the first available printer. Administration of the printers is also simplified because all printers in the printer pool are consolidated under one driver. If you modify the properties for the single logical printer, all physical printers in the printer pool use the same settings.

To set up a printer pool or change the port settings for a printer, complete the following steps:

1. In the Printers And Faxes folder, right-click the printer you want to modify and select Properties from the shortcut menu.

2. Click the Ports tab.

3. Select the Enable Printer Pooling check box.

4. To add additional printers to the printer pool, select the ports to which the additional printers are connected.

5. To change the settings for a port, select the port and click Configure Port.

Caution   All printers in a printer pool must be able to use the same printer driver.

Changing Spool Settings

Print spooling, or storing a print job on disk before printing, affects the actual printing speed as well as how clients perceive printing performance. You can change the way print spooling works to correct printing problems or to hold printed documents in the printer queue in case a user needs to print the document again. To change the spool settings for a printer, right-click the printer you want to modify, select Properties from the shortcut menu, and then use the Advanced tab (Figure 11-10) to modify the spool settings.

Following is a description of the print spool settings on the Advanced tab:

- **Spool Print Documents So Program Finishes Printing Faster**   Spools the print documents to the print server, freeing the client to perform other tasks more quickly.

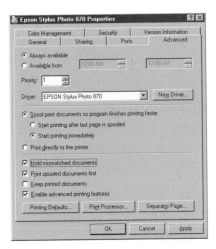

Figure 11-10. *Print spool settings can be modified on the Advanced tab of a printer's Properties dialog box.*

- To ensure that the entire document is available to the printer when printing begins, select Start Printing After Last Page Is Spooled. This step might correct some printing problems, and also helps high-priority documents print before low-priority documents.

- To reduce the time it takes to print a document, select Start Printing Immediately.

- **Print Directly To The Printer**   Turns off spooling, causing a performance hit on the server (though it might fix some printing problems).

- **Hold Mismatched Documents**   Holds documents in the queue that don't match the current printer settings (for example, documents that require legal-size paper when letter paper is currently in the printer). Other documents in the print queue are unaffected by held documents.

- **Print Spooled Documents First**   Prints the highest priority document that is already spooled first, ahead of higher priority documents that are still spooling. This step speeds overall printer throughput by keeping the printer from waiting for documents.

- **Keep Printed Documents**   Keeps a copy of print jobs in the printer queue in case users need to print the document again. In this circumstance, the user can resubmit the document directly from the queue rather than printing from his or her application a second time.

- **Enable Advanced Printing Features** Enables metafile spooling and printer options such as page order, booklet printing, and pages per sheet (if available on the printer). Disable this when you're experiencing printer problems.

- **Separator Page** Allows you to specify a separator page to insert between printed documents. Windows Small Business Server 2003 comes with three default separator pages located in the *%systemroot%*\System32 folder: Pcl.sep for PCL printers, Pscript.sep for PostScript printers that support Printer Job Language (PJL), and Sysprint.sep for PostScript printers that don't support PJL.

Setting Print Server Options

Although most printer configuration occurs in the printer driver for a particular printer, you can also configure print server settings that affect all printers hosted by the print server. These settings include determining which forms are available and which ports and printer drivers are available to use, as well as some spool settings.

1. In the Printers And Faxes folder, choose the Server Properties command from the File menu to open the Print Server Properties dialog box, shown in Figure 11-11.

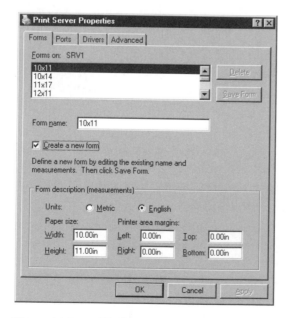

Figure 11-11. *The Forms tab of the Print Server Properties dialog box.*

2. To create a new form corresponding to a special paper size on which users can print, select the Create A New Form check box, type a name for the form in the Form Name box, use the Form Description (Measurements) section to define the form, and then click Save Form.

3. To view the ports available on the print server, click the Ports tab. Select a port and click Configure Port to modify the port settings, or click Add Port or Delete Port to add or remove a port from the system.

4. Click the Drivers tab to view and modify the list of currently installed drivers on the print server.

   - To view the driver details for a printer driver, select the driver and then click Properties to display the Driver Properties dialog box.

   - To reinstall a printer driver, select the driver and click Reinstall.

   - To add a printer driver that you want to make available to clients to download, click Add to launch the Add Printer Driver Wizard, which guides you through the driver installation process.

   - To remove a printer driver, select the driver and click Remove.

5. Click the Advanced tab. In the Spool Folder text box, type the location in which you want to store the spool folder. Make sure the drive is big enough to hold all the documents in the print queue. If you choose to enable the holding of printed documents, the drive needs to be big enough to archive all print jobs.

6. Select the check boxes next to the events to be logged.

7. To be notified of errors while printing remote documents, select Beep On Errors Of Remote Documents. Windows XP clients display an unobtrusive balloon tip in the System Tray for 10 seconds (or until clicked) when a document has finished printing. To notify earlier clients when a document has finished printing, select Notify When Remote Documents Are Printed. To display a notification message on the computer the document was printed on (even if the user who printed it is currently logged on elsewhere), select Notify Computer, Not User, When Remote Documents Are Printed.

Tip The Notify When Remote Documents Are Printed feature can be useful to earlier clients on busy print servers when a significant delay might occur between the time a client sends a document and the time the document reaches the head of the queue and actually prints. However, on less busy print servers or for users who need to print frequently, this feature can be annoying. If this situation occurs for users, you can turn off the option to eliminate the problem.

Managing Printers

Windows makes the job of managing printers easy and flexible. You can manage printers from virtually any Windows computer using the standard Windows print queue, you can use a Web browser interface, or you can use the Windows Small Business Server 2003 command-line interface.

Managing Printers from Windows

You can manage printers shared by a Windows Small Business Server 2003 computer using any machine running Windows Server 2003, Windows XP, or Windows 2000 (including the Windows Small Business Server computer, of course). To manage printers from within Windows, double-click a printer in the Printers And Faxes folder to view and manage the print queue, as shown in Figure 11-12.

Tip To open the Printers And Faxes folder using an account with Administrator privileges without logging off and then logging on again, launch Windows Explorer using the Run As command, display the Address Bar if it's not already present, type **Control Panel** in the Address Bar, and then double-click Printers And Faxes. For more information about the Run As command, see Chapter 9, "Users, Groups, and Security."

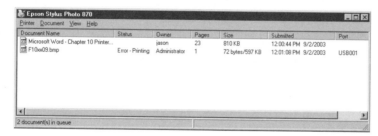

Figure 11-12. *The print queue window.*

You can manage the print queue using the following simple processes:

- To temporarily stop a *single* document from printing, right-click the selected document and choose Pause from the shortcut menu. To resume printing, right-click the document and choose Resume.

- To temporarily stop *all* documents from printing, choose Pause Printing from the Printer menu. To resume printing all documents, select Pause Printing a second time from the Printer menu.

- To cancel one or more print jobs, select the documents, right-click and choose Cancel from the shortcut menu. (You can also cancel print jobs by selecting them and pressing Delete.)

- To cancel *all* print jobs in the print queue, choose Cancel All Documents from the Printer menu.

- To restart a print job (force the document to print from the beginning again), right-click the document and choose Restart from the shortcut menu.

- To change the priority of a print job, right-click the print job, choose Properties from the shortcut menu, and then use the Priority slider to adjust the priority of the document, with 1 being the lowest priority and 99 being the highest priority.

- To specify that a print job should be printed only during a certain period, right-click the print job, choose Properties from the shortcut menu, select the Only From option, and choose the time range to allow the document to print. This feature is useful when you want to set a large document to print only during a time when you anticipate the printer to be free.

Note Sometimes a print job appears stuck in the queue and cannot be deleted. Try turning the printer off and then on again, or stop the Print Spooler service on the print server and restart it. See the "Deleting Stuck Documents" section of this chapter for more information.

Managing Printers from a Web Browser

Windows Small Business Server 2003 lets you manage printers from any browser, provided you have Internet Printing support installed. To install Internet Printing support, double-click Add Or Remove Programs in Control Panel, click Add/ Remove Windows Components, select Application Server, click Details, select Internet Information Services (IIS), click Details, select Internet Printing, and then click OK.

Once Internet Printing support is installed, complete the following steps to manage printers using a Web browser:

1. Type the URL of the print server followed by **/printers** in the browser's Address window.

2. To display a printer's queue, click the hyperlink of the printer you want to manage.

3. Click a hyperlink under the Printer Actions heading to pause, resume, or cancel the printing of all documents in the print queue.

4. To pause or cancel a specific print job, select the option button to the left of the document, and then click the Pause hyperlink or the Cancel hyperlink under the Document Actions heading (Figure 11-13).

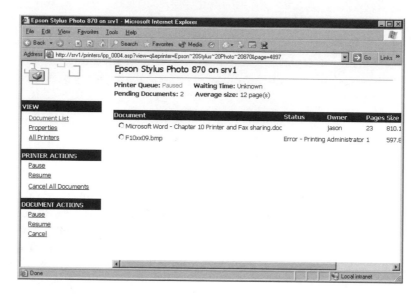

Figure 11-13. *The Document List page for a printer.*

5. To view the properties for the printer, click the Properties hyperlink under the View heading. Note that you can only view properties in the browser; to change them, you must use the Printers And Faxes folder.

Managing Printers from a Command Line

Windows Small Business Server 2003 makes command-line administration really practical for administrators. Open a command prompt window and then use the following commands to get started. To view a list of parameters, type the command followed by /? at a command prompt, or use the Help and Support Center.

- **Print** Prints the specified text file to the specified printer.

- **Lpr** Prints the specified text file to the specified LPD print queue.

- **Net print** Displays information about the specified print queue or print job. Can also hold, release, or delete print jobs.

- **Lpq** Displays information about the specified LPD print queue.

- **Net start** Starts the specified service. Can be used to start or stop the spooler service.

Windows Small Business Server 2003 also comes with the following print management scripts that you can run from a command line—as long as you switch to the %windir%\system32\ folder first:

- **Cscript Prnmngr.vbs** Adds, deletes, or lists printers on a Windows print server

- **Cscript Prnjobs.vbs** Lets you view and manage the print jobs of printer shares on a Windows print server

- **Cscript Prncfg.vbs** Allows you to view and change the settings of printers on a Windows print server

- **Cscript Prnqctl.vbs** Pauses or resumes printing, clears the print queue, or prints test pages

- **Cscript Prnport.vbs** Administers all things related to printer ports

- **Cscript Prndrvr.vbs** Adds, deletes, or lists printer drivers on a Windows print server

Using Printer Migrator to Back Up or Migrate Print Servers

You can use the free Microsoft Printer Migrator utility (also called the Print Migrator) to back up, restore, or migrate print server settings including printer drivers and print queues. This utility makes moving to a new server much easier—simply back up the print server configuration on the old server and restore it to the new one—even when the servers are running different versions of Windows. (Don't try to restore a Windows Server 2003 print server configuration on a Windows NT 4.0 server, though).

To use this program, you can download it from the Microsoft Web site. Then launch the program (Figure 11-14) and choose Backup from the Actions menu. This saves the configuration to a compressed .CAB file. Move the .CAB file to the desired server and run Printer Migrator again, this time choosing Restore from the Actions menu. Voilà! The settings and drivers are restored. (Keep in mind that if you migrate from Windows NT 4.0, you'll want to promptly upgrade the migrated level 2 drivers to native level 3 drivers for maximum stability.)

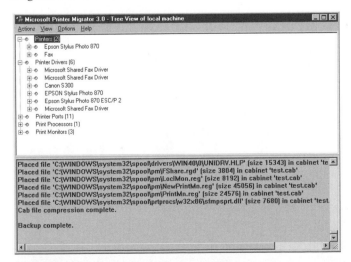

Figure 11-14. *The Printer Migrator utility.*

Under the Hood **Level 2 and Level 3 Printer Drivers**

Windows Small Business Server 2003 can use two types of printer drivers: level 2 printer drivers, which are written for Windows NT 4.0; and level 3 printer drivers, which are written for the Windows 2000, Windows XP, and Windows Server 2003 families. Level 2 drivers run in kernel mode, and can destabilize the operating system or force a reboot when they crash. Level 3 drivers run in protected user mode, where unstable drivers can't cause operating system instability (at worst they can crash the spooler service, which restarts automatically without requiring a reboot). Level 2 drivers can be used only on an upgraded system—they can't be installed on a running Windows Small Business Server 2003 system, except by using the Printer Migrator utility.

Troubleshooting Printing Problems

The following sections address a number of common printing problems. If you're having trouble pinpointing the problem or solution, first use the following steps to troubleshoot the printing process:

1. **Print from the client experiencing the problem and pay attention to any errors.** If the document prints properly, you probably have a user error, in which case you might need to educate the users as to the proper printing procedure. Otherwise, you might have a problem with a particular program, or the printer driver might be improperly configured for the users.

2. **Check the print server status.** When no errors are listed, check to see whether any documents are printing correctly. If not, check that sufficient free disk space exists on the drive holding the spool folder. If documents print garbled, the printer might be using the wrong data type (EMF or raw). Try using the raw data type to see whether this corrects the problem. You might also want to clear the Enable Advanced Printing Features check box on the Advanced tab of the printer's Properties dialog box. (See "Changing Spool Settings" earlier in this chapter for more information.)

   If some documents in the print queue don't print and you can't delete them, the print spooler might be stalled. Restart the Print Spooler service to see whether this corrects the problem. You might also want to add another logical printer (printer driver) for the printer to try to rule out the possibility of a corrupt printer driver.

Tip To prevent documents with certain languages from printing slowly, install on the print server the fonts for all languages that the clients will use to print. To do this, copy the fonts to the *%SystemRoot%*\Fonts folder on the print server and open the Fonts folder (or reboot the server).

3. **Print from another client machine.** If the second client prints properly, go back to the original client and perform more in-depth troubleshooting, such as reinstalling the printer drivers and testing the printing subsystem. If the second client can't print to the specified printer, you most likely have a problem with the print server or printer.

4. **Check the printer.** If no documents are printing, pause the print queue and then go check the actual printer. Are any errors reported on the printer? Make sure that the ready or online light is illuminated and that the printer cable is securely attached, or that the network cable is properly plugged in and the light next to the network port is illuminated (if available). Print a test page directly from the printer. If the test page prints properly and the printer is connected directly to the network, use the Ping.exe program from a command prompt to test the ability to reach the printer. If you still can't print to the printer, try installing the printer on a different computer temporarily to rule out the original print server.

Document Fails to Print

When the document doesn't print, error messages frequently appear that might help you identify the problem. Here are some solutions to try:

- If you receive an error stating that the appropriate printer driver wasn't available for download, you need to install the appropriate client drivers on the print server (or manually install drivers on the client).

- If you receive an error stating that the print device was unavailable, you might have a network connectivity problem, or the client might lack sufficient permissions. Try using the Ping command to test connectivity, or print using a user account with administrative privileges.

- Determine whether you can see and connect to the print server across the network. Try copying a file to the print server to see whether you can access the print server. (Generally, if you can't access the print server, you can't access any attached printers.)

- If you experience a lot of disk access and the document fails to print, verify that the drive holding the client's spool folder contains enough free disk space to hold the spooled document.

- Print a test document from Microsoft Notepad. If you can print with Notepad but not with the user's application, the printer drivers are correct and the application is likely to be the problem.

- If you can't print with Notepad, you can try printing from the command line by typing the following command: *dir > [printer port name]*, using the share name of the network printer as the printer port name.

- If you still can't print at all, run the Add Printer Wizard, choose the Local Printer option, select Create A New Port, choose Local Port, type the share name of the printer (*servername**printername*) for the port name, and complete the rest of the wizard. Then print a test page.

Document Prints Incorrectly

When a document prints but appears garbled or has some other defect, a compatibility problem exists between the client, the printer driver, and the printer. Make sure that the client is using the proper client printer driver and that the server is also using the proper printer driver.

Install a duplicate logical printer to test whether the printer driver is corrupt. If this isn't the problem, try changing the spool settings on the client driver (or, if multiple clients experience the same problem, try changing the settings on the server's printer driver). Specifically try changing the following options on the Advanced tab of the printer's Properties dialog box:

- To ensure that the entire document is available to the printer when printing begins, select the Start Printing After Last Page Is Spooled option.

- If you continue to have printing problems, choose the Print Directly To The Printer option to turn off spooling. This action causes a performance reduction on the server.

- Clear the Enable Advanced Printing Features check box on the print server to turn off metafile spooling, which disables some printer options such as page order, booklet printing, and pages per sheet (if available on the printer).

More Info   For more information about the Advanced tab options, see the "Changing Spool Settings" section earlier in this chapter.

Printing from Windows 3.x and MS-DOS Applications

Although the Windows 3.x and MS-DOS operating systems have no place on a modern network, most Windows 3.x and MS-DOS applications run fine under newer versions of Windows. With that said, you need to know a few things to use a shared printer from Windows 3.x and MS-DOS programs:

- Windows 3.x applications generally can print only to the default printer.

- To print from an MS-DOS program in Windows 98 or Windows 95, you must first capture a local printer port, either by choosing Yes in the Add Printer Wizard when asked whether you print from MS-DOS programs, or by opening the printer's Properties dialog box, clicking the Details tab, and then clicking Capture Printer Port.

- To print from MS-DOS programs running in Windows Small Business Server 2003, Windows XP, Windows 2000, or Windows NT 4.0, you must manually map the LPT1 printer port to the remote printer by typing the following command (replace printserver\printersharename with the server and printer share name of the remote printer as shown in this example):

  net use lpt1 *printserver**printersharename* /persistent:yes

  To disconnect LPT1 from the remote printer, type the following command:

  net use ltp1 /delete

Deleting Stuck Documents

When you can't delete documents in the print queue or documents don't print, the print spooler might be stalled. This stalling also affects any fax services the server is running. To restart the Print Spooler service, complete the following steps:

1. Launch the Computer Management snap-in from the Administrative Tools folder, expand Services And Applications in the console tree, and then select Services.

2. Select the Print Spooler service in the right pane, shown in Figure 11-15, and then click the Restart Service toolbar button.

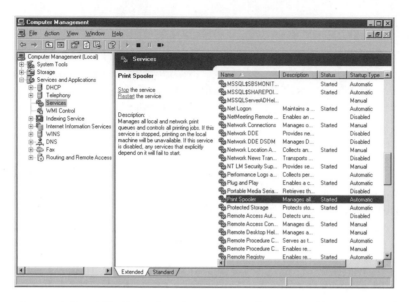

Figure 11-15. *The Print Spooler service in Computer Management.*

3. To view the services (such as remote procedure call) on which the print spooler depends, double-click the Print Spooler service and then click the Dependencies tab. You can also use this tab to view the services that depend on the print spooler to function properly.

4. To configure a recovery process to take place should the Print Spooler service fail, click the Recovery tab, and then specify whether you want to restart the service, reboot the computer, or run a program after each print spooler failure.

Restarting the service is usually a good option—it saves time. Automatic rebooting of the computer is a last option.

Tip To restart the print spooler from a command prompt, type **net stop "print spooler"**, press Enter, and then press Y to stop any dependant services. When all services have stopped, type **net start "print spooler"**, press Enter, and then restart any dependant services using the same method (for example, **net start "Fax"**).

Summary

Printing is a vital service to most networks, and this chapter showed you how to accomplish virtually any printing administration task you might need to accomplish including installing and managing printers, troubleshooting print problems, and using the shared fax service to set up a network fax server. In the next chapter, we discuss an equally important topic—managing computers on a network.

Chapter 12
Managing Computers on the Network

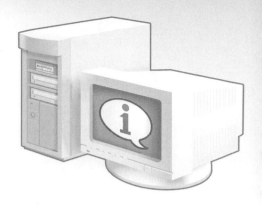

As you'll learn in this chapter, Microsoft Windows Small Business Server 2003 streamlines client management tasks by making it easy to connect computers to the network and manage them remotely from the server. Windows Small Business Server doesn't directly address keeping client machines up-to-date. See "Security Basics" in Chapter 6, "Completing the To Do List and Other Post-Installation Tasks," for details about Microsoft Software Update Services (SUS), a free service that enables administrators to approve which Windows updates are applied to client computers.

Microsoft recommends using Microsoft Windows XP Professional, Microsoft Windows XP Tablet Edition, Microsoft Windows XP Media Center Edition, or Microsoft Windows 2000 Professional for all client computers on the network. (Member servers should use Microsoft Windows Server 2003 or Microsoft Windows 2000 Server.) Microsoft Windows NT 4.0 and Microsoft Windows 98 computers function adequately on a Windows Small Business Server 2003 network, but some features aren't supported (such as automated software deployment and Microsoft Outlook 2003), and clients using these operating systems require extra management time and effort. Computers running Mac OS X or other operating systems usually can be made to work with Windows Small Business Server 2003 for basic tasks (as discussed later in this chapter), but have significant limitations and require more work on the part of the administrator. Therefore, this chapter focuses on clients running Windows XP Professional or Windows 2000 Professional but also includes discussions of other operating systems.

Connecting Computers to the Network

Connecting computers running Windows XP Professional, Windows Server 2003, or Windows 2000 to a Windows Small Business Server 2003 network is easy: just create computer accounts for the computer, establish basic network connectivity, and then use the Small Business Server Network Configuration Wizard to configure the rest of the client's settings.

Tip Add all routinely connected VPN clients to the domain. This enables computer authentication as well as user authentication, eliminates the need for remote users to provide credentials for every domain resource they access, and lays a foundation for L2TP VPN deployment. Because VPN client computers that are domain members must authenticate with the domain during logon, remote users can log onto their computers either via a dial-up VPN connection to the domain or by using cached credentials when they don't want to establish a VPN connection.

Creating Computer Accounts for Client Computers

Before you connect a client computer to the network, you need to run the Set Up Computer Wizard on the Windows Small Business Server computer. This wizard creates computer accounts and optionally assigns software to the computers.

More Info For information about connecting additional servers to the network, see the next section, "Creating Computer Accounts for Server Computers."

To run the Set Up Computer Wizard, complete the following steps:

1. Log on to the Windows Small Business Server 2003 computer, click Start, and then click Server Management to open the Server Management console.

2. Click Computers and then click Set Up Client Computers to open the Set Up Computer Wizard.

3. Click Next. On the Client Computer Names page (Figure 12-1), create computer accounts for all client computers, and then click Next:

   - To create a new computer account, type the computer name in the Client Computer Name box and click Add.

   - To rename or remove a computer account you added, select the computer account and click Rename or Remove.

4. On the Client Applications page (Figure 12-2), select the applications to install on each client computer. To allow users to change which applications are installed during Client Setup, select the During Client Setup, Allow The Selected Applications To Be Modified check box. To force the client computer to log off after Client Setup completes processing, select the After Client Setup Is Finished, Log Off The Client Computer check box. Click Next to continue.

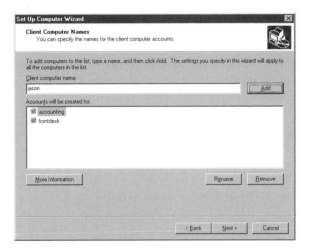

Figure 12-1.   *The Client Computer Names page of the Set Up Computer Wizard.*

Note   Users of Windows Small Business Server 2003, Premium Edition, should also assign the ISA Server Firewall Client to client computers (unfortunately, it's not assigned by default). To do so, first add the Firewall Client to the list of available applications, as described in the "Assigning Applications to Client Computers" section of this chapter.

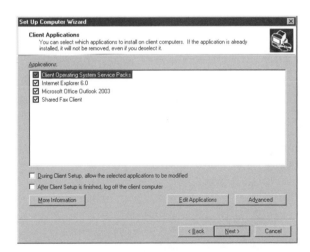

Figure 12-2.   *The Client Applications page of the Set Up Computer Wizard.*

5. On the Mobile Client And Offline Use page, select the Install Connection Manager and Install ActiveSync 3.7 check boxes to facilitate the client computers connecting remotely via VPN and synchronizing Microsoft Pocket PC and Microsoft SmartPhone devices. Click Next to continue.

6. Review the settings and then click Finish.

> **More Info** To edit the list of applications, see the "Assigning Applications to Client Computers" section of this chapter. To change client computer settings, see the "Viewing and Modifying Client Computer Settings" section of this chapter.

Creating Computer Accounts for Server Computers

Before connecting an additional server to the network, first run the Set Up Server Wizard on the Windows Small Business Server computer to create the computer account and optionally assign software to the computer:

1. Select Sever Management from the Start menu.

2. Click Server Computers in the console tree, and click Set Up Server Computers to launch the Set Up Server Wizard.

3. Click Next. On the Server Computer Name page, type the computer name you want to use for the server in the Server Name box, and then click Next.

4. On the IP Address Configuration page (Figure 12-3), select Obtain An IP Address Automatically By Using DHCP, or select Use The Following Static IP Address and type the static IP address of the server. Click Next when you're finished.

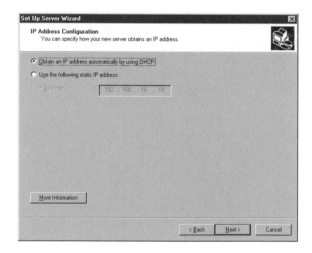

Figure 12-3. *The IP Address Configuration page of the Set Up Server Wizard.*

5. Review the settings and then click Finish.

Establishing Basic Network Connectivity

The first step in connecting a computer to a Windows Small Business Server 2003 network is to connect to the network and obtain a valid IP address. This process is pretty simple: plug the computer into an Ethernet switch on the internal network, and configure the system for Dynamic Host Control Protocol (DHCP). Wireless clients must first associate with an access point and provide a WPA/WEP key.

Configuring Windows XP and Windows Server 2003 to Use DHCP

To configure computers running Windows XP or Windows Server 2003 to use DHCP for TCP/IP configuration, complete the following steps:

1. In the Network Connections folder (available in Control Panel), right-click the appropriate network adapter (most likely Local Area Connection), and choose Properties from the shortcut menu.

2. In the Local Area Connection Properties dialog box, select the Internet Protocol (TCP/IP) component, and click Properties. The Internet Protocol (TCP/IP) Properties dialog box appears (Figure 12-4).

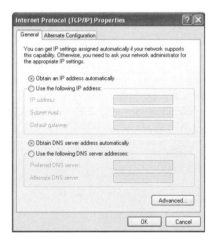

Figure 12-4. *The General tab of the Internet Protocol (TCP/IP) Properties dialog box.*

3. Verify that the Obtain An IP Address Automatically and Obtain DNS Server Address Automatically options are selected, and then click OK.

Note You might want to use static IP addresses for additional servers (print servers and additional domain controllers are two likely candidates). If you choose to use a static IP address, configure the server with an IP address in the excluded IP address range of 192.168.16.3 through 192.168.16.9, or add an appropriate exclusion in DHCP.

Configuring Windows 2000 to Use DHCP

To configure Windows 2000 clients and servers to use DHCP for TCP/IP configuration, complete the following steps:

1. In the Network And Dial-Up Connections folder (available in Control Panel), right-click the appropriate network adapter (most likely Local Area Connection), and choose Properties from the shortcut menu.

2. In the Local Area Connection Properties dialog box, select the Internet Protocol (TCP/IP) component and click Properties. The Internet Protocol (TCP/IP) Properties dialog box appears (Figure 12-5).

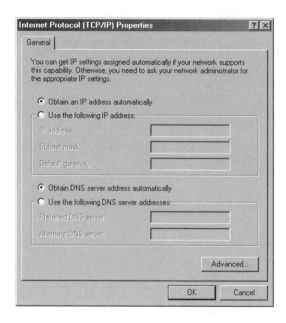

Figure 12-5. *The General tab of the Internet Protocol (TCP/IP) Properties dialog box.*

3. Verify that both the Obtain An IP Address Automatically and Obtain DNS Server Address Automatically options are selected, and then click OK.

Associating with a Wireless Access Point

Windows XP clients can use the Zero Configuration Wireless feature to easily associate with wireless access points and provide appropriate network keys, as discussed in the following steps. All other clients must use the interface provided by the network adapter drivers.

Note Pocket PC 2003 devices provide a feature called Zero Configuration Wi-Fi, which works almost identically to the Zero Configuration Wireless feature in Windows XP.

1. After installing and configuring a wireless network adapter, right-click the Wireless Network Connection icon in the system tray, and choose View Available Networks from the shortcut menu.

2. Select your wireless network in the Wireless Network Connection dialog box, shown in Figure 12-6.

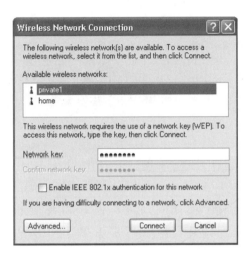

Figure 12-6. *The Wireless Network Connection dialog box.*

3. Type the network key (WPA or WEP) in the Network Key and Confirm Network Key boxes, and then click Connect. If you're using 802.1X authentication, as discussed in Chapter 17, "Customizing a SharePoint Web Site," leave the Network Key box empty and select the Enable IEEE 802.1X Authentication For This Network check box. (See Chapter 15, "Managing Connectivity," for more help with 802.1X.) If you're using WPA, see the Real World sidebar, "Getting Connected with WPA Authentication."

Real World **Getting Connected with WPA Authentication**

Using Wi-Fi Protected Access (WPA) for wireless client authentication and encryption is one convenient method of securely connecting wireless clients to an internal network, though you must clear a few implementation hurdles before everything works properly.

To use WPA for wireless authentication, clients must run Windows Server 2003 or Windows XP SP1 with the Microsoft WPA client program (discussed in Microsoft Knowledge Base Article 815485 and likely included in future service packs). To use WPA on other operating systems, purchase a third-party WPA supplicant unless one is provided with the network adapter drivers. Two popular third-party WPA supplicants are Funk Software's Odyssey client (*http://www.funk.com/radius/wlan /wlan_c_radius.asp*) and Meetinghouse Data Communications AEGIS client (*http://www.mtghouse.com/products/client/index.shtml*).

Because many wireless network adapters rely on the Microsoft WPA client program for WPA support, computers that don't have this or a third-party WPA supplicant installed might have to connect to the network via Ethernet cable to download and install WPA support, or install the latest service pack and WPA client from removable media before connecting to the network.

Using the Small Business Server Network Configuration Wizard

After you create a computer account and establish network connectivity, the next step in connecting a Windows XP, Windows Server 2003, or Windows 2000 computer to a Windows Small Business Server 2003 network is to log on to the computer, open Microsoft Internet Explorer, and launch the Small Business Server Network Configuration Wizard. This wizard configures the computer to run on the network by performing the following actions:

- Changes the computer's workgroup or domain membership to be a member of the Windows Small Business Server's domain.

- Installs operating system service packs and the Previous Versions client.

- Optionally migrates existing local user profiles stored on the computer to new domain user profiles, preserving the data and settings of local user accounts.

- Optionally installs Outlook 2003, the shared fax client, and any other software you assign to computers (as discussed later in this chapter in the "Assigning Applications to Client Computers" section).

- Optionally installs printer drivers and changes various Windows settings, as discussed later in this chapter in the "Viewing and Modifying Client Computer Settings" section.

More Info   Computers running operating systems other than Windows XP Professional; Windows XP Tablet Edition; Windows XP Media Center Edition; Windows Server 2003; or Windows 2000 must be manually connected to the network, as discussed in the "Connecting Alternate Clients" section of this chapter.

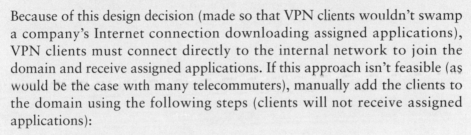

Real World   Connecting Clients Across VPN Links

Clients that frequently connect to the network via a VPN connection, such as telecommuters and wireless clients, should be added to the domain. This makes accessing domain resources easier, improves security by implementing computer authentication, and reduces the complexity of deploying L2TP VPNs. However, VPN clients can't use the Network Configuration Wizard to join the network, and they can't receive assigned applications either.

Because of this design decision (made so that VPN clients wouldn't swamp a company's Internet connection downloading assigned applications), VPN clients must connect directly to the internal network to join the domain and receive assigned applications. If this approach isn't feasible (as would be the case with many telecommuters), manually add the clients to the domain using the following steps (clients will not receive assigned applications):

1. Open the System tool in Control Panel.

2. On Windows XP and Windows Server 2003 clients, click the Computer Name tab and then click Change. On Windows 2000 clients, click the Network Identification tab and then click Properties.

3. Select Domain, type the name of the Windows Small Business Server 2003 domain, and then click OK. Reboot the computer when prompted.

Caution   If clients are running previous versions of Outlook and you want to upgrade them to Outlook 2003, disable any COM add-ins before running the Client Setup Wizard.

To use the Small Business Server Network Configuration Wizard to join a computer to the network, complete the following steps:

1. Log on to the client computer using an account with local administrator privileges.

2. Open Internet Explorer. If the Internet Connection Wizard appears, use the wizard to connect to the Internet via a LAN connection.

3. In the Address bar, type **http://*sbssrv*/ConnectComputer** (where *sbssrv* is the computer name of the Windows Small Business Server computer) and press Enter.

4. On the Network Configuration page, click the Connect To The Network Now link.

5. If a Security Warning dialog box appears asking whether you want to install and run the SBS Network Configuration Wizard, click Yes. After a few moments, the Small Business Server Network Configuration Wizard appears.

6. On the User Account And Password Information page, type the user name and password of a domain user account, and then click Next.

7. On the Assign Users To This Computer And Migrate Their Profiles page of the wizard (Figure 12-7), select all domain user accounts that will use the computer from the Available Users list, and then click Add.

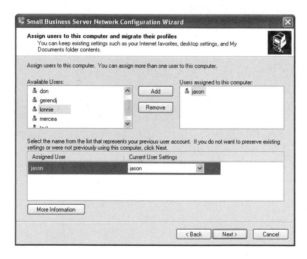

Figure 12-7. *The Assign Users To This Computer And Migrate Their Profiles page.*

8. To migrate existing documents and program settings that are stored in a local user profile to the new domain user profile, select the domain user account in the Assigned User column, and then select the local user profile to migrate in the Current User Settings box. Click Next when you're finished assigning users to the computer and migrating user accounts.

Note Use the Files And Settings Transfer Wizard provided with Windows XP to transfer user data and settings from a different computer, or to migrate user settings from an account in an existing domain to the new Windows Small Business Server 2003 domain. (See the Real World sidebar "Migrating Profiles from an Existing Domain" for a more thorough procedure.)

9. On the Computer Name page, select the computer name to use and then click Next. Only names created using the Set Up Computer Wizard and not already taken by another computer are listed.

More Info For more information about the Set Up Computer Wizard, see the sections "Creating Computer Accounts for Client Computers" and "Creating Computer Accounts for Server Computers" in this chapter.

10. On the Completing The Network Configuration Wizard page, review the settings and then click Finish. The Small Business Server Network Configuration Wizard adds the computer to the domain and then restarts the computer (typically two times).

11. Log on to the client computer using a domain user account. A Client Setup Wizard dialog box will appear automatically.

12. In the Client Setup Wizard dialog box, click Start Now to install assigned service packs and software immediately, or click Postpone to do it later.

13. On the first page of the Client Setup Wizard, click Next. On the Assigned Applications page (Figure 12-8), which appears if you selected the During Client Setup, Allow The Selected Applications To Be Modified check box when you created the client computer account, clear the check boxes next to any applications you don't want to install and then click Next.

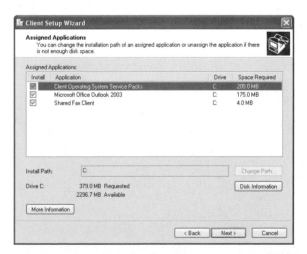

Figure 12-8. *The Assigned Applications page of the Client Setup Wizard.*

14. If the Automatic Logon Information page appears, either type your password to permit the Client Setup Wizard to automatically log on during the Client Setup Wizard (one or more reboots might be necessary) or select Manual Logon to do it yourself. The automatic logon feature is disabled after Client Setup completes. Click Next when you're finished.

The Application Setup Progress page appears. The Client Setup Wizard installs the specified applications and service packs and reboots the computer a couple of times, if necessary.

Real World Migrating Profiles from an Existing Domain

Although the Files And Settings Transfer Wizard in Windows XP is the simplest way to preserve settings in a domain account when switching domains or migrating from an old server, it doesn't preserve all settings. To preserve the entire user profile, use the following steps to create a new local user account and copy the domain profile to that account.

1. On the client computer, create a new local user account using the Local Users and Groups MMC snap-in (accessible via the Computer Management snap-in) and add the account to the local Administrators group (you can make the local group memberships more appropriate after joining the domain).

2. Log on with the new local user account.

3. Open the System tool in Control Panel, click the Advanced tab, and then click Settings in the User Profiles section.

4. Select the domain account you want to migrate, click Copy To, and in the Copy To Profile box, type the path to a suitable folder on the hard drive (most likely a subfolder of the C:\Documents And Settings folder).

5. Click Change, click Locations, select the local computer in the Locations dialog box, and then click OK. This returns you to the Select User Or Group dialog box.

6. Type the name of the local user account you created and then click OK. Click OK again twice to finish copying the profile.

7. Open the Local Users And Groups snap-in, double-click the local user account you created, click the Profile tab, and then type the location of the folder to which you copied the profile in the Profile Path box. Click OK when you're finished.

8. Open the System tool in Control Panel, click the Computer Name tab, and then click Change (on Windows XP and Windows Server 2003 computers). On Windows 2000 computers, click the Network Identification tab and then click Properties.

9. Select Workgroup, type a workgroup name (**WORKGROUP** is always popular), and then click OK. Reboot the computer when prompted, log on using the newly minted local user account, and then use the Network Configuration Wizard to join the domain and migrate the new local user account, which now stores the settings of the domain account you want to migrate.

Connecting Alternate Clients

Windows XP and Windows 2000 clients provide the best client experience on a Windows Small Business Server 2003 network and take the least amount of time to administer. However, clients running other versions of Windows as well as computers running Mac OS X can be connected to a Windows Small Business Server network if you're willing to expend a little extra effort. The following sections show you how.

Note   Windows XP Home Edition isn't suitable for full-time use on a Windows Small Business Server network and should be upgraded to Windows XP Professional. However, for occasional use, Windows XP Home Edition can be made to work if you enable DHCP, join it to a workgroup with the same name as the Windows Small Business Server domain, and provide a domain user name and password when connecting to shared resources.

Connecting Windows 98 and Windows Me Clients

To connect Windows 98 and Microsoft Windows Millennium Edition (Me) clients to a Windows Small Business Server 2003 network, configure TCP/IP, install Windows Small Business Server clients, and connect to network printers and the shared fax service.

Note   Microsoft Windows 95 clients should be upgraded to Windows 98 (at a minimum). If you can't easily upgrade Windows 95 clients, install the Active Directory client extensions or disable signed communications, as discussed in the "Disabling SMB Signing" section of this chapter.

Caution   Sensitive data stored on a Windows 98 machine is completely exposed to anyone with local access to the computer. If file security is important, upgrade the client to Windows 2000 or Windows XP and use NTFS permissions and EFS to encrypt files as necessary.

Configuring TCP/IP Settings To connect to the Windows Small Business Server 2003 computer, Windows 98 and Windows Me clients must first configure TCP/IP properly, as discussed in the following steps:

1. On the Windows 98 or Windows Me client, uninstall existing versions of the Shared Fax Client, Shared Modem Client, and Firewall client.

2. Open Control Panel on the client and double-click Network.

3. Select the TCP/IP component bound to the network adapter used to connect to the Windows Small Business Server computer, as shown in Figure 12-9, and then click Properties.

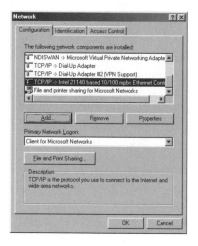

Figure 12-9. *The Network dialog box of a Windows 98 client.*

4. On the IP Address tab, select Obtain An IP Address Automatically.

5. Click the WINS Configuration tab and select Use DHCP For WINS Resolution, and then click OK.

6. In the Network dialog box, click the Identification tab, type the appropriate computer name in the Computer Name box, type the Windows Small Business Server domain name (**EXAMPLE**, for example) in the Workgroup box, and optionally type a description of the computer.

7. Click the Access Control tab and select Share-Level Access Control.

8. Click the Configuration tab, select Client For Microsoft Networks, and then click Properties.

9. In the Client For Microsoft Networks Properties dialog box, select the Log On To Windows NT Domain check box (Figure 12-10), type

the NetBIOS name of the Windows Small Business Server domain, click OK, and then click OK once more. Restart the computer when prompted.

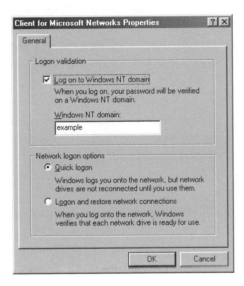

Figure 12-10. *The Client For Microsoft Networks Properties dialog box of a Windows 98 client.*

10. Open Control Panel, double-click Internet Options, and then click the Connections tab.

11. In the Dial-Up And Virtual Private Network Settings section of the Connections tab, specify if and when the client should establish a dial-up or VPN connection, and then click LAN Settings. (If the options in the Dial-Up And Virtual Private Network Settings section are unavailable, install the Dial-Up Network and Virtual Private Networking components from the Windows Setup tab in Add Or Remove Programs.)

12. If you're using Windows Small Business Server 2003, Standard Edition, clear the Use A Proxy Server check box. If you're using Windows Small Business Server 2003, Premium Edition with ISA Server, select the Use A Proxy Server check box, type the NetBIOS name of the Windows Small Business Server Computer in the Address box (**SBSSRV**, for example), type **8080** in the Port box (unless you changed it to something else), select the Bypass Proxy Server For Local Addresses check box, click OK, and then click OK again.

Installing Windows Small Business Server Client Software   After getting a Windows 98 or Windows Me client up and running on the network, you should perform some additional tasks before considering the system ready for use:

- **Install Active Directory client extensions for Windows 95/98**   These extensions provide stronger authentication (NTLM version 2), site awareness for businesses with branch offices, and Distributed Files System (DFS) client support. Install the Dsclient.exe file from the \Clients \Win9X folder of a Windows 2000 Server CD.

- **Install the firewall client**   If you're using Windows Small Business Server 2003, Premium Edition, install the ISA Server firewall client by running Setup.exe from the *sbssrv*\mspclnt share (where *sbssrv* is the computer name of the Windows Small Business Server computer).

- **Install Previous Versions client (shadow copy client)**   This provides access to previous versions of files stored on the Windows Small Business Server computer. To install the Previous Versions client, launch the Shadowcopyclient.msi file from the *sbssrv*\ClientApps\Shadow-Copy share where *sbssrv* is the name of the Windows Small Business Server computer. (To install the Previous Versions client, you must have Windows 98 Second Edition or Windows Me.)

- **Install Internet Explorer 6**   Installing Internet Explorer 6 ensures that the client can use the Intranet properly and increases the security and compatibility of general Web browsing as well (although you can, of course, use a different Web browser). To install Internet Explorer 6, launch the Ie6setup.exe file from the *sbssrv*\ClientApps\Ie6 share where *sbssrv* is the name of the Windows Small Business Server computer.

- **Install the latest updates from Windows Update**   Use Windows Update on the client to download the latest security patches and updates.

- **Configure Outlook to work with Exchange**   Outlook 2003 won't install on Windows 98 computers, so you're stuck with earlier versions or Microsoft Outlook Web Access (OWA). If you're going to use an earlier version of Outlook, configure Outlook to use the Exchange Server by opening Control Panel, double-clicking Mail, clicking either E-Mail Accounts (Outlook 2002) or Add (Outlook 2000), and then using the resulting dialog boxes to add a new Microsoft Exchange Server account.

Connecting to Printers and Shared Faxes   To connect to printers and shared faxes, complete the following steps:

1. Click Start, choose Run, type *sbssrv* in the Open box, and then press Enter (where *sbssrv* is the computer name of the Windows Small Business Server computer).

2. Double-click the printer or fax to which you want to connect and then click Yes to set up the printer.

3. On the first page of the Add Printer Wizard, specify whether to enable printing from MS-DOS–based programs and then click Next. If you chose to enable printing from MS-DOS–based programs, click Capture Printer Port, select the first available printer port (LPT1), click OK, and then Click Next.

4. If the wizard does not recognize your printer, you are asked to select the printer manufacturer and model. If the printer isn't listed, use the installation disk that came with your printer.

5. Type a name for the printer, specify whether you want to use it as the default printer, and then click Next.

6. If asked to print a test page, make a selection and then click Finish. If prompted, provide the location of the printer drivers. If you chose to connect to the shared fax printer, the first time you send a fax you are asked whether you want to install the Shared Fax Client so that you can monitor faxes as they're sent. Click Yes to install the Shared Fax Client, which also creates shortcuts on the Start menu for sending faxes.

Connecting Windows NT 4.0 Clients

To connect Windows NT 4.0 clients to a Windows Small Business Server 2003 network, configure TCP/IP, add the computers to the domain, install Windows Small Business Server clients, and connect to network printers and the shared fax service.

Configuring TCP/IP Settings and Domain Membership   To connect to the Windows Small Business Server 2003 computer, Windows NT 4.0 clients must first configure TCP/IP and create computer accounts in the Windows Small Business Server domain. Follow these steps:

1. On the client, open Control Panel and double-click Network.

2. Click the Protocols tab, select TCP/IP Protocol, and then click Properties.

3. Select the network adapter used to connect to the Windows Small Business Server computer, and then select Obtain An IP Address From A DHCP Server.

4. Click the WINS Address tab, and select the Enable DNS For Windows Resolution check box. Click OK, click Close, and then restart the computer. Once the connection process completes, Windows NT obtains an IP address and subnet mask from the DHCP server, as well as the IP addresses of the default gateway, DNS server, and WINS server.

5. Open Control Panel and double-click Network.

6. Click Change on the Identification tab to display the Identification Changes dialog box (Figure 12-11). Select Domain and type the domain name of the Windows Small Business Server. Select the Create A Computer Account In The Domain check box, type a domain user name and password, and then click OK. Close the Network dialog box, and then restart the computer when prompted.

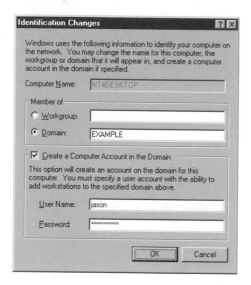

Figure 12-11. *The Identification Changes dialog box of a Windows NT 4.0 client.*

7. Open Control Panel, double-click Internet Options, and then click the Connections tab. (If you're still using Internet Explorer 2, install Internet Explorer 6 before performing this step.)

8. In the Dial-Up And Virtual Private Network Settings section of the Connections tab, specify if and when the client should establish a dial-up or VPN connection, and then click LAN Settings.

9. If you're using Windows Small Business Server 2003, Standard Edition, clear the Use A Proxy Server check box. If you're using Windows Small Business Server 2003, Premium Edition with ISA Server, select

the Use A Proxy Server check box, type the NetBIOS name of the Windows Small Business Server Computer in the Address box (**SBSSRV**, for example), type **8080** in the Port box (unless you changed it to something else), select the Bypass Proxy Server For Local Addresses check box, click OK, and then click OK again.

Installing Windows Small Business Server Client Software   After getting a Windows NT 4.0 client up and running on the network, you should perform some additional tasks before considering the system ready for use:

- **Install Service Pack 6a**   Service Pack 6a is required by many software packages. Download it from *http://www.microsoft.com*.

  Oddly enough, a clean installation of Windows NT 4.0 can't connect to the Microsoft Web site to download SP6a or install Internet Explorer 6. However, it can download Netscape (*http://www.netscape.com*) or Mozilla (*http://www.mozilla.org*), which can then be used to install updates.

  Note   Windows NT 4.0 clients prior to SP4 don't support Server Message Block (SMB) signing, and consequently can't access files (such as service packs) on the Windows Small Business Server 2003 computer, unless you disable SMB signing, as discussed in the "Disabling SMB Signing" section of this chapter.

- **Install the firewall client**   If you're using Windows Small Business Server 2003, Premium Edition, install the ISA Server firewall client by running Setup.exe from the *sbssrv*\Mspclnt share (where *sbssrv* is the computer name of the Windows Small Business Server computer).

- **Install Internet Explorer 6**   Installing Internet Explorer 6 ensures that the client can use the intranet (and the Internet) and install the Windows Small Business Server 2003 client applications properly. To install Internet Explorer 6, launch the Ie6setup.exe file from the *sbssrv*\ClientApps\Ie6 share on the Windows Small Business Server 2003 computer.

- **Install Active Directory client extensions for Windows NT 4.0**   These extensions provide stronger authentication (NTLM version 2), site awareness for businesses with branch offices, and Distributed Files System (DFS) client support. To install the Active Directory client extensions, launch the Dsclient.exe file from the Windows Small Business Server 2003 Disk 3 in the \SBSSUPPORT\ADCLIENT folder.

- **Install the latest updates from Windows Update**   Connect to the Windows Update site (*http://windowsupdate.microsoft.com*) on the client to download the latest security patches and updates.

- **Configure Outlook to work with Exchange**   Outlook 2003 won't install on Windows NT 4.0 computers, so you'll have to stick with earlier versions or Outlook Web Access (OWA). If you're going to use an earlier version of Outlook, configure Outlook to access the Exchange Server by opening Control Panel, double-clicking Mail, and clicking either E-Mail Accounts (for Outlook 2002) or Add (for Outlook 2000), and then using the resulting dialog boxes to add a new Microsoft Exchange Server account.

Note   Windows NT 4.0 doesn't support the Previous Versions client.

Connecting to Printers and Shared Faxes   To connect to printers and shared faxes, complete the following steps:

1. Click Start, choose Run, type *sbssrv* in the Open box, and then press Enter.

2. Double-click the printer or fax to which you want to connect and then click Yes to install the printer. If prompted, provide the location of the needed drivers. Click Yes to restart the computer if prompted.

Connecting Mac OS X Clients

Mac OS X is the most compatible Macintosh operating system ever. Out of the box, Mac OS X 10.2.x and Mac OS X 10.3.x can connect to file shares and printers hosted by a Windows Small Business Server 2003 computer and use Internet Explorer 5 for Mac OS X to participate on SharePoint intranet Web sites. Besides the built-in support, Microsoft Office is available on Mac OS X; Microsoft Entourage v.X 10.1.4 and later have native support for Microsoft Exchange; and there's a free Remote Desktop Connection client for Mac OS X available at *http://www.microsoft.com/mac*.

There are some caveats. First, the Windows Small Business Server domain shouldn't use a domain name with the .local top-level domain (for example, example .local) because it conflicts with the Rendezvous automatic network configuration feature of Mac OS X 10.2.x and later. (See the Real World sidebar "Can't Connect to .local Domains" for a somewhat awkward workaround.) Second, Mac OS X 10.2.x can't log on natively to the domain (though Mac OS X 10.3.x can)—instead it acts as a workgroup member (unless you use Thursby Software's ADmitMac). Even with these issues addressed, Mac OS X computers are still second-class citizens on a Windows Small Business Server 2003 network, with no support for the Previous Versions or Shared Fax clients, no remote administration capabilities, and limited support for the Remote Web Workplace.

Nonetheless, a few hurdles rarely stop a Mac user, so the following sections show how to use a Mac OS X 10.2.x computer with Windows file shares and shared printers, and how to disable SMB signing on the Windows Small Business Server network for Mac OS X 10.2.x clients (Mac OS X 10.3.x clients work fine with SMB signing enabled).

Connecting to Windows File Shares   To connect to a Windows file share from a computer running Mac OS X 10.2.x, use the following steps. (Mac OS X 10.3.x clients look slightly different.)

1. Disable SMB signing on the Windows Small Business Server, as described in the "Disabling SMB Signing" section of this chapter. (This isn't necessary for Mac OS X 10.3.x clients.)

2. Configure the computer to obtain its IP address using DHCP, if it doesn't already.

3. Select Connect To Server from the Go menu of Finder.

4. In the Connect To Server window shown in Figure 12-12, browse to the computer or type the address of the Windows file share, using one of the following formats:

smb://*fullyqualifieddomainname/sharename*

smb://*domain.name;servername/sharename*

For example, to connect to the Data share on the sbssrv.example.office computer in the example.office domain, type **smb://sbssrv.example.office/Data**.

Figure 12-12.   *Connecting to a Windows file share.*

5. Verify the workgroup or domain name, type an appropriate user name and password in the SMB/CIFS Filesystem Authentication dialog box, and then click OK. If you browsed to the computer, select a share and then click OK. The Windows file share appears on the desktop.

Real World   Can't Connect to .local Domains

Apple computers running Mac OS X version 10.2 and later support automatic network configuration using a technology called Rendezvous. This is all fine and good until you try to use one of these systems on a domain that uses the .local DNS extension (which Windows Small Business Server 2003 uses by default). Simply put, the Mac system isn't able to connect to any Windows systems via Server Message Blocks (SMBs)—the default file sharing protocol of Windows.

To remedy this situation, install a newer version of Mac OS X that fixes this issue (if one is ever released), read article 107800 in Apple's Knowledge Archive (*http://search.info.apple.com*), or use the following procedure (unless you want to follow the advice from Microsoft and rename your domain to some other extension, such as .office or .work):

1. Open the Terminal program located in the Utilities folder, which opens a full-fledged UNIX command line. (OK, technically it's not UNIX; it's Darwin—an open-source variant of FreeBSD.)

2. Change to the /etc/resolver/ directory by typing the following commands, pressing Enter after each line:

   Cd /

   Cd etc/resolver

3. Log on as the root (administrator) user by typing **sudo tcsh**, and then typing the administrator password for the system.

4. Edit the local file using the text editor of your choice. To use pico (a simple text editor), type **pico local**.

5. Replace the listed *nameserver* IP address with the correct IP address of a DNS server on the .local domain that you want the Mac OS X system to access.

6. Replace the port number with 53.

7. Save the file by pressing Ctrl+X, and then Y, and then Enter.

Connecting to Networked Printers   The easiest way to print to a printer shared by a Windows computer from a Mac OS X 10.2.x client is to install Print Services For UNIX on the Windows Small Business Server computer and then print using IP printing. (Mac OS X 10.3.x clients can connect directly to Windows print servers and don't need this section.) To do so, complete the following steps:

1. On the Windows Small Business Server computer, open Add/Remove Programs and then click Add/ Remove Windows Components.

2. In the Windows Components Wizard, select the Other Network File And Print Services option, click Details, select Print Services For Unix, and then click OK. Click Next to install the component.

3. On the Mac OS X client, open the Applications folder, and then open the Utilities folder.

4. Double-click Print Center to open the Printer List dialog box.

5. Click Add.

6. Choose IP Printing from the box at the top of the sheet shown in Figure 12-13.

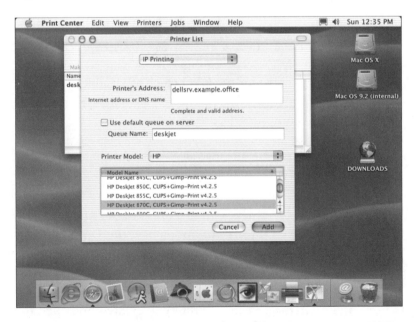

Figure 12-13.   *Connecting to a Windows print server using an LPR connection on a Mac OS X 10.2.x system.*

7. Type the IP address or DNS name of the print server.

8. To specify a printer on the print server, clear the Use Default Queue On Server check box and type the share name of the printer in the Queue Name box.

9. Select the appropriate printer driver from the Printer Model box. If a driver isn't available from the printer manufacturer, try using Gimp-Print (*http://gimp-print.sourceforge.net*), though these drivers are unsupported.

10. Click Add when you're finished. The printer is then added to the list of printers available on the Mac OS X client system.

Disabling SMB Signing   To use Mac OS X 10.2.x on a Windows Small Business Server 2003 network, you need to first disable SMB signing on the domain. (This is unnecessary for Mac OS X 10.3.x systems.) To do so, complete the following steps:

1. Open the Group Policy Management console in the Administrative Tools folder on the Start menu.

2. In the console tree, navigate to Domains, then to example.local (or whatever the domain is called), and then to Group Policy Objects.

3. Create a new Group Policy Object (GPO) for the settings by right-clicking the Group Policy Objects container, choosing New from the shortcut menu, typing a name for the GPO (such as Disable SMB Signing), and then clicking OK.

Tip   Don't make changes to the default GPOs—instead create new GPOs with your settings. That way you can easily undo your changes by disabling the GPO. Use the Group Policy Results and Group Policy Modeling tools to ensure that your GPO is being applied properly.

4. Link the new GPO to the Domain Controllers container by dragging it from the Group Policy Objects container into the Domain Controllers container. Click OK when asked whether you want to create the link.

5. Select the Domain Controllers container. On the Linked Group Policy Objects tab (Figure 12-14), select the GPO you created and click the Move Link To Top button to ensure that the GPO overrides the settings in the Default Domain Controllers Policy. The GPO you created appears at the top of the list, with a link order of one (the lower the

link order, the later the policy is processed, with each policy overwriting any preceding policies that conflict).

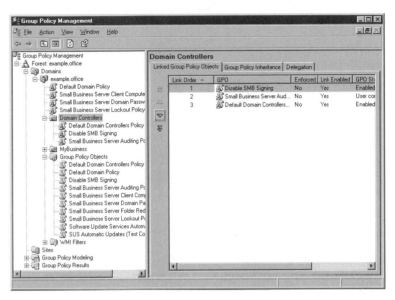

Figure 12-14.   *The Linked Group Policy Objects tab showing the Disable SMB Signing GPO processed last (and thus having the highest priority).*

6. Right-click the GPO you created and choose Edit from the shortcut menu. This opens the Group Policy Object Editor.

7. Navigate to Computer Configuration, Windows Settings, Security Settings, Local Policies, and finally Security Options (Figure 12-15).

8. Double-click the Microsoft Network Server: Digitally Sign Communications (Always) policy.

9. In the Microsoft Network Server: Digitally Sign Communications (Always) dialog box, select the Define This Policy check box, choose Disabled, and then click OK. Close the Group Policy Object Editor window.

10. Open a command prompt window and type **gpupdate** to refresh Group Policy.

Tip   To verify that the policy is being applied to the Windows Small Business Server 2003 computer, right-click the Group Policy Results container in the Group Policy Management console, choose Group Policy Results Wizard from the shortcut menu, and then use the wizard to create a report detailing which settings are applied to the server.

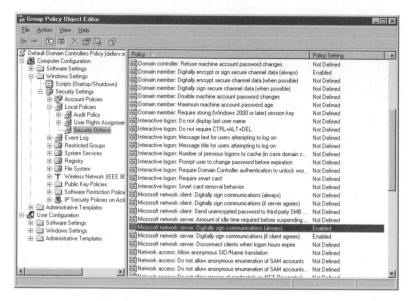

Figure 12-15. *The Security Options container of the Group Policy Objects Editor window.*

Using the Remote Web Workplace

Windows Small Business Server 2003 automatically creates a special Web site on the server called the Remote Web Workplace that provides access to Exchange e-mail (via Outlook Web Access), the SharePoint intranet site, Windows Small Business Server usage reports, Remote Desktop connections, and a couple of methods for connecting to the internal network from across the Internet.

The Remote Web Workplace is available on the local network to all clients with correct TCP/IP settings, Internet Explorer 5 or later, and a valid domain user account—no other connection steps are required. The Remote Web Workplace can also be accessed by properly authenticated users on the Internet, provided that you selected Remote Web Workplace in the Web Services Configuration page of the Configure E-mail and Internet Connection Wizard.

More Info For more information about the Configure E-Mail and Internet Connection Wizard, see Chapter 6.

Following is a brief overview of how to use the Remote Web Workplace:

1. To open the Remote Web Workplace, launch Internet Explorer and type **https://*sbssrv.example.local*/Remote** in the Address bar (where *sbssrv.example.local* is the DNS address of the Windows Small Business Server computer). If you're connecting from across the Internet, use the registered domain name used by the Small Business Server (or the IP address of the firewall device if there isn't a registered domain name that refers to the Small Business Server computer).

2. On the Remote Web Workplace logon page (Figure 12-16), type your user name and password (you must be a member of the Mobile Users group), select the connection speed, clear the I'm Using A Public Or Shared Computer check box if you're using a secure computer, and then click Log On.

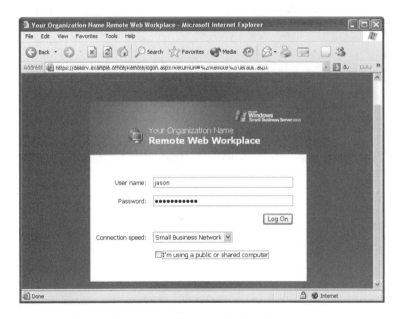

Figure 12-16.   *The Remote Web Workplace logon page.*

3. On the main Remote Web Workplace page (Figure 12-17), click the link that corresponds to the action you want to perform. (Some links might not work over an Internet connection, depending on which services you allow through the firewall.)

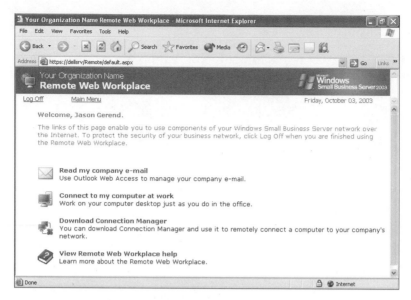

Figure 12-17. *The Remote Web Workplace page.*

The Remote Web Workplace page can include the following options:

- **Read My Company E-Mail**   This opens Outlook Web Access (OWA) to display your Exchange folders, as shown in Figure 12-18. Outlook Web Access provides almost all the functionality of the full-fledged Outlook 2003 application, allowing you to work with your Exchange folders as you would normally. You can also log on directly to OWA by typing **https://*sbssrv.example.local*/Exchange** in the Address bar (where *sbssrv.example.local* is the DNS address of the Windows Small Business Server computer).

- **Connect to Server Desktops**   This displays a list of servers on the network to which you can connect via Remote Desktop, and is only available if you log on using an account that's a member of the Domain Administrators group. Select a computer (assuming it supports Remote Desktop connections), click Optional Settings to change the connection behavior, and then click Connect.

- **Connect To My Computer At Work**   This displays a list of computers on the network to which you can connect via Remote Desktop. (This option is called Connect To Client Desktops if you log on using an administrator account.) Select your computer (assuming it supports Remote Desktop connections), click Optional Settings to change the connection behavior, and then click Connect.

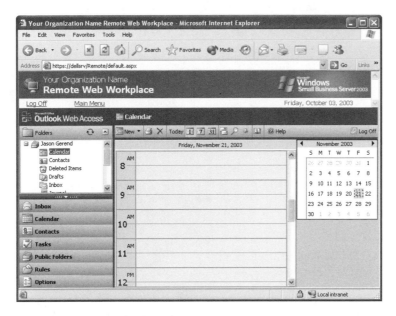

Figure 12-18. *Outlook Web Access.*

- **Use My Company's Internal Web Site** This displays the SharePoint intranet site (accessible to internal clients via *http://companyweb*). For information about SharePoint, see Chapter 17.

- **View Server Usage Reports** This displays the current usage data for the server, as discussed in Chapter 20, "Monitoring and Fine-Tuning Performance."

- **Download Connection Manager** This downloads Connection Manager, which installs a secure VPN connection to the Windows Small Business Server.

- **Configure Your Computer To Use Outlook Via Internet** This displays instructions for setting up Outlook 2003 to connect to the Exchange Server over the Internet without a VPN connection (via RPC over HTTP).

- **View Remote Web Workplace Help** This displays the Help pages for Remote Web Workplace.

Note Instruct users always to log off when they're finished using Remote Web Workplace by clicking the Log Off link.

Managing Computers from the Server

Most aspects of Windows XP and Windows 2000 clients (and some aspects of Windows NT 4.0) can be easily managed across the network from a Windows Small Business Server 2003 computer using the Server Management console. The following sections cover assigning applications (including the ISA Server firewall client) to computers, creating a Remote Connection disk for VPN access, remotely managing client computers and settings, as well as removing computers from the network.

More Info   For information about using the Microsoft Baseline Security Analyzer tool to scan client systems for security issues and missing updates, see Chapter 6.

Real World   Virus and Spam Strategies

Viruses and spam are two of the biggest hazards for networks today. To mitigate these risks, maintain consistent backups, install software updates as they are released, keep on top of network security, and take the following actions.

Install self-updating antivirus software on the Windows Small Business Server 2003 server as well as on all clients. The best way to do this is to use a small-business antivirus package that includes client, server, and Exchange Server virus scanning. This package is often no more expensive than purchasing consumer antivirus software for each client, and it provides additional scanning and management capabilities. Users of Windows Small Business Server 2003, Premium Edition, might want to evaluate ISA Server third-party antivirus and spam filtering plug-ins. Companies that have a lot of remote users connecting to their SharePoint site should also investigate SharePoint antivirus software.

To reduce the effects of spam on your business, test the built-in spam filtering capabilities of Outlook 2003 in your environment By default, Outlook 2003 blocks HTML e-mail messages from connecting to the Internet without your expressed permission, which might confuse some users but prevents spammers from confirming an e-mail address. Outlook also makes it easy to set up lists of blocked senders and safe senders, which can be uploaded to Exchange Server, though once again, this might require some user training. If these features don't make a large enough impact, supplement or replace them with third-party spam filtering software on the Exchange Server or the client, or both.

Assigning Applications to Client Computers

Windows Small Business Server provides a way to easily assign applications to client computers running Windows 2000 Professional, Windows XP Professional, Windows XP Tablet PC Edition, or Windows XP Media Center Edition (additional servers should install software manually or by using Group Policy). To do so, complete the following steps:

1. Open the Server Management console on the Windows Small Business Server 2003 computer.

2. Click Computers to open the Client Computers container, shown in Figure 12-19.

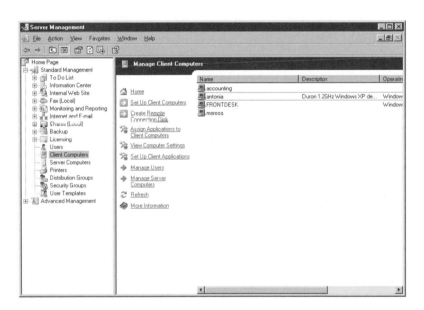

Figure 12-19.   *The Client Computers container of the Server Management console.*

3. Click Assign Applications To Client Computers, and then click Next in the first page of the Assign Applications Wizard.

4. On the Client Computers page, select the computers to which you want to assign applications and then click Add. Click Next to continue.

5. On the Client Applications page (Figure 12-20), select which applications you want to assign to the specified computers. Click Next when you're finished.

- To allow users to change which applications are installed during Client Setup select the During Client Setup, Allow The Selected Applications To Be Modified check box.

- To force the client computer to log off once Client Setup is complete, select the After Client Setup Is Finished, Log Off The Client Computer check box.

- To change whether Windows Small Business Server configures such settings as Outlook Profiles and Internet Explorer settings, click Advanced.

- Click Edit Applications to edit or add to the list of available applications. See the Real World sidebar "Adding Your Own Applications" in this chapter for information about how to add other applications (including the ISA Server firewall client) to the Client Applications list.

More Info Refer to the "Viewing and Modifying Client Computer Settings" section later in this chapter for information about changing client settings such as Internet Explorer Favorites.

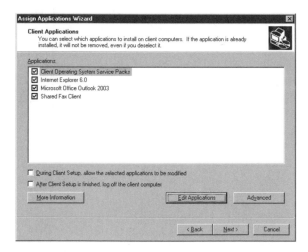

Figure 12-20. *The Client Applications page of the Assign Applications Wizard.*

6. On the Mobile Client And Offline Use page, check the Install Connection Manager and Install ActiveSync 3.7 check boxes to facilitate the client computers connecting remotely via VPN connection and synchronizing Microsoft Pocket PC and Microsoft SmartPhone devices.

(You must run the Remote Connection Wizard before Connection Manager will work.) Click Next to continue.

7. Review the settings and then click Finish. The next time a domain user logs on to the computer to which applications are assigned, the applications automatically install. For programs that you manually added to the list of client applications, a shortcut to the installation program is placed on the desktop instead.

Real World   Adding Your Own Applications

Windows Small Business Server 2003 makes it easy to assign service packs, Internet Explorer 6, Outlook 2003, and the Shared Fax Client to client computers, but this isn't exactly a comprehensive list of applications. In fact, there is a very important omission for users of Windows Small Business Server 2003 Premium Edition—the ISA Server Firewall Client. To add applications to this list, complete the following steps:

1. Perform an administrative installation of the desired program to a new folder in the C:\ClientApps folder on the Windows Small Business Server computer, or copy the setup files to a new folder in the C:\ClientApps folder (assuming the \ClientApps folder is located on the C:\ drive). To perform an administrative installation of Microsoft Office, for example, use the **setup.exe /a** command.

   The ISA Server Firewall Client installation files are already shared as \mspclnt on Windows Small Business Server 2003, Premium Edition installations, and don't need to be copied anywhere else.

2. Start the Assign Applications Wizard.

3. On the Client Applications page of the Assign Applications Wizard, click Edit Applications, which displays the first page of the Set Up Client Applications Wizard. Click Next.

4. On the Available Applications page, click Add.

5. In the Application Information dialog box, shown in Figure 12-21, type the application name and network path, including any setup parameters (such as those that automate setup), and enclose the path in quotation marks. For the ISA Server Firewall Client, type "*sbssrv*\mspclnt\setup.exe" (where *sbssrv* is the computer name of the Windows Small Business Server computer). Click OK.

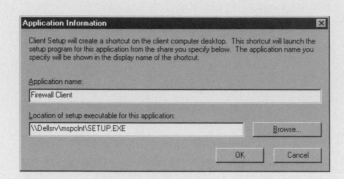

Figure 12-21. *The Application Information dialog box.*

6. If Windows Small Business Server asks whether it can change the permissions of the folder to Read and Execute, click Yes.

7. Add or remove any additional programs, click Next, and then click Finish to return to the Assign Applications Wizard.

Under the Hood   How Applications Are Assigned

Windows Small Business Server 2003 assigns applications to computers using a logon script (SBS_LOGIN_SCRIPT.BAT) that is assigned to all domain users. When a user logs on, the script is run and the Windows Small Business Server client setup program starts (*sbssrv*\Clients\Setup\Setup.exe). The client setup program then parses the XML response file (Apps.dat) located in the *sbssrv*\clients\response*computername* folder (where *sbssrv* is the name of the Windows Small Business Server 2003 computer, and *computername* is the name of the computer the user is logging on to). This XML file provides the location of the setup program for each assigned application, as well as any setup parameters. The Apps.dat file can be edited to force a reboot after an application is installed (change the *needsReboot*="*0*" value to "*1*").

Using the Windows Small Business Server 2003 method of application deployment is the most painless way to deploy applications in Windows Small Business Server 2003; however, the Software Installation And Maintenance feature of Group Policy is also present, and can be used by savvy administrators (though be careful when mixing the two). For in-depth coverage of software deployment using Group Policy, refer to *Microsoft Windows Server 2003 Administrator's Companion* (Microsoft Press).

Creating a Remote Connection Disk

Windows Small Business Server 2003 can create a Remote Connection disk to automate the process of connecting a client computer to the Windows Small Business Server 2003 computer using a VPN connection. (This is the same as installing Connection Manager on a client.)

More Info   For more information about VPN connections, see Chapter 15, "Managing Connectivity."

To use this feature, which requires that you've already run the Remote Access Wizard, complete the following steps:

1. In the Client Computers container of the Server Management console, click Create Remote Connection Disk.

2. Click Next in the first page of the Create Remote Connection Disk Wizard, specify the floppy drive to use as well as the number of disks to create, and then click Next.

3. Insert a blank floppy disk into the Windows Small Business Server computer and click Finish.

Tip   You can turn the Remote Connection disk into a Remote Connection CD, USB Key, or E-mail by taking the contents of the disk and putting it on the media of your choice—the total size is less than 600 KB. Or you can open the Remote Web Workplace and click Download Connection Manager to download Connection Manager.

To use the Remote Connection disk on a client computer, insert the floppy disk, run the Setup.exe program, and click Yes when asked whether you want to install the connection to Small Business Server. To use the new VPN connection, double-click the Connect To Small Business Server icon on the desktop, type the appropriate user name and password (Figure 12-22), and then click Connect.

Note   The first time you double-click the Connect To Small Business Server icon on a Windows 98 machine, you'll be asked to install some components. Click Yes, insert the Windows 98 CD-ROM when prompted, and then click Yes when prompted to reboot the computer.

Note   The Remote Connection disk won't work on Windows NT 4.0 systems unless Internet Explorer 5.0 or later is installed.

Figure 12-22. *The Connect To Small Business Server window.*

Viewing and Modifying Client Computer Settings

Windows Small Business Server 2003 makes viewing and changing the settings it applies to client computers on the network easy. To view or change the settings, open the Server Management console, click Computers, and click View Computer Settings. In the View Or Change Client Computer Settings dialog box, perform the appropriate tasks:

- To view the settings for a computer, click the plus sign next to the computer name, and then click the plus sign next to Assigned Applications, Client Setup Settings, or Client Setup Configuration Options (Figure 12-23).

- To add applications to a specific computer, right-click Assigned Applications under the appropriate computer and choose Run Assigned Applications Wizard.

- To unassign or reinstall an application on a computer, click the plus sign (+) next to Assigned Applications, right-click the application, and choose either Unassign This Application or Reinstall from the shortcut menu. Unassigning an application doesn't uninstall it.

- To toggle Client Setup Settings or Client Setup Configuration Options on or off, right-click the setting or option and choose Change from the shortcut menu.

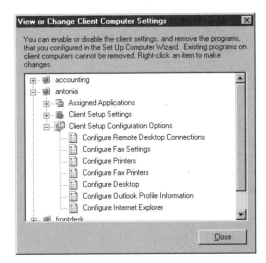

Figure 12-23.   *The View Or Change Client Computers Settings dialog box.*

Under the Hood   Settings Applied to Client Computers

Besides installing applications, the Small Business Server Network Configuration Wizard configures the following settings:

- **Internet Explorer**   Sets the Home Page to *http://companyweb* and adds links to the Favorites menu for a Windows Small Business Server help page, the official Microsoft Small Business Server Web site, a remote server management page, and a remote e-mail access page (Outlook Web Access).

- **Outlook Profile Settings**   Configures Outlook to use Exchange Server for the default e-mail account, installs the fax mail transport allowing MAPI applications (including Outlook) to send faxes, and configures manual synchronization of offline folders for computers that are assigned Connection Manager.

- **Desktop Settings**   Creates a My Network Places link to the /General Documents folder in the SharePoint Intranet Web site (*http://companyweb/General Documents*).

- **Fax Printer**   Installs a fax printer so that the client computer can send faxes by "printing" to the Windows Small Business Server Shared Fax service.

- **Printers** If a single printer is published in Active Directory, the printer is installed on the client and made the default printer, unless a local printer is installed on the client. If multiple printers are published in Active Directory, all are installed, but no default printer is specified.

- **Fax Configuration Information** Configures the client fax software with the default sender information from the server so that cover sheets automatically contain the correct sender information.

- **Remote Desktop** Enables Remote Desktop and Remote Assistance on the client computer.

Remotely Managing Computers and Viewing Event Logs

Checking the health of client computers can be a time-consuming task when it involves physical visits to each machine. Windows Small Business Server 2003 reduces the time involved by allowing you to remotely check event logs, open the Computer Management console, and even establish a Remote Desktop connection to client computers, all from within the Server Management console.

To perform these tasks, open the Client Computers or Server Computers container in the Server Management console, select the computer, and then use the following list to perform certain tasks. Unless otherwise noted, these tasks can be performed only on computers running Windows XP Professional, Windows XP Tablet PC Edition, Windows XP Media Center Edition, Windows Server 2003, and Windows 2000.

- To open Computer Management on the client computer, click Manage Computer. The Computer Management console provides access to event logs, Device Manager, Services, Shared Folders, local users and groups, and other important tools.

- To go straight to the event logs, click View Event Logs.

- To establish a Remote Desktop connection to the computer, giving you complete control over the computer, click Connect To Computer Via Terminal Services. This feature doesn't work on computers running Windows 2000 Professional.

- To go straight to the Services console of a selected server computer, click View Services. This feature appears for server computers.

Tip   You can use the Server Management console to remotely perform the following tasks on Windows NT 4.0 computers: check Event Logs; start and stop services; and to a limited extent, use the Computer Management console.

More complex administrative tasks can be accomplished using Windows Management Instrumentation (WMI), although learning WMI is worth the time only if you do a *lot* of remote administration. Use the Scriptomatic Tool (available at *http://www.microsoft.com/technet/scriptcenter*) to get started, which makes it easy to create simple scripts that remotely obtain useful information from client computers running most versions of Windows. You can also use the Windows Management Instrumentation Console (WMIC), a relatively easy-to-use command-line interface for WMI, from within Windows XP or Windows Small Business Server 2003. (Type **wmic /?** at a command prompt for more information.)

Removing Computers from the Network

To permanently remove a computer from the network, delete the associated computer account by completing the following steps:

1. In the Server Management console, click Client Computers or Server Computers.

2. Select the computer you want to remove and then click Remove Computer From Network. Click Yes when prompted. This deletes the computer account in Active Directory.

3. On the client, open System in Control Panel.

4. On Windows XP and Windows Server 2003 clients, click the Computer Name tab and then click Change. On Windows 2000 clients, click the Network Identification tab and then click Properties.

5. Select Workgroup (Figure 12-24), type a suitable workgroup name (**WORKGROUP** is always popular), and then click OK. Reboot the computer when prompted.

Deleting the computer account prevents the computer from connecting to the domain. To reinstate the computer on the network, create a new computer account (see the "Connecting Computers to the Network" section of this chapter), and then use the Small Business Server Network Configuration Wizard on the client computer.

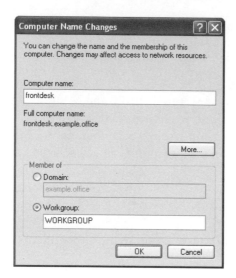

Figure 12-24. *The Computer Name Changes dialog box.*

Note To remove computers running other operating systems such as Mac OS X 10.2.x that don't create computer accounts in Active Directory, simply configure them to no longer log on to the domain.

Removing Windows 98 and Windows Me Clients from the Network

To remove a Windows 98 or Windows Me computer from the network, open Control Panel on the client, double-click Network, select Client For Microsoft Networks and then click Properties. Clear the Log On To Windows NT Domain check box, and then click OK. Windows 98 or Windows Me doesn't use computer accounts, so there's no need to delete one.

To reinstate a Windows 98 or Windows Me computer, simply reselect the Log On To Windows NT Domain check box in the Client For Microsoft Network Properties dialog box.

Removing Windows NT 4.0 Clients from the Network

To remove a Windows NT 4.0 computer from the network, delete its computer account as described previously, open Control Panel on the client, double-click Network, click Change on the Identification tab, select Workgroup, type a workgroup name, and then click OK. Reboot the computer when prompted.

To reinstate a Windows NT 4.0 computer, double-click Network in Control Panel, click Change on the Identification tab, select Domain, select the Create A Computer Account In The Domain check box, type your user name and password, and then click OK. Click OK to close the Network dialog box and then restart the computer when prompted.

Summary

Managing computers on a network can be a lot of work, but Windows Small Business Server 2003 reduces the effort involved by streamlining the process of connecting computers to the network, deploying software, remotely managing computers, and connecting from across the Internet.

The next part of this book addresses advanced tasks, starting with the setup and use of Microsoft Exchange Server.

Chapter 13
Backing Up and Restoring Data

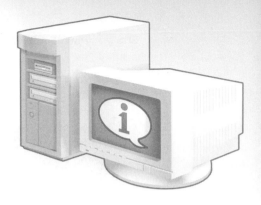

Backing up the data on your network is a chore that everyone knows is important but which all too many ignore or don't take seriously. Microsoft Windows Small Business Server 2003 includes a dedicated backup utility that makes the task simple and straightforward. Although businesses at the upper end of the range covered by Windows Small Business Server might find they need a more full-featured backup program with all the bells and whistles, most businesses will find the included Backup Utility quite adequate, especially given the integration into the Server Management console.

Backup Terminology and Methods

You'll need to understand a number of different terms when dealing with backups. Here's a short list of the most important ones:

- **Backup device**   The hardware device on which backups are saved.
- **Backup media**   The actual tape, disk, or DVD on which the backup is stored.
- **Full backup**   What it says—this backup includes *all* files in a given selection set.
- **Incremental backup**   All the files in a given selection set that have changed since the last full or incremental backup. To restore, you need the last full backup and all the incremental backups since then.
- **Differential backup**   All the files in a given selection set that have changed since the last full backup. To restore, you need the last full backup and the latest differential backup.

Backup Devices

Windows Small Business Server supports writing to either a tape device or a hard drive. The hard-drive backup option includes both fixed and removable hard drives. There is no support, however, for using a CD or DVD writer as a backup device. In theory, you could use a CD or DVD device by using third-party software that makes them appear to be just another hard drive, albeit a removable one.

Caution Windows Small Business Server 2003 does not directly support using writeable CD or DVD drives as backup devices. Using these drives as backup devices requires third-party software that is designed for consumer use to make the CD or DVD drive appear as a hard drive, allowing the Backup Utility to use it. Using consumer-grade software for your backup strategy is not tested on Windows Small Business Server 2003 and is not a supported scenario. You should carefully assess the risks to your business and make an informed decision before using a solution based on CDs or DVDs.

The preferred backup device has always been tape of one variety or another. Tape drives are not cheap; and large, fast tape drives are very definitely not cheap. But tape is a proven technology that has many advantages, including portability, easy off site storage, and a predictable life span. It does, however, have some very real disadvantages—probably the most important is that it is slower than the alternatives. This can create a problem with the length of time a backup takes, as well as the time to recover a specific file or files.

The alternatives to tape have their own problems, however. Extra hard drives, even removable ones, are not ideal for off site storage, and if you use any sort of rotation, they aren't exactly cheap, either. CDs simply don't hold enough any more. And even writeable DVDs really don't hold enough for most backups without having to span multiple DVDs, and, most importantly, they are not a supported solution.

Caution Although CDs and DVDs seem like the sort of backup media that should last forever, recent studies show that their actual data-integrity life is really quite short. They should not be used for long-term archival storage. They have sufficient life for ordinary backups that will be rotated and replaced on a regular schedule, but they are best *not* depended on for longer than a year.

Backup Media

Whatever backup device you choose, you will need to have sufficient media for it to manage a full schedule of backups. Don't stint here. If the price for a batch of DDS4 or DLT tapes seems too good to be true, it probably is.

Once you've decided on your backup strategy, you'll have a good idea of the number of media you'll need to support it, whether tapes or disks. Keep in mind that media *does* fail, and there will be times you want or need to do something special, so order accordingly. If your backup strategy calls for 25 tapes used in rotation, you'll probably want 30 or 35, plus a couple of cleaning tapes. Backup strategies are covered in the next section, "Designing a Backup Strategy."

Before you spend your money on a batch of tapes, buy one of the brand you are considering and test it. And test it some more. Some brands of tapes do have problems with some tape drives. You want to make sure there aren't any incompatibilities before you spend your money on a bunch of tapes.

Designing a Backup Strategy

To effectively back up a network, you must plan your approach to this complex task. Backups are more complicated than simply putting a tape in the drive and starting up the software. Your backup strategy should address all the following questions:

- How much data do you have to back up?
- How much time do you have to perform backups?
- How often should you back up the data?
- Who is going to be responsible for seeing that backups are completed?
- How many tapes (or other media) do you plan to use?

Even if you use a fairly simple and straightforward tape rotation schedule, you'll want to spend some time answering each of these questions to make sure your strategy answers them appropriately for your environment.

- **How much data**   With Windows Small Business Server, the standard backup strategy backs up *all* the files on your server. Make sure that you plan for the amount of growth you expect when you decide what backup hardware to use. Ideally, you want a tape type that will store all your files on a single tape. Or, if that's not possible, you'll need to buy a tape library that holds several tapes and can automatically change tapes as needed.

- **How much time**   The total amount of data you need to back up, divided by the effective backup speed your backup device can support, yields the total time your backup will take. Ideally the backup should happen during a relatively quiet time on your network to reduce the overall load on the network and your server. Different tape technologies yield different speeds, but also have different costs. Balance your need for speed with your aversion to spending money to get the best tape drive you can afford.

- **How often**   This is simple, really. How much data can you and your business afford to lose? In the event of the death of a server, you'll need to restore from your most recent backup onto your new server. If the last time you did a backup was a week ago, you've just lost a week's worth of work. Realistically, most businesses should plan on a daily backup.

- **Who**   Who is responsible for doing backups? And more importantly, who is responsible when that person is out sick, on vacation, or out of town? Don't count on a single person being the only one who is responsible. Make sure that at least one other person knows the routine for changing tapes and handling the offsite backup plan, and so on.

- **How many tapes** This will depend on how often you overwrite your tapes, and how many days are in your rotation. We'll go over some more details in the next section, "Backup Schedules."

Backup Schedules

It sometimes seems like there are as many different backup schedules as there are system administrators, but it really isn't quite that complicated. Your backup schedule should meet the needs of your company for data protection and disaster recovery, but should also recognize the reality of the resources available.

Frequency

For most businesses, a full *daily* backup is the core of their backup schedule. Once a week you should plan on archiving your backup tape—that is, removing it from the daily rotation and storing it someplace safe.

Why once a day? Because most businesses can't really afford to lose more than a day or two's worth of work. In the event of a disaster, you might need to restore your most current backup, or even the one before that if there are problems. If you're comfortable with losing up to a week's work, you could do once-a-week backups. But if there's a problem with that most recent tape, you've lost two week's work.

Reusing Tapes

Magnetic tape is a reusable medium. You can write on it repeatedly, and read it repeatedly without noticeable problem, up to the limits of the particular type of tape. Each type of tape has an expected life span. Most system administrators plan on throwing away their tapes at about half that life span. Nothing is more frustrating when you're in the middle of trying to restore a file or a whole directory than discovering that your backup has failed and you have to go to an earlier tape.

For most scenarios, a simple tape rotation of individual tapes for each day of the week, with a once-a-week archive tape, makes a reasonable compromise between simplicity and security. In this scenario you have a "Monday" tape, a "Tuesday" tape, and so on. Each week you put the Monday tape in the drive on Monday morning when you pull out the previous tape. Then on Tuesday morning, when you come in, you swap the Monday tape for Tuesday.

Whereas this simple one-week rotation is adequate for many scenarios, many businesses use a two-week or four-week rotation. This has the advantage of making it easier to keep the most current tapes readily available while still having an off-site archive set that is only a week old.

Archive and Off-Site Storage

In addition to maintaining a daily backup, it is important to keep archival and off-site backups that allow you to recover in the event of a total disaster, or to recover to a point in time. You might well have legal requirements that require you to keep archival tapes also.

Why off-site storage? Well, if your business burns down, or is damaged by a hurricane or earthquake, it's a real mess. But if your only backup copies are in the burned-out server room, it's a disaster. There are commercial services that will pick up your backup tapes weekly (or as often as you want) and store them in a secure facility. They're not inexpensive, but they do provide a reliable, secure, and predictable service.

> **Tip**   Off-site storage is an essential part of any backup and recovery strategy. If your business really can't afford to use a commercial off-site storage service, you can get some of the same benefits by simply having someone take the archive tape home every week. It's not as good as having it in a secure storage facility, but it does protect from the most common disasters. It is essential, however, that you treat this as a serious responsibility and standardize how it is done if you're to be able to depend on it in an emergency.

Which tape should you send off-site? Well, not yesterday's! That's the one you're most likely to need, and need in a hurry. If your pickup day for tapes is Wednesday, send off the Wednesday tape, and put a new tape in your rotation on Wednesday. Keep at least a month's worth of weekly backups off-site, and then have them bring back the tape from a month ago, and put it back into your rotation.

Using Shadow Copies to Supplement Backups

Windows Small Business Server enables Volume Shadow Copy automatically on the drive that houses the Users share and sets save points or snapshots twice a day. You can enable Volume Shadow Copy on additional volumes as appropriate to your business. This allows users to quickly recover to a previous version of a lost, damaged, or deleted file without administrative involvement and without having to load up yesterday's backup tape and restore it.

If you have the disk space, and your comfort window for lost data is not very high, you can increase the frequency of scheduled snapshots to more often than twice a day. Keep in mind, however, that disk space is finite. For most situations, the default setting of twice a day is sufficient.

> **More Info**   For more information about enabling and configuring volume shadow copies, see Chapter 8, "Storage Management."

Backing Up Your Data

Windows Small Business Server provides an excellent wizard that configures and executes backups. For most users and situations, using the provided wizard is definitely the way to go. You can also manually run Backup Utility (located by accessing Start, All Programs, Accessories, System Tools folder) for a greater set of options and choices. However, for daily full backups, automatically scheduled, using the wizard is the way to go.

> **Real World** **Test Your Backups!**
>
> A wise and perspicacious system administrator once explained to me that there were only two kinds of backups: ones that had been tested and verified, and ones that were worthless. Strong words, but worthy of some serious consideration. Magnetic tapes are not a perfect medium and they are subject to all kinds of possible errors and corruption. Until you have actually taken your backup tape and restored it, you don't actually know you can. Although in the real world not every single backup will get a full restore test, you really should test a full restore regularly, and a partial restore of a randomly selected set of files and folders more often, at least once a week and on a different day each week. Also check the Event Log and all your backup logs for any error messages that Backup Utility has generated. By carefully monitoring logs, and regularly checking the integrity of your tapes by restoring from them, you have at least reduced the likelihood of undetected problems causing a failed restore.

Configuring the Backup Utility

The first time you use the Backup Configuration Wizard for Windows Small Business Server, you will also be configuring your regular backup schedule. To get started, click Backup in the Server Management console. If you haven't yet configured Backup, your details pane will look like Figure 13-1.

Figure 13-1. *The Backup Utility in Server Management console, before configuring.*

To configure the Backup Utility, complete the following steps:

1. Click Configure Backup to start the Backup Configuration Wizard shown in Figure 13-2. Click Next.

2. On the Backup Location page, set the backup location, as shown in Figure 13-3. A tape drive is the preferred backup location. If you're backing up to a hard drive, you can browse to find the location, or

simply type the location in the Store BackUp Files At This Location box. Click Next.

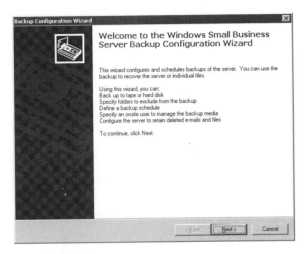

Figure 13-2. *The Backup Configuration Wizard.*

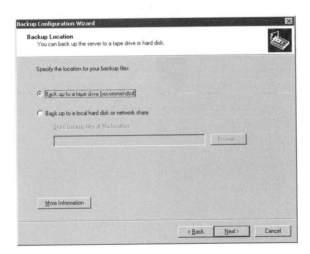

Figure 13-3. *The Backup Location page.*

3. On the Backup Data Summary page, the default is for everything to be backed up. If you want to exclude certain folders from the standard backup, click Exclude Folders to open the Exclude Folders dialog box, shown in Figure 13-4.

4. Add folders to the exclusion by clicking the Add Folder button, or highlight an existing exclusion and click Remove to add it back into the backup set. Click OK to return to the Backup Data Summary page. If you've excluded any folders, they will now show on the list.

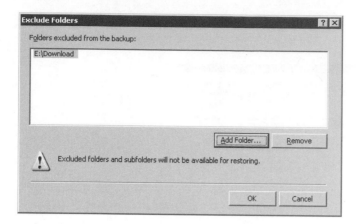

Figure 13-4. *The Exclude Folders dialog box.*

5. Click Calculate Folder Sizes to update the display to show how much space you've excluded. Click Next.

6. On the Define Backup Schedule page, shown in Figure 13-5, the default schedule calls for backups to be performed Monday through Friday evenings at 11 P.M. Make any changes you need to here, and click Next.

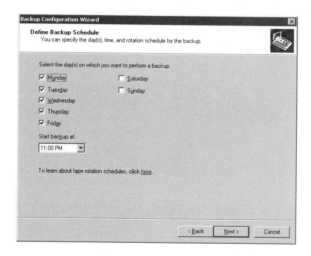

Figure 13-5. *The Define Backup Schedule page.*

7. If you are backing up to a tape, the Onsite Tape Changer page appears (Figure 13-6). (If you're backing up to a hard drive, you won't see this page, so skip to the next step.) Designate the person who will be responsible for changing tapes, known as the Onsite Tape Changer, and select the time when he or she will get an automatic reminder to change the tape. You can also send this person a monthly reminder to clean the tape drive by selecting the Send A Monthly Tape Drive Cleaning Reminder check box. Click Next.

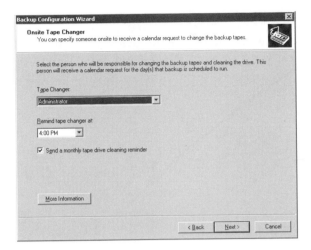

Figure 13-6.   *The Onsite Tape Changer page.*

Tip   Windows Small Business Server will automatically remind you to do a monthly tape cleaning, which is good, but we prefer weekly cleanings. Cleaning tapes is cheap, but failed backups are potentially very expensive.

8. On the Storage Allocation For Deleted Files And E-Mail page (Figure 13-7), choose how long to retain copies of deleted e-mail messages, and how much space to allocate for snapshots of the files in shared folders (Volume Shadow Copy). Clearing the check boxes will disable that functionality. Click Next.

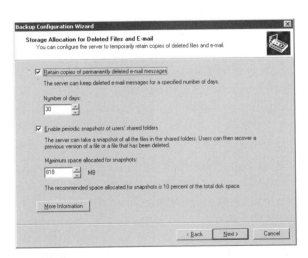

Figure 13-7.   *The Storage Allocation For Deleted Files And E-Mail page.*

9. The final page of the wizard shows a summary of your backup configuration. If everything is OK, click Finish to implement the configuration.

Running a Backup Manually

Windows Small Business Server will schedule your backup for you, but there are often situations where you want to manually execute a back up. You can use the Backup Utility directly, or if you prefer, use your already-configured selections for Windows Small Business Server.

Full Manual Backup

To use your already-configured backup selections, target, and so on, you can run the Backup Utility from within the Server Management console by clicking Backup, and then clicking Backup Now.

> **Under the Hood   Backup Scripts**
>
> The Backup Utility uses backup scripts (*.bks) to control the backup process. Small Business Server creates a "Small Business Backup Script.bks" file in the %SystemDrive%\Program Files\Microsoft Windows Small Business Server\Backup directory to control the automated backups. When you run the configuration wizard, this script gets updated. But if you run the Backup Utility directly, the utility stores the scripts you create in user-specific directories—%USERPROFILE%\Local Settings\Application Data\Microsoft\Windows NT\NTBackup\Data—not terribly helpful when you have multiple users who might have responsibility for initiating a backup.

Back Up Selected Files and Folders

Rather than use the Windows Small Business Server Backup Configuration Wizard to change the standard backup selections, you can manually run the Backup Utility to make specific backups of important files or folders, or whenever you need to manually run a backup without backing up the entire server. To do this, start the Backup Utility by clicking Start, All Programs, Accessories, System Tools, Backup. Start the Backup Utility in Advanced Mode, as shown in Figure 13-8. From here you can use the Backup Wizard to select files, or click the Backup tab and manually select the files you want to back up.

Whether you use a wizard to help you select files or go straight to the Backup tab and select them yourself, you use a Microsoft Windows Explorer–like hierarchical display, as shown in Figure 13-9, to browse your drives and make selections using the check boxes. You can select entire drives or individual files and directories for backup. The System State item backs up the registry and the Active Directory database on the local machine, as well as other system elements required in a disaster recovery situation.

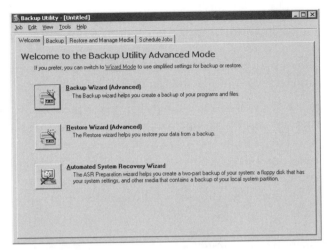

Figure 13-8. *The Advanced Mode of the Windows Small Business Server 2003 Backup Utility.*

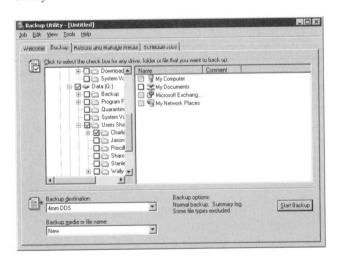

Figure 13-9. *Choosing files and folders to back up.*

Creating Selection Scripts After you select the files and directories to back up, you can create a selection script that contains the job configuration you created. After choosing Save Selections from the Job menu, you specify a filename with a .BKS extension for the selection script and the directory where the program should create it. You can use selection scripts to create an identical backup job during a subsequent session by loading the selection script from the Job menu. When you do this, the same system elements you selected before creating the script are selected again. You can then run the job as is or make additional selections. You can also use the script to execute the job from the Ntbackup.exe command line.

Accessing Files and Folders for Backup   To back up any files and folders, the account used to run the job must have the appropriate permissions granting access to those files and folders. A user who is an Administrator is automatically granted permission to back up any and all files and folders on the server. Other users will have permission to back up their own files and folders.

Selecting the Backup Target   After you specify what you want to back up, you must tell the program where to write the data. In the Backup Destination drop-down list, the File option is the default. If you used the Backup Configuration Wizard to specify a tape device as a destination, you'll also have an option to use that tape device. After you make a selection, use the Backup Media Or File Name box to specify a tape or disk name or the path and filename the program should use to create a backup file.

> **Note**   The Server Management Backup wizards will not let you select a CD or DVD writeable drive as a backup device. But if you are manually running the Backup Utility, and you have third-party software that formats the CD or DVD to let it be treated as a hard drive, you can use a writeable or rewriteable CD or DVD drive as your backup destination.

When you select a tape device, you can then select one of the existing tapes already created by the Windows Small Business Server Backup Utility Wizard, or use the name New. When you have all your selections made, click Start Backup.

This opens the Backup Job Information dialog box shown in Figure 13-10. From here, type a description for the backup and a new name for the tape or disk file.

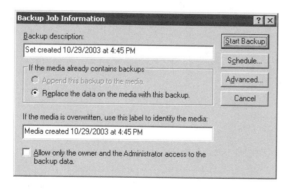

Figure 13-10.   *The Backup Job Information dialog box.*

Now all you need to do is click Start Backup and the backup begins. If you want to set advanced backup options, click Advanced. The options that you can set are:

- Back Up Data That Is In Remote Storage
- Verify Data After Backup
- If Possible, Compress The Backup Data To Save Space

- Automatically Backup System Protected Files When Backing Up The System State
- Disable Volume Shadow Copy
- Backup Type

Some of these might not apply to your selections or backup destination, and will be unavailable.

You can also schedule this backup to occur later by clicking Schedule. You'll have to save your selections before you can schedule the backup for later because the scheduler uses backup scripts to manage the backups. You'll be prompted for a name for the selection script, and for a user account and password to use to run the scheduled job. Finally, you can give the job a name, select the scheduled properties, and add the job to the schedule.

Caution   If you run a manual job that writes a backup to tape, make sure that the person responsible for changing tapes knows about the job and that the job doesn't interfere with the normal backup schedule. It's all too easy to have your job overwritten, and the nightly backup job fail as well.

Modifying the Backup Configuration

Instead of running the full Windows Small Business Server Backup Configuration Wizard to change one element of the backup configuration, you can run a shortened version of the Configuration Wizard to just change one portion. The options are listed on the left side of the Backup pane, as shown in Figure 13-11.

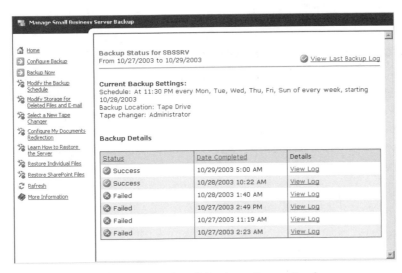

Figure 13-11.   *The Manage Small Business Server Backup pane.*

To change an element of the backup configuration, click:

- **Modify The Backup Schedule**   This allows you to modify the default backup schedule without affecting other configuration items. You'll see the Define Backup Schedule page shown in Figure 13-5.

- **Modify Storage For Deleted Files And E-Mail**   This allows you to modify the storage and retention settings for deleted files and e-mail without affecting other configuration items. You'll see The Storage Allocation For Deleted Files And E-Mail page shown in Figure 13-7.

- **Select A New Tape Changer**   If you are using a tape backup, this allows you to change the person designated to change tapes without affecting other configuration items. You can also set the notification options for the new designee. You'll see the Onsite Tape Changer page shown in Figure 13-6.

Restoring Data

Windows Small Business Server 2003 gives you two different and powerful tools for restoring lost, damaged, or corrupted data. The first tool is the traditional method of restoring files, folders, or the entire server using a tape or file system backup made with the Backup Utility. The second tool takes advantage of the Volume Shadow Copy feature to allow you to restore files or folders to a previous snapshot version of them. Since the two approaches use very different methods and technologies, we'll treat them quite separately.

Tip   In almost all cases, it's a lot quicker to restore a few files or folders using the Previous Versions client than to restore from tape. You should always use the Previous Versions client when the option is available.

Using the Backup Utility to Restore Files and Folders

The traditional method of backup and restore uses the Backup Utility we've discussed earlier in the chapter to make a backup of your Windows Small Business Server onto tape or a hard drive. This allows you to restore individual files or the entire server. The ability to restore files is not limited to files stored on a shared directory, and you can restore to the original location, or to a new location, giving you excellent flexibility.

More Info   For details about how to restore in the event of a totally failed server, see Chapter 21, "Disaster Planning and Fault Tolerance."

To restore individual files or folders with the Backup Utility, complete the following steps:

1. If you're restoring from a tape backup, insert the tape from the backup version of the file or folder that you want to restore into the tape drive and wait for any blinking lights to stop.

2. Open the Backup Utility by clicking Start, All Programs, Accessories, System Tools, Backup. Open in Advanced Mode.

3. Click the Restore And Manage Media tab to open the screen shown in Figure 13-12.

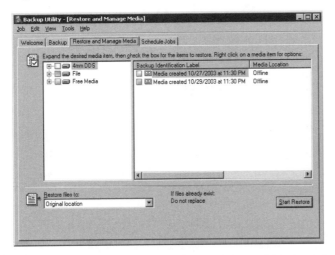

Figure 13-12. *The Restore And Manage Media tab of the Backup Utility.*

4. Highlight the media you will be restoring from and select the check box next to the file or folder you want to restore, as shown in Figure 13-13.

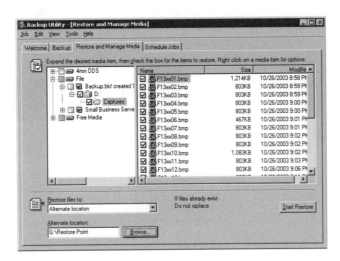

Figure 13-13. *Selecting the files and folders to restore using the Backup Utility.*

5. Choose whether to restore to the original location (not recommended) or to an alternative location or single folder.

6. Click Start Restore to open the Confirm Restore dialog box, shown in Figure 13-14. You can click Advanced in this dialog box to change mount point settings if you have mounted volumes to worry about; otherwise, click OK to restore your selected files and folders.

Figure 13-14. *The Confirm Restore dialog box.*

7. Once the restore is complete, the Restore Progress dialog box will show that the restore is complete. You can click Close to exit the restore, or click Report to view a report of the restoration.

Real World   **Restore to an Alternate Location**

It's almost always best when restoring only a few files or folders to choose an alternative location to restore the files to. This prevents inadvertently overwriting files that you don't want to overwrite and makes sure that all the files from that restored point in time are available together. If the user that needs the restored file finds out that the version needed wasn't part of Wednesday's backup but rather Thursday's, for example, you're covered. And you don't have to worry about overwriting their current version of it only to discover that they have the wrong file name and it's really in a different file. Of course, if you're restoring an entire drive because you had to replace a failed drive, you'll simply restore to the original location.

Using the Previous Versions Client to Restore Files and Folders

Windows Small Business Server 2003 includes the new Volume Shadow Copy technology of Windows Server 2003 that allows the creation of shadow or snapshot copies of files that are shared to the network. This enables files and folders to be restored to a point in time when the snapshot was taken. By default, shadow copy snapshots are taken twice a day, at 7 A.M. and noon.

To restore files that have been saved by Volume Shadow Copy, you need to use the Previous Versions client. This client is installed by default on all Microsoft Windows XP and Windows 2000 client computers, and can be installed on earlier versions of the Windows operating system as well, as described in Chapter 12, "Managing Computers on the Network."

The procedure for restoring files and folders using the Previous Versions client is quite straightforward and seems pretty simple. And it is—until you realize that someone just deleted the payroll file for today's payroll, the CFO and CEO are standing in the server room looking over your shoulder wanting to know where it is, the telephone is ringing because the Finance Department just realized it's gone, and to top it off, you just spilled hot coffee on your lap. If you've never restored a file or folder using the Previous Versions client, you really don't want this to be your first attempt. Wouldn't you feel a lot more comfortable about the whole process knowing you'd tested and practiced the whole thing on some innocuous files you created for the purpose?

To restore snapshot copies of an individual file or folder using the Previous Versions client, complete the following steps:

1. Log on to a client workstation using an account with permission to view and restore the file or folder you want to recover. Generally this will be the owner of the missing or corrupted file.

2. In Windows Explorer, right-click the network share where the file or folder resided and choose Properties from the shortcut menu.

3. Click the Previous Versions tab, as shown in Figure 13-15.

Figure 13-15. *The Previous Versions client.*

4. Select the folder version and then click View, Copy, or Restore.

- **View** Opens the shadow copy in Windows Explorer. You can then open or copy the files just like in a normal folder (although you can't delete anything or save to these folders).

- **Copy** Copies the shadow copy to the location you specify.

- **Restore** Rolls back the shared folder to its state as of the snapshot image you selected.

Tip To access shadow copies from the Windows Small Business Server machine itself, connect to the shared folder using its UNC path (for example, \\sbssrv\Users) instead of using a local path.

Tip As with the Backup Utility, we think it's a good idea to always restore files to a different location. With the Previous Versions client, this means using the Copy or View options and avoiding the Restore option. Restore will always restore the highlighted version of the file or folder over any existing version. It's much safer to copy it to a new location and inspect it there—you can always copy it back to its original location if that's what you want. But be sure. You can't undo a restore that has overwritten your current version.

Summary

In this chapter, we covered the essentials of backing up your server and the files and data on it. Windows Small Business Server 2003 provides an easy-to-use Backup Utility that, combined with the Volume Shadow Copy feature, can help protect your business from loss due to data corruption, server crash, or simple user error.

In Chapter 14, "Using Exchange Server," we'll cover e-mail and the Microsoft Exchange Server 2003 that is the e-mail engine of Windows Small Business Server.

Part IV
Performing Advanced Tasks

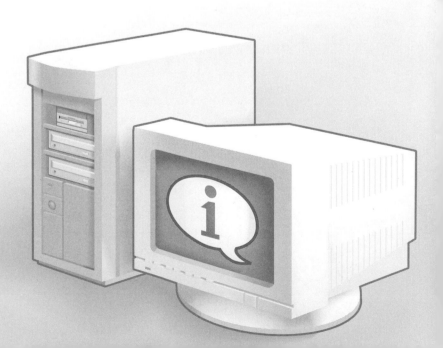

Chapter 14
Using Exchange Server

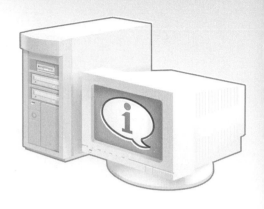

One of the most used and important parts of the Microsoft Windows Small Business Server 2003 package is Microsoft Exchange Server 2003. Installed as part of both the Windows Small Business Server 2003 Standard Edition and Premium Edition, Exchange Server provides a full-featured, flexible, and robust e-mail and collaboration infrastructure. Windows Small Business Server gives you the wizards and tools to make managing Exchange Server a straightforward process. This chapter covers basic e-mail configuration and goes on to address some of the advanced configuration options that allow you to tweak Exchange Server to your needs, including ways to block unwanted e-mail *before* it gets to your users.

Basic E-Mail Configuration

The default Exchange Server configuration is set up when you first run the Configure E-Mail and Internet Connection Wizard, which was described in Chapter 6, "Completing the To Do List and Other Post-Installation Tasks." If you haven't yet run this wizard to connect to the Internet, you'll need to do that first. The first part of the wizard sets up your Internet connection. Once you configure the Internet connection, the wizard guides you through initial configuration of your Exchange server, starting with the Internet E-Mail page shown in Figure 14-1.

If you've got the Exchange snap-in open when you click Next, you get a warning message about refreshing the snap-in when you're done so you'll see any changes. Next, you need to decide how you want your outgoing e-mail configured. You can either use DNS to route outgoing e-mail or forward all your outgoing e-mail to a server specified by your ISP, as shown in Figure 14-2.

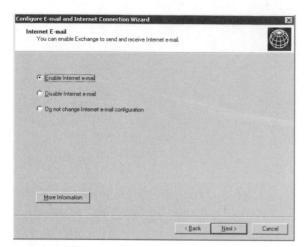

Figure 14-1. *Enabling Internet e-mail as part of the Configure E-Mail and Internet Connection Wizard.*

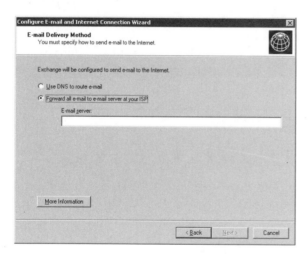

Figure 14-2. *Choosing between DNS e-mail routing or forwarding through your ISP's server.*

Real World   Use DNS E-Mail Routing

Choosing forwarding as your e-mail delivery mechanism has some serious drawbacks, not the least of which is that all e-mail from your Windows Small Business Server will show that it has been forwarded from your ISP. Because spam e-mails use this technique, often forwarding from unsuspecting and poorly configured mail servers, using a forwarder can result in undelivered e-mail. Some very fussy e-mail domains refuse to accept mail that has passed through a mail forwarder, and even those who are not that absolute can end up blocking your e-mail when your ISP gets on their black list—something you have no control over.

In the early days of e-mail on the Internet, forwarding was a sensible way to configure many Simple Mail Transfer Protocol (SMTP) servers. Configuring an SMTP server, most commonly one running sendmail, was an arcane and difficult task for even experienced UNIX administrators. Many opted instead to use "smart hosts" that were configured to accept mail and send it on to the right place. Sadly, the flood of Unsolicited Commercial E-Mail (UCE, or more commonly *spam*) has made that practice no longer possible or desirable. Fortunately, Exchange Server 2003 does most of the SMTP heavy lifting in the background, so you don't need to understand all the complexities.

Once you configure your sending method, click Next to open the E-Mail Retrieval Method page shown in Figure 14-3, where you define how e-mail gets delivered to you. Your ISP will have a preferred method, so make sure you consult with them before filling this out. You can also configure POP3 mailboxes at this point, but save that for later. Configuring POP3 e-mail will be discussed later in the "POP3 E-Mail" section. Click Next after you make your selections.

Caution   Incorrectly configuring your e-mail retrieval method will result in e-mail not being delivered to your server. Your ISP's configuration will determine what the correct method is.

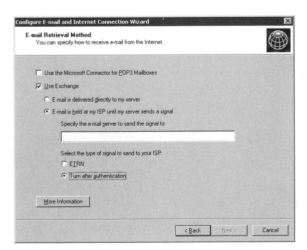

Figure 14-3. *Configuring how your e-mail gets delivered to your server.*

Under the Hood   E-Mail Retrieval Methods

There are two basic methods for e-mail retrieval: e-mail is directly delivered to your Exchange server, or e-mail is first delivered to your ISP, which holds it until your Exchange server specifically asks for it. Which method is used is controlled by the DNS records for your domain—specifically the MX record.

Direct Delivery

If you want e-mail delivered directly to your server, the MX record for your domain must point to your server. If you want it delivered first to your ISP, and to you only when you ask for it, the MX record must point to your ISP's server. Many ISPs support a mixture of the two methods—the primary MX record points to your server, but a secondary one points to your ISP. If for some reason your server is not available, your e-mail will go to your ISP. Once your e-mail server comes back online, you can either trigger delivery directly if your ISP supports that or wait until their automatic process recognizes that your e-mail server is back online.

Indirect Delivery: ETRN

The Extended Turn (ETRN) command is used by most ISPs to initiate a download of queued e-mail messages that are stored while waiting for a server to be online to receive them. The ETRN command is documented in the Request for Comments (RFC) 1985, available at *http://www.ietf.org /rfc/rfc1985.txt*. The ETRN command is an extension of the TURN command, which had serious security issues and is generally not used any longer.

Indirect Delivery: TURN After Authentication

The TURN After Authentication command gets around the most serious security issues of the TURN command by requiring your Exchange server to authenticate to your ISP's SMTP server before the SMTP server accepts a TURN command from it. This methodology is useful when your Exchange server doesn't have a fixed IP address but uses a dynamic IP address. Dynamic IP addresses are not supported for the ETRN method.

Manual ETRN Trigger

If you normally have e-mail directly delivered to your Exchange server and have secondary MX records that allow your ISP to hold e-mail when you're offline, once your server is back up and available, you can wait for normal processing to send your e-mail to you, or you can manually initiate the transfer if your ISP supports doing that. The following procedure starts a mail queue to send e-mail to your domain. It assumes that your ISP's SMTP server is smtp.example.com and your domain is microsoft.com.

```
telnet smtp.example.com 25
220 smtp.example.com ESMTP Mon, 3 Nov 2003 15:18:30 -0800 (PST)
ETRN @microsoft.com
250 2.0.0 Queuing for node @microsoft.com started
quit
221 2.0.0 smtp.example.com closing connection
```

The 220, 250, and 221 lines are the responses from the remote server.

If you're using TURN After Authentication as your retrieval method, you get prompted for an account name and a password, which are used to authenticate your Exchange server to your ISP, as shown in Figure 14-4. Fill in the authentication information you received from your ISP and click Next.

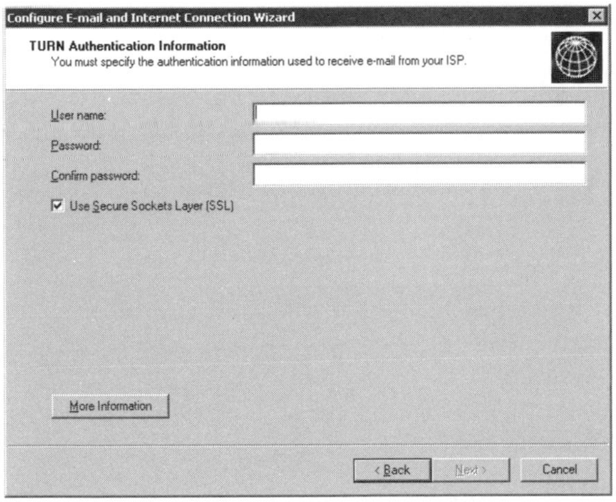

Figure 14-4. *The TURN authentication information used to ensure that only your Exchange server can retrieve your e-mail.*

The E-Mail Domain Name page is shown in Figure 14-5. Type your Internet domain name, which should be different from your internal domain name, and click Next.

The Remove E-mail Attachments page of the Configure E-Mail and Internet Connection Wizard, shown in Figure 14-6, lets you automatically strip certain attachments from incoming e-mail received from the Internet. E-mail that has an attachment removed will have a text note attached to it so that the recipient knows the attachment was stripped. You can edit this list to add additional extensions or to remove ones that your business routinely uses.

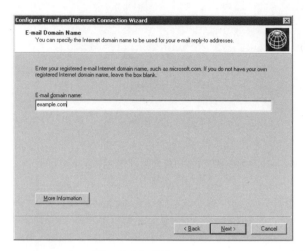

Figure 14-5. *The E-Mail Domain Name page of the Configure E-Mail and Internet Connection Wizard.*

Security Alert If you routinely need to receive e-mail from the Internet with an attachment that can be used maliciously, don't simply enable that particular extension, but rather create a policy for how to change the extension so that both sender and recipient know what to use (for example, *.vb* for *.vbs*). This strategy enables you to get your work done efficiently while still providing some protection.

Security Alert E-mail sent from one Exchange mailbox to another Exchange mailbox that does not go outside your internal network will not be checked nor have attachments removed.

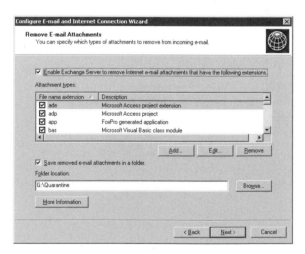

Figure 14-6. *Removing potentially hazardous attachments is one way to help protect your network.*

If you want any stripped attachments to be saved into a safe area for inspection, select the Save Removed E-Mail Attachments In A Folder check box and specify a location where the attachments will be saved.

Security Alert Although automatically removing some attachments from your e-mail is a good thing to do, it just isn't enough these days. You should be running an antivirus suite that protects your network at multiple points of attack and includes at least file scanning and e-mail attachment scanning.

Click Next to display a final confirmation page that summarizes all your selections. If everything looks right, click Finish to implement them.

Tip You can run the Configure E-Mail and Internet Connection Wizard again at any time if you need to change one or more of the configuration items. The wizard will start with your existing configuration and let you change just the items that need changing.

POP3 E-Mail

Many small businesses prefer their ISPs to handle all the configuration and maintenance of the public side of their e-mail. This responsibility can take the form of handling individual e-mail boxes for each employee or function within the company, or it can be managing a single, global e-mail box that receives all the mail for the entire domain. Windows Small Business Server can automatically download e-mail from Post Office Protocol version 3 (POP3) e-mail boxes and distribute it into the correct Exchange mailbox using the Microsoft Connector for POP3 Mailboxes.

Configuring POP3 E-Mail

To configure and enable the Microsoft Connector for POP3 Mailboxes, you first need to add one or more POP3 mailboxes. If you haven't defined any POP3 mailboxes, the connector is disabled and the service doesn't start.

Adding, Removing, and Editing POP3 E-Mail Boxes

You can add, remove, and edit an existing POP3 e-mail box using the POP3 Connector Manager shown in Figure 14-7. To open the POP3 Connector Manager, open Server Management, expand Advanced Management in the console tree, click POP3 Connector Manager in the console tree, and then click Open POP3 Connector Manager in the details pane.

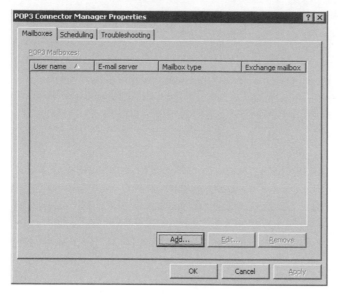

Figure 14-7. *The POP3 Connector Manager, before any mailboxes have been created.*

Adding a POP3 E-Mail Box

To add a POP3 e-mail box or to create your first one, complete the following steps:

1. Open the POP3 Connector Manager.

2. Click Add to open the POP3 Mailbox dialog box shown in Figure 14-8.

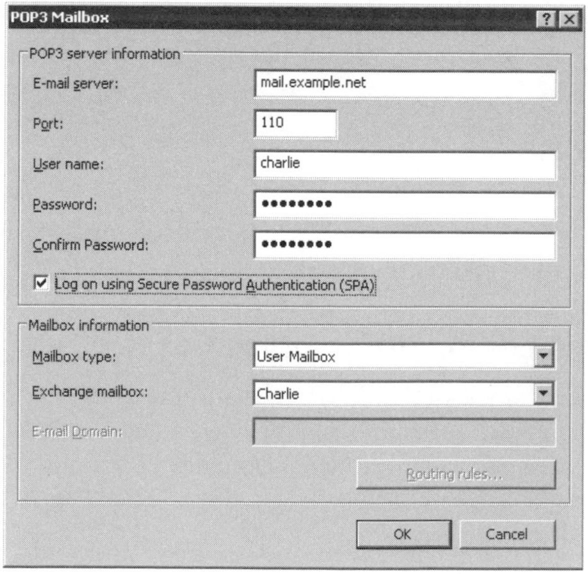

Figure 14-8. *The POP3 Mailbox dialog box for a new mailbox.*

3. Fill in the fields. The fields are:

- **E-Mail Server**   Your ISP's e-mail server or the server of the e-mail hosting service you use.

- **Port**   The TCP/IP port number your ISP uses. The default value of 110 should be correct unless your ISP specifies something else.

- **User Name**   The ISP's account name for this POP3 e-mail box. This might not be the same as the user's name or Exchange mailbox.

- **Password and Confirm Password**   Type the password used for this account.

- **Log On Using Secure Password Authentication (SPA)**   Some ISP and e-mail hosting services permit or even require a secure logon to your POP3 account. If your ISP supports SPA, use it!

- **Mailbox Type**   Either a User Mailbox that is directly tied to a specific Exchange mailbox or a Global Mailbox that can contain e-mail for multiple users.

- **Exchange Mailbox**   If you selected User Mailbox as the mailbox type, you need to link it to a specific Exchange mailbox from the drop-down list.

- **E-Mail Domain**   If you selected Global Mailbox as the mailbox type, you need to specify the e-mail domain used as the return address for users of this e-mail box.

- **Routing Rules**   If each user of the Global Mailbox maps directly to an identical Exchange mailbox, you don't need to add routing rules. See the section "Routing POP3 E-Mail" for more information about routing rules.

4. Once you've filled in all the fields, click OK to return to the POP3 Connector Manager.

5. Click Add again to add additional mailboxes. When you're finished adding e-mail boxes, click OK. If this is the first POP3 e-mail box you've created, you get a message that the Microsoft Connector for POP3 Mailboxes service is not running. Click OK to start the service and create the mailbox.

Removing a POP3 E-Mail Box

To remove a POP3 e-mail box, complete the following steps:

1. Open the POP3 Connector Manager, shown in Figure 14-7.

2. Select the mailbox you want to remove and click Remove.

3. Confirm the removal, and the POP3 e-mail box is removed. This action does not affect the regular Exchange mailbox—that's tied to the user account in Active Directory.

Editing an Existing POP3 E-Mail Box

To edit an existing POP3 e-mail box, complete the following steps:

1. Open the POP3 Connector Manager, shown in Figure 14-7.

2. Select the e-mail box you want to modify, and click Edit to open the POP3 Mailbox dialog box, shown in Figure 14-8.

3. Edit any fields you need to change. The fields are:

   - **E-Mail Server** Your ISPs e-mail server or the server of the e-mail hosting service you use.

   - **Port** The TCP/IP port number your ISP uses. The default value of 110 should be correct unless your ISP specifies something else.

   - **User Name** The ISP's account name for this POP3 e-mail box. This might not be the same as the user's name or Exchange mailbox.

   - **Password and Confirm Password** Type the password used for this account.

   - **Log On Using Secure Password Authentication (SPA)** Some ISP and e-mail hosting services permit or even require a secure logon to your POP3 account. If your ISP supports SPA, use it!

   - **Mailbox Type** Either a User Mailbox that is directly tied to a specific Exchange mailbox or a Global Mailbox that can contain e-mail for multiple users.

   - **Exchange Mailbox** If you selected User Mailbox as the mailbox type, you need to link it to a specific Exchange mailbox from the drop-down list.

   - **E-Mail Domain** If you selected Global Mailbox as the mailbox type, you need to specify the e-mail domain used as the return address for users of this e-mail box.

   - **Routing Rules** If each user of the Global Mailbox maps directly to an identical Exchange mailbox, you don't need to add routing rules. See the section "Routing POP3 E-Mail" for more information about routing rules.

4. Click OK to return to the POP3 Connector Manager, and click OK again to exit.

Setting a POP3 Delivery Schedule

The default is for the Microsoft Connector for POP3 Mailboxes to download messages from POP3 mailboxes once an hour, every hour, 7 days a week. You can change this as appropriate for your business, but the minimum time between download intervals is 15 minutes.

To change the default schedule, complete the following steps:

1. Open the POP3 Connector Manager and click the Scheduling tab, as shown in Figure 14-9.

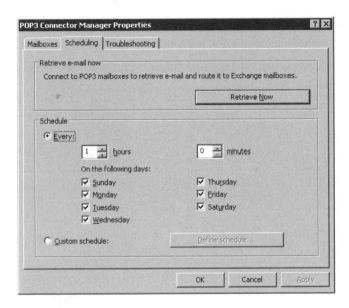

Figure 14-9. *Setting the download schedule for POP3 e-mail boxes.*

2. For a standard schedule, with the same frequency all day every day, select the appropriate check boxes and specify how often to schedule a download. Click OK when you're finished.

3. To define a custom schedule, select the Custom Schedule option and click Define Schedule to open the Define Schedule dialog box shown Figure 14-10.

4. Highlight a section of time and select from the download choices: None, Once Per Hour, Twice Per Hour, or Four Times Per Hour. You can select multiple periods and define each of the periods differently, as shown in Figure 14-10.

5. When you're finished defining your schedule, click OK and then OK again to exit the POP3 Connector Manager.

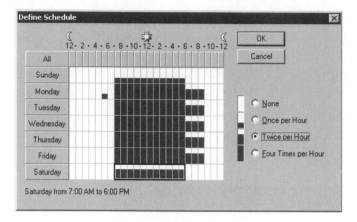

Figure 14-10. *A custom POP3 download schedule for a business that doesn't work much on the weekends.*

To immediately download POP3 e-mail, complete the following steps:

1. Open the POP3 Connector Manager and click the Scheduling tab, as shown in Figure 14-9.

2. Click the Retrieve Now button. (This button is unavailable when the connector is in the midst of a download or the service is stopped.) You get an informational message.

3. Click OK to begin the download.

Routing POP3 E-Mail

Windows Small Business Server and Exchange Server support using a single, global POP3 mailbox for your domain. This allows you to have all e-mail that is sent to your domain automatically delivered to the same mailbox maintained by your ISP. There's no need to assign individual POP3 e-mail boxes to individual Exchange users, no worry about your customers getting bounced e-mail, and so on.

When mail is retrieved from the POP3 e-mail box by the Microsoft Connector for POP3 Mailboxes, it is automatically distributed to the corresponding Exchange mailboxes. So if there's a message with Charlie@example.com in the To field, and Wally@example.com and Priscilla@example.com are in the Cc field, each account gets a copy of the message.

If you get mail that is sometimes addressed to a particular function, such as sales@example.com or orders@example.com, you'll need to create a rule that routes them to the appropriate Exchange mailbox. Also, many mailing list servers hide the recipient's address, so mail to Security_List@TreyResearch.net might actually be intended for Stanley@example.com. But Exchange won't know that without an explicit routing rule.

Adding a Routing Rule

To add a routing rule, complete the following steps:

1. Open the POP3 Connector Manager.

2. Select the global mailbox you want to set routing rules for and click Edit to open the POP3 Mailbox dialog box.

3. Click Routing Rules to open the Routing Rules dialog box, shown in Figure 14-11.

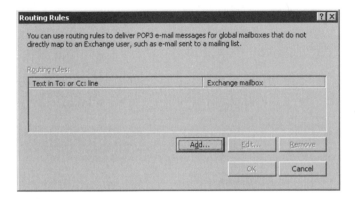

Figure 14-11.   *The Routing Rules dialog box.*

4. Click Add to open the Routing Rule dialog box, shown in Figure 14-12.

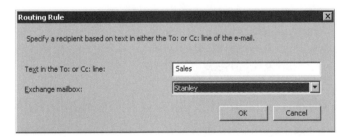

Figure 14-12.   *Determining how specific text in the To and Cc fields will be routed.*

5. Type the text that will control the routing rule. This text will appear in either the To or Cc fields of the message. Rules based on Subject lines are not supported, nor are Bcc-based rules.

6. Select the mailbox to route to from the Exchange Mailbox drop-down list, and then click OK to return to the Routing Rules dialog box. You can add additional rules here, modify existing rules, or delete rules that are no longer required. When you complete your changes, click OK again.

Changing a Routing Rule

To change a routing rule, complete the following steps:

1. Open the POP3 Connector Manager.

2. Select the global mailbox you want to modify the routing rules for, and click Edit to open the POP3 Mailbox dialog box.

3. Click Routing Rules to open the Routing Rules dialog box, shown in Figure 14-11.

4. Select the rule you want to modify, and then click Edit to open the Routing Rule dialog box, shown in Figure 14-12.

5. Make the necessary changes and then click OK.

Removing a Routing Rule

To remove a routing rule, complete the following steps:

1. Open the POP3 Connector Manager.

2. Select the global mailbox you want to remove a routing rule from and click Edit to open the POP3 Mailbox dialog box.

3. Click Routing Rules to open the Routing Rules dialog box, shown in Figure 14-11.

4. Select the rule you want to remove, and click Remove. You get a confirmation dialog box. Click Yes and then click OK in the Routing Rules dialog box. The rule is removed.

Troubleshooting POP3

Windows Small Business Server includes several helpful features to enable you to troubleshoot POP3 problems. These features are available on the Troubleshooting tab of the POP3 Connector Manager and include:

- Service Status
- Logging
- Undeliverable POP3 E-Mail

Microsoft Connector for POP3 Mailboxes Service Status

To view the current status of the Microsoft Connector for POP3 Mailboxes, open the POP3 Connector Manager and click the Troubleshooting tab. In the Service Status box, you'll see the number of messages in the Failed Mail Folder and the state of the connector service, as shown in Figure 14-13.

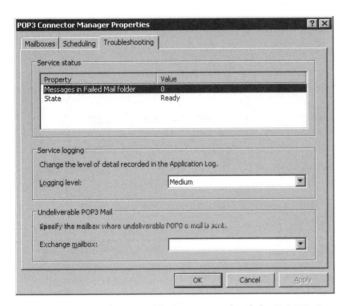

Figure 14-13.   *The Troubleshooting tab of the POP3 Connector Manager.*

Messages that are in the Failed Mail Folder can be resent once the cause of the failure is identified. Before you try to resend the message, make sure that the other important Exchange Server services are running. At a minimum, the Microsoft Exchange Information Store, Microsoft Exchange Routing Engine, Microsoft Exchange System Attendant, and Simple Mail Transfer Protocol (SMTP) services should be up and running before attempting to retry delivery of the messages.

To try delivering failed messages again, complete the following steps:

1. Log on to the Windows Small Business Server machine with an account that has administrative privileges.

2. Open Microsoft Windows Explorer and navigate to the %ProgramFiles%\ Microsoft Small Business Server\Networking\POP3\Failed Mail folder.

3. Select the files you want to retry delivery for, and move them to the %ProgramFiles%\Microsoft Small Business Server\Networking\POP3\ Incoming Mail folder.

4. The next time a POP3 connection is made—either a normal, scheduled connection or an immediate one—the delivery will be retried.

5. To trigger an immediate retry, open the POP3 Connector Manager, click Scheduling, and then click Retrieve Now.

Configuring Logging

Windows Small Business Server allows you to log connection information for the Microsoft Connector for POP3 Mailboxes service. Four levels of logging are supported:

- **None** No logging at all is done.

- **Minimum** Logs only critical error messages and security-audit success and failure messages.

- **Medium** Logs additional informational messages beyond that of the Minimum setting.

- **Maximum** Logs additional troubleshooting messages in addition to logging the Medium setting.

Caution Enabling Maximum logging can fill up the Application Event Log quickly! You should enable Maximum logging only when actively trying to troubleshoot a connector problem. Once the problem is identified and resolved, return the logging level to your preferred normal level.

All logging messages are sent to the Application Event Log and can be viewed with the Event Viewer. Changes in logging level require stopping and restarting the Microsoft Connector for POP3 Mailboxes service.

Configuring Undeliverable POP3 E-Mail

When using a global POP3 mailbox, normal messages are routed to the Exchange Server mailbox for the recipients that appear in the To and Cc fields. Any messages that are retrieved by the Microsoft Connector for POP3 Mailboxes service and addressed to a recipient without an associated Exchange mailbox are delivered to the Administrator's mailbox. To change where undeliverable POP3 e-mail is sent, specify a different e-mail box on the Troubleshooting tab of the POP3 Connector Manager.

Note Many mailing list managers hide the individual recipients. Messages sent to mailing lists require specific routing rules. Messages with recipients in the Bcc fields can not be delivered to their intended recipients because this information is stripped off when the messages are delivered to the POP3 mailbox and are no longer available to Exchange.

Advanced E-Mail Configuration and Management

There are a number of advanced e-mail configuration and management tasks available through the Server Management console. Click Advanced Management in the console tree, and then click Exchange Server in the details pane to open the Exchange Server console, which is shown in Figure 14-14.

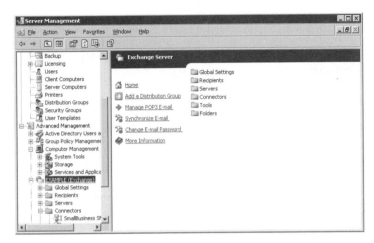

Figure 14-14. *Exchange Server Advanced Management.*

Changing E-Mail Password

If your e-mail is configured to use TURN After Authentication, to collect your e-mail, you must supply an account name and password to connect to the ISP's e-mail server. When you initially configure your e-mail using the Configure E-Mail and Internet Connection Wizard, you supply this information, but if the data changes at any point in the future, you'll need to change the account information used by Exchange to connect and collect e-mail.

To change this information, complete the following steps:

1. Select your Exchange server in the Advanced Management section of the Server Management console, as shown in Figure 14-14.

2. Click Change E-Mail Password in the details pane to open the Change E-Mail Password dialog box (Figure 14-15).

3. Edit the user name if necessary, and type the new password provided by your ISP. Retype the password and select or clear the Use Secure Sockets Layer (SSL) check box as required by your ISP.

4. Click OK to make the change, and click OK again to acknowledge the password was changed.

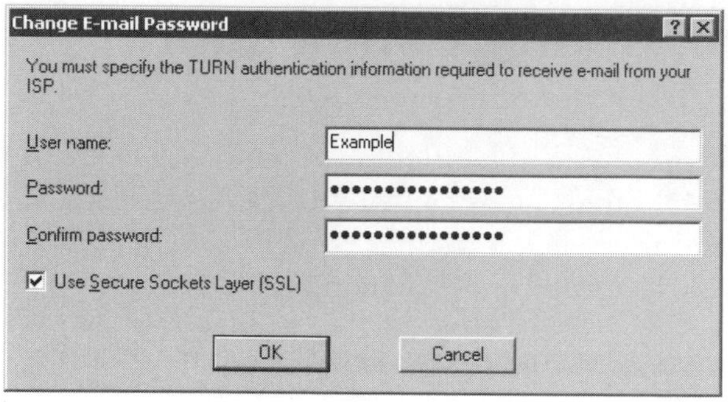

Figure 14-15. *Changing the e-mail password for an Exchange server that uses TURN After Authentication.*

Synchronize E-Mail

E-mail is normally delivered according to the schedule you established when you initially configured your Exchange server using the Configure E-Mail and Internet Connection Wizard. If your e-mail is delivered directly, without your ISP holding it for you, there's no need to synchronize e-mail. If your ISP holds your mail until you request it either using ETRN or TURN After Authentication, your e-mail is delivered only as often as you scheduled it initially. You can initiate an asynchronous connection, however, at any time by clicking Synchronize E-Mail in Exchange Server Advanced Management, as shown in Figure 14-14. When you click Synchronize E-Mail, you get an informational message. Click OK. Exchange Server connects to your ISP and downloads any pending messages while uploading any outgoing messages in your outgoing e-mail queue.

Managing E-Mail Distribution Lists

Windows Small Business Server uses distribution groups to manage how e-mail is delivered to various groups of users in your organization. These distribution groups are different from the security groups used to control access to specific features or directories, though there is often significant overlap, obviously.

When you initially run the Configure E-Mail and Internet Connection Wizard, a distribution group is created that includes all users. The name of this group is based on your organization's name (Example.com in our organization). Whenever a new user is created using one of the user templates, the user is automatically added to this distribution group. If you create a new user and do not use one of the default templates, make sure you include the user in this distribution group.

Creating a New Distribution Group (List)

Distribution groups, or distribution *lists*, as they are more commonly called when talking about e-mail, are a convenient mechanism for ensuring that e-mail gets consistently routed to the appropriate individuals without each user having to maintain his or her own individual list. You might have one list that goes to Finance, for example, that your sales people use to send in their expense reports. Rather than sending e-mail to a specific individual—who might be on vacation or no longer with the company—the user sends the e-mail to the list. The list ensures the e-mail gets routed as necessary, even when a key person is absent.

To create a new distribution list, complete the following steps:

1. Select your Exchange server in the Advanced Management section of the Server Management console.

2. Click Add A Distribution Group to open the Add Distribution Group Wizard.

3. Click Next to open the Distribution Group Information page, shown in Figure 14-16.

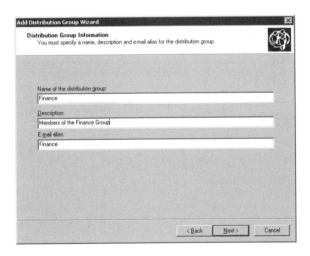

Figure 14-16.   *Specifying the information for a new distribution group.*

4. Type the name of the distribution group. An e-mail alias for the group is automatically created based on that name, although you can modify the alias as needed. Also type a description for the group.

5. Click Next to display the Group Membership page, shown in Figure 14-17.

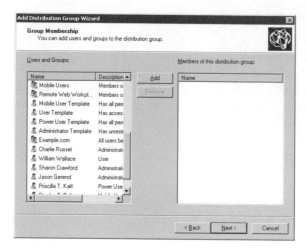

Figure 14-17. *Add members to the new distribution group.*

6. Select users or other groups from the left pane and click Add to add them to the new distribution group.

7. Click Next to display the Group Manager page, shown in Figure 14-18. The user or security group specified here will have permission to modify the membership of the group, regardless of whether that user or security group has any other administrative rights.

Note The group manager for a distribution group must be a member of the distribution group.

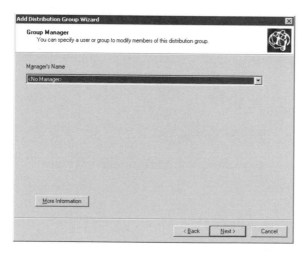

Figure 14-18. *The Group Manager page of the Add Distribution Group Wizard.*

8. Click Next to display the Group Options page, shown in Figure 14-19.

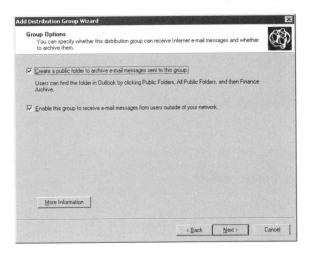

Figure 14-19.   *Setting options for a new distribution group.*

9. Clear the appropriate check boxes if you do *not* want messages to this distribution group to be automatically archived in Public Folders, or if you want the group to be able to receive messages from the Internet.

10. Click Next to display the summary page, and then click Finish to create the distribution group.

Modifying a Distribution Group (List)

Inevitably, the membership of a distribution group changes over time. If you've assigned a group manager to the distribution group, that manager (along with Domain Admins) can modify the membership of the group, adding or removing members as needed using Microsoft Outlook.

Note   Configuring Outlook to work with Exchange is discussed in Chapter 12, "Managing Computers on the Network."

Modifying Group Membership with Outlook 2003   To modify group membership, open Outlook 2003 on a client computer and complete the following steps:

1. If the distribution list isn't in your Contacts folder, add it.

Note   In Outlook, distribution groups are referred to as distribution lists.

2. Open your Contacts folder and select the distribution list you want to modify. Double-click the list to open the Distribution List dialog box, as shown in Figure 14-20.

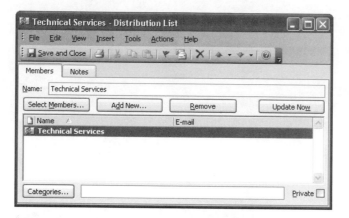

Figure 14-20. *The Distribution List dialog box.*

3. Double-click the name of the distribution list to open the Properties dialog box, as shown in Figure 14-21.

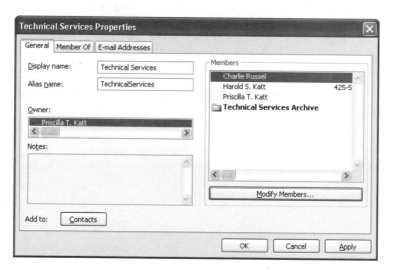

Figure 14-21. *The properties of the Technical Services distribution list.*

4. Click Modify Members to open the Distribution List Membership dialog box, shown in Figure 14-22.

5. Click Add to add members or click Remove to remove members from the list. To see the properties of a current list member, highlight the member and click Properties. After you make the changes, click OK to return to the Properties dialog box, and click OK again to return to the Distribution List dialog box. Click Save and Close to save the changes and exit the dialog box.

Figure 14-22. *The Distribution List Membership dialog box lets you add or remove members from a distribution list.*

Modifying Group Membership with the Server Management Console Administrators can modify group membership, change the group's manager, and enable or disable group options using the Server Management console. To modify a distribution group using the Server Management console, complete the following steps:

1. Select Distribution Groups from the Standard Management section of the Server Management console, as shown in Figure 14-23.

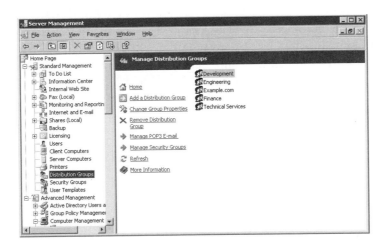

Figure 14-23. *The Manage Distribution Groups pane of the Server Management console.*

2. Double-click the group you want to modify to open the Properties dialog box, as shown in Figure 14-24 for the Technical Services group.

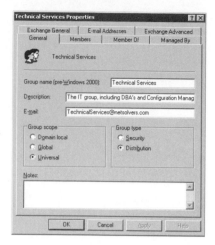

Figure 14-24. *The Properties dialog box for the Technical Services distribution group.*

3. Modify the properties of the group as needed, and click OK when you're finished.

Deleting A Distribution Group (List)

To remove a distribution group from Windows Small Business Server, select Distribution Groups from the Standard Management section of the Server Management console and highlight the group you want to remove. Click Remove Distribution Group. A confirmation dialog box appears, as shown in Figure 14-25. If you also want to remove the public folder associated with the distribution group, select the check box and click Yes. You get a confirmation message that the group was removed, along with its public folder archive, if specified.

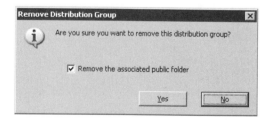

Figure 14-25. *Deleting a distribution group, as well as its public folder archive.*

Setting the Reply To Address

If you need to change the Reply To address on your outgoing e-mail, either for an individual user or for everyone, you can easily do it. You can also use this process to add e-mail domain addresses that Exchange Server will recognize as yours and accept e-mail for.

Changing the Reply To Address for All Users

To change the Reply To address for all users, complete the following steps:

1. Select your Exchange server in the Advanced Management section of the Server Management console.

2. Double-click Recipients, and then double-click Recipient Policies.

3. Double-click Default Policy to open up the Default Policy Properties dialog box. Click the E-Mail Addresses (Policy) tab, as shown in Figure 14-26.

Figure 14-26.   *Default Policy controls the SMTP Reply To address for all users.*

4. To change the default SMTP Reply To address, highlight the current primary SMTP address. It is displayed in boldface (Figure 14-26). Click Edit and type the new domain address.

5. To add an additional SMTP address, click New.

6. Select SMTP as the address type for normal Internet e-mail addresses and click OK.

7. Type the new address you want to receive mail for in the form *@domainname*, as shown in Figure 14-27.

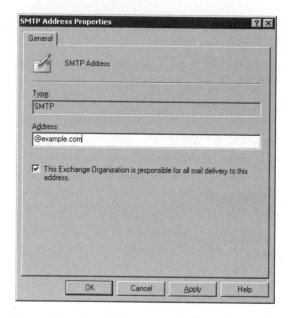

Figure 14-27. *Adding a new SMTP address that Exchange will receive.*

8. Click OK to return to the Default Policy Properties dialog box. To enable the new SMTP address, select the SMTP check box.

9. To make an address the primary address and appear as the Reply To address in outgoing e-mail, highlight the address and click Set As Primary.

10. Click OK when you are finished making changes.

Changing the Reply To Address for a Specific User

To change the Reply To address for a specific user, complete the following steps:

1. Select Users from the Standard Management section of the Server Management console.

2. Double-click the user whose Reply To address you want to change; this opens the Properties dialog box for the user.

3. Click the E-Mail Addresses tab, shown in Figure 14-28.

4. Click New to add an additional address. To change an existing address, highlight it and click Edit.

5. If the address is new, highlight the SMTP Address type (or other type, as appropriate) in the New E-Mail Address dialog box, as shown in Figure 14-29. Click OK.

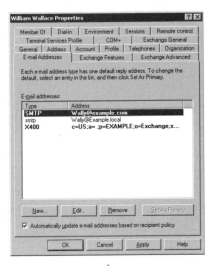

Figure 14-28.   *Changing the e-mail address of user William Wallace.*

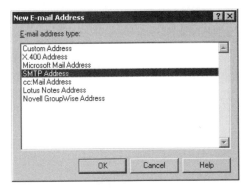

Figure 14-29.   *Adding an SMTP address type.*

6. Type the new address in the Internet Address Properties dialog box, as shown in Figure 14-30. Click OK to return to the E-Mail Addresses tab.

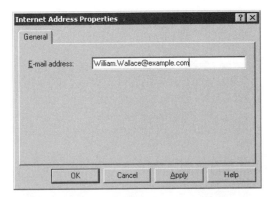

Figure 14-30.   *Adding a new address for user William Wallace.*

7. If you want the new address set as the primary address (and have it used in the Reply To field), click Set As Primary.

8. Click OK to exit the user's Properties dialog box.

Managing E-Mail Delivery

The Advanced Management section of the Server Management console allows you to manage a number of Exchange Server features that affect the delivery and sending of e-mail. You can set default values for messages including the maximum size of individual messages, both sent and received, and the maximum number of individual recipients per message.

To set the message defaults, complete the following steps:

1. Select your Exchange server under the Advanced Management section of the Server Management console.

2. Double-click Global Settings in the details pane.

3. Right-click Message Delivery and select Properties to open the Message Delivery Properties dialog box.

4. Click the Defaults tab, shown in Figure 14-31. Set the maximum values for the size of incoming and outgoing messages, as well as the maximum number of recipients allowed for a message.

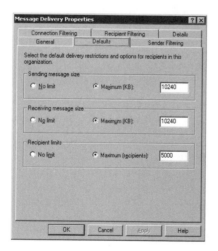

Figure 14-31. *Managing message defaults and delivery options in the Message Delivery Properties dialog box.*

5. Click Apply or OK after you set the defaults.

Setting an Individual User's Message Properties

Windows Small Business Server gives you the ability to override the default values for messaging to handle special users and circumstances. Avoid the temptation whenever possible, however, because the default values are quite generous and it's much more work to try to manage multiple individual mailboxes. If the default values are inappropriate for many users, that's a good indication that it's time to change the defaults rather than override the values for many individual users.

To set message properties for users, complete the following steps:

1. Select Users from the Standard Management section of the Server Management console.

2. Double-click the user whose message limits you want to change; this opens the Properties dialog box for the user.

3. Click the Exchange General tab, shown in Figure 14-32.

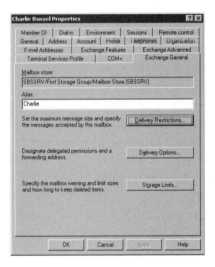

Figure 14-32.   *The Exchange General tab for user Charlie.*

4. Click Delivery Restrictions to set the maximum sending and receiving message size for this user, as shown in Figure 14-33.

5. Make the changes to the delivery restrictions, and then click OK to return to the Exchange General tab.

6. Click Delivery Options to open the Delivery Options dialog box, shown in Figure 14-34.

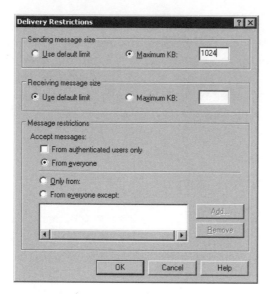

Figure 14-33. *Setting user Charlie's maximum message sending size to 1MB.*

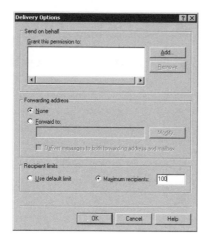

Figure 14-34. *Setting the delivery options for an Exchange user.*

7. Click Maximum Recipients and type the maximum number of recipients the user can send a message to. Use this dialog box to set a Send On Behalf permission as well.

8. Click OK to return to the Exchange General tab.

9. Click Storage Limits to open the Storage Limits dialog box. Here you can set the user's maximum mailbox size and the number of days a deleted message is retained.

SMTP Filtering

Exchange Server 2003 has a rich set of filtering options to let you control what e-mail you allow. You can't stop all the spam sent to your organization with Exchange filtering, but you can definitely put a dent in it. Exchange Server supports three basic types of filtering:

- **Sender filtering**   Messages are blocked based on who the sender is.

- **Connection filtering**   Messages are blocked based on the connection they use.

- **Recipient filtering**   Messages are blocked based on whom they are sent to.

Sender Filtering

By default, no domains or senders are filtered. You can add individual senders or entire domains that will be blocked. You can also control how blocked messages are treated.

1. Select your Exchange server under the Advanced Management section of the Server Management console.

2. Double-click Global Settings in the details pane.

3. Right-click Message Delivery and select Properties to open the Message Delivery Properties dialog box. Click the Sender Filtering tab, as shown in Figure 14-35.

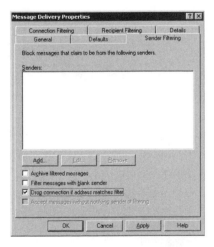

Figure 14-35.   *Automatically block messages from known bad senders.*

4. Click Add to open the Add Sender dialog box where you can type the sender's e-mail address. You can use wildcards to block an entire domain, as shown in Figure 14-36. After typing the new address, click OK to return to the Sender Filtering tab.

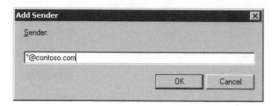

Figure 14-36. *Blocking the entire contoso.com domain.*

5. Click Edit to modify a current blocked sender, or click Remove to remove the sender from the list.

6. Select the Archive Filtered Messages check box if you want to archive messages that you've blocked.

Caution If you archive filtered messages, there is no automatic process to clean up the archive, which can grow very large very quickly. Make sure that cleaning up this archive is part of your regular Exchange maintenance.

7. Select the Filter Messages With Blank Sender check box to disallow messages that have a blank From field.

8. Clear the Drop Connection If Address Matches Filter check box if you don't want to automatically drop the SMTP connection when you recognize that a message should be blocked.

Tip The Drop Connection If Address Matches Filter check box is selected by default—and we think that's a good thing.

9. Click Apply to apply your filters. You get the message shown in Figure 14-37, warning you that the filtering won't actually happen until you enable it for specific SMTP virtual servers. Click OK, and then click the Connection Filtering tab to configure filtering by IP address and block list service providers.

Figure 14-37. *Warning indicating that filtering must be manually enabled.*

Connection Filtering

By default, connection filtering is not configured. To configure blocking by block lists and by specific IP addresses, use connection filtering.

1. Make sure the Message Delivery Properties dialog box is open and click the Connection Filtering tab, as shown in Figure 14-38.

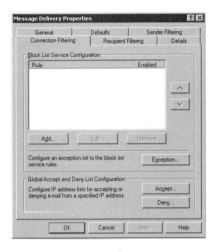

Figure 14-38.   *Connection filtering can include block lists and specific blocks of IP addresses.*

2. Click Add in the Block List Service Configuration box to add a new block list provider and configure the details for it.

3. After you add any block list providers you're going to use, click Exception to add exceptions for recipients who shouldn't be blocked regardless of what a block list says. Use this option to add addresses of any recipients who absolutely can't have an important message blocked.

4. Click Accept to specify an IP address or range of addresses that Exchange will always accept e-mail from.

5. Click Deny to specify an IP address or range of addresses that Exchange will always reject e-mail from.

Real World   Block List Providers

Block lists are an attempt to provide a central resource that accurately identifies known spammers and the IP addresses they use. These lists include real-time block lists (RBLs) and open relay lists. There are both free and commercial lists, and they range from those that contain only verified, known spam sources to those that are quite aggressive at deciding who and what is spam. Which type of list you choose will have a lot to do with how tolerant you are of false positives. One list of block lists you can start with is *http://www.email-policy.com/Spam-black-lists.htm*. Another useful resource is a list of resources related to spam and block lists: *http://dmoz.org/Computers/Internet/Abuse/Spam/Blacklists/*.

A word of caution, however: using an RBL means that you are trusting someone else to make the decisions about what e-mail you will receive and what e-mail you will block. There are inherent problems with this approach, but it *does* make your decisions easier. If you do use an RBL, you should probably archive blocked messages to make sure you're not inadvertently blocking something you really want. But then make sure you actually check your archive and clean it up regularly.

Recipient Filtering

Use recipient filtering to filter messages sent to addresses that you know are only spam catchers. These filters will not apply to authenticated users or internal Exchange servers, so they won't interfere with any normal internal e-mail.

1. If you don't have the Message Delivery Properties dialog open, open it, and click the Recipient Filtering tab as shown in Figure 14-39.

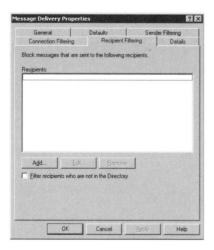

Figure 14-39. *Using recipient filtering to catch e-mail sent to addresses that get only spam sent to them.*

2. Click Add to type a recipient e-mail address to block (you can use wildcards here), and click OK after you type it in.

3. Click Edit to modify a currently blocked recipient, or click Remove to remove the recipient from the list.

4. Select the check box to filter recipients who are not in Active Directory.

Security Alert Although it might seem like a good idea to filter out any e-mail sent to non-existent addresses in your domain, that filtering process is actually one way spammers can tell what *is* a valid address. So we think it's probably not a good idea.

5. Click OK when you're finished.

Managing Queues

Exchange Server uses queues to handle incoming and outgoing messages. Some of the things you can do with queues are:

- View and monitor queues
- Find messages that are in a queue
- Shut down all outgoing queues immediately

Viewing and Monitoring Queues

To view the queues on your server, open the Server Management console, expand Advanced Management, expand your Exchange server, expand Servers, expand your server name, and then click Queues to open the Queue Viewer shown in Figure 14-40.

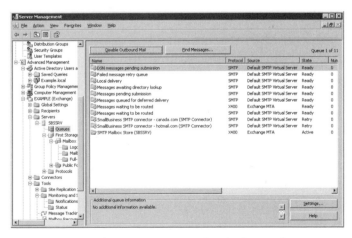

Figure 14-40. *The Queue Viewer for Exchange Server.*

From here you can see a number of queues, most of which you'll never have to do anything with. But if you see a queue with a bunch of messages in it, chances are there's a problem.

Finding the Messages In a Queue

If you have a queue with one or more messages in it, you can see what those messages are and take steps to either remove the messages or retry sending them once the reason they got stuck is resolved. Sometimes the problem is simply a bad message and the only resolution is to remove it. Or, if the message is generated by spam, it might be trying to reach a nonexistent domain or addressee within a domain. To find the messages in a queue:

1. Open the Queue Viewer as described in the preceding section, "Viewing and Monitoring Queues."

2. Highlight the queue you want to view the messages in, as shown in Figure 14-41.

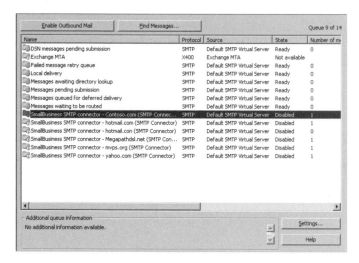

Figure 14-41. *The Queue Viewer, with the SMTP connector to Contoso.com highlighted.*

3. Double-click the queue to open the Find Messages dialog box, as shown in Figure 14-42.

4. You can specify search parameters, or to search for all messages in the queue, leave the fields blank and click Find Now.

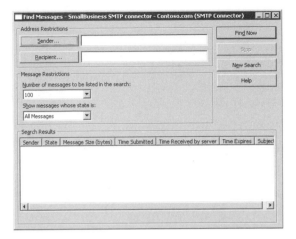

Figure 14-42.   *The Find Messages dialog box for an SMTP connector.*

5. When the search returns, double-click any of the messages to see the message properties, as shown in Figure 14-43.

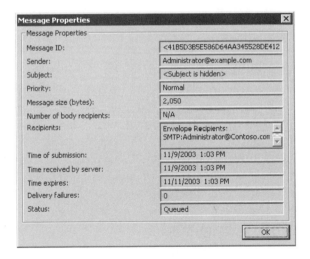

Figure 14-43.   *The message properties of a message in the Contoso.com SMTP connector queue.*

6. To freeze, unfreeze, or delete a message in the queue, highlight the message in the Search Results window and right-click it, as shown in Figure 14-44.

7. If you delete the message, you can choose whether to send the sender a non-delivery report (NDR).

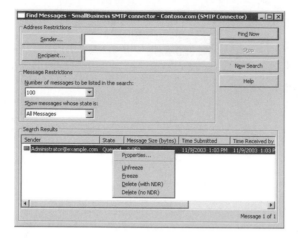

Figure 14-44. *You can freeze, unfreeze, or delete a message, with or without a non-delivery report from the queue.*

Shutting down All Outgoing Queues Immediately

If you have a virus loose on the network that is trying to send itself to every e-mail address it can find in one or more of your client address books, you have a problem! Long term, you need to get to the root of why and how the virus got loose on your network and take steps to make sure it can't happen again. But first and foremost, you need to *stop the spread outside your organization—now.*

There are a number of ways to do that, up to and including pulling the power plug out of the back of your Windows Small Business Server machine, but that's just a bit drastic. Probably the smartest and quickest way to make sure you don't create more problems is to quickly pull the network plug that connects your network to the outside world if you have physical access to the server room. Once that is done, or if you don't have quick and ready access to the server room when the problem is discovered, you can stop all outgoing e-mail in its tracks on the server itself, without interrupting any other functions on the server—including incoming e-mail—by shutting down all outbound e-mail queues. To shut down all outgoing queues:

1. Open the Queue Viewer as described in the section "Viewing and Monitoring Queues."

2. Click Disable Outbound Mail.

ZAP! That's it—the e-mail stops. Now you can deal with finding the virus, disabling and removing it, and removing the messages in the outbound queues that have the virus in them. Once you get all that sorted, and it's safe to start sending mail, click Enable Outbound Mail, and the queues will start sending mail again.

Summary

In this chapter, we covered all the basics of setting up and maintaining Microsoft Exchanger Server 2003, which is a core component of Microsoft Windows Small Business Server 2003. We discussed connecting to your ISP to send and deliver e-mail, setting up and maintaining the Microsoft Connector for POP3 Mailboxes, changing e-mail passwords, managing distribution groups, changing the e-mail Reply To address, managing e-mail queues, and filtering e-mail to reduce spam.

In the next chapter, we'll cover the details of managing the connectivity of your Windows Small Business Server network.

Chapter 15
Managing Connectivity

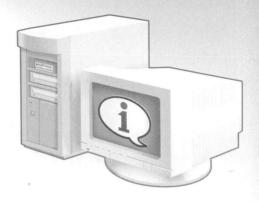

Managing network connectivity is a complicated task that Microsoft Windows Small Business Server distills into a relatively simple process handled by two wizards—the Configure E-Mail and Internet Connection Wizard, and the Remote Access Wizard.

More Info   For more information about these wizards, see Chapter 6, "Completing the To Do List and Other Post-Installation Tasks."

Though these wizards are the best way to change network settings, you might want to perform additional network administration tasks that aren't handled by them. This chapter covers the most common and useful tasks, including managing Dynamic Host Control Protocol (DHCP), viewing Dynamic Name Service (DNS) and Windows Internet Naming Service (WINS) records, and changing VPN settings using Routing and Remote Access and Internet Authentication Service (IAS).

This chapter also details three complex tasks that can increase network security and usability: creating a Public Key Infrastructure (PKI) to deploy certificates, setting up L2TP VPN connections, and implementing 802.1X authentication for wireless clients.

Administering TCP/IP Services

Windows Small Business Server 2003 manages DHCP, DNS, and WINS with no user intervention required. However, if clients experience trouble connecting to the server or other computers on the network, check DHCP, DNS, and WINS to verify that the clients are properly registered with each service.

More Info   See Chapter 20, "Monitoring and Fine-Tuning Performance," for additional network troubleshooting help. For an in-depth discussion about DHCP, DNS, and WINS, see *Microsoft Windows Server 2003 Administrator's Companion* (Microsoft Press).

Managing DHCP

DHCP automatically provides computers on the local network segment with valid IP addresses, and the addresses of the DNS server, WINS server, and default gateway. Windows Small Business Server manages most DHCP settings automatically, but you nonetheless might want to view the addresses currently leased to clients or change the range of excluded IP addresses to accommodate devices and computers with static IP addresses.

To view the addresses currently leased to clients, complete the following steps:

1. Open Server Management, and expand Advanced Management, Computer Management, Services And Applications, and finally DHCP.

2. Expand the Scope container, and then select Address Leases (Figure 15-1) to view a list of currently assigned IP addresses and their corresponding host names.

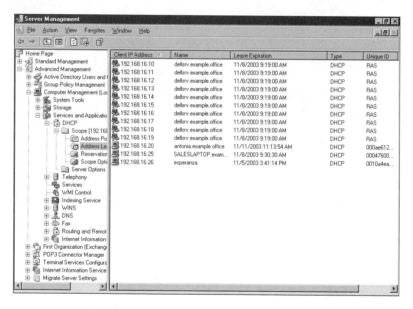

Figure 15-1. *Viewing assigned IP addresses.*

More Info To set up a client computer to use DHCP, see Chapter 12, "Managing Computers on the Network."

The pool of addresses a DHCP server can lease to clients is called a *scope*. If any devices on the network have static IP addresses in the scope, create an exclusion for the address or address range so that the DCHP server doesn't lease out these addresses. To do so, complete the following steps:

1. Right-click Address Pool in the Server Management console and choose New Exclusion Range from the shortcut menu.

2. In the Add Exclusion dialog box (Figure 15-2), use the Start IP Address and End IP Address boxes to specify the range of IP addresses you want to exclude. To exclude a single IP address, type it in the Start IP Address box.

3. Click Add to create the exclusion. Create any additional exclusions, and then click Close when you're finished.

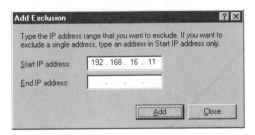

Figure 15-2. *The Add Exclusion dialog box.*

Viewing DNS Records

DNS is a TCP/IP service that maps IP addresses (192.168.16.2) to names (sbssrv.example.local). As such, it's an essential service for the Internet (the Web in particular) and Windows Small Business Server–based networks (which rely on TCP/IP).

Under the Hood **Default DNS Settings**

Windows Small Business Server 2003 uses the DNS server service for local name resolution only. If the name doesn't belong to the local domain, the DNS server forwards the query to your ISP's DNS server, which resolves the name on the Internet.

Windows Small Business Server 2003 automatically creates a couple types of zones for local name resolution. It creates a forward lookup zone for the domain (example.local), which allows you to use a DNS name to resolve an IP address. It also creates a reverse lookup zone, which enables you to resolve the DNS name associated with a particular IP address (a useful trick for troubleshooting). Both zones use secure dynamic updates so that Microsoft Windows 2000, Windows XP, and Windows Server 2003 clients can automatically and securely update their own DNS records.

Windows Small Business Server 2003 manages DNS automatically and there is little need to manually administer it. If you have trouble reaching hosts on the network by name (but can reach them by IP address), check their DNS resource records using the following steps:

1. Open Server Management, and expand Advanced Management, Computer Management, Services And Applications, and finally DNS.

2. Expand the *SBSSRV* container (where SBSSRV is the name of the Windows Small Business Server computer), expand Forward Lookup Zones, and then select *example.local* (assuming the name of the domain is *example.local*). This displays all resource records in the forward lookup zone (Figure 15-3). A Host (A) record for each computer in the domain, listing its current IP address and DNS name, should be visible.

3. To view records in the reverse lookup zone, expand the Reverse Lookup Zone container, and then 192.168.16.x Subnet. All Pointer (PTR) records in the reverse lookup zone are displayed.

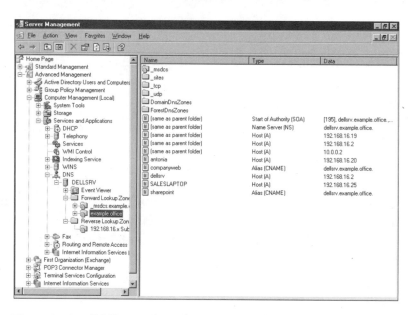

Figure 15-3. *DNS records in the DNS console.*

Viewing WINS Registrations

If clients have trouble Browsing the network or contacting a server by NetBIOS name, check to make sure that the clients are properly registered in Windows Internet Naming Service (WINS). To do so, complete the following steps:

1. Open Server Management, and expand Advanced Management, Computer Management, Services And Applications, and finally WINS.

2. Select the Active Registrations container.

3. Right-click Active Registrations and choose Display Records from the shortcut menu.

4. Click Find Now to display a list of all records in the WINS database (Figure 15-4), along with their status (Active or Released).

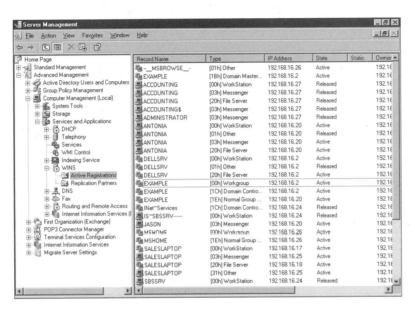

Figure 15-4. *WINS records in the WINS console.*

WINS and NetBIOS Name Resolution

NetBIOS is an interface originally developed to allow applications to access network resources in the MS-DOS operating system. As such, it was the primary networking API and naming method for Microsoft networks until the release of Windows 2000, and it is still required by older operating systems and network applications.

NetBIOS host names are up to 15 characters long and part of a flat namespace, so all names on a given network must be unique. Normally, host names are resolved by broadcast—not the most efficient means in terms of either time or network bandwidth. Routers also usually do not forward NetBIOS broadcasts, eliminating the ability to resolve host names on a different subnet.

WINS was created to provide a solution to this problem by maintaining a dynamic database of IP addresses and their associated NetBIOS names. Although many of us might be eager to do away with WINS, it is still used in Windows Small Business Server 2003 to provide NetBIOS name resolution services to clients that don't function properly in a NetBIOS-free network, for example, Microsoft Windows 98 and Windows NT 4.0. (Windows Server 2003, Windows XP, and Windows 2000 don't require NetBIOS support.)

Administering Routing and Remote Access

Routing and Remote Access serves as the router, firewall, and remote access (VPN and dial-up) server for a Windows Small Business Server 2003, Standard Edition network. Windows Small Business Server 2003, Premium Edition, uses Routing and Remote Access in combination with ISA Server 2000 for this functionality.

To configure Routing and Remote Access, use the Configure E-Mail and Internet Connection Wizard and the Remote Access Wizard, both of which are covered in Chapter 6. To view connected remote access clients, increase the allowed number of VPN connections, or increase VPN security, read the following sections.

Viewing Remote Access Clients

To view the clients currently connected to the server via a VPN or dial-up connection, complete the following steps:

1. Open Server Management, and expand Advanced Management, Computer Management, Services And Applications, and finally Routing And Remote Access.

2. Select Remote Access Clients to view a list of connected clients, as shown in Figure 15-5.

   - Double-click a client to view detailed status information on the connection.

   - Right-click a client and choose Disconnect from the shortcut menu to close the connection.

- Right-click a client and choose Send Message to send a pop-up message to the client, or choose Send To All to send a pop-up message to all connected clients.

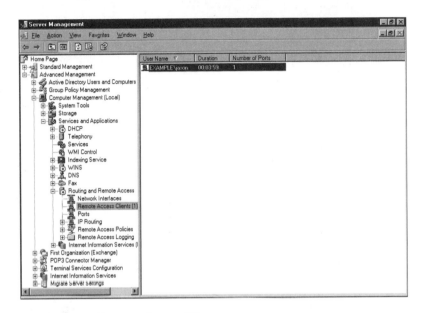

Figure 15-5.   *Remote Access Clients.*

Configuring Ports

Windows Small Business Server 2003 automatically creates 10 VPN ports that clients can use to connect to the server—five Point To Point Tunneling Protocol (PPTP) ports and five Layer 2 Tunneling Protocol (L2TP) ports. VPN clients can't use the L2TP protocol without some additional work, as discussed in "Creating L2TP VPN Connections" later in this chapter, which leaves five available ports for VPN connections. To support additional connections, you must increase the number of PPTP ports available. To do this, or to increase the number of L2TP ports available, complete the following steps:

1. In the Routing And Remote Access container of Server Management, right-click Ports and choose Properties from the shortcut menu.

2. In the Ports Properties dialog box (Figure 15-6), select WAN Miniport (PPTP) or WAN Miniport (L2TP), and click Configure.

3. In the Configure Device dialog box, use the Maximum Ports box to specify the number of connections you want to allow and click OK when you're finished.

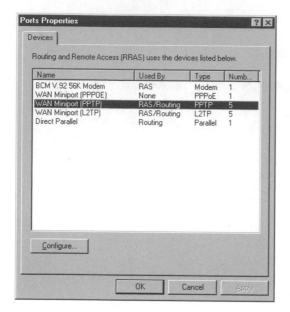

Figure 15-6. *The Ports Properties dialog box.*

Using Internet Authentication Service to Increase VPN Security

To maximize compatibility, VPNs in Windows Small Business Server 2003 aren't locked down as tightly as they could be. However, you can increase VPN security significantly with no compatibility problems as long as all clients run Windows 98 or later with High Encryption (128 bit) support. To do so, first install Internet Authentication Service (IAS), Microsoft's implementation of a Remote Authentication Dial-In User Service (RADIUS) server. (IAS is also needed for L2TP VPNs and 802.1X wireless authentication.)

To install IAS, complete the following steps:

1. Open Add Or Remove Programs in Control Panel and then click Add/Remove Windows Components. The Windows Components Wizard opens.

2. On the Windows Components page, select Networking Services and click Details.

3. In the Networking Services dialog box, select the check box next to Internet Authentication Service, click OK, and then click Next. The Windows Components Wizard installs IAS. Click Finish when it's done.

Once IAS is installed, use the following steps to modify the Windows Small Business Server Remote Access Policy to disable the use of Microsoft Challenge

Handshake Authentication Protocol (MS-CHAP) authentication and require 128-bit encryption:

1. From the Start menu, choose the Administrative Tools folder and then select Internet Authentication Service. This opens the Internet Authentication Service console.

2. Select Remote Access Policies and then double-click Small Business Remote Access Policy (Figure 15-7).

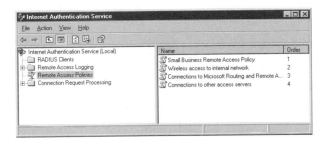

Figure 15-7. *The Internet Authentication Service console.*

3. In the Small Business Remote Access Policy Properties dialog box, click Edit Profile. The Edit Dial-In Profile dialog box appears.

4. Click the Authentication tab and then clear the Microsoft Encrypted Authentication (MS-CHAP) check box.

5. Click the Encryption tab (Figure 15-8) and clear all check boxes except Strongest Encryption (MPPE 128 bit), and then click OK.

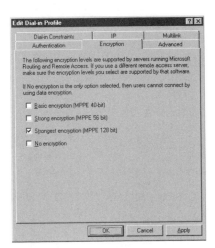

Figure 15-8. *The Encryption tab of the Edit Dial-In Profile dialog box.*

> **Note** Disabling MS-CHAP authentication prevents Microsoft Windows 95 clients from establishing remote access connections unless you install the Dial-Up Networking 1.3 Performance And Security Update for Windows 95, or upgrade the clients to Windows 98 or newer.

Deploying Certificate Services

Most networks use password-based authentication to secure network communications such as VPN and wireless connections. When used with secure authentication methods such as MS-CHAP v2 (for PPTP VPN connections) or WPA (for wireless connections), password-based security can be quite secure. However, password-based authentication can be inconvenient (you must remember a password or network key), and doesn't ensure the integrity of transmitted data—an industrious hacker could intercept, replay, and tamper with data.

One way of addressing these issues is to sign communications with a digital certificate. Doing so also enables clients to verify the identity of the server (reducing the risk of rogue servers), and to digitally sign and encrypt e-mails. Digital certificates are required by L2TP VPN connections and 802.1X authentication of wireless networks.

Installing Certificate Services

The first step in setting up 802.1X authentication or L2TP VPNs is to install Certificate Services and create an enterprise root Certificate Authority (CA), which can then be used to deploy certificates to users and computers on the network. To do so, complete the following steps:

1. Open Add Or Remove Programs in Control Panel and then click Add/Remove Windows Components. The Windows Components Wizard appears.

2. On the Windows Components page, select Certificate Services in the component list. The installer warns you that after the CA software is installed, you can't change the name of the server or move it into or out of an Active Directory domain. Click Yes, and then click Next.

3. On the CA Type page (Figure 15-9), select Enterprise Root CA and then click Next.

4. On the CA Identifying Information page (Figure 15-10), type a descriptive name for the CA (most likely including the company name) and then click Next.

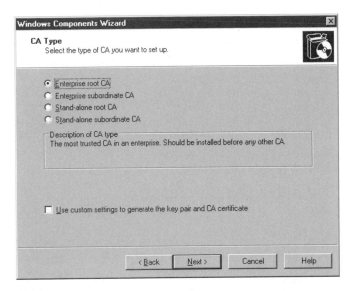

Figure 15-9. *The CA Type page of the Windows Components Wizard.*

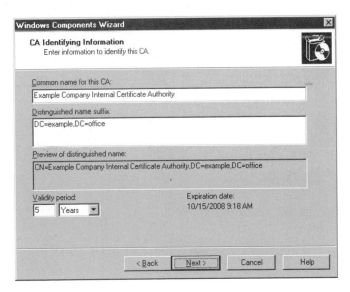

Figure 15-10. *The CA Identifying Information page of the Windows Components Wizard.*

5. On the Certificate Database Settings page, accept the default storage location for the certificate database and log files and configuration information. Note that the location you specify *isn't* where issued certificates are stored; it's where the CA's own certificates are stored. Click Next.

Note If the computer acting as the Enterprise Root CA crashes and you lose the CA database, you must reissue every certificate. Consider this extra motivation to regularly back up your entire Windows Small Business Server installation.

6. Click Yes when prompted to stop Microsoft Internet Information Services. When prompted, insert the appropriate Windows Small Business Server 2003 CD or DVD and then click OK. The Windows Components Wizard completes the installation of Certificate Services. Click Finish when it's done.

Creating a Local Computer and Current User Certificates Console

To request computer and user certificates for client computers, first create a console on the client computer that displays the Certificates (Local Computer) and Certificates (Current User) snap-ins. To do so, complete the following steps:

1. On a client computer, click Start, choose Run, type **mmc** in the Open box and then click OK. This opens a blank Microsoft Management Console (MMC).

2. Choose Add/Remove Snap-In from the File menu. The Add/Remove Snap-In dialog box appears.

3. Click Add, and select Certificates in the Add Standalone Snap-In dialog box, and then click Add again.

4. In the Certificates Snap-In dialog box (Figure 15-11), select Computer Account, click Next, select Local Computer, and then click Finish.

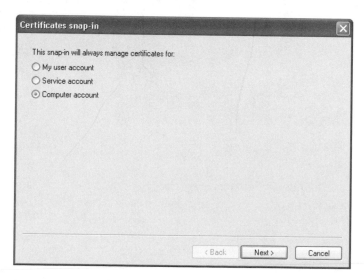

Figure 15-11. *The Certificates Snap-In dialog box.*

5. In the Add Standalone Snap-In dialog box, select Certificates again and click Add. The Certificates Snap-In dialog box appears.

6. Select My User Account and then click Finish. Click Close and then OK. This displays the MMC console with the two Certificates snap-ins.

7. Choose Save As from the File menu and then save this to a network share so that you can use the console from any computer on the network.

Requesting Computer and User Certificates

After creating a console that displays the Certificates (Local Computer) and Certificates (Current User) snap-ins, use the following steps to request and install computer and user certificates on a client computer. (But first join the computer to the domain, as described in Chapter 12.)

1. While connected to the network using a wired network connection, a wireless connection using 802.1X authentication with PEAP-MS CHAP v2, or an existing (PPTP) VPN connection, expand the Certificates (Local Computer) container, right-click Personal, choose All Tasks from the shortcut menu, and then choose Request New Certificate.

2. Click Next on the first page of the Certificate Request Wizard. Select Computer on the Certificate Types page (Figure 15-12), and then click Next.

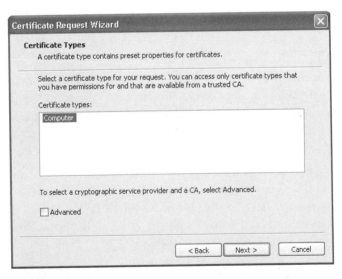

Figure 15-12. *Requesting a new certificate for the local computer.*

3. On the Certificate Friendly Name And Description page, type a friendly name and description for the certificate. Click Next and then Finish. Click OK in the dialog box that appears if the request was

successful. A new certificate is then created in the Certificates (Local Computer)\Personal\Certificates folder.

4. Expand the Certificates (Current User) container, right-click Personal, choose All Tasks from the shortcut menu, and then choose Request New Certificate.

5. Click Next on the first page of the Certificate Request Wizard, select User on the Certificate Types page (Figure 15-13), and then click Next.

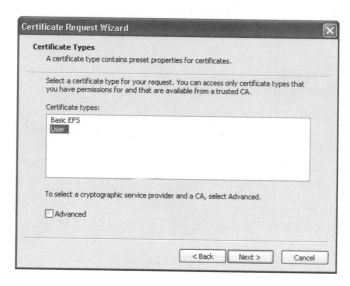

Figure 15-13. *Requesting a new certificate for a user.*

6. On the Certificate Friendly Name And Description page, type a friendly name and description for the certificate, click Next, and then click Finish. Click OK in the dialog box that appears if the request was successful. A new certificate is then created in the Certificates (Current User)\Personal\Certificates folder.

7. Just to be safe, expand the Trusted Root Certification Authorities container in either snap-in, select Certificates, and verify that the enterprise root CA that you created on the Windows Small Business Server computer appears in the list. (In our case, the enterprise root CA is Example Company Internal Certificate Authority.)

Tip You can configure clients to automatically request computer certificates, install the trusted root certificate from the Windows Small Business Server, and receive the proper 802.11 settings by using Group Policy. This is the best way to deploy 802.1X authentication settings to clients once you've tested the system. For information on how to do this, see the "Using Group Policy to Automatically Configure 802.11 and Certificate Settings" section later in this chapter.

Requesting a Certificate for the Windows Small Business Server Computer

The Windows Small Business Server computer should obtain a domain controller certificate so that it can validate its identity to clients for L2TP VPN connections and 802.1X authentication. To do so, first install Certificate Services as an enterprise root CA (as discussed earlier in this chapter), and then use the following procedure to request a certificate from the CA.

1. Open the Certificates (Local Computer) console. See the "Creating A Local Computer and Current User Certificates Console" section earlier in this chapter if you have yet to create this console.

2. Right-click the Personal container, choose All Tasks from the shortcut menu, and then choose Request New Certificate. The Certificate Request Wizard opens.

3. Click Next on the first page of the Certificate Request Wizard, and on the Certificate Types page, select Domain Controller. Click Next to continue.

4. On the Certificate Friendly Name And Description page, type **SBS Server Certificate** in the Friendly Name box, optionally type a description, and then click Next.

5. Review the settings and then click Finish. Click OK in the dialog box that appears, which states that the certificate request was successful. (If this doesn't appear, there's a problem with Certificate Services.)

Creating L2TP VPN Connections

Layer 2 Tunneling Protocol (L2TP) is currently the most secure VPN protocol available in Windows Small Business Server 2003, offering significantly higher levels of security than PPTP. Unfortunately, setting up L2TP is a complex process involving a number of different services and tasks. The following sections reduce this complexity into a series of straightforward steps that make deploying L2TP almost easy.

Deploying Certificates

The first step in setting up L2TP is to deploy user and computer certificates to all VPN clients, and to request a computer certificate for the Windows Small Business Server computer. (Even though the computer already has several certificates, it needs a domain controller certificate signed by the certificate authority.) Follow the steps in the "Deploying Certificate Services" section of this chapter to do this.

Modifying the Small Business Remote Access Policy

After deploying user and computer certificates to VPN clients and the Windows Small Business Server computer, edit the Small Business Remote Access Policy to allow authentication via certificates. To do so, install Internet Authentication Service, if it's not already (as described in the "Using Internet Authentication Service to Increase VPN Security" section of this chapter), and then complete the following steps:

1. From the Start menu, choose the Administrative Tools folder and then select Internet Authentication Service. This opens the Internet Authentication Service console.

2. Select Remote Access Policies and then double-click Small Business Remote Access Policy.

3. In the Small Business Remote Access Policy Properties dialog box, click Edit Profile. The Edit Dial-In Profile dialog box appears.

4. Click the Authentication tab and then click EAP Methods. The Select EAP Providers dialog box appears.

Security Alert   To increase the security of VPN connections, disable MS-CHAP authentication and require 128-bit encryption using the Authentication and Encryption tabs, as discussed in the "Using Internet Authentication Service to Increase VPN Security" section of this chapter.

5. Click Add, select Smart Card Or Other Certificate, and then click OK. The Select EAP Providers dialog box (Figure 15-14) lists the newly added EAP type.

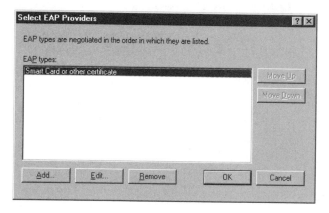

Figure 15-14.   *The Select EAP Providers dialog box.*

6. Select Smart Card Or Other Certificate and click Edit. In the Smart Card Or Other Certificate Properties dialog box that appears, select the certificate the server should use to authenticate itself with VPN clients and then click OK. Click OK, and then click OK again to finish updating the profile.

Tip   Add the Protected EAP (PEAP) authentication method as well if you want to allow L2TP connections authenticated with MS-CHAP v2 instead of certificates. PEAP authentication provides a way of gradually moving to a certificate-based authentication—implement L2TP connections using certificates when possible, and PEAP when not. PEAP authentication also makes troubleshooting L2TP VPN connections easier.

Opening Ports in the Firewall

After deploying certificates and modifying the default remote access policy, open ports in the firewall to allow L2TP VPN connections to pass through to the internal network. The following sections show how to open the appropriate ports in ISA Server 2000 (for Windows Small Business Server 2003, Premium Edition, users) and in the Routing and Remote Access firewall (for Windows Small Business Server, Standard Edition, users).

Opening Ports in ISA Server 2000

If you're using ISA Server 2000, complete the following steps to open ports for L2TP:

1. Click Start, choose All Programs, Microsoft ISA Server, and finally ISA Management.

2. Expand Servers And Arrays, then *SBSSRV* (assuming the server is named SBSSRV), and finally select Network Configuration. The Configure Network Connection taskpad appears.

3. Click Configure A Client Virtual Private Network (VPN). The ISA VPN Server Wizard appears.

4. Click Next and then Finish (it's a short wizard). An ISA Virtual Private Network (VPN) Wizard dialog box appears.

5. Click Yes to install the Routing And Remote Access service, and then click Yes to restart the service.

Caution   The first time you run the ISA VPN Server Wizard, the wizard clears any Routing And Remote Access settings you might have customized.

Note If you have a stand-alone firewall, open UDP port 500 for Internet Key Exchange (IKE), UDP port 4500 for IPSec NAT-Traversal traffic, and IP Protocol port 50 for IPSec ESP traffic.

Real World **The Configure E-Mail and Internet Connection Wizard Disables L2TP Packet Filters**

Changing firewall settings using the Configure E-Mail and Internet Connection Wizard disables packet filters created by the ISA VPN Server Wizard for L2TP VPN connections. To get L2TP connections working again, complete the following steps:

1. In the ISA Management console, expand Servers And Arrays, then *SBSSRV* (assuming the server is named SBSSRV), and finally select Access Policy. The Configure Access Policy taskpad appears.

2. Double-click Allow L2TP Protocol IKE Packets, select the Enable This Filter check box in the Properties dialog box, and then click OK.

3. Double-click Allow L2TP Protocol Packets, select the Enable This Filter check box in the Properties dialog box, and then click OK.

Opening Ports in Routing and Remote Access

If you're using Windows Small Business Server 2003, Standard Edition, complete the following steps to open ports for L2TP in the Routing and Remote Access firewall:

1. Open Server Management, and expand Advanced Management, Computer Management, Services And Applications, and finally Routing And Remote Access.

2. Expand IP Routing, and then NAT/Basic Firewall. Right-click Network Connection and choose Properties from the shortcut menu. The Network Connection Properties dialog box appears.

3. Click the Services And Ports tab (Figure 15-15), select the following protocols, and then click OK:

   - IP Security (IKE)
   - IP Security (IKE NAT Traversal)
   - VPN Gateway (L2TP/IPSec—running on this server)

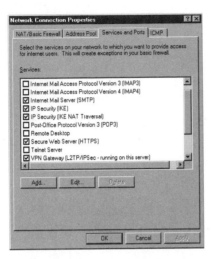

Figure 15-15. *The Services And Ports tab of Network Connection Properties dialog box.*

Note   If you have a stand-alone firewall, open UDP port 500 for Internet Key Exchange (IKE), UDP port 4500 for IPSec NAT-Traversal traffic, and IP Protocol port 50 for IPSec ESP traffic.

Enabling EAP in Routing and Remote Access

The final step in preparing a server to accept incoming L2TP VPN connections is to enable Extensible Authentication Protocol (EAP) in Routing and Remote Access. To enable EAP in Routing and Remote Access, complete the following steps:

1. Open Server Management, and expand Advanced Management, Computer Management, Services And Applications, and finally Routing And Remote Access.

2. Right-click Routing And Remote Access and choose Properties from the shortcut menu. The Routing And Remote Access Properties dialog box appears.

3. Click the Security tab, and then click Authentication Methods. The Authentication Methods dialog box appears (Figure 15-16).

4. Select Extensible Authentication Protocol (EAP), click OK, and then click OK again.

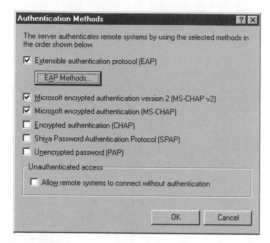

Figure 15-16. *The Authentication Methods dialog box.*

Creating the VPN Connection

After the server is properly configured to accept incoming L2TP connections, manually create a VPN connection on the client computer using the following steps:

1. On the client computer, open the Network Connections (Windows XP) or Network and Dial-Up Connections folder (Windows 2000).

Note VPN connections created using the Windows Small Business Server 2003 Connection Manager automatically connect using PPTP.

2. Choose New Connection from the File menu. When the New Connection Wizard appears, click Next.

3. On the Network Connection Type page, choose Connect To The Network At My Workplace (Windows XP) or Connect To A Private Network Through The Internet (Windows 2000), and then click Next.

4. On the Network Connection page, choose Virtual Private Network Connection and then click Next. (This page doesn't appear in Windows 2000.)

5. On the Connection Name page, type the name for the connection and then click Next. (This page doesn't appear in Windows 2000.)

6. On the Public Network page, choose whether to establish a dial-up Internet connection before using the VPN connection and then click Next. (This page doesn't appear in Windows 2000.)

7. On the VPN Server Selection page (Windows XP) or Destination Address page (Windows 2000), type the Internet-accessible IP address of the Windows Small Business Server computer and then click Next.

8. On the Connection Availability page, choose whether to allow other users access to the VPN connection and then click Next. Type a name for the connection (if creating a connection in Windows 2000) and then click Finish to complete the wizard. The Connect dialog box appears.

9. In the Connect dialog box, click Properties.

10. Click the Networking tab (Figure 15-17) and choose L2TP IPSec VPN (Windows XP) or Layer-2 Tunneling Protocol (L2TP) (Windows 2000) from the Type Of VPN box.

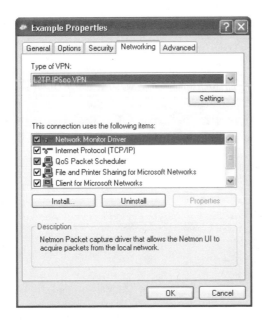

Figure 15-17. *The Networking tab.*

11. Click the Security tab, choose Advanced, and then click Settings. The Advanced Security Settings dialog box appears.

12. Choose Use Extensible Authentication Protocol (EAP), select Smart Card Or Other Certificate, as shown in Figure 15-18, and then click Properties. The Smart Card Or Other Certificate Properties dialog box appears.

Figure 15-18. *The Advanced Security Settings dialog box.*

13. Choose Use A Certificate On This Computer, as shown in Figure 15-19, select Validate Server Certificate, and then select the name of the Windows Small Business Server computer in the Trusted Root Certification Authorities section of the dialog box. Click OK when you're finished. Click OK, and then click OK again. The VPN connection is then established.

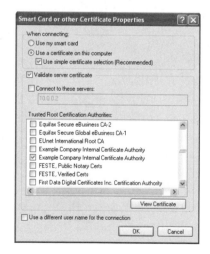

Figure 15-19. *The Smart Card Or Other Certificate Properties dialog box.*

14. In the Validate Server Certificate dialog box, click OK to accept the server's credentials and connect to the network.

Tip   Once you've got L2TP VPN connections working, automate the process of creating L2TP VPN connections for clients using the Connection Manager Administration Kit, which can be installed using the Windows Component Wizard, accessible from Add Or Remove Programs.

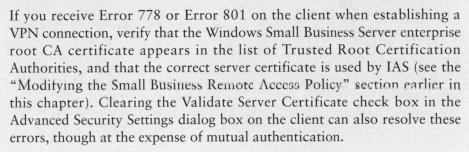

Real World   **L2TP Troubleshooting**

If you have trouble connecting via L2TP, try establishing an L2TP VPN connection from inside the internal network (this tests whether the problem is in the firewall configuration). Check Event Viewer and use Network Monitor to perform a network capture, if necessary. L2TP connections might not work properly if the client computer is behind a NAT firewall.

If you receive Error 778 or Error 801 on the client when establishing a VPN connection, verify that the Windows Small Business Server enterprise root CA certificate appears in the list of Trusted Root Certification Authorities, and that the correct server certificate is used by IAS (see the "Modifying the Small Business Remote Access Policy" section earlier in this chapter). Clearing the Validate Server Certificate check box in the Advanced Security Settings dialog box on the client can also resolve these errors, though at the expense of mutual authentication.

Wireless Security Using 802.1X Authentication

Securing 802.11 (Wi-Fi) networks is a subject of much debate and a myriad of options. (See the Real World sidebar, "Wireless Security Strategies," appearing later in this chapter.) One of the most sophisticated methods of securing an 802.11 network is using 802.1X authentication in conjunction with WEP or WPA encryption. Although setting up 802.1X authentication evokes panic in the hearts of many administrators due to its complexity, it's not as hard as you might think, especially when done in a simplified manner suitable for small businesses, as discussed in the following sections.

Caution   Deploying 802.1X authentication is a complex process, so it's extremely important to carefully follow the steps in each section, double-check your work, and not skip any sections.

Real World   Wireless Security Strategies

There are a number of strategies for securing wireless 802.11a/b/g networks:

- **MAC address filtering** Usually combined with disabling SSID broadcasting and using static IP addresses for clients, MAC address filtering can be hacked easily with a network sniffer, requires a lot of administrative work and hassle, and is a complete waste of time.

- **Wired Equivalent Privacy (WEP) Encryption** This method secures a network against casual hacking attempts, but is easily defeated by monitoring network traffic for an extended period of time (which can be as short as several hours on a busy network—even when 128-bit keys are used). WEP encryption also requires manually typing long encryption keys on all clients and access points, which can be a nuisance. To maximize security with WEP, change encryption keys weekly if possible.

- **Wi-Fi Protected Access (WPA)** WPA provides good security for wireless networks, but you must manually type network keys on all clients and access points, unless 802.1X authentication is used. Not all client operating systems support WPA yet—only newer access points support it—and WPA can be easily compromised when the keys used aren't long (128 bits), randomly generated strings.

- **VPNs** An extremely popular, secure, and easily set up method of securing wireless networks is to place access points in a perimeter network and have clients establish a VPN connection to access the internal network. However, there is some performance impact; Group Policy Computer Configuration doesn't work over VPN links; and remote administration of clients only works while the VPN is connected.

- **802.1X Authentication** 802.1X authentication using WEP or WPA encryption is very secure (keys are generated dynamically and mutual authentication occurs) and offers the most seamless client experience—authentication takes place using the user account and digital signatures. This is the preferred wireless solution by Microsoft; however, it does require additional configuration on the server and clients, as well as access points that support 802.1X authentication.

Choosing Authentication Protocols

The 802.1X authentication standard requires the use of an authentication protocol. There are two worth considering:

- Protected Extensible Authentication Protocol (PEAP) combined with Microsoft Challenge Handshake Authentication Protocol version 2 (MS-CHAP v2)

- Extensible Authentication Protocol-Transport Layer Security (EAP-TLS)

PEAP is the easiest protocol to implement—only the Windows Small Business Server computer requires a certificate. However, because PEAP relies on user credentials for authentication, Group Policy computer configuration information won't work, nor will remote administration while the user is logged off.

EAP-TLS provides higher security and greater functionality by requiring client authentication using computer and user certificates. This allows a client computer to remain connected to the network while the user is logged off (the computer is authenticated), and also permits Group Policy computer configuration processing. However it does mean installing computer and user certificates on the client.

Because PEAP is easier to configure, start by implementing PEAP and switch to a full-blown EAP-TLS configuration when you're ready—immediately or at a later date.

> **Tip** A wireless client receives updated Computer Configuration policies every time it restarts while connected to the network via an Ethernet connection, including during the initial process of joining the computer to the Windows Small Business Server network. For companies that rarely change Group Policy settings, updating Computer Configuration policies in this manner might be satisfactory.

Under the Hood 802.1X Authentication Process

Here's a summary of the 802.1X authentication process for a client.

1. The client associates with an access point.

2. The client asks for the RADIUS server's certificate to authenticate the server.

3. The client sends its computer account credentials to the RADIUS server.

4. The RADIUS server contacts Active Directory to verify the computer account credentials, and checks any remote access policies to verify that the computer belongs to a group with access permissions.

5. If the client's computer account has the proper permissions, the client and RADIUS server generate WEP (or WPA) keys and establish a secure session, logging the computer onto the domain.

6. The client sends user credentials, which the RADIUS server also checks in Active Directory.

7. If successful, the user is logged onto the domain and given network access.

Real World   PEAP and Group Policy Processing

Although PEAP provides great wireless security and is easier to implement than EAP-TLS authentication, there are two significant drawbacks. The first is that you won't be able to remotely administer wireless clients unless someone's logged on. The second is that Group Policy Computer Configuration won't work.

Group Policy Computer Configuration is used by Windows Small Business Server to apply the following Group Polices to computers in the network:

- Password policies

- Account lockout policies

- Tightened Kerberos policies

- Prohibit installation of Network Bridge on internal network

- Prohibit use of Internet Connection Firewall on internal network

- Prohibit use of Internet Connection sharing on internal network

- Enable Domain Admins to offer remote assistance without invitation

Additionally, Group Policy Computer Configuration is the easiest way to enable clients to connect to Software Update Services for patches (as discussed in Chapter 6.)

Deploying Certificates

The first step in deploying 802.1X authentication is to deploy user and computer certificates to all wireless clients (when implementing EAP-TLS), and request a computer certificate for the Windows Small Business Server computer. (Even though the computer already has several certificates, it needs a domain controller certificate signed by a trusted certificate authority for PEAP and EAP-TLS.)

Follow the steps in the "Deploying Certificate Services" section of this chapter to do this.

Adding Access Points as RADIUS Clients

After deploying user and computer certificates to wireless clients and the Windows Small Business Server computer, set up IAS to recognize wireless access points as RADIUS clients. To do so, install Internet Authentication Service if you haven't already (as described in the "Using Internet Authentication Service to Increase VPN Security" section), and then complete the following steps:

1. Open Internet Authentication Service from the Administrative Tools folder.

2. Right-click the RADIUS Clients container and choose New RADIUS Client from the shortcut menu. This opens the New RADIUS Client Wizard.

3. On the Name And Address page (Figure 15-20), type a descriptive name for the access point in the Friendly Name box. In the Client Address (IP or DNS) box, type the IP address of the access point, and then click Next.

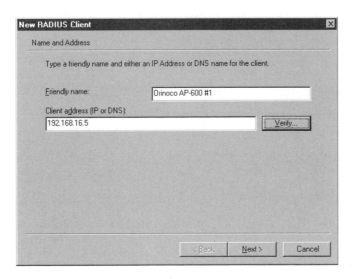

Figure 15-20. *The New RADIUS Client Wizard.*

Caution   The access point should use a static IP address or a DHCP reservation. When using a static IP address, either make sure that the address is in the range of addresses automatically excluded from the DHCP scope by Windows Small Business Server (192.168.16.3 to 192.168.16.9), or add an exclusion range that includes the IP address of the access point, as discussed in "Managing DHCP" earlier in this chapter.

4. On the Additional Information page, type a complex password in the Shared Secret and Confirm Shared Secret boxes. You must type this password into each access point as well, as discussed in the "Configuring Wireless Access Points" section of this chapter. Click Finish when you're done.

Note A *shared secret* is a password used between an IAS server and any wireless access points. The shared secret must be the same on both the IAS server and all access points and must follow general password rules: it's case sensitive, can use alphanumeric and special characters, and can be up to 255 characters long. Use a long (16-characters or longer) and complex string to maximize security—because the shared secret is embedded in the software and is only typed once, you don't need to memorize it.

Creating a Remote Access Policy

The next step in configuring wireless security is to create a new remote access policy that allows clients that use 802.1X authentication (and have proper domain logon permissions) to connect to the network. To do so, complete the following steps:

1. Open Internet Authentication Service from the Administrative Tools folder.

2. Right-click Remote Access Polices and choose New Remote Access Policy from the shortcut menu. This displays the New Remote Access Policy Wizard. Click Next on the first page.

3. On the Policy Configuration Method page, type a policy name such as **Wireless access to internal network**. Click Next.

4. On the Access Method page, select Wireless (Figure 15-21) and then click Next.

5. On the User Or Group Access page, select Group and then click Add.

6. In the Select Groups dialog box, type **Domain Users; Domain Computers** and then click OK. The User Or Group Access page updates to show the Domain Users and Domain Computers groups (Figure 15-22). Click Next to continue.

Tip To limit wireless access to certain users, create a new security group named Wireless Users, add the desired users and their associated computer accounts to the group, and then specify this group in the Select Groups dialog box instead of Domain Users and Domain Computers.

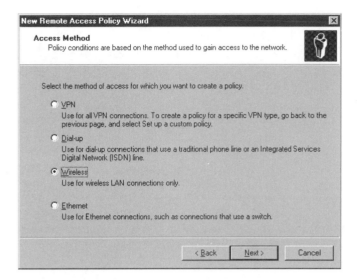

Figure 15-21. *The Access Method page of the New Remote Access Policy Wizard.*

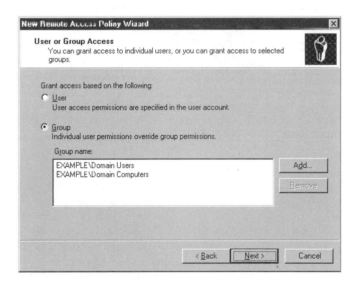

Figure 15-22. *The User Or Group Access page of the New Remote Access Policy Wizard.*

7. On the Authentication Methods page, select the type of authentication to use and then click Next.

- **Protected EAP (PEAP)** Choose this if you've decided not to deploy user and computer certificates to all wireless clients, or you want to simplify initial testing and client deployment.

- **Smart Card Or Other Certificate** Choose this if you've decided to implement EAP-TLS authentication, which requires that wireless clients have valid user and computer certificates. See the "Enabling EAP-TLS" section later in this chapter for the additional steps required to deploy EAP-TLS.

8. Review the settings and then click Finish. If you have trouble getting to this page, check to make sure that the certificate was properly issued to the server.

9. In the Remote Access Policies container, double-click the remote access policy you just created and click Edit Profile in the Properties dialog box.

10. Click the Encryption tab and clear all check boxes except Strongest Encryption (MPPE 128 bit) to maximize the security of the connection. Click OK twice.

Configuring Wireless Access Points

Once the Windows Small Business Server computer is properly configured for 802.1X authentication, it's time to set up the wireless access points. The procedure varies from access point to access point, but here are the settings to configure:

- Set up the access points with static IP addresses in the range of 192.168.16.3 through 192.168.16.9, a subnet mask of 255.255.255.0, and a gateway address of 192.168.16.2. (If you need more addresses, see the "Managing DHCP" section earlier in this chapter for information about creating new exclusion ranges.)

- Disable the DHCP server feature of the access point.

- Change the SSID to one that's appropriate for the network but doesn't reveal the location or name of the business.

- Change all access point passwords to secure passwords.

- Enable Primary RADIUS Server, and type the IP address of the Windows Small Business Server in the Primary RADIUS Server IP Address field (most likely 192.168.16.2). In the Destination Port, type **1812**.

- Type the shared secret you typed when adding the access points as RADIUS clients. (See the "Adding Access Points as RADIUS Clients" section in this chapter for more information.)

- Enable WEP encryption or WPA if all access points and clients support it.

- Enable 802.1X Authentication with 128-bit keys.

Configuring Clients to Use PEAP

Most companies set up 802.1X authentication using PEAP before implementing EAP-TLS authentication. PEAP is simpler to set up (clients don't need certificates) and is easier to test. To configure clients for 802.1X authentication using PEAP, complete the following steps. (See the next section to set up EAP-TLS authentication.)

1. Using a wired network connection, join the computer to the Windows Small Business Server network using the Network Configuration Wizard, if you haven't already. See Chapter 12 for help with this step.

2. While still connected via wired network connection, click Start, choose Run, type *sbssrv*\CertEnroll in the Open box (where sbssrv is the name of the Windows Small Business Server computer), and then click OK.

3. In the list of certificates, double-click the certificate corresponding to the Windows Small Business Server computer.

4. In the Certificate dialog box (Figure 15-23), click Install Certificate. The Certificate Import Wizard appears.

Tip If there are a large number of wireless clients on the network, use Group Policy to automate the deployment of certificates and 802.11 settings after verifying that 802.1X authentication is working properly. For information about how to do this, see the "Using Group Policy to Automatically Configure 802.11 and Certificate Settings" section later in this chapter.

Figure 15-23. *The Certificate dialog box.*

5. Click Next on the first page of the Certificate Import Wizard, click Next on the Certificate Store page, and then click Finish to install the certificate automatically. This places it in the root store.

6. Disconnect from the wired network (if you're connected), right-click the Wireless Network Connection icon in the system tray, and choose View Available Networks from the shortcut menu. Clients running operating systems other than Windows XP should follow the instructions provided with their wireless network card.

7. In the Wireless Network Connection dialog box, click Advanced.

8. In the Available Networks section of the Wireless Network Connection Properties dialog box (Figure 15-24), select the correct network and then click Configure. (This dialog box looks different on computers running Windows XP Service Pack 2 or later.)

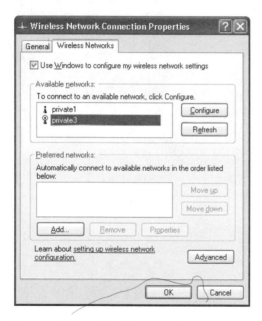

Figure 15-24. *The Wireless Network Connection Properties dialog box on a computer running Windows XP Service Pack 1.*

9. If the client is running Windows XP Service Pack 1 without the WPA patch, verify that the Data Encryption (WEP Enabled) and The Key Is Provided For Me Automatically check boxes are selected in the Wireless Network Properties dialog box (Figure 15-25). If the client has the WPA patch installed or is running Windows XP Service Pack 2 or later, select Open from the Network Authentication box (or WPA if using WPA), and WEP from the Data Encryption box (or TKIP if using WPA). The dialog box might look somewhat different in Windows XP Service Pack.

10. Click the Authentication tab (Figure 15-26), select the Enable IEEE 802.1x Authentication For This Network check box, choose Protected

EAP (PEAP) from the EAP Type box, select Authenticate As Computer When Computer Information Is Available, and then click OK. After clicking OK again, the computer authenticates and connects to the network.

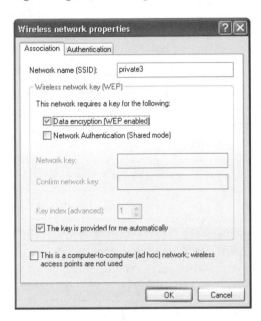

Figure 15-25. *The Wireless Network Properties dialog box on a computer running Windows XP Service Pack 1.*

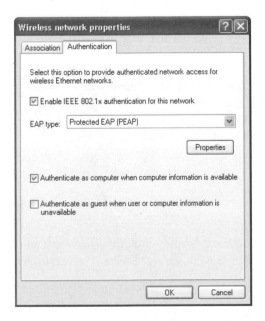

Figure 15-26. *The Authentication tab of the Wireless Network Properties dialog box.*

Real World   Troubleshooting 802.1X Authentication

If clients can't connect using 802.1X authentication, check Event Viewer on the Windows Small Business Server computer for clues. Enable all encryption levels in the Remote Access Policy, and verify that the client computer has the Windows Small Business Server computer's certificate properly installed. Installing Network Monitor and performing a network capture while the client attempts to connect can also be helpful.

If the client loses a connection when roaming between access points in the same network, click Properties on the Authentication tab of the Wireless Network Properties dialog box and select the Enable Fast Reconnect check box.

Enabling EAP-TLS

Once 802.1X authentication is working with PEAP, implementing EAP-TLS authentication is relatively easy. (PEAP is often deployed first to simplify initial testing.) To enable EAP-TLS, use the following sections to modify the wireless remote access policy and configure the clients to authenticate using certificates.

More Info   User and computer certificates must be installed on wireless clients before they can authenticate using EAP-TLS. To request user and computer certificates, see the "Requesting Computer and User Certificates" section of this chapter.

Enabling EAP-TLS in Remote Access Policy

If you created a remote access policy that permits PEAP authentication (in the "Creating a Remote Access Policy" section of this chapter), use the following steps to add EAP-TLS to the list of allowed authentication protocols. If you chose Smart Card Or Other Certificate on the Authentication Methods page when creating the remote access policy, skip this section.

To add EAP-TLS authentication to the remote access policy you created earlier in this chapter, complete the following steps:

1. Open Internet Authentication Service from the Administrative Tools folder.

2. Select Remote Access Policies and then double-click the wireless access policy you created in the "Creating a Remote Access Policy" section of this chapter.

3. In the Properties dialog box, click Edit Profile.

4. In the Edit Dial-In Profile dialog box, click the Authentication tab (Figure 15-27).

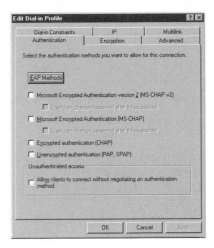

Figure 15-27.   *The Authentication tab of the Edit Dial-In Profile dialog box.*

5. Click EAP Methods. In the Select EAP Providers dialog box, click Add.

6. In the Add EAP dialog box, select Smart Card Or Other Certificate and then click OK.

7. In the Select EAP Providers dialog box (Figure 15-28), select Protected (EAP) and click Remove. If you want to leave PEAP enabled until EAP-TLS is deployed and operating on all clients, select PEAP and click Move Down so that it is used only by clients who can't authenticate using EAP-TLS. When you're finished, click OK, and then click OK again twice to return to the Internet Authentication Service console.

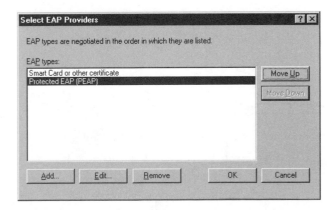

Figure 15-28.   *The Select EAP Providers dialog box.*

Configuring Clients to Use EAP-TLS

After enabling EAP-TLS in the remote access policy and deploying computer and user certificates to wireless clients (as discussed in the "Requesting Computer and User Certificates" section of this chapter), complete the following steps to configure clients for 802.1X authentication using EAP-TLS.

1. On a client computer, disconnect from the wired network (if you're connected), right-click the Wireless Network Connection icon in the system tray, and choose View Available Networks from the shortcut menu. Clients running operating systems other than Windows XP should follow the instructions provided with their wireless network card.

2. In the Wireless Network Connection dialog box, click Advanced. (Computers running Windows XP Service Pack 2 or later might appear somewhat different.)

3. In the Available Networks section of the Wireless Network Connection Properties dialog box (Figure 15-29), select the correct network and then click Configure.

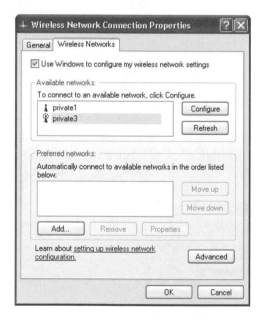

Figure 15-29. *The Wireless Network Connection Properties dialog box.*

4. If the client is running Windows XP Service Pack 1 without the WPA patch, verify that the Data Encryption (WEP Enabled) and The Key Is Provided For Me Automatically check boxes are selected in the Wireless Network Properties dialog box. If the client has the WPA patch installed or is running Windows XP Service Pack 2 or later, select Open in the

Network Authentication box (or WPA if using WPA), and WEP in the Data Encryption box (or TKIP if using WPA on the network). The dialog box might look somewhat different in Windows XP Service Pack 2.

5. Click the Authentication tab (Figure 15-30), select the Enable IEEE 802.1x Authentication For This Network check box, choose Smart Card Or Other Certificate in the EAP Type box, select Authenticate As Computer When Computer Information Is Available, and then click OK. After clicking OK again, the computer authenticates and connects to the network.

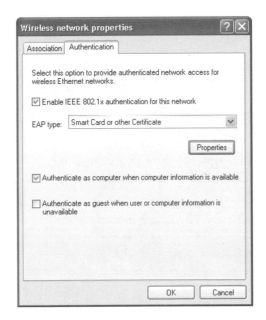

Figure 15-30.   *The Authentication tab of the Wireless Network Properties dialog box.*

Using Group Policy to Automatically Configure 802.11 and Certificate Settings

You can streamline the process of deploying computer certificates and 802.11 settings using Group Policy, making the deployment process for L2TP VPNs and 802.1X wireless authentication much simpler. The only steps left to perform manually are obtaining user certificates and creating L2TP VPN connections. To automate the enrollment of user certificates, you need a Windows Server 2003 Enterprise Edition Certificate Authority, which is solidly outside of the reach of small businesses.

Use the following sections to create a new Group Policy Object (GPO) and configure it to automate computer certificate enrollment and 802.11 wireless settings deployment.

> **Tip** You can easily obtain a user certificate using the Microsoft Certificate Services Web site (*http://sbssrv/CertSrv*, where the Windows Small Business Server computer's name is sbssrv). You can automate the creation of L2TP VPN connections using the Connection Manager Administration Kit (CMAK).

Creating and Linking a New Group Policy Object

It's a best practice to create a new Group Policy Object (GPO) any time you want to apply settings via Group Policy. This makes it easy to undo changes—simply disable the GPO.

Complete the following steps to create a new GPO and link it to the appropriate domain or organizational unit (OU):

1. From the Start menu, choose the Administrative Tools folder and then open the Group Policy Management console.

2. In the console tree, navigate to Domains, then to example.local (or whatever the domain is named), and then to Group Policy Objects.

3. Right-click Group Policy Objects (Figure 15-31). Choose New from the shortcut menu, type a name for the GPO, and then click OK.

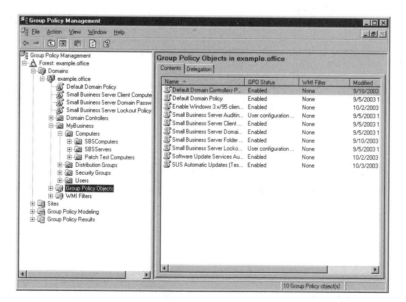

Figure 15-31. *The Group Policy Objects container and the Group Policy Management console.*

4. Link the new GPO by dragging it from the Group Policy Objects container to the appropriate OU or container:

- Use the Computers OU in the MyBusiness OU to link the GPO to all client and server computer accounts created with the Set Up Client Wizard and Set Up Server Wizard.

- Use the SBSComputers OU in the MyBusiness\Computers OU to link the GPO to all client computer accounts created with the Set Up Client Wizard.

- Use the SBSServers OU in the MyBusiness\Computers OU to link the GPO to all server computer accounts created with the Set Up Server Wizard.

Note   There's no harm in deploying computer certificates and 802.11 settings to desktop computers.

Tip   Use the Group Policy Results and Group Policy Modeling tools to ensure that your GPO is being applied properly. For more information, see Chapter 10, "Shares, Permissions, and Group Policy."

Modifying Certificate Settings

After creating a new GPO for your settings, use the following steps to enable client computers to automatically obtain computer certificates and install the Windows Small Business Server computer's certificate in the Trusted Root Certificate Authorities certificate store.

1. Right-click the GPO you created in the Group Policy Management Console and choose Edit from the shortcut menu. This opens the Group Policy Object Editor.

2. Navigate to Computer Configuration, Windows Settings, Security Settings, and finally Public Key Policies (Figure 15-32).

3. Right-click Automatic Certificate Request Settings, choose New from the shortcut menu, and then choose Automatic Certificate Request. When the Automatic Certificate Request Setup Wizard appears, click Next.

4. On the Certificate Template page, select Computer, click Next, and then click Finish.

5. Right-click Trusted Root Certificate Authorities and choose Import from the shortcut menu. When the Certificate Import Wizard appears, click Next.

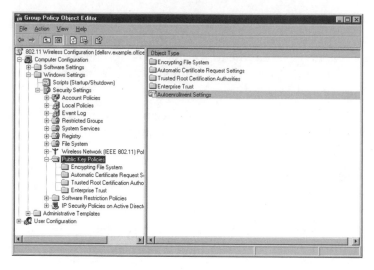

Figure 15-32. *The Group Policy Object Editor displaying the Public Key Policies container.*

6. On the File To Import page, click Browse, select the certificate file for the Windows Small Business Server Certificate Authority, and then click Open. (The certificate should be located in the root directory of the C:\ drive.) Click Next.

7. On the Certificate Store page, click Next to place certificates in the Trusted Root Certification Authorities certificate store. Review the settings and then click Finish. If the import was successful, a message will appear.

8. In the Group Policy Object Editor, verify that the certificate appears in the Trusted Root Certification Authorities container.

Creating a Wireless Network Policy

After creating a new GPO for your settings, complete the following steps to create a new wireless network policy that automates the deployment of 802.11 network settings to clients:

1. In the Group Policy Management Console, right-click the GPO you created and choose Edit from the shortcut menu. This opens the Group Policy Object Editor.

2. Navigate to Computer Configuration, Windows Settings, Security Settings, and finally Wireless Network (IEEE 802.11) Policies.

3. Right-click Wireless Network (IEEE 802.11) Policies and choose Create Wireless Network Policy from the shortcut menu. When the Wireless Network Policy Wizard appears, click Next.

4. On the Wireless Network Policy Name page, type a name and description for the policy, click Next, and then click Finish. The policy Properties dialog box appears.

5. Click the Preferred Networks tab and then click Add. The New Preferred Setting Properties dialog box (Figure 15-33) appears.

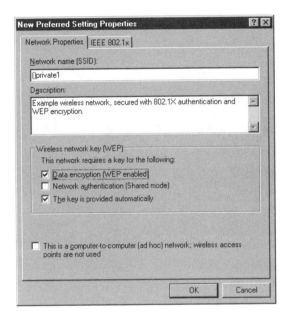

Figure 15-33. *The New Preferred Settings Properties dialog box.*

6. Type the SSID of your wireless network in the Network Name box.

7. Click the IEEE 802.1X tab and choose the EAP type used on the network (Smart Card Or Other Certificate, or Protected EAP) from the EAP Type box. Configure other settings as necessary and then click OK. Add other networks to which clients should automatically connect, and then click OK.

Summary

This chapter covers the painless process of administering DHCP, DNS, WINS and Routing and Remote Access on a Windows Small Business Server network. It also walks, step by step, through the complicated process of deploying certificate services, L2TP VPN connections, and 802.1X authentication for wireless networks.

Chapter 16, "Using ISA Server 2000," discusses administering ISA Server 2000, a component of Windows Small Business Server 2003, Premium Edition.

Chapter 16
Using ISA Server 2000

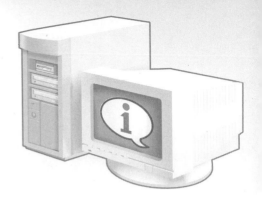

Microsoft Windows Small Business Server 2003, Premium Edition, includes Microsoft Windows Internet Security and Acceleration Server 2000 Standard Edition (ISA Server) on the Premium Technologies CD. ISA Server is a full-featured, robust, and powerful firewall that can play an important role in:

- Securing your network from attacks

- Managing the use of your company's Internet resources

- Improving the effective bandwidth of your Internet connection

More Info The installation and configuration of ISA Server as part of Windows Small Business Server is covered in Appendix B, "Installing ISA Server 2000 and SQL Server 2000."

Real World   Stand-Alone Firewall

The ISA Server 2000 Standard Edition that is included as part of Windows Small Business Server 2003, Premium Edition, can be installed only on the main Windows Small Business Server machine. Although this is sufficient for most small business environments, it does limit your options. For maximum security, your firewall should not reside on the same machine as your domain controller. You can add a server that acts only as a host for ISA Server 2000 (or the new ISA Server 2004, not yet released at the time this book was published) when you want to maximize the overall security of your network. This server will not, however, be managed by the Configure E-Mail and Internet Connection Wizard but instead will need to be separately configured and managed.

Concepts

The main goals of ISA Server are to insulate the network from attack, improve Internet performance for clients on the internal network, and control client access to the Internet.

ISA Server maintains control of connectivity and isolates the internal network by having two completely separate physical connections—one to the Internet and one to the internal network. Each network is connected to a different network card, and all packets must pass through the ISA Server software to get from one connection to the other.

The mechanisms that ISA Server uses to achieve these aims are fairly straightforward. The following three basic techniques are used:

- Network address translation
- Packet filtering
- Caching

The following sections discuss each of these techniques, as well as the different methods available to support clients. They also describe some of the core concepts used with ISA Server.

Network Address Translation

Network Address Translation (NAT) hides your actual IP address from machines beyond the device doing the translation. Only the device doing NAT needs to have a valid Internet IP address; all clients and servers on the internal network are given private addresses from the address ranges reserved for private networks. (See the Real World sidebar, "IP Addresses for Internal Networks.")

To provide NAT, you can use a stand-alone router or firewall device, a proxy server or firewall software package such as ISA Server, or the built-in NAT functionality of Windows Small Business Server 2003.

Although NAT is the backbone of any Internet connection sharing technique, and the first line of your security perimeter, it isn't sufficient by itself to truly protect your network. ISA Server supplements NAT with additional security measures, most notably packet filtering.

Real World   IP Addresses for Internal Networks

Back when folks were deciding how to parcel out IP addresses (and long before anyone figured out how to perform NAT), the need for addresses that could be used for test networks was recognized. A special set of IP addresses called *private network addresses* was defined in RFC 1918 (*http://www.faqs.org/rfcs/rfc1918.html*) for test networks or other networks not physically connected to the Internet.

These private network addresses allow a much larger address space than would be possible with officially assigned addresses while protecting the integrity of the Internet. If a machine with one of these addresses were to connect to the Internet, it wouldn't cause a conflict with another machine because routers automatically filter out these addresses.

The following addresses are designated for private networks that won't be directly connected to the Internet. They can, of course, be connected to the Internet through ISA Server or another method that performs NAT:

- 10.0.0.0 through 10.255.255.255 (a single "Class A" network)
- 172.16.0.0 through 172.31.255.255 (16 contiguous "Class B" networks)
- 192.168.0.0 through 192.168.255.255 (256 contiguous "Class C" networks)

Quotation marks enclose the Class in the preceding list because the Internet Assigned Numbers Authority (IANA) no longer uses classes to define IP address spaces. But the terminology is still in common use to describe the size of the resulting address space.

One other block of addresses is important to NAT and internal networks: the "link local" block, 169.254.0.0 through 169.254.255.255. This block of addresses, defined in RFC 3330 (*http://www.faqs.org/rfcs/rfc3330 .html*), is self-configured by a network device whenever the device fails to get an assigned address from DHCP or other means. As with the private networks defined in RFC 1918, these addresses are locally unique but not globally unique, and should never appear on the public Internet.

ISA Server automatically includes these addresses in its local address table (LAT) when you initially install the program.

Another byproduct of using NAT is that all the machines on a network *appear* to have the same single address to the outside world—the external address of the Windows Small Business Server machine itself. This allows your company to connect to the Internet with only a single public IP address.

Packet Filtering

Because every packet that passes to or from the Internet must first pass through Windows Small Business Server, ISA Server is in a perfect position to act as a gatekeeper. Besides performing simple NAT, ISA Server can inspect each packet and permit only packets that use approved protocols and ports to enter or leave the internal network. (This process is called *packet filtering*.) When packet filtering is enabled, you can also restrict access to specific external sites or enable only certain external sites to be seen. In addition, third-party ISA Server plug-ins can add controls and functionality.

In addition to basic packet filtering, ISA provides Stateful Packet Inspection (SPI), which analyzes the origin of every packet and allows only unaltered packets from approved hosts or networks to pass through the firewall. This prevents hackers from tampering with packets and provides the ability to block incoming packets that aren't specifically requested by network clients.

Caching

Every company has certain Web sites that users visit regularly. ISA Server can cache information from these frequently accessed sites, so when users connect to the site, much of the information is actually delivered by the ISA server, not the remote site. Caching significantly improves the apparent speed of the connection to the Internet and leaves more Internet bandwidth available.

ISA Server uses off hours, when few users are connected to the Internet, to check frequently accessed sites to make sure the information it has stored for those sites is current. This monitoring, called *active caching*, helps to balance and smooth out demand, providing improved throughput during busier times because fewer pages and images need to be downloaded.

ISA Server also performs fancy tricks like splitting audio or video streams and sharing them with multiple users on the network, and performing reverse caching, which accelerates the perceived performance of the Web servers to Internet clients.

Client Types

Clients can connect to the ISA Server using the Firewall client, the SecureNAT client, or the Web Proxy client. For Windows clients, only the Firewall client is a supported method with Windows Small Business Server, and the ISA Server installation will prompt you to add the Firewall client to the automatically installed client software. For Macintosh and UNIX clients and for network devices, SecureNAT is used. Each client using SecureNAT should have its default gateway set to point to Windows Small Business Server. All systems should have their Web browsers configured to use the Web Proxy service. This is done automatically when installing the Firewall client software, but needs to be done manually for SecureNAT clients.

ISA Server Policies and Policy Elements

ISA Server is customized with rules. Setting an ISA Server rule requires two separate steps: creating the policy elements that define to what protocol, client group, time of day, address, or other element the policy will apply; and then creating the actual policy that will be applied to one or more policy elements. You might define a schedule policy element that is "Weekends"—that is, all day Saturday and Sunday. Then you might create a policy that prohibits the use of FTP. When you combine those two, you have a rule that doesn't allow anyone to download files onto their computers on the weekend.

So when you create or modify a policy element such as a Client Address Set, Protocol Definition, or Schedule, you aren't actually creating any rules; you're just changing the options to which the rules apply. Policies are the rules you actually create, and you apply them to policy elements.

Installing the Firewall Client

The installation and deployment of the Firewall client to your Windows Small Business Server clients must be completed by the administrator after the ISA Server installation has completed. There are three basic steps to the installation:

1. Setting permissions on the Firewall Client deployment folder

2. Adding the Firewall client to Client Applications

3. Deploying the Firewall client

Setting Permissions on the Firewall Client Deployment Folder

Before the ISA Server Firewall Client can be deployed to client computers, the permissions on the shared folder it is installed from need to be set to allow Read and Execute permissions for users. To set these permissions, complete the following steps:

1. Using Windows Explorer, browse to the %ProgramFiles%\Microsoft ISA Server\Clients folder.

2. Right-click the Clients folder and select Sharing And Security.

3. Click the Security tab to bring up the Security page, shown in Figure 16-1.

4. Click Add. The Select Users, Computers, Or Groups dialog box appears. In the Enter The Object Names To Select box, type **Domain Users**.

5. Click OK. The default permissions are Read & Execute, List Folder Contents, and Read, as shown in Figure 16-2.

6. Click OK to accept the default permissions and close the Properties dialog box.

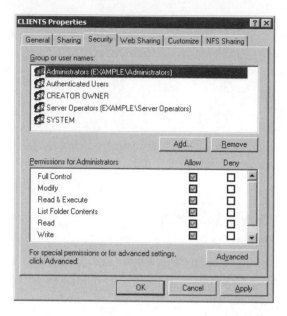

Figure 16-1. *The Security page for the Clients folder.*

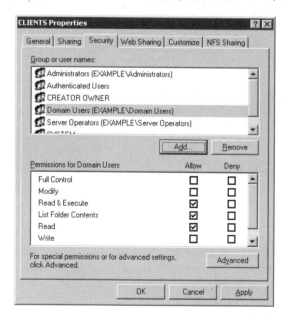

Figure 16-2. *Default permissions for Domain Users.*

Adding the Firewall Client to Client Applications

Once you've set the folder permissions so that users have the necessary access to be able to run the installation, you need to assign the Firewall Client application to the client machines. To do this, run the Assign Applications Wizard, as described in the following steps:

1. In the Server Management console, click Client Computers and then Assign Applications To Client Computers to open the Assign Applications Wizard.

2. Click Next to bring up the Client Computers page, as shown in Figure 16-3.

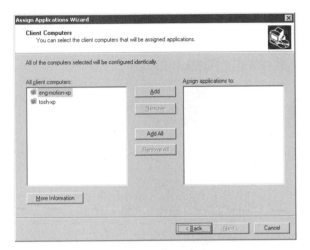

Figure 16-3. *The Client Computers page of the Assign Applications Wizard.*

3. Click Add All to assign the Firewall client to all client computers. Remove any client computers that will never be allowed access to the Internet.

4. Click Next to bring up the Client Applications page, shown in Figure 16-4.

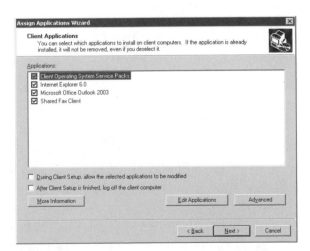

Figure 16-4. *The Client Applications page of the Assign Applications Wizard.*

5. Click Edit Applications to open the Set Up Client Applications Wizard. Click Next at the Welcome screen to open the Available Applications page.

6. Click Add to bring up the Application Information dialog box. Type **ISA Server Firewall Client** in the Application Name box, and in the Location Of Setup Executable For This Application box, type **"\\<servername>\mspclnt\setup.exe"** (including the quotation marks, but replacing <servername> with the actual name of your server), as shown in Figure 16-5.

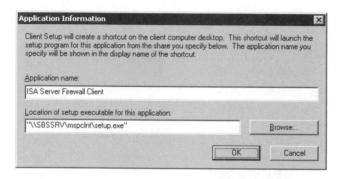

Figure 16-5. *Setting the application information for the Firewall client.*

7. Click OK to return to the Available Applications page. You might see the warning shown in Figure 16-6.

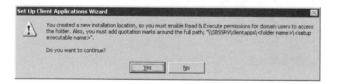

Figure 16-6. *The New Installation Location warning.*

8. Click Yes to continue. If you need to add quotation marks around the location, click the Edit button to return to the Application Information dialog box.

9. Click Next and then click Finish to complete the Setup Client Applications Wizard and return to the Assign Applications Wizard.

10. Click Next to open the Mobile Client And Offline Use page of the Assign Applications Wizard. You can add Connection Manager and ActiveSync here.

11. Click Next to display a summary of your settings, and then click Finish to complete the assignment.

Deploying the Firewall Client

Once you assign the Firewall client to client computers, the next time users log on to the computers, a shortcut is placed on the desktop to install the Firewall client. All the users need to do to start the installation is double-click the shortcut.

Unfortunately, automated installation works only on Microsoft Windows 2000 and Windows XP clients. Older clients will need to manually connect to the shared installation point and run the Setup.exe directly. To run the setup directly, log on to the client computer, click Start, Run, and type **\\\<*servername*>\Mspclnt\Setup.exe**, where <servername> is replaced by your server's actual name or internal IP address.

Administering ISA Server

The initial configuration of ISA Server is handled automatically as part of the Configure E-Mail and Internet Connection Wizard, which is run as the final step of installing ISA Server. All the necessary protocol and publishing rules are set up, and if your installation never changes, you really don't need anything else. But inevitably there will be changes—there always are. If the changes are covered by the Configure E-Mail and Internet Connection Wizard, your first step should always be to rerun the wizard. The tasks that you can use the Configure E-Mail and Internet Connection Wizard to perform include:

- Changing your broadband or dial-up connection
- Enabling or disabling services through the ISA Server, specifically:
  - E-mail (enabled by default when you are running Microsoft Exchange)
  - Virtual Private Networking
  - Terminal Services
  - File Transfer Protocol (FTP)
- Enabling or disabling Web Publishing of internal Web site services, specifically:
  - Outlook Web Access
  - Remote Web Workplace
  - Server performance and usage reports
  - Outlook Mobile Access
  - Outlook via the Internet
  - Business Web site (your public Web site)

- Changing the Web server certificate
- Enabling or disabling Internet e-mail

Caution If you are using L2TP for your VPN protocol, as described in Chapter 15, "Managing Connectivity," running the Configure E-Mail and Internet Connection Wizard to modify your Firewall Configuration will disable your VPN configuration. You'll need to re-enable the packet filters manually, as described in Chapter 15.

Changing Your Broadband or Dial-Up Connection

You can use the Configure E-Mail and Internet Connection Wizard to change your Internet connection type, or to change the specific parameters of your current connection type. When you run the wizard, the wizard will make the necessary changes to ISA Server as well. See Chapter 6, "Completing the To Do List and Other Post-Installation Tasks," for details about setting or changing your Internet connection type.

Enabling or Disabling Services Through the ISA Server

You can use the Configure E-Mail and Internet Connection Wizard to control which services running on your Windows Small Business Server network are available directly from the Internet. When you run or rerun the Configure E-Mail and Internet Connection Wizard, the wizard makes the necessary changes to packet filters and publishing rules in ISA Server to support the changes you're making. The services you can enable for direct Internet access are:

- E-mail
- Virtual Private Networking
- Terminal Services
- File Transfer Protocol (FTP)

To make changes to these services, complete the following steps:

1. In the Server Management console, click Internet And E-Mail, and then click Connect To The Internet to open the Configure E-Mail and Internet Connection Wizard.

2. Click Next to open the Connection Type page. Select Do Not Change Connection Type and click Next to open the Firewall page.

3. Select Enable Firewall, and click Next. You are warned that any custom packet filters you defined will be disabled, such as L2TP VPN packet filters, as shown in Figure 16-7. See Chapter 15 for more information about L2TP and how to re-enable the filters.

Figure 16-7. *The Configure E-Mail and Internet Connection Wizard disables any custom packet filters you defined, including L2TP VPN connections.*

4. Click OK to bring up the Services Configuration page, shown in Figure 16-8.

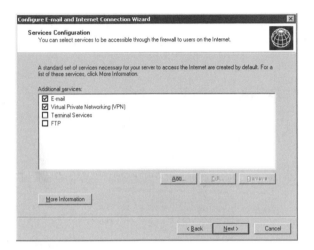

Figure 16-8. *The Services Configuration page of the Configure E-Mail and Internet Connection Wizard.*

5. Select the check boxes of any service you want available directly through the Internet. Clear the others. If you enable Virtual Private Networking (VPN), these other services will be available to client computers once they have established a VPN connection to your network.

6. You can add custom services that are available directly from the Internet, or edit existing ones you created. If you click Add, you see the Add Or Edit A Service dialog box, shown in Figure 16-9. You need to know the port used by the service, the protocol type (TCP or UDP), and whether the service is an inbound or outbound service. Type and select the appropriate information, and then click OK to return to the Services Configuration page.

7. After you make the necessary changes on the Services Configuration page, click Next.

8. Step through the rest of the Configure E-Mail and Internet Connection Wizard. Don't change any additional settings as you step through it. When you reach the end, click Finish, and the changes are implemented.

Figure 16-9. *Adding or editing a custom service allows it to be used through the ISA Server.*

9. Once the configuration is implemented, you see a confirmation message, as shown in Figure 16-10. Click Close and you're finished.

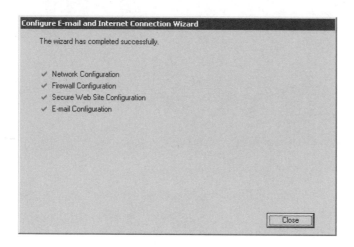

Figure 16-10. *Confirmation message showing that the Configure E-Mail and Internet Connection Wizard completed successfully.*

Enabling or Disabling Web Services

You can use the Configure E-Mail and Internet Connection Wizard to control which Web services running on your Windows Small Business Server are available directly from the Internet through your firewall. When you run or rerun the Configure E-Mail and Internet Connection Wizard, the wizard makes the necessary changes to packet filters and publishing rules in ISA Server to support the changes you're making. The Web services you can enable for direct Internet access are:

- Outlook Web Access
- Remote Web Workplace
- Server performance and usage reports

- Outlook Mobile Access
- Outlook via the Internet
- Business Web site (your public Web site)

To make changes to these Web services, complete the following steps:

1. In the Server Management console, click Internet And E-Mail, and then click Connect To The Internet to open the Configure E-Mail and Internet Connection Wizard.

2. Click Next to open the Connection Type page. Select Do Not Change Connection Type, and click Next to open the Firewall page.

3. Select Enable Firewall, and click Next. You are warned that any custom packet filters you defined will be disabled, as shown earlier in Figure 16-7.

4. Click OK to bring up the Services Configuration page. Don't make any changes here, and click Next to bring up the Web Services Configuration page, shown in Figure 16-11.

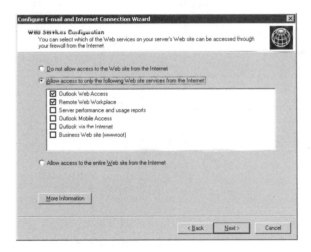

Figure 16-11.   *The Web Services Configuration page of the Configure E-Mail and Internet Connection Wizard.*

5. Select the check boxes of those Web services you want available directly from the Internet. If you have Virtual Private Networking enabled, the other services will be available from the Internet by first establishing a VPN connection to your network.

6. After you make your changes, click Next.

7. Step through the rest of the Configure E-Mail and Internet Connection Wizard. Don't change any additional settings as you step through it.

When you reach the end of the wizard, click Finish, and the changes are implemented.

8. After the configuration is implemented, you see a confirmation message (Figure 16-10). Click Close and you're finished.

Creating Protocol Definitions

ISA Server is automatically configured with definitions for most protocols, and you can create other definitions by using the Configure E-Mail and Internet Connection Wizard and adding a service. However, you might need to use a protocol that ISA Server doesn't already know about. If so, you need to create a protocol definition first and then a protocol rule enabling the use of the new protocol definition. To create a protocol definition, complete the following steps:

1. Open the ISA Management console by clicking Start, All Programs, Microsoft ISA Server, and then ISA Management.

2. Open Policy Elements and then Protocol Definitions in the console tree, as shown in Figure 16-12.

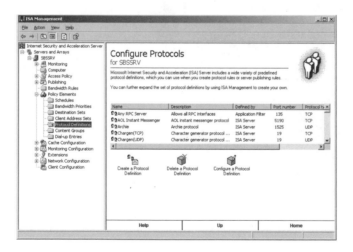

Figure 16-12. *Protocol Definitions in the ISA Management console.*

3. Scan the list of protocol definitions to make sure there isn't already a suitable definition, and if there isn't, click Create A Protocol Definition.

4. On the first page of the New Protocol Definition Wizard, type the protocol name and then click Next to open the Protocol Connection Information page, shown in Figure 16-13.

5. Type the port number used by the protocol, the protocol type, and the direction of information transfer, and then click Next.

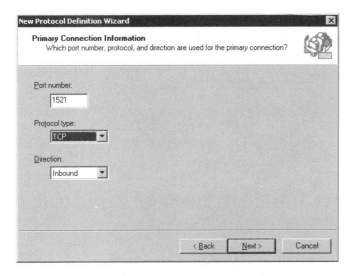

Figure 16-13. *The Protocol Connection Information page of the New Protocol Definition Wizard.*

6. If the protocol uses secondary connections, select the Yes option on the Secondary Connections page, and then click New to specify a port range, type, and direction for secondary connections. Click Next to continue.

7. Review the settings and then click Finish. To use the protocol definition, either add it to an existing protocol rule or create a new Allow protocol rule for it.

Creating a Protocol Rule

ISA Server is automatically configured with protocol rules for the protocol definitions that are configured as part of the Windows Small Business Server Configure E-Mail and Internet Connection Wizard, but if you create new, custom protocol definitions without using the wizard, you'll also need to create a protocol rule enabling the use of the new protocol definition. To create a protocol rule, complete the following steps:

1. In the ISA Management console tree, open Access Policy and then Protocol Rules, as shown in Figure 16-14.

2. Click Create A Protocol Rule in the details pane to open the New Protocol Rule Wizard.

3. Type a name for the rule. Include Allow or Deny as part of the name to make it easy to identify the rule later. Click Next.

4. On the Rule Action page, select Allow or Deny to specify whether this is a rule to allow or deny the use of the protocol.

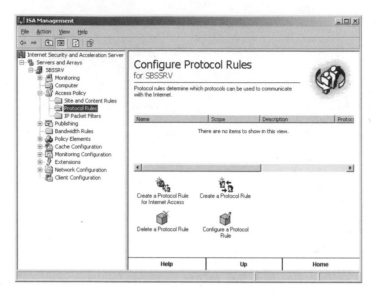

Figure 16-14. *Protocol Rules in the ISA Management console.*

5. On the Protocols page, select Selected Protocols from the Apply This Rule To drop-down list, locate the protocol you want to create a rule for, and then select the check box for it, as shown in Figure 16-15. Click Next.

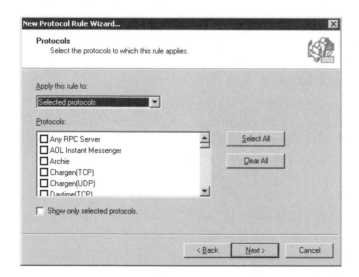

Figure 16-15. *The Protocols page of the New Protocol Rule Wizard.*

6. On the Schedule page, select from the available schedules. Click Next.

7. On the Client Type page, select Specific Users And Groups, as shown in Figure 16-16. This selection will maintain consistent security with existing Windows Small Business Server rules. Click Next.

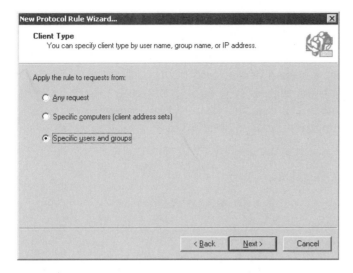

Figure 16-16. *For Windows Small Business Server, you should choose Specific Users And Groups.*

8. On the Users And Groups page, Click Add to bring up the Select Users Or Groups dialog box. To allow all Internet users to use this protocol, click Object Types, select Groups in the Object Types dialog box, and then click OK to return to the Select Users Or Groups dialog box.

9. In the Enter Object Names To Select box, type **Internet Users.** Click OK to return to the Users And Groups page, as shown in Figure 16-17.

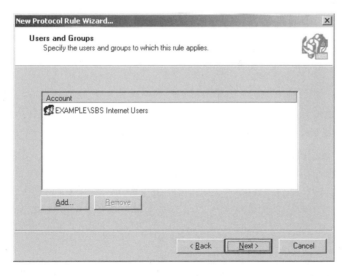

Figure 16-17. *The Internet Users group, consisting of all SBS Domain Users permitted to use the Internet.*

10. Click Next and then click Finish to create the protocol rule.

Configuring Schedules

ISA Server automatically sets up a Work Hours schedule (9–5 Monday through Friday) and a Weekends schedule (all day Saturday and Sunday). You can use these schedules to control when certain protocols or features are enabled by way of protocol rules. If the default schedules don't really match up with your business, you can modify the existing ones or create new ones. Create new schedules rather than modify the existing ones to make problems easier to trouble-shoot later.

Creating a Schedule

To create a new schedule, complete the following steps:

1. In the ISA Management console tree, open Policy Elements and then Schedules, as shown in Figure 16-18.

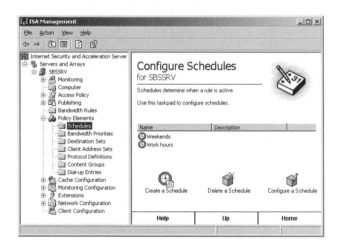

Figure 16-18. *Schedules in the ISA Management console.*

2. Click Create A Schedule in the details pane to open the New Schedule dialog box, shown in Figure 16-19.

3. Type a name for the schedule and a description, and then highlight the hours you want the rule to apply to (shown in blue if you are using the default color scheme). Activate or inactivate times by selecting a region with your mouse and then clicking the Active or Inactive options.

4. Click OK and your new schedule is created.

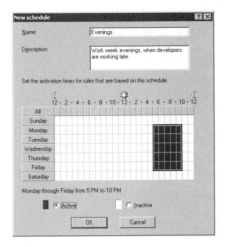

Figure 16-19.   *Creating a new Evenings schedule to use with protocol rules.*

Deleting a Schedule

You can delete a schedule that isn't being used any longer, but you need to be certain that the schedule isn't being used by any existing protocol rules. Navigate to the Schedules in ISA Management. Highlight the schedule you want to delete and click Delete A Schedule. You get the Confirm Delete dialog box shown in Figure 16-20. Make sure that the Verify That No Rules Use This Element check box is selected, and then click Yes.

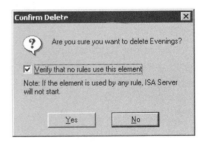

Figure 16-20.   *Never delete a schedule without checking whether it is being used somewhere.*

Changing Cache Properties

Although most cache configuration is performed when you install ISA Server, you can configure additional settings or modify the ones that were created during the initial configuration. Use the following sections to change the size of the cache and which drives are used for caching, and to set up specific Web sites or objects for scheduled downloading into the ISA Server cache.

Changing the Size and Location of the Cache

To change which drives are used to store the ISA Server cache and how much disk space is used on each drive, complete the following steps:

1. In the ISA Management console tree, click Cache Configuration.

2. Select the Windows Small Business Server system in the details pane.

3. Click the Configure Cache Size link to open up the Cache Drives dialog box, which is shown in Figure 16-21.

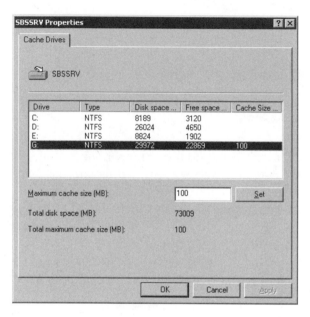

Figure 16-21. *Configuring the cache size for SBSSRV server.*

4. Select a drive from the list, and type the size of cache you want on that drive in the Maximum Cache Size box.

5. Click Set to add the cache. Click OK. You get a warning dialog box, as shown in Figure 16-22.

6. Choose either to save the changes and not restart the service, in which case the settings are not immediately applied; or to restart the Web Proxy service now to immediately enable the new cache settings. Then click OK.

Figure 16-22. *Changes in cache size require a restart of the Web Proxy service.*

Setting Up Content for Scheduled Downloading

You can set up ISA Server to automatically download individual Web pages or even entire Web sites on a set schedule. This ensures that the desired content is always available and fresh in the ISA Server cache.

Use this feature of ISA Server when you have a particular site or set of sites that many users in the company need access to regularly, such as a reference site or the site of a partner company.

If you have a separate internal Web server, you can also use ISA Server's scheduled download functionality to accelerate performance of the internal Web server for external (Internet) clients. Set up the ISA server to automatically download the Web site from the internal Web server, and then when Internet clients request pages from the Web site, the clients are served directly from the ISA server.

To schedule ISA Server to download content automatically, complete the following steps:

1. In the ISA Management console tree, open Cache Configuration and then Scheduled Content Download Jobs.

2. On the Action menu, choose New, Job to start the New Scheduled Content Download Job Wizard.

3. Type a descriptive name for the download job and then click Next.

4. On the Start Time page, specify the date and time the download job should begin, and then click Next.

5. On the Frequency page, specify how often ISA Server should download content from the Web site, and then click Next.

6. On the Content page, type the URL of the content to download. Select the Content Only From URL Domain check box if you want to prevent download of material from other sites that this site links to.

7. Select the Cache Dynamic Content check box if you want dynamic content cached. Click Next.

Note   If the dynamic content requires user authentication or identification (including the use of cookies), it won't cache properly.

8. On the Links And Downloaded Objects page, specify how ISA Server should deal with the Time to Live (TTL) of objects it downloads. The choices are:

   - **Always Override Object's TTL**   Gives all downloaded objects the TTL you specify in the box provided (default is 60 minutes)

   - **Override TTL If Not Defined**   Writes the TTL you specify on downloaded objects only if they don't have a specified TTL

Note   Web page authors can specify a Time to Live (TTL) for Web pages to indicate how long the content is "fresh" (in other words, how long the page should hang around before getting checked for a new copy). When the TTL expires, ISA Server considers the page invalid and automatically checks for an updated copy if active caching is enabled and the page is popular. If active caching isn't enabled, ISA Server updates the page the next time the page is requested.

9. Choose to set a maximum depth to cache or to set no limits on cache depth, which is the default. ISA Server follows all links on the page you specified and continues following all links on each linked page up to the maximum link depth.

10. Optionally change the maximum number of objects ISA Server caches during the scheduled download operation, and then click Next. Click Finish to enable the caching job.

Backing Up the ISA Server Configuration

You should always run a full Windows Small Business Server backup as soon as practical after any major change, such as installing ISA Server. Follow the instructions in Chapter 13, "Backing Up and Restoring Data," for performing an immediate backup once you have your ISA Server installed and working correctly.

You can also back up just the ISA Server configuration using the ISA Server backup tool. This will store a complete copy of your current configuration on disk to allow for a quick restore in case of problems. To back up the ISA Server configuration, complete the following steps:

1. In the ISA Management console tree, right-click your ISA Server and select Back Up from the shortcut menu to open the Backup Array dialog box, shown in Figure 16-23.

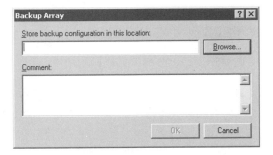

Figure 16-23. *Backing up the ISA Server configuration to disk.*

2. Type a file name and location for the backup, and then type a description. Click OK to begin the backup of the configuration.

3. When the backup completes, you get an informational message that tells you the backup succeeded. Click OK and return to the ISA Management console.

Tip   Always back up the ISA Server configuration before making any changes. If your configuration changes cause problems, you can quickly return to a known good working configuration by restoring the backup you made before you started.

Publishing SharePoint Through ISA

Unfortunately, installation of ISA Server 2000 disables remote access to the *http://companyweb* home page. To correct this and make companyweb available from the Remote Web Workplace after you have installed ISA Server 2000, you need to do the following:

1. Create a new protocol definition for Inbound TCP/444 as described in the "Creating Protocol Definitions" section. Give this definition the name "Companyweb Inbound." The port number is 444, the protocol type is TCP, and the direction is Inbound.

2. Create a server publishing rule to publish the new protocol:

   • In the ISA Management console tree, open Publishing and then Server Publishing Rules.

- Click Publish A Server in the details pane to open the New Server Publishing Rule Wizard. Type **Publish Companyweb** in the Server Publishing Rule Name box and click Next.

- On the Address Mapping page (Figure 16-24), specify the internal and external IP addresses of your Windows Small Business Server. Click Next.

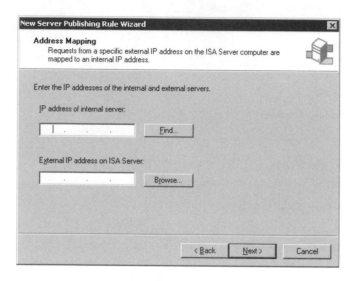

Figure 16-24. *Specifying IP addresses on the Address Mapping page.*

- On the Protocol Settings page (Figure 16-25), select Companyweb Inbound from the drop-down list. Click Next.

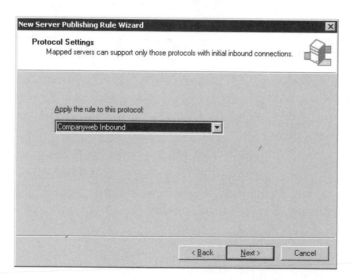

Figure 16-25. *Selecting the protocol for the rule.*

- On the Client Type page, select Any Request. Click Next. Make sure everything is as you expect on the final summary page, and then click Finish to create the publishing rule.

3. Use the following steps to assign the FQDN Certificate to the company-web with SSL port set to 444.

   - Open the Internet Information Services Manager from the Start menu, point to All Programs, Administrative Tools, and select Internet Information Services (IIS) Manager.

   - In the Internet Information Services Manager console tree, open Web Sites and then companyweb (Figure 16-26). Right-click company-web and select Properties.

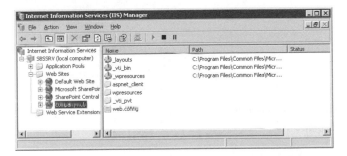

Figure 16-26. *Internet Information Services (IIS) Manager console.*

   - In the Properties dialog box, click the Directory Security tab, and then click Server Certificate to open the IIS Certificate Wizard. Click Next.

   - On the Server Certificate page, select Assign An Existing Certificate, as shown in Figure 16-27.

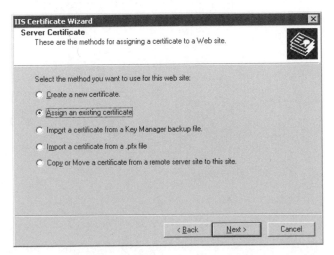

Figure 16-27. *The Server Certificate page of the IIS Certificate Wizard.*

- On the Available Certificates page, select the certificate for your official, fully qualified, public domain name from the list of certificates, as shown in Figure 16-28. Click Next.

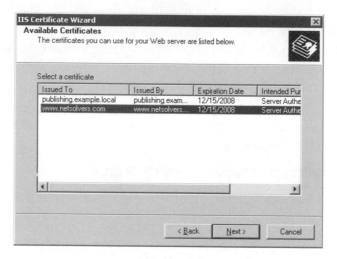

Figure 16-28. *The Available Certificates page.*

- On the SSL Port page, type **444** in the SSL Port This Web Should Use box (Figure 16-29). Click Next.

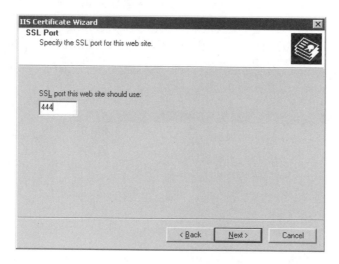

Figure 16-29. *The SSL Port page.*

- Click Next again, and finally Finish to complete the change.

4. Edit the Registry to display the correct links in the Remote Web Workplace:

- Open the Registry Editor by selecting Run from the Start Menu and typing **regedit** in the Open box.

- Navigate to HKEY_LOCAL_MACHINE\SOFTWARE\Microsoft \SmallBusinessServer\RemoteUserPortal\KWLinks and set the value for STS to **1**, as shown in Figure 16-30.

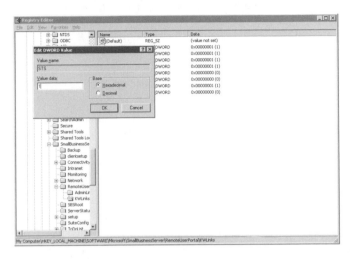

Figure 16 30. *The Edit DWORD Value dialog box for KWLinks.*

- Navigate to HKEY_LOCAL_MACHINE\SOFTWARE\Microsoft \SmallBusinessServer\RemoteUserPortal\AdminLinks and set the value for STS to **1**.

- Set the value for HelpDesk to **1**.

- Close the Registry Editor.

5. Open a command window and type **iisreset** at a command prompt. This will stop and restart the IIS services.

6. In the Server Management console tree, open Advanced Management, Computer Management, Services and Applications, Services. Restart the Microsoft ISA Server Control.

Note If your remote client is connecting from behind another ISA Server, you're not done. ISA does not allow HTTPS traffic on port 444 by default. Setting up the packet filters as described in the preceding procedure will affect only server-based communications. Clients that are behind another ISA server use the protocol rules and if the HTTP Redirector is enabled it will also use the site and content rule for its HTTPS requests. You need to follow the instructions on Knowledge Base article 283284, "Blank Page or Page Cannot Be Displayed When You View SSL Sites Through ISA Server" (*http://support.microsoft.com /?id=283284*). You'll need to change the port range to 444,444 on the ISA server.

Monitoring ISA Server

You can use the monitoring functions of the ISA Server to create and view reports on the usage and statistics of ISA Server, as well as to view alerts about the functioning of the server.

Reporting

ISA Server supports a number of reports, but before you can use any of them, you need to set up Monitoring Configuration on the ISA Server. Once you have configured monitoring, you can view reports or save the information to a Microsoft Excel workbook for additional reporting and manipulation.

Monitoring

To configure monitoring, complete the following steps:

1. In the ISA Management console tree, click Monitoring Configuration. Right-click Report Jobs, select New, Report Job from the shortcut menu to open the Report Job Properties dialog box, shown in Figure 16-31.

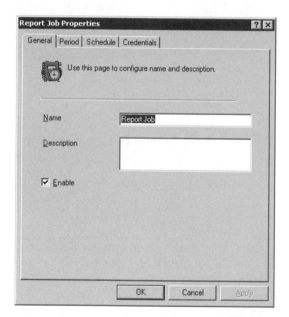

Figure 16-31. *The General page of the Report Job Properties dialog box.*

2. On the General page, type a name and a description for the new report job, and select the Enable check box.

3. Click the Period tab and choose whether the report is a Daily, Weekly, Monthly, or Yearly report. You can also create a custom period for the report.

4. Click the Schedule tab to create a schedule for this report. The default is an immediate report that isn't repeated. If you want a daily report, make sure you change the recurrence pattern to Generate Every Day, as shown in Figure 16-32.

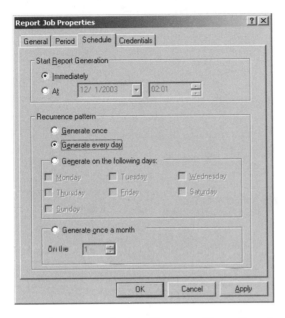

Figure 16-32. *Selecting Generate Every Day for a daily report.*

5. Click the Credentials tab, and type the user name and password information that will be used to generate the report. This should be an administrative account.

6. After you make all your selections, click OK. If you specified immediate report generation, the report is generated now; otherwise, it will be generated when you scheduled it to run.

Under the Hood   Report Period vs. Report Schedule

One of the most confusing aspects of reports is the difference between the period of the report and the schedule that the report runs on. The *period* is the length of time that the report covers—daily, weekly, monthly, or yearly. You specify the time period for the statistics that the report will cover. The *schedule* is the frequency with which the report is generated. These two might well line up, but they don't really have to. For example, you might want a monthly report that covers the usage over the last year so that you can easily track trends. In this case, you'd set the period for the report job to yearly, but set the schedule to generate the report once a month.

Viewing a Report

To view a report, complete the following steps:

1. In the ISA Management console tree, open Monitoring and then Reports. There are five report types listed: Summary, Web Usage, Application Usage, Traffic & Utilization, and Security.

2. Click the type of report you want to see, and then in the details pane, double-click the Report Job that you want to view. The report opens in Internet Explorer, as shown in Figure 16-33.

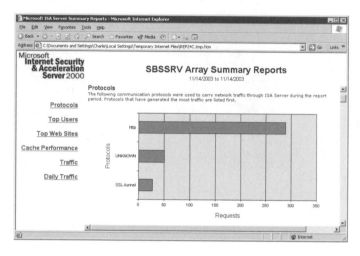

Figure 16-33. *A daily Summary report for SBSSRV showing the protocols used in the last 24 hours.*

Saving a Report to Excel

To save the report information to an Excel workbook, complete the following steps:

1. In the ISA Management console tree, open Monitoring and then click Reports.

2. Right-click the Report Job you want to save and select Save As to save the report to an Excel file.

Sessions

You can use the ISA Management console to view the current ISA Sessions on your network. You can also disconnect sessions if necessary.

To view the current sessions, complete the following steps:

1. In the ISA Management console tree, open Monitoring and then Sessions. You see a list of the current sessions in the details pane, as shown in Figure 16-34.

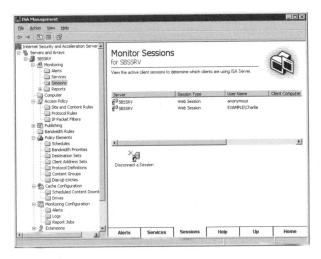

Figure 16-34.   *Monitoring the ISA sessions of server SBSSRV.*

2. If you want to disconnect a session, select it and click Disconnect A Session.

Alerts

ISA Server comes with more than 40 alerts that are monitored. These include intrusion attempts, startup, shutdown, and status of various parts of the ISA Server. Most of these are automatically enabled during the initial configuration of ISA Server with a default action of reporting to the Event Log. You can configure additional actions, enable or disable various alerts, change the events that trigger the alert, or create custom alerts.

Viewing Current Alerts

To view any current alerts, or alerts that haven't been reset, complete the following steps:

1. In the ISA Management console tree, open Monitoring and then click Alerts. You'll see a list of alerts in the details pane, as shown in Figure 16-35.

2. If you want to reset an alert, select it and click Reset Alert.

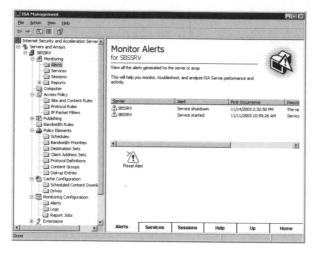

Figure 16-35. *The current ISA Server alerts on SBSSRV.*

Enabling or Disabling an Alert

To enable or disable an alert, complete the following steps:

1. In the ISA Management console tree, open Monitoring Configuration and then click Alerts.

2. Select the alert you want to enable or disable in the details pane. If the alert is currently disabled, the alert icon will include a red down arrow, as shown in Figure 16-36.

Enable

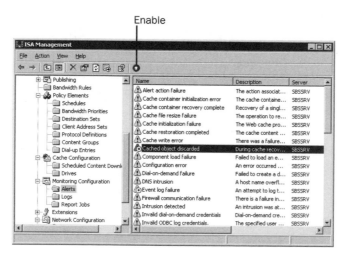

Figure 16-36. *The cached object's discarded alert, currently disabled.*

3. To enable an alert that is currently disabled, click the Enable button (green up arrow) on the toolbar.

4. To disable an alert that is currently enabled, click the Disable button (red down arrow) on the toolbar.

Creating a New Alert

To create a new alert, complete the following steps:

1. In the ISA Management console tree, click Monitoring Configuration.

2. Right-click Alerts, select New, Alert from the shortcut menu to open the New Alert Wizard.

3. Type a name for this alert and click Next.

4. On the Events And Conditions page, select the type of event that will trigger the alert from the Event drop-down list, as shown in Figure 16-37. If there are additional conditions associated with the event, select the conditions that control the trigger. Click Next.

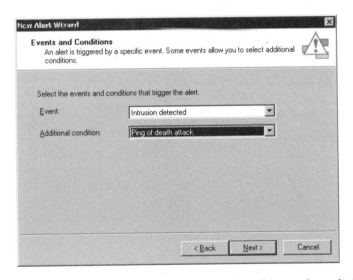

Figure 16-37.   *Adding an event and the additional conditions that trigger the alert.*

5. On the Actions page select the actions that will be taken when the alert is triggered, as shown in Figure 16-38. Click Next.

6. If you selected an e-mail action, you are prompted to fill in the details of the e-mail server and accounts, as shown in Figure 16-39.

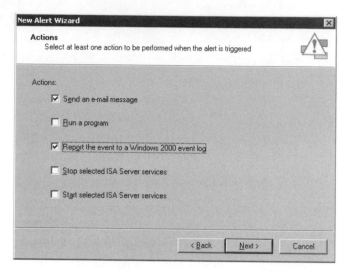

Figure 16-38. *Selecting the actions that will be triggered by the alert.*

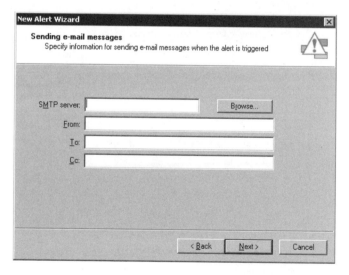

Figure 16-39. *Specifying the SMTP server and the accounts to use for the e-mail event.*

7. If you selected a program action, you are prompted to fill in the details of the program, as shown in Figure 16-40.

Tip You can use the program action to handle actions that aren't easily configured using the New Alert Wizard by itself. For example, you can run a script to execute a complicated action or send e-mail that requires more advanced configuration.

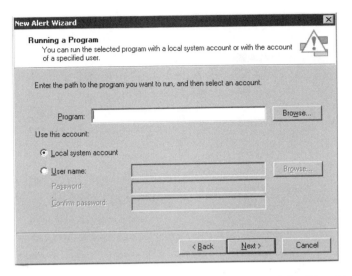

Figure 16-40. *The Running A Program page of the New Alert Wizard.*

8. If you selected a stop service action, you'll see the Stopping Services page that lets you select which ISA Server services you want to stop. If you want to stop other services not part of ISA Server, you'll need to use a program action to run a script that stops those services.

9. If you selected a start service action, you see the Starting Services page that lets you select which ISA Server services you want to start. If you want to start other services not part of ISA Server, you need to use a program action to run a script that starts those services.

10. Click Next on the action pages as necessary. You get a final summary page of the new alert that will be created. Review the settings and then click Finish to create the alert. If an error is displayed indicating that ISA Server cannot save the new object, an alert with the same settings might already be defined.

Modifying an Alert

To modify an existing alert, complete the following steps:

1. In the ISA Management console tree, open Monitoring Configuration and then Alerts.

2. In the details pane, double-click the alert you want to modify. The Properties dialog box opens.

3. Click the Events tab, as shown in Figure 16-41.

4. Change the events, conditions, number, or frequency of events necessary to trigger the alert, or change when the recurring actions are performed.

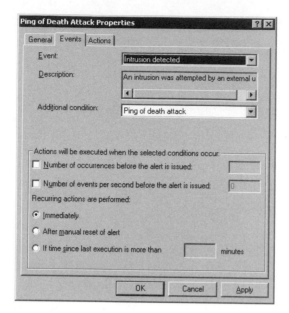

Figure 16-41. *Changing the details of which and how many events trigger an alert.*

5. Click the Actions tab to modify the actions that will be taken when an alert is triggered.

6. Click OK when you complete your changes to the alert.

Summary

The ISA Server 2000 that is included as part of the Premium Edition gives Windows Small Business Server 2003 a full-featured, robust, and flexible Internet firewall. In this chapter, we covered configuring, administering, and monitoring of your ISA Server installation.

In Chapter 17, "Customizing a SharePoint Web Site," we cover how to customize your Windows SharePoint Services intranet site, including using Microsoft FrontPage 2003, which is part of the Premium Edition.

Part V
Administering Server Components

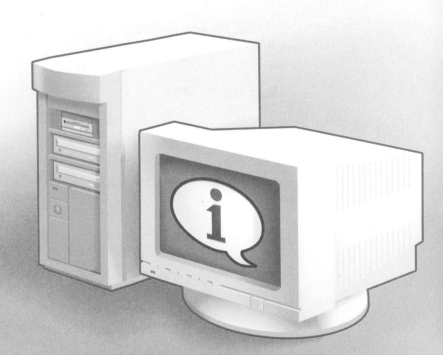

Chapter 17
Customizing a SharePoint Web Site

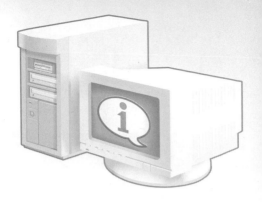

Microsoft Windows Small Business Server 2003 automatically creates a Microsoft Windows SharePoint Services Web site (*http://companyweb*) during installation. This Web site provides a central location for employees to collaborate and share information. Consider it a bulletin board, digitized and turbo-boosted.

You don't need to do anything special to get started using Windows SharePoint Services, and many companies should experiment with Windows SharePoint Services to discover its usefulness before spending a significant amount of time customizing it. By default, all domain users are given Web Designer privileges, which let them view the site, upload information, and change the design of the site. The site is accessible from the internal network and also from the Internet via the Remote Web Workplace (which requires a secure logon), if you enabled this when configuring your Internet connection.

This chapter gives you an overview of the default Windows SharePoint Services Web site, and then shows you how to edit, manage, and customize the site using Microsoft FrontPage 2003. For more sophisticated design work, you'll probably want to hire a professional Web developer.

Note Windows SharePoint Services is an update and revision to Microsoft SharePoint Team Services version 1.0. Windows SharePoint Services, or Share-Point, is an outgrowth of the Microsoft Office Server Extensions, which are themselves a superset of the Microsoft FrontPage Server Extensions.

Getting Familiar with Windows SharePoint Services

Familiarizing yourself with the default SharePoint Web site is helpful regardless of whether you're a company employee or an independent network consultant (in fact, network consultants will be very happy about the Help Desk list). Connect to the Web site directly at *http://companyweb* or via Remote Web Workplace (when at a remote location), and then use the following section to get familiar with the site, which is shown in Figure 17-1.

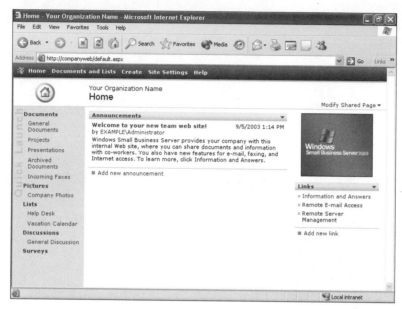

Figure 17-1. *The default SharePoint Web site created by Windows Small Business Server.*

Note The SharePoint Web site officially works best with Microsoft Internet Explorer 6 or later; however, it works fine in other browsers as well. (However, you should test any non-PC platforms before you rely on them.)

Understanding SharePoint Items

A SharePoint Web site contains several types of items:

- **Document and Picture Libraries** Web pages that make it easy to view, upload, and organize documents of all sorts (spreadsheets, presentations, pictures, faxes, and other Web pages), as shown in Figure 17-2.

- **Lists** Web pages that contain postings by users in the same way newsgroups do (however, lists are not threaded for conversations as newsgroups are). Some sample lists are Announcements, Help Desk, Links, and Vacation Calendar (which works a little differently from the other lists by also presenting the information in calendar form).

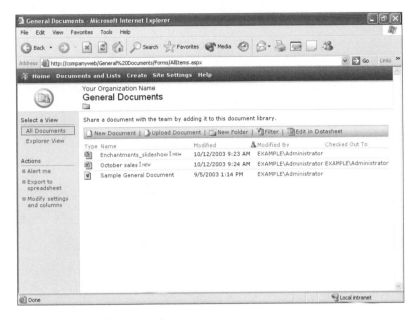

Figure 17-2. *The General Documents page.*

- **Discussion Boards** Web pages that are set up to very closely mimic newsgroups—users can carry on threaded conversations (Figure 17-3).

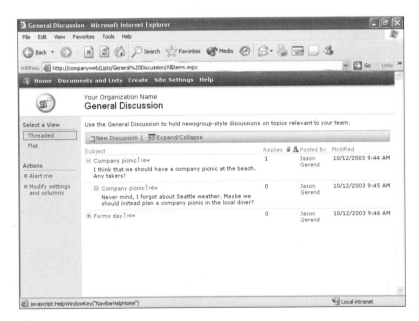

Figure 17-3. *The General Discussion page.*

- **Surveys** Web pages designed to poll users on topics of your choice.

Interacting with a SharePoint Site

You can interact with pages on a SharePoint site in a number of ways:

- **Change the view** Each item on a SharePoint site can be viewed in a number of different ways depending on the item (similar to the Views feature in Microsoft Windows Explorer). For example, documents can be viewed in the All Documents or Explorer View; Picture Libraries (Figure 17-4) can be viewed in Details, Thumbnails, Filmstrip, or Explorer View.

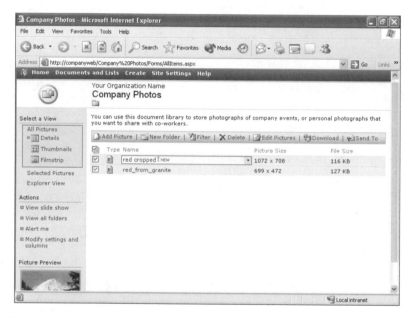

Figure 17-4. *The Company Photos page in Details view.*

- **Add items** Create or upload new messages, documents, or pictures by using the New Document and Upload Document options, or by clicking the similarly named buttons prominently placed on each page of the site. Creating a new document opens Microsoft Word (if it is installed), which by default saves the file back into the SharePoint site (when using Microsoft Word 2003 or Microsoft Word 2002).

- **Check out items** Documents and pictures can be easily checked out, preventing other users from modifying the files until the files are checked back in. To check out a file, move the mouse over the file name, click the down arrow next to the file name, and then choose Check Out from the pop-up menu. Check in documents the same way.

- **Get alerted to changes**   Click the Alert Me link in the Actions section of a page to create alerts that notify you of changes made to the item.

- **Import and export files**   Many pages in the SharePoint Web site allow you to export data to Microsoft Excel by clicking the Edit In Datasheet button or clicking the Export To Spreadsheet link. You must have Excel installed to use these options. You can also import Calendar items and Contacts from Outlook or export them to Outlook.

- **Discuss pages and documents**   Click the Discuss toolbar button in Internet Explorer to write comments about the current page. These comments can then be viewed and replied to by other viewers of the site. (To view comments, the Discuss button must be toggled on, as shown in Figure 17-5.)

Note   The Discussions feature stores comments in a database on the discussion server (the SharePoint Web site), not in the page or document itself.

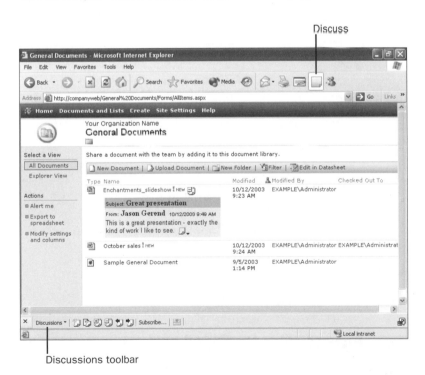

Figure 17-5.   *The General Documents page showing a comment and the Discussions toolbar, which appears at the bottom of the page.*

Changing the Appearance of the Site

Once you're familiar with how the default SharePoint Web site works, you might want to change the way the overall site looks—the visual theme, title, and description. To do so, display the Site Settings page (Figure 17-6) by clicking the Site Settings link at the top of a page in the SharePoint Web site.

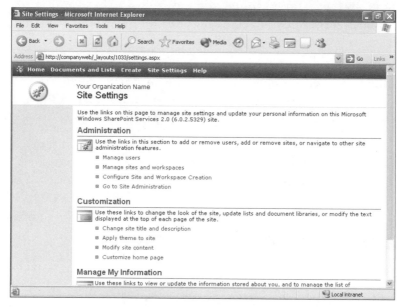

Figure 17-6. *The main Site Settings page.*

You can do the following to change the site's appearance:

- **Change the title and description** Click the Change Site Title And Description link and type the new title and description in the Title and Description boxes. Click OK when you're finished. The title of the site (by default, "Your Organization Name") appears on all pages; the site description appears only on the home page.

- **Apply a theme** Click the Apply Theme To Site link, select a theme, and then click Apply to change the fonts and color scheme used for the site.

Changing Home Page Content

After customizing the look of the overall SharePoint site, you might want to change the content of the home page to better suit the needs of your users. The home page is made up of several different parts: the Quick Launch link bar, which runs vertically down the left side of the page and contains links to commonly used pages on the site; a link bar across the top of the page, which appears on all pages of the site; and multiple Web Parts in the main body of the page.

Note   A Web Part is a single-purpose component that you can place on a Web page to present data such as images or the current contents of a SharePoint list, or to filter data such as announcements or links.

To change the content of the home page, display the SharePoint home page (*http://companyweb*) and then use the following list:

- **Add a Web Part**   Click the Modify Shared Page link, choose Add Web Parts from the pop-up menu, and click Browse. Locate the desired Web Part from the Add Web Parts tool pane (Figure 17-7) and then drag it to the desired location on the page. When dragging a Web Part on the page, acceptable locations will be indicated with a blue rectangle appearing around the Web Part. A thick blue line indicates where the top of the Web Part will be positioned. When finished, click the Close button in the top right corner of the Add Web Parts tool pane.

Figure 17-7.   *The Add Web Parts tool pane.*

Note   Form Web Parts allow users to filter data from the SharePoint Web site, in essence acting as a search form. Once you have added a Form Web Part to the page, you can connect it to a data source. To connect the form to a data source, click the down arrow in the top right corner of the Web Part, and then choose Connections, Provide Form Values To, and then the appropriate data source (such as Announcements or Links).

- **Move Web Parts around** Switch the page into design mode by clicking the Modify Shared Page link and then selecting Design This Page from the menu. When you are in design mode, gray rectangles appear around each Web Part and a check mark will appear next to the Design This Page option in the pop-up menu. Drag each Web Part to the location you want. To switch off design mode, click Modify Shared Page link and click Design This Page again.

- **Minimize or close a Web Part** Click the down arrow in the top right corner of the Web Part and choose Minimize or Close from the pop-up menu.

- **Modify a Web Part** Click the down arrow in the top right corner of the Web Part and choose Modify Shared Web Part from the pop-up menu. A yellow dotted rectangle appears around the Web Part. Use the tool pane shown in Figure 17-8 to change the view, appearance, layout, and other settings related to the Web Part. When finished, click OK.

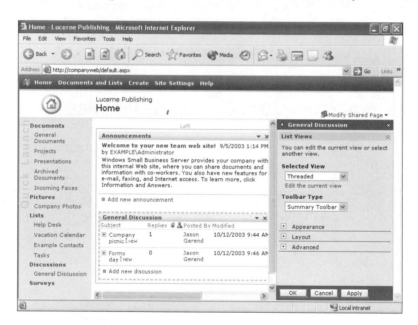

Figure 17-8. *Modifying a Web Part.*

Note The Home Page has two views that you can customize. The Shared View is the home page view shared by all users of the site and is displayed by default. Any customizations to this view affect all users. The Personal View, on the other hand, can be customized to suit the preferences of each user because customizations are kept private to that user. To switch between the views, click the Modify Shared Page link and select Shared View or Personal View from the pop-up menu. When you switch to Personal View, some of the option names will change accordingly.

Customizing Pages

The home page isn't the only page on a SharePoint Web site that can be easily customized, though other pages have somewhat different options. To modify other pages, click the Site Settings link at the top of a page in the SharePoint Web site, click the Modify Site Content link and then click the link corresponding to the item that you want to customize. This displays the Customization page (Figure 17-9) for the specified item.

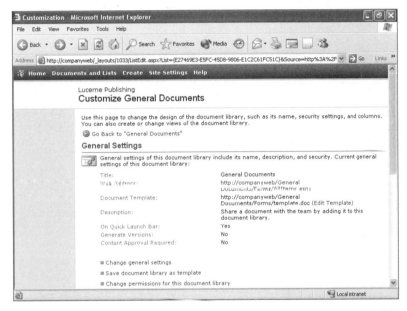

Figure 17-9.   *The Customization page for the General Documents library.*

Note   To create a new item, click the Create link at the top of the SharePoint Web site, click the type of item you want to create, and then provide the general settings for the item.

On the Customization page, you can:

- **Modify settings on pages other than the home page**   Use the Change General Settings link to open the Change General Settings page (Figure 17-10), which you can use to change the following settings. (Not all settings are available for all item types.)

  - Page name and description.

  - Whether a link to the page appears in the Quick Launch bar.

  - Whether user-submitted items and files require approval before being posted for general viewing on the site.

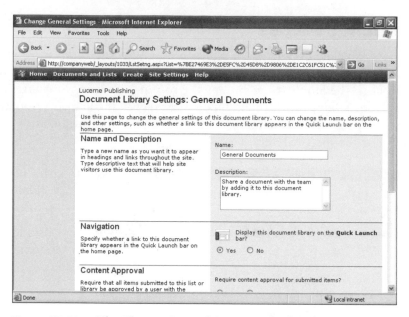

Figure 17-10. *The Change General Settings page for the General Documents library.*

Note Members of the Administrator site group or another site group with Manage Lists rights can accept or reject posted items in a SharePoint page for which content approval is enabled. To do so, open the page, click the Approve/Reject Items view, move the mouse over the item, click the down arrow to the right of the item, and choose Approve/Reject from the pop-up menu. Rejected and Pending items remain on the site until the creator of the items or an Administrator deletes them.

- Whether new versions of documents or pictures in the library are created with each edit. When versioning is enabled, users can access older versions of a file by clicking the down-arrow next to the item name and choosing Version History. Office 2003 programs also support the Version History command directly from within files saved to a SharePoint library with versioning enabled.

- Whether users are allowed to attach files to posted items.

- Which permission levels users have for items created by other users.

- Which file is used as the template for new files created in the library.

- **Create a template from the item** Use the Save Item As Template link to create a template from the current SharePoint item. This allows users to create new items based on the settings from the template.

- **Alter site group permissions for an item** Use the Change Permissions For This Item link to alter the permissions each site group of users has for the item. You can also change which level of access to this item anonymous users have, if any, and whether to allow restricted users to request increased access privileges.

> **Note**   Anonymous users can gain access to an item only when anonymous access is enabled on the *http://companyweb* site in Microsoft Internet Information Services (IIS) and anonymous access is enabled for the site in SharePoint Top-Level Site Administration. See the "Managing Site Groups and Access Permissions" section of this chapter for more information.

- **Delete the item**   Use the Delete This Item link to delete the item and all data (posts, documents, and so on) stored within it. You probably don't need to be told to be careful with this.

- **Make columns and views available for the item**   In the Columns and Views sections use the available links to modify which columns and views are available in the item.

Administering a SharePoint Web Site

So far this chapter has provided an overview of how to use and customize a SharePoint Web site using the default tools. This section discusses how to administer the site.

To administer a SharePoint Web site, click Site Settings at the top of a page in the SharePoint Web site, click the Go To Site Administration link, and then use the Top-Level Site Administration page (Figure 17-11) to administer site settings.

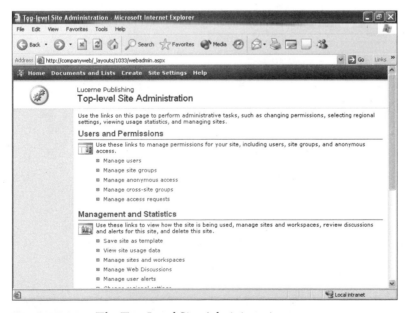

Figure 17-11.   *The Top-Level Site Administration page.*

Tip You can administer SharePoint from the command line using the Stsadm.exe command-line tool (C:\Program Files\Common Files\Microsoft Shared\Web server extensions\60\BIN\Stsadm.exe).

Managing Site Users

Active Directory user accounts are given differing levels of access and change permissions on a SharePoint Web site depending on their SharePoint site group membership. (You must have a user account in Active Directory to use a SharePoint site.) To manage users, click the Manage Users link in the Top-Level Site Administration page. This displays a list of users that you can administer, as described in the following list:

- To remove SharePoint site access permissions from a user, select the check box next to the user and click Remove Selected Users. (This doesn't delete the user's account in Active Directory.)

- To change the SharePoint site group memberships for the user, select the check box next to the user and click Edit Site Groups Of Selected Users.

- To add an Active Directory user account that doesn't have permissions on the SharePoint Site, complete the following steps:

    1. Click Add Users. This displays the Add Users page, shown in Figure 17-12.

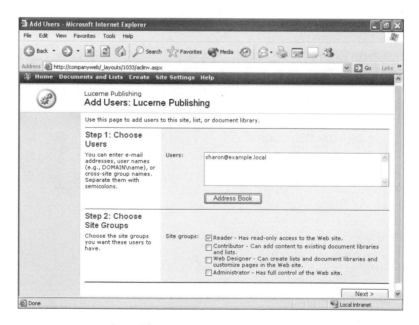

Figure 17-12. *The Add Users page.*

2. Type the user's e-mail address (or click Address Book to find the user in your Address Book), specify which site groups the user should belong to, and then click Next.

3. In the second Add User page, optionally modify the user name and display name of the user, and then customize the e-mail that is sent to the user inviting them to participate in the SharePoint Web site. Click Finish when you're finished.

Under the Hood   Site Groups and Rights

The groups used by SharePoint (site groups) to assign rights to users are different from standard Windows user groups:

- **Guest**   An implicit site group to which users are added by granting them access to an item or page without adding them to the list of site users. As such, they can only access the items to which they are explicitly given access. This site group is never seen and can't be deleted.

- **Reader**   This site group gives members read-only access to the site, though if Self-Service Site Creation is enabled on the virtual server (it's not by default), users with Reader rights can create new sites (in which they are given Administrator rights).

- **Contributor**   This site group gives members Reader rights plus the ability to add content to existing items.

- **Web Designer**   This site group gives members Contributor rights plus the ability to create new items and customize existing items. Active Directory Domain Users and Mobile Users are automatically members of this site group.

- **Administrator**   This site group is the typical administrator group—members have full control of the site and can create and delete additional sites as well. Active Directory Domain Administrators and Domain Power Users are automatically members of this site group.

Managing Site Groups and Access Permissions

To change SharePoint site group memberships, enable anonymous access, or deny users the ability to request access to items they don't have permission to access, use the Users And Permissions section of the Top-Level Site Administration page, as discussed in the following list:

- To add or delete site groups, click the Manage Site Groups link.

- To add or delete cross-site groups, which have permissions on all SharePoint sites created on the virtual server, click the Manage Cross-Site Groups link.

- To enable anonymous access to the site, first enable anonymous access to the *http://companyweb* site in IIS (as discussed in Chapter 18, "Managing an Intranet Web Server"), then click Manage Anonymous Access and use the Change Anonymous Access Settings page (Figure 17-13) to control what anonymous users should be able to access. (You'll still have to explicitly enable anonymous access on each item, as described in the "Customizing Pages" section of this chapter.) Click OK when you're finished.

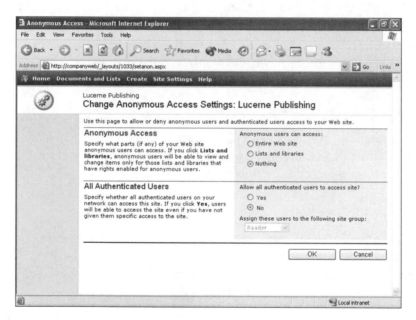

Figure 17-13. *The Change Anonymous Access Settings page.*

- To permit authenticated users on the network who aren't members of the SharePoint site access to the site, click Manage Anonymous Access to open the Change Anonymous Access Settings page. In the Allow All Authenticated Users To Access Site section of the page select Yes and choose a site group in which to place these users. Click OK when you're finished.

- To change whether users can request access to the site, click the Manage Access Requests link, enable or disable access requests, and specify an e-mail address to which requests should be sent. Click OK when you're finished.

Managing Templates, Usage Data, and Other Settings

To manage sites and templates, view usage data, manage alerts and Web discussions, delete a site, or change regional settings, open the Top-Level Site Administration page and use the following list:

- **Save the site as a template** Click Save Site As Template to save the entire SharePoint site as a template for new sites. You can manage site templates and item templates by clicking the Manage Site Template Gallery and Manage List Template Gallery links in the Site Collection Galleries section of the page.

- **See usage data for the site** Click View Site Usage Data to see usage data for the site, including the number of hits and which users have been accessing the site. Use the View Site Collection Usage Summary and View Storage Space Allocation links in the Site Collection Administration section of the page for additional statistics.

- **View a list of child sites and control creation of new sites** Click Manage Sites And Workspaces to view a list of child sites (Figure 17-14), change which site groups can create new sites (by default, only the Administrator site group), as well as create new sites. This allows you to create extra sites for specific projects, while keeping a unified company site.

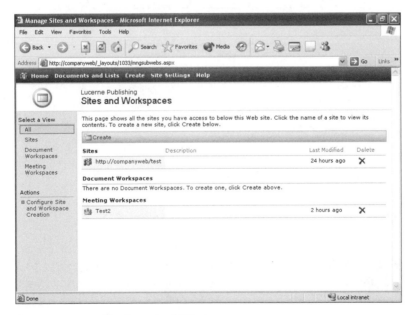

Figure 17-14. *The Sites And Workspaces page.*

- **View comments and delete discussions** Click the Manage Web Discussions link to view a list of pages with discussion comments and delete discussions as desired.

- **View and delete alerts**   Click the Manage Users Alerts link to view all alerts set on the site, and optionally delete alerts.

- **Change regional settings**   Click the Change Regional Settings link to change the time zone and format as well as other regional options.

- **Delete the site**   Click Delete This Site to permanently delete the site, including all content. Once again, be careful with this link.

Administering SharePoint Virtual Servers

Besides administering SharePoint at the site level, you can also administer the IIS virtual server in which SharePoint sites run. This is useful for tweaking security settings and changing how SharePoint works with e-mail. To do so, open the SharePoint Central Administration page (Figure 17-15) from the Administrative Tools folder on the Windows Small Business Server computer, and then use the following list to perform some notable tasks.

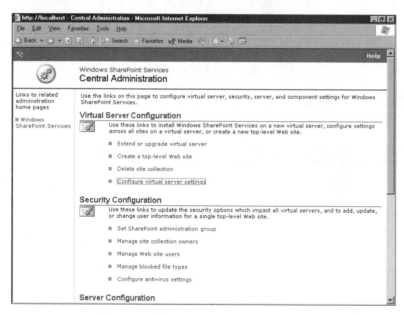

Figure 17-15.   *The Central Administration page.*

- **Change settings for a virtual server**   To change settings specific to a single virtual server, click the Configure Virtual Server Settings link, click companyweb (or the appropriate virtual server), and then use the following list:

  - To change which user rights are available to site groups on the virtual server, click Manage User Rights For Virtual Server, and then clear the check boxes next to any rights you want to prohibit. Click OK when you're finished.

- To disable the ability to create connections between Web Parts, click Manage Security Settings For Web Part Pages. This generally breaks Web Parts that include forms; however, if you don't use any of these Web Parts, disabling this ability can improve site security by reducing the surface area open to attack.

- To change general settings such as the maximum size of uploaded files, or to permit properly configured document libraries on the virtual server to automatically publish attachments posted in Exchange public folders, click the Virtual Server General Settings link.

- To enable Self-Service Site Creation, click the Configure Self-Service Site Creation link. This enables users with the Use Self-Service Site Creation right to create sites.

- **Control ability to upload and download file types**   To change which file types users are blocked from uploading or downloading, click Manage Blocked File Types.

- **Control antivirus program interaction**   To change how a third-party SharePoint antivirus program interacts with SharePoint, click Configure Antivirus Settings.

- **Change how e-mail is sent**   To change how e-mail is sent from SharePoint sites, click Configure Default E-Mail Server Settings. This configures such settings as the outbound SMTP server and the e-mail address used for the From and Reply-To fields.

- **Enable full-text searching**   To enable full-text search of Windows SharePoint Services sites, click the Configure Full Text Search link, select the Enable Full-Text Search And Index Component check box, and then click OK. Doing so places a search form on all SharePoint sites, utilizing Microsoft SQL Server 2000 for search results. To use this feature, you must be using Windows Small Business Server 2003, Premium Edition, with the Full-Text Search component of SQL Server installed. For information about installing SQL Server, see Appendix B, "Installing ISA Server 2000 and SQL Server 2000."

- **Log usage data**   To enable logging of usage data (which enables the viewing of site usage reports), click the Configure Usage Analysis Processing link, select the Enable Logging and Enable Usage Analysis Processing check boxes, optionally change the default settings, and then click OK.

Real World   The Microsoft Office HTML Viewer Service

The Configure HTML Viewer link leads to a page that you can use to enable on-the-fly, high-quality translations of .DOC, .XLS, .PPT, and .PPS files in the Windows SharePoint Services site to .HTML files for clients who don't have appropriate Microsoft Office viewers installed. However, this nifty feature requires the use of a dedicated HTML Viewer server running on Microsoft Windows XP Professional with Office 2003 and the Microsoft Office HTML Viewer Service installed (because the HTML Viewer computer services only the SharePoint server, a server operating system is unnecessary).

The Microsoft Office HTML Viewer Service won't work properly when installed on the Windows Small Business Server computer, and doing so can cause significant security vulnerabilities and performance issues. For more information, download the Microsoft Office HTML Viewer from the Microsoft Office 2003 Resource Kit Web site (*http://www.microsoft.com /office/ork/2003*) and read the HTML Viewer Whitepaper included with the package.

Using FrontPage 2003 to Customize Windows SharePoint Services

FrontPage 2003 is a full-featured Web page editor that you can use to edit or create sophisticated Windows SharePoint Services sites as well as normal Web pages. Although entire books have been written about FrontPage, the coverage here focuses on accomplishing some select tasks on your SharePoint site. For a thorough grounding in FrontPage, see *Microsoft Office FrontPage 2003 Inside Out* (Microsoft Press).

Note Microsoft FrontPage 2002 and earlier versions don't work with the version of Windows SharePoint Services installed on Windows Small Business Server. However, a copy of FrontPage 2003 is included with Windows Small Business Server 2003, Premium Edition.

Customizing Existing SharePoint Sites

Although you can customize most aspects of a SharePoint Web site using a Web browser, as discussed earlier in this chapter, FrontPage provides the ability to exert complete control over the SharePoint site. From a client computer, you can easily modify the contents of link bars, work with Web Parts, create new pages, and do anything else you want.

> **Tip**   You can also use FrontPage to customize the default Web site created
> by Windows Small Business Server. For security purposes, use a Web host-
> ing company to host your public Internet site, and don't publish your default
> Web site to the Internet. Employees will still be able to access the Share-
> Point site from the Internet using the Remote Web Workplace, which is available
> on the Internet at *http://www.example.com/remote*, if you configure your firewall
> appropriately (where *http://www.example.com* is the Internet domain name
> of the Windows Small Business Server computer).

Opening the SharePoint Site And Getting Comfortable

To open the SharePoint Web site (*http://companyweb*) in FrontPage 2003, complete
the following steps:

1. In FrontPage, choose Open Site from the File menu.

2. In the Open Site dialog box, type **http://companyweb** in the Site Name
   box and then click Open. To open the default Web site for the Windows
   Small Business Server computer, type **http://sbssrv** (where sbssrv is the
   computer name of the Windows Small Business Server computer).

3. The site is opened in Folders view (Figure 17-16), which shows a listing
   of folders and pages on the site:

   - To open a folder, double-click it. To return to the previous folder,
     click the Up One Level button on the right side of the view.

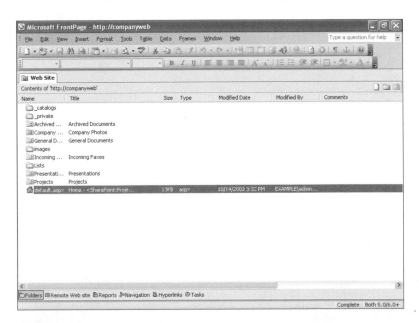

Figure 17-16.   *The http://companyweb site in FrontPage 2003.*

- To open a page for editing, double-click it. This displays the page in Design view, a What You See Is What You Get (WYSIWYG) view that you can use to edit the page as if it were a normal Microsoft Office document.

- To change the Design view of a page to match a specific screen resolution, click the Page Size display on the Status bar and choose the desired resolution; 760 × 420 (800 × 600 Maximized) is usually a good choice.

- To change the Estimated Time To Download reading to reflect a different speed network connection, click it on the Status bar and choose the desired connection speed. As a rule, pages shouldn't take more than 15 seconds to download over the targeted connection speed, if possible.

- To disable tools that create pages incompatible with certain browser versions, choose Page Options from the Tools menu and then use the Authoring tab (Figure 17-17) to specify Web browser compatibility options.

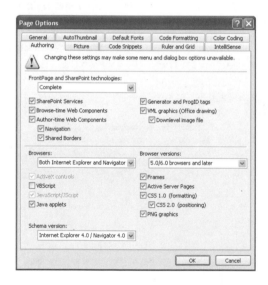

Figure 17-17.   *The Page Options dialog box.*

- To select a specific area of a Web page by using an HTML tag (a trick Macromedia Dreamweaver users are accustomed to), click the desired tag at the top of the page in Design view.

- To change the view to show HTML code or view the page as it would appear rendered in Internet Explorer 6, click the Split, Code, and Preview buttons at the left side of the Status bar.

- To preview a page in the Web browser of your choice, click the down arrow next to the Preview toolbar button and select the desired browser and resolution. To add browsers to the list, choose Edit Browser List.

Tip   To back up the entire Web site, choose Server and then Backup Web Site from the Tools menu. To package a group of pages and all dependant files into a Web Package that can be imported into any other site, choose Packages and then Export from the Tools menu.

Adding Links and Customizing the Link Bar

Two essential tasks that you can't perform using the SharePoint Web interface are adding links to pages and customizing the link bar that appears across the top and left side of a SharePoint site. These are easy to accomplish in FrontPage—just open the page in FrontPage 2003 and follow this list of options:

- To add a link to a link bar, click + Add Link on the appropriate link bar (Figure 17-18). This opens the Add To Link Bar dialog box, which you can use to link to another item in the site or a page anywhere on the Internet.

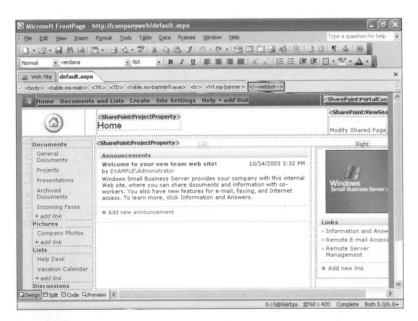

Figure 17-18.   *The http://companyweb Home page in FrontPage.*

- To edit a link bar, right-click a link bar and choose Link Bar Properties. This displays the Link Bar Properties dialog box (Figure 17-19). Select the link bar you want to edit from the Choose Existing box, and use the following list:

- Click Create New to make a new link bar.

- To add, remove, or edit links, click the Add Link, Remove Link, and Modify Link buttons, respectively.

- To rearrange links, click the Move Up and Move Down buttons.

- Click the Style tab to change the link bar style, orientation, and appearance.

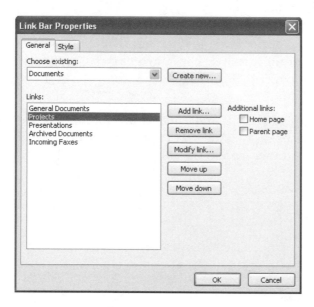

Figure 17-19. *The Link Bar Properties dialog box.*

- To add a bookmark in a page so that you can create hyperlinks to that specific location in the page (such as the top of the page), place the cursor at the location to which you want to link, choose Bookmark from the Insert menu, type a name for the bookmark, and then click OK.

- To add a normal hyperlink, place the cursor in the desired location or select the desired element, and click the Insert Hyperlink toolbar button. Use the Insert Hyperlink dialog box to specify where the hyperlink should send users. To send users to a bookmark in the current page, click Place In This Document on the Link To bar, select the appropriate bookmark, and then click OK.

Adding Web Parts

To add Web Parts to a Windows SharePoint Services page with FrontPage, complete the following steps:

1. Open the SharePoint page and place the cursor in the location you want to insert a Web Part.

2. Choose Insert Web Part from the Data menu to display the Web Parts task pane.

3. If you want the Web Part to be customizable using the SharePoint Web site, first create a new Web Part zone in which to place the Web Part. To do so, click New Web Part Zone.

4. Select the Web Part that you want to insert and then click Insert Selected Web Part. The new Web Part is placed on the page (in the newly created Web Part zone, if you made one), as shown in Figure 17-20.

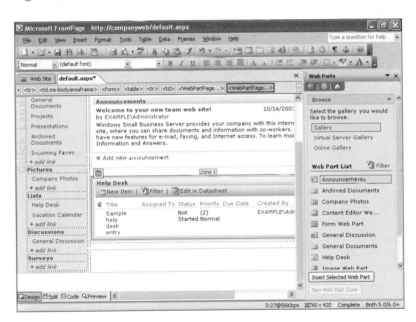

Figure 17-20. *A Web Part in a newly created Web Part zone.*

5. To connect a Web Part to a data source (for those Web Parts that support connections), right-click the newly inserted Web Part and choose Web Part Connections from the shortcut menu. This displays the Web Part Connections Wizard, which walks you through the connection process.

Tip   To change whether a user can customize a Web Part zone, right-click the zone and choose Web Part Zone Properties from the shortcut menu.

Creating New SharePoint Web Sites

FrontPage 2003 makes it easy to create powerful SharePoint Web sites from templates or from scratch. Once again, without going into detail about this, here's how to get started:

1. In FrontPage, choose New from the File menu.

2. In the New task pane, click More Web Site Templates.

3. In the Web Site Templates dialog box (Figure 17-21), click the Share-Point Services tab.

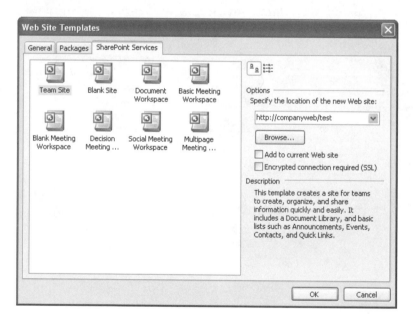

Figure 17-21.   *The Web Site Templates dialog box.*

Tip   You can use the Packages tab of the Web Site Templates dialog box to create a News And Reviews Site or a Web Log (blog) site.

4. Select the desired template, specify where to save the new site, and then click OK. FrontPage creates the new site and displays it.

Summary

This chapter showed you how to use the SharePoint Web site created by Windows Small Business Server (*http://companyweb*), as well as how to customize and administer it. The chapter also discussed administering SharePoint virtual servers and how to use FrontPage 2003 to perform more sophisticated authoring of SharePoint sites.

In the next chapter, you will move on to performing common Web server administration tasks using Windows Small Business Server's built-in Web server—Internet Information Services (IIS).

Chapter 18
Managing an Intranet Web Server

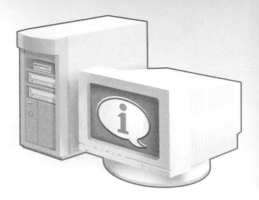

Microsoft Windows Small Business Server 2003 automatically installs and configures Microsoft Internet Information Services (IIS) 6.0 to serve as an intranet Web server. As such, Windows Small Business Server enables such features as the *http://companyweb* SharePoint intranet site (discussed in Chapter 17, "Customizing a SharePoint Web Site"), the Network Configuration Wizard, Remote Web Workplace, and Outlook Web Access (all discussed in Chapter 12, "Managing Computers on the Network").

In general, IIS doesn't require much configuration for use on an intranet; however, you might occasionally need to create additional virtual directories, enable or disable anonymous access to a site, place limits on network bandwidth and CPU utilization, or configure File Transfer Protocol (FTP) or the Indexing Service. This chapter helps you perform these tasks and a few other tasks appropriate for small businesses hosting intranet Web sites.

More Info Sources for more information about IIS include *Microsoft IIS 6.0 Administrators Companion* by William Stanek (Microsoft Press, 2003) and the *Microsoft Internet Information Services (IIS) 6.0 Resource Kit* (Microsoft Press, 2004).

Real World **Hosting Your Own Internet Web Site**

Internet-accessible Web servers sit on the front lines of a virtual battlefield, exposed to continual assault by hackers and script-kiddies (neophyte hackers using polished hacking applications and pre-built scripts to launch attacks). For this reason, small businesses should use a Web hosting company to host their public Internet Web sites. Alternatively, companies can use dedicated Windows Server 2003 Web Edition computers placed in a perimeter network to host their public Web sites, and keep these computers locked down and updated with the latest patches. Public Web sites shouldn't be hosted by Windows Small Business Server 2003.

Although these recommendations are standard best practices for server security, you'll probably want to stray a little bit and open your firewalls to allow your Windows Small Business Server to act as an Internet-accessible Web server for the purpose of hosting your Remote Web Workplace. You can reduce the risks involved by configuring your Windows Small Business Server firewall to publish only the Remote Web Workplace, not the default Web site.

Creating New Virtual Directories

If you want to create a new Web site or a series of Web pages on the internal network, the best way to do this is to create a new virtual directory in Internet Information Services. A *virtual directory* is a directory name or alias that corresponds to a physical directory on the server. Virtual directories appear as subfolders on a Web site but in reality can point to a folder located anywhere on the network.

Real World **Creating New Web Sites**

It's usually more convenient to create new virtual directories in an existing site such as the Windows SharePoint Services site (*http://companyweb*) or the Default Web Site instead of creating a completely new site in IIS. Creating new sites requires managing host headers as well as manually adding alias (CNAME) records to the DNS reverse lookup zone, which is a nuisance and unnecessary for most small businesses. If you need to create a new site, right-click the Web Sites container in the Internet Information Services console, choose New, Web Site from the shortcut menu to start the Web Site Creation Wizard—just remember to create the alias record in DNS corresponding to the Web site's host header.

To create a new virtual directory, complete the following steps:

1. Open the Server Management console, expand the Advanced Management container, and then expand Internet Information Services.

2. Expand the SBSSRV (local computer) container (assuming your server is named SBSSRV), and select the Web Sites container (Figure 18-1).

3. In the details pane, right-click Default Web Site, and choose New, Virtual Directory from the shortcut menu. The Virtual Directory Creation Wizard appears.

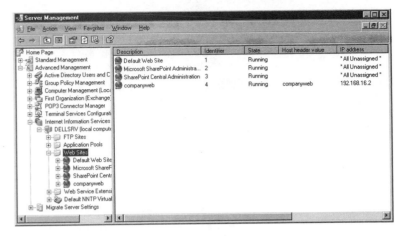

Figure 18-1.   *The Server Management console showing the Web Sites container.*

Tip   You can also publish from Microsoft FrontPage directly into a new virtual directory without first creating the directory in IIS if you publish with a user account that has the appropriate permissions.

4. On the first page of the Virtual Directory Creation Wizard, click Next.

5. On the Virtual Directory Alias page, type a folder name and then click Next.

6. On the Web Site Content Directory page, specify the path to the real folder that will contain the Web site content (for example, **c:\inetpub \training**), and then click Next.

Tip   Placing content in a subfolder of the c:\inetpub folder is usually the most convenient approach because this folder already has the proper NTFS permissions applied to it, and the Windows Small Business Server default and *http://companyweb* sites are located here as well.

7. On the Virtual Directory Access Permissions page, clear the Run Scripts check box (unless you plan on using scripts or dynamic Web pages in the virtual directory). Click Next and then click Finish.

Using Web Sharing

You can make any folder on a Windows Small Business Server computer directly accessible from your Web site by using the Web Sharing feature. This feature provides a handy way to quickly make a virtual directory for a folder that stores a Web site or to simulate an FTP site. To do either, complete the following steps:

1. In Microsoft Windows Explorer, right-click the folder you want to share on your Web site and choose Properties from the shortcut menu.

2. Click the Web Sharing tab (Figure 18-2), and then select the Web site on which you want to share the folder (most likely Default Web Site).

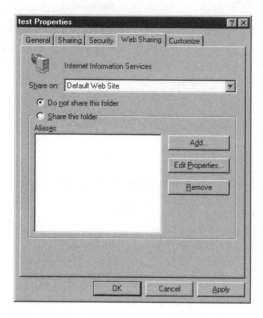

Figure 18-2. *The Web Sharing tab.*

3. Choose Share This Folder. This opens the Edit Alias dialog box, shown in Figure 18-3.

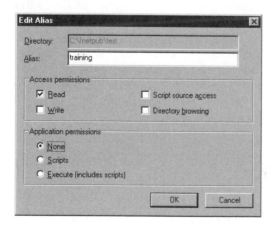

Figure 18-3. *The Edit Alias dialog box.*

4. Type the virtual directory name you want to use in the Alias box.

5. Specify the Access Permissions and Application Permissions for the folder.

   - To use the folder as a standard Web site with the home page (Default.htm or Index.htm) linking to all relevant files, select the Read check box for the Access Permissions and the None option for the Application Permissions.

   - To use server-side scripting or dynamic Web pages in the virtual directory, select both the Read check box and Scripts option.

   - To allow users to browse the folder as if it were an FTP site, select the Directory Browsing check box.

Security Alert   Directory Browsing is usually disabled on Web sites to improve security—visitors can view only those linked pages or files for which they know the exact URL. Although this is of less concern on an internal Web site, it's still wise to leave this feature disabled when unneeded.

6. Click OK when you're finished.

7. Click Add to create any additional aliases, and click OK when you're finished.

Changing Security Settings

Windows Small Business Server 2003 does a pretty good job of locking down IIS while still allowing all its relevant features to work. Nonetheless, there are several security settings that you might want to change, such as which sites are externally accessible or which allow anonymous users, as well as which server certificate is used for secure communications.

Note   WebDAV support is disabled in IIS by default to maximize security. If you need to enable it, open the Web Service Extensions folder in Internet Information Services (IIS) Manager, select WebDAV, and click Allow.

Changing Which Sites Are Externally Accessible

You can use three methods to control whether a site hosted by Windows Small Business Server is accessible to external users who don't have a Virtual Private Network (VPN) connection to your network:

- Change the firewall settings to prohibit or allow access to the Remote Web Workplace, Outlook Web Access, the Default Web Site or the *http://companyweb* site. This permits or denies all external users (though some sites such as *http://companyweb*, Remote Web Workplace, and Outlook Web Access are still password protected).

- Change the IP addresses to which a Web site responds in the Internet Information Services console. Configuring the Web site (Default Web Site or *http://companyweb*) to respond only to the internal IP address blocks all external users to the site and all virtual directories within it.

- Change the Directory Security for a Web site or a virtual directory to block or allow a range of IP addresses or a specific domain. For example, you could block all external IP addresses.

The first method is covered in Chapter 6, "Completing the To Do List and Other Post-Installation Tasks." To use the other two methods, follow these steps:

1. Open the Server Management console, expand the Advanced Management container, and then expand Internet Information Services.

2. Expand the SBSSRV (local computer) container (assuming your server is named SBSSRV), select the Web Sites container, right-click the Web site or virtual directory with which you want to work, and then choose Properties from the shortcut menu.

   If you chose a Web site, complete Step 3. If you chose a virtual directory, continue with Step 4.

3. If you chose a Web site, use the Web Site tab of the Properties dialog box (Figure 18-4) to identify the IP address or addresses on which you want the Web site to be available.

Caution Choosing an internal IP address for a Web site blocks external access to all virtual directories hosted by the Web site. Doing this on the Default Web Site will block external access to the Remote Web Workplace and Outlook Web Access, even if the firewall is configured to allow it.

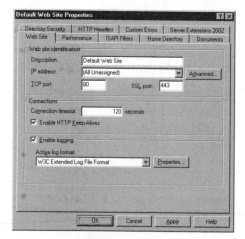

Figure 18-4. *The Web Site tab of the Properties dialog box.*

4. To specify access permissions by IP address, which is the only way to change access to virtual directories, click the Directory Security tab of the Properties dialog box. Click the Edit button in the IP Address And Domain Name Restrictions section of the dialog box. This displays the IP Address And Domain Name Restrictions dialog box shown in Figure 18-5.

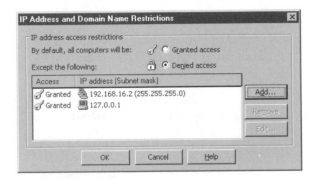

Figure 18-5. *The IP Address And Domain Name Restrictions dialog box.*

5. Choose Granted Access or Denied Access to allow or block all computers by default.

6. Click the Add button to create a rule allowing or denying a computer, group of computers, or all computers belonging to a specific domain name.

   Depending on the default condition you chose, either the Grant Access (Figure 18-6) or Deny Access dialog box is displayed.

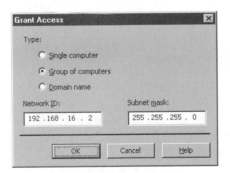

Figure 18-6. *The Grant Access dialog box.*

7. In the Grant Access or Deny Access dialog box, choose Single Computer or Group Of Computers. To block or allow a single computer, type the computer's IP address in the Network ID box. To block or allow a group of computers, type the IP address of the first computer in the group in the Network ID box and then type a subnet mask indicating how many computers are in the group. Click OK when you're finished.

8. Add any additional rules and then click OK when you're finished.

Caution Don't allow or block computers by Domain Name—doing so requires that a reverse DNS lookup be performed on every visitor, which can generate excessive network traffic.

Real World **What Subnet Mask to Use**

When including or excluding a group of computers by IP address and subnet mask, use the following subnet masks to include or exclude entire Class A, B, or C networks:

- Use the 255.255.255.0 subnet mask to include all computers in a Class C network (for example, 192.168.16.1 through 192.168.16.254).

- Use the 255.255.0.0 subnet mask to include all computers in a Class B network (for example, 192.168.0.1 through 192.168.255.254).

- Use the 255.0.0.0 subnet mask to include all computers in a Class A network (for example, 10.0.0.1 through 10.255.255.254).

To include or exclude a subset of these networks, you need to use a variable length subnet mask such as 255.255.255.192 (which includes 62 addresses starting with the IP address you type in the Network ID box). For in-depth information about subnet masks, hop on the Web and download a custom subnet mask calculator.

Enabling or Disabling Anonymous Access

You can enable or disable anonymous (unauthenticated) users, controlling access to particular Web sites. This is probably most significant with the *http: //companyweb* SharePoint site—anonymous users won't be able to access the site even when you give them permission within Windows SharePoint Services unless you enable anonymous access in Internet Information Services.

To enable or disable anonymous access to a Web site or virtual directory, complete the following steps:

1. Open the Server Management console, expand the Advanced Management container, and then expand Internet Information Services.

2. Expand the SBSSRV (local computer) container (assuming your server is named SBSSRV), select the Web Sites container, right-click the Web site or virtual directory with which you want to work, and then choose Properties from the shortcut menu.

3. Click the Directory Security tab, and then click Edit in the Authentication And Access Control section of the dialog box.

4. In the Authentication Methods dialog box (Figure 18-7), select or clear the Enable Anonymous Access check box depending on whether you want to allow or prohibit anonymous access.

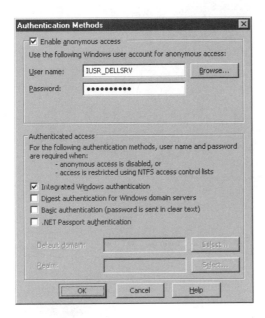

Figure 18-7. *The Authentication Methods dialog box.*

5. Use the Authenticated Access section of the dialog box to control which methods are available for client authentication. These methods are used when anonymous access is disabled, or when the NTFS permissions on the folder storing the content don't give Read permissions to the Domain Users group. Click OK when you're finished.

More Info See the Under the Hood sidebar "Anonymous Access and NTFS Folder Permissions," appearing later in this chapter, for more information about how anonymous access works.

Security Alert Integrated Windows Authentication and .NET Passport Authentication are the only authentication methods that don't have significant security problems. .NET Passport Authentication is complex and outside the scope of this book. Digest Authentication, although secure over the network, requires that passwords be stored in plaintext unencrypted form on the Windows Small Business Server computer; and Basic Authentication sends passwords in clear text (unencrypted form) over the network.

Under the Hood   Anonymous Access and NTFS Folder Permissions

Anonymous access is controlled using the IUSR_SBSSRV user account (where SBSSRV is the name of the Windows Small Business Server computer), which is a member of the Guests and Domain Users groups.

To determine whether anonymous users can access a folder with NTFS permissions applied, right-click the folder in Windows Explorer, choose Properties from the shortcut menu, and then click the Security tab and look for the Users or Domain Users groups. To explicitly check on IUSR_SBSSRV permissions, click Advanced, click the Effective Permissions tab, and then click Select. In the Select User, Computer, Or Group dialog box, type **IUSR_SBSSRV** (where SBSSRV is the NetBIOS name of the Windows Small Business Server computer), and then click OK. This displays the Effective Permissions for anonymous Web site users, as shown in Figure 18-8.

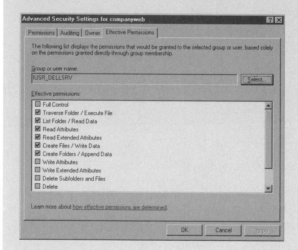

Figure 18-8. *The Advanced Security Settings dialog box.*

Changing Server Certificates and SSL Settings

When you run the Configure E-mail and Internet Connection Wizard, the Web Server Certificate page lets you create a new self-signed certificate used to authenticate the Web server for Secure Sockets Layer (SSL) communication, or you can use an existing certificate obtained from a trusted Certificate Authority (such as Verisign or a locally installed CA). Rerunning the wizard is the easiest way to change the certificate used by Internet Information Services, but doing so is cumbersome for viewing and choosing certificates, and the wizard can't create certificate requests to send to commercial or locally hosted CAs. For these tasks, complete the following steps:

1. Open the Server Management console, expand the Advanced Management container, and then expand Internet Information Services.

2. Expand the SBSSRV (local computer) container (assuming your server is named SBSSRV), select the Web Sites container, right-click the Web site or virtual directory with which you want to work, and then choose Properties from the shortcut menu.

3. Click the Directory Security tab. In the Secure Communications section of the dialog box, click View Certificate to view the currently assigned certificate, or click Edit to enable or disable SSL.

Caution   Don't enable SSL on the *http://companyweb* site—doing so makes the site inaccessible. This is because SSL encrypts host headers, preventing IIS from sending users to sites that make use of host headers, including the *http://companyweb* site.

---

4. To manage certificates, click Server Certificate on the Directory Security tab, and then click Next on the first page of the IIS Certificate Wizard.

5. If a certificate is currently installed, use the Modify The Current Certificate Assignment page (Figure 18-9) to choose the action that you want to perform and then click Next. You can choose from the following actions:

   • Renew The Current Certificate

   • Remove The Current Certificate

   • Replace The Current Certificate

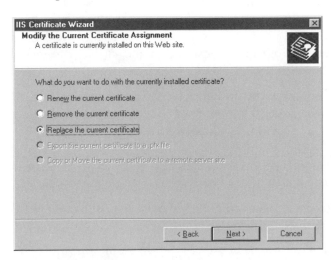

Figure 18-9.   *The Modify The Current Certificate Assignment page of the IIS Certificate Wizard.*

6. If no certificate is currently installed, the Server Certificate page (Figure 18-10) appears instead of the Modify The Current Certificate Assignment page. Choose one of the following actions and then click Next:

   - Create A New Certificate
   - Assign An Existing Certificate
   - Import A Certificate From A .PFX File

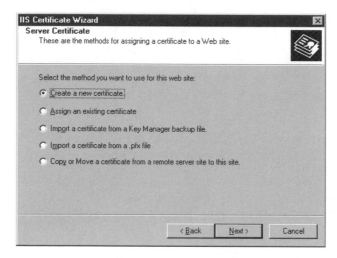

Figure 18-10. *The Server Certificate page of the IIS Certificate Wizard.*

7. If you chose to assign an existing certificate or replace the current certificate, click Next, select a certificate (only certificates that have been installed on the computer are displayed), click Next, accept the default SSL port, click Next, verify the settings, and then click Next to install the certificate for use with IIS.

8. If you chose to create a new certificate, click Next and, on the Delayed Or Immediate Request page, select whether to send the request later or send it immediately to a local CA. Click Next.

More Info   For more information about installing Certificate Services and creating your certificate authority, see Chapter 15, "Managing Connectivity."

9. On the Name And Security Settings page, type a descriptive name for the certificate and then click Next.

10. On the Organization Information page, type the name of your company and organizational unit, and then click Next.

11. On the Your Site's Common Name page, type the DNS name of the Web site and then click Next. (If this is a publicly accessible Web site, make sure to use the public DNS name of the site.)

12. On the Geographical Information page, type the country, state, and city in which the server is located, and then click Next.

13. If you chose to submit the certificate request later, type a file name for the certificate request and click Next. Review the settings and click Next to complete the request.

14. If you chose to submit the request immediately, click Next on the SSL Port page to accept the default SSL port (443).

15. On the Choose A Certificate Authority page, select the internal CA, click Next, review the settings, and then click Next again to submit the certificate request. Click Finish when prompted.

Limiting Network Usage by Web Sites

By default, IIS allows Web site visitors to consume as much network bandwidth as is available. When you have a lot of remote users or a slow Internet connection, visitors can consume all available bandwidth, preventing users of the internal network from accessing the Internet for Web browsing and e-mail. While it is easy to place limits on the maximum number of people who can concurrently connect to the Web site and the maximum amount of network bandwidth a Web site (virtual server) can consume, there is a catch—internal and external (Internet) users are treated the same. Therefore, it's best not to apply this feature to the *http://companyweb* site, and you should think about your usage patterns before applying it to the Default Web Site as well.

Caution IIS must install Packet Scheduler to enable *bandwidth throttling*, which will drop all currently connected users of the server—not just Web site users. Make sure you do *not* do this while users are connected to the Windows Small Business Server computer.

To limit network bandwidth or the number of concurrent connections, complete the following steps:

1. Open the Server Management console, expand the Advanced Management container, and then expand Internet Information Services.

2. Expand the SBSSRV (local computer) container (assuming your server is named SBSSRV), select the Web Sites container, right-click the Web site on which you want to limit bandwidth, and then choose Properties from the shortcut menu.

3. Click the Performance tab (Figure 18-11), select the Limit The Network Bandwidth Available To This Web Site check box, and specify the maximum bandwidth that IIS should allow the Web site and all virtual directories on the virtual server to use.

Figure 18-11. *The Performance tab of the Default Web Site Properties dialog box.*

4. To limit the number of concurrent users who can use the site, select the Connections Limited To option and type the maximum number of connections to allow.

5. Click OK when you're finished.

Setting Up an FTP Server

Although it might seem like a throwback to the days of Archie, Gopher, and Mosaic, File Transfer Protocol (FTP) is still occasionally useful as a quick and efficient way of sharing large files with external users. It contains no security worth using (passwords are sent in plaintext), so enable FTP on an as-needed basis, and disable it while not in use.

FTP in Windows Small Business Server 2003 is implemented as a component of Internet Information Services and is administered using the standard Internet Information Services consoles. Before you can use it, you must install it.

Installing FTP

To install the FTP service, complete the following steps:

1. Click Add Or Remove Programs in Control Panel, and then click Add/ Remove Windows Components. This opens the Windows Components Wizard.

2. Select Application Server, click Details, select Internet Information Services (IIS), and then click Details again.

3. Select the File Transfer Protocol (FTP) Service check box, click OK twice, and then click Next to install the service. Click Finish when it's done. Windows Small Business Server installs the FTP service and creates the default FTP site in the C:\Inetpub\FTProot directory.

Security Alert   Once FTP is installed, to allow external users to access FTP, you must rerun the Configure E-Mail and Internet Connection Wizard to open the firewall. If you have a non-UPnP external firewall in addition to Windows Small Business Server, make sure you open port 21 as well. Once you're finished transferring files, close the port again to prevent hackers from attacking your server over this port.

Configuring FTP

Although Windows Small Business Server sets up FTP with no additional help, you will probably want to change some settings, such as the welcome messages and directory security To do so, complete the following procedure:

1. Open the Server Management console, expand the Advanced Management container, expand Internet Information Services, and finally expand the SBSSRV (local computer) container (assuming your server is named SBSSRV). Then expand the FTP Sites container.

2. Right-click Default FTP Site and choose Properties from the shortcut menu. This displays the Default FTP Site Properties dialog box.

3. On the FTP Site tab, click the Current Sessions button to view currently connected users and optionally disconnect them.

4. Click the Security Accounts tab and select the Allow Only Anonymous Connections check box. This increases security by preventing users with valid accounts from sending their credentials in clear text over the Internet.

5. Click the Messages tab to type welcome messages that appear to visitors when they enter the site.

6. Click the Home Directory tab to specify where the FTP site should be stored.

7. Click the Directory Security tab to selectively block or enable access to certain IP addresses. This is useful for enabling the FTP site for a small number of users with known IP addresses. Click OK when you're finished.

Tip For maximum security, when you're finished using the FTP site, temporarily disable it by right-clicking it and choosing Stop from the shortcut menu. If you don't anticipate using it again, uninstall it using Add Or Remove Programs in Control Panel.

Configuring the Indexing Service

The Indexing Service is a built-in service that builds a searchable catalog of files on the server. This service vastly increases the speed of search operations as long as you perform the search locally on the Windows Small Business Server computer or use a search form created on a Web page hosted by the Windows Small Business Server computer. (Web page search forms hosted by IIS won't work until the Indexing Service is enabled or the form is rewritten to use a different technology such as CGI.)

Although the Indexing Service is installed by default, it's not turned on because it reduces overall server performance a small amount because of its background indexing of files.

Note Windows SharePoint Services can't use Indexing Service—it requires the full version of Microsoft SQL Server to perform searches. The SQL Server Desktop Engine included with Windows Small Business Server 2003 Standard Edition won't work either—you need the full version included with Windows Small Business Server 2003, Premium Edition.

If you want to enable a search form on a non-SharePoint Web site, complete the following steps to enable Indexing Service:

1. Open the Server Management console, expand Advanced Management, Computer Management, Services And Applications, and then select Services.

2. Right-click Indexing Service in the Services container and choose Properties from the shortcut menu.

3. Choose Manual in the Startup Type box, click Apply, and then click Start to start the service. Click OK when you're finished.

To view what the Indexing Service is cataloging, select the Indexing Service container (located under the Services And Applications container in the Advanced Management section of the Server Management console) and then use the following list:

- To view a list of folders included in and excluded from the catalog, expand the System or Web containers and then select Directories (Figure 18-12).

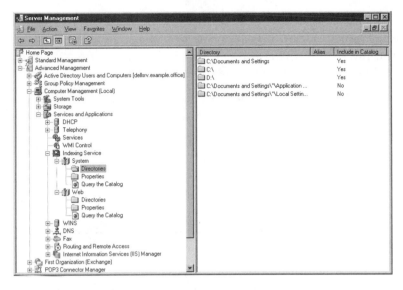

Figure 18-12. *The Server Management console showing the Indexing Service container.*

- To add rules including folders in or excluding folders from the catalog, right-click the Directories container, and choose New, Directory from the shortcut menu. Then use the Add Directory dialog box to specify which folder or network share to include or exclude.

- To perform a search against the catalog, select the Query The Catalog object and use the search form to perform your query.

Security Alert   When including network shares not located on the Windows Small Business Server computer, you should be aware that catalog searches will show all matches on the network share, even if the user isn't permitted access to the files.

Backing Up and Restoring the IIS Configuration

IIS has a couple of backup and restoration features that can complement a regular system and data backup schedule. Specifically, IIS lets you save configuration data for Web sites to XML files, which can be used to re-create the Web site settings. IIS also performs general configuration backups automatically. Neither of these features restores Web site data—you'll still need a full-fledged backup program for that, but they can help protect your IIS configuration.

To use these features, use the following list as a guide:

- To save the configuration of a Web site to a file, right-click the Web site in the Internet Information Services console, choose All Tasks, Save Configuration To File from the shortcut menu.

- To restore a previously saved Web site configuration, right-click the Web Sites container, choose New, Web Site (From File) from the shortcut menu.

- To back up or restore the IIS configuration, right-click the computer name in the Internet Information Services console, choose All Tasks, Backup/Restore Configuration from the shortcut menu.

Reinstalling IIS

Windows Small Business Server 2003 is much more than the sum of its parts—it is a synthesis of many discrete features. This is especially true with regard to IIS, which is closely integrated with Windows SharePoint Services, the Microsoft SQL Server Desktop Engine, Exchange Server, Routing and Remote Access, client deployment, remote access, and even Internet Security and Acceleration (ISA) Server.

The downside to this high level of integration is that fixing things can be a delicate operation. If IIS, Windows SharePoint Services, or a related product becomes corrupted, do some research on the Microsoft Knowledge Base and the Windows Small Business Server newsgroups, and contact Microsoft Product Support, if necessary. Before attempting to fix things, make a current backup, save your IIS configuration to a file, and try creating a duplicate Web site to experiment with.

If your problems persist, here's a last-ditch approach you can attempt before resorting to a complete reinstall or restore from backup. Proceed with caution.

1. Launch Windows Small Business Server Setup by selecting it in the Add Or Remove Programs tool and clicking Change/Remove.

2. Use the Microsoft Window Small Business Server Setup Wizard to remove intranet support.

3. Use Add Or Remove Programs to uninstall Microsoft Window SharePoint Services 2.0 and, possibly, uninstall Microsoft SQL Server Desktop Edition. It will appear in the Add Or Remove Programs list as Microsoft SQL Server Desktop Edition (SHAREPOINT).

> **Tip** If the automatic uninstall doesn't work, see the Microsoft Knowledge Base Article 320873 for the lengthy procedure to manually uninstall Microsoft SQL Server Desktop Edition.

4. Open the Server Management console, expand Advanced Management, Internet Information Services, and then expand your server (local computer). Expand the Web Sites container, select companyweb, and click Delete.

5. Open Registry Editor, export the following keys to backup files, and then delete them:

```
HKEY_LOCAL_MACHINF\SOFTWARE\Microsoft\SmallBusinessServer\Intranet
HKEY_LOCAL_MACHINE\SOFTWARE\Microsofl\Microsoft SQL Server\SHAREPOINT
```

> **Caution** Editing the registry can cause serious damage to your Windows Small Business Server software installation, which might be fixable only by reinstalling Windows Small Business Server. Use extreme caution.

6. Open Windows Explorer and delete C:\Program Files\Microsoft SQL Server\MSSQL$SHAREPOINT folder. (You might have to reboot into Safe Mode to do this.)

7. Reboot the computer and use Windows Small Business Server Setup to reinstall the intranet feature.

Summary

This chapter covered how to create new virtual directories, share folders on a Web site directly from within Windows Explorer, change security settings and network usage, and set up an FTP server as well as how to configure the Indexing Service. You've also learned to back up and restore the IIS configuration and what to do in the event of major troubles.

In the next chapter, you'll learn how to use SQL Server 2000, included in Windows Small Business Server 2003, Premium Edition.

Chapter 19
Using SQL Server

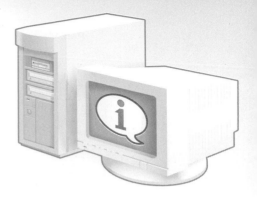

The Premium Edition of Microsoft Windows Small Business Server 2003 includes Microsoft SQL Server 2000. SQL Server 2000 is a set of components, based around a relational database, that work together to meet the data storage and analysis needs of some of the largest Web sites and enterprise data-processing systems and can equally well meet the day-to-day business needs of the small business.

In this chapter, we will *not* pretend to tell you everything you need to know about SQL Server 2000—frankly, that's the subject of many books already out there and beyond the scope of what we can do in this book. But what we will do is give you a quick overview of some of the features of SQL Server 2000.

More Info Installation of Microsoft SQL Server 2000 from the Premium Technologies CD is covered in Appendix B, "Installing ISA Server 2000 and SQL Server 2000."

Architecture

At the core of Microsoft SQL Server 2000 is the relational database, which is made up of the actual database files that store the data, and the database management system (DBMS) that both manages the structure of the database, including the relationship between various portions, and maintains the integrity of the data, including handling system failures by restoring the data to a point in time when it was consistent.

In addition to the DBMS components, at the core of the database are communications components that ensure the database can communicate with clients, manage encryption, and accept or provide streaming data as required. There are also additional server components that help integrate the database into the overall Microsoft .NET architecture.

Administration

Microsoft SQL Server 2000 administration is not integrated into the Server Management console, but instead uses its own MMC snap-in, the SQL Server Enterprise Manager console (SQL Server Enterprise Manager.MSC). You can open this console from All Programs, Microsoft SQL Server, Enterprise Manager. In addition to the Enterprise Manager, there are individual management utilities for other tasks, including:

- **Client Network Utility (Cliconfg.exe)** Creates the network protocol connections for SQL Server

- **Configure SQL XML Support in IIS (SQL IIS Admin.MSC)** Configures a virtual directory that allows HTTP access to SQL Server 2000

- **Import and Export Data (Dtswiz.exe)** The Data Transformation Services Import/Export Wizard is used to move data to and from other database formats

- **Profiler (Profiler.exe)** Allows administrators to monitor the events in a SQL Server 2000 database instance

- **Query Analyzer (Isqlw.exe)** Used to run interactive queries against the database and also to analyze the execution plan of the query

- **Server Network Utility (Svrnetcn.exe)** Manages the server's network properties, including protocols, encryption, and proxies

- **Service Manager (Sqlmangr.exe)** Controls SQL Server 2000 related services

Start, Stop, and Pause

Although it's easy enough to start or stop instances on your local machine using the Server Management console or even the Net Start and Net Stop commands from a command line, using the SQL Server Service Manager shown in Figure 19-1 enables you to start, stop, or pause a database on a remote server as well. You can also set a service to automatically start by selecting the Auto-Start Service When OS Starts check box.

Figure 19-1. *The SQL Server Service Manager lets you start, stop, and pause the services for both local and remote databases.*

Backup

Backing up your SQL Server databases should be done on a regular schedule as part of a comprehensive backup and disaster recovery program. The SQL Server 2000 database backup is *not* integrated into the Windows Small Business Server Backup utility and so must be run separately. SQL Server 2000 supports both standard tape and file backups, and logical backups using the export utility covered in the section titled "Import and Export Data," later in this chapter.

More Info For more information about backups in general, see Chapter 13, "Backing Up and Restoring Data." For detailed information about off-site backups and disaster recovery scenarios, see Chapter 21, "Disaster Planning and Fault Tolerance."

Defining a Backup Device

To simplify backing up a database, and to allow you to create the backup from within TransactSQL, the SQL Server interactive query application, you can first define one or more backup devices. Both tape drives and file backups are supported, but you should back up to a tape drive whenever possible to enable you to store critical backups off site.

Tip Backing up to a CD or DVD burner directly is not supported, but using third-party software that makes the CD or DVD drive appear as a normal file system allows SQL Server backups to write directly to the CD or DVD.

Caution Writeable and rewriteable CDs and DVDs are not considered a suitable medium for long-term archival storage and should not be used for reference archival storage. They can be appropriate for providing a fast and cost-effective short-term backup medium, however.

To add a backup device, complete the following steps:

1. Open the SQL Server Enterprise Manager if it isn't already open.

2. In the console tree, expand Microsoft SQL Servers, SQL Server Group, (local) (Windows NT), Management, and then select Backup, as shown in Figure 19-2.

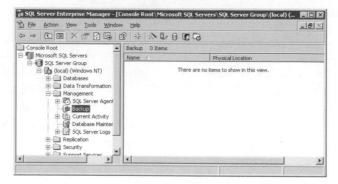

Figure 19-2. *The Backup utility of the SQL Server Enterprise Manager.*

3. Right-click Backup and select New Backup Device. If you select a Tape device, this device must be physically connected to the Windows Small Business Server machine—remote tape devices are not supported. If the device is a File device, as shown in Figure 19-3, you must give it both a logical name ("Default" in the figure) and a physical file name ("R:\SQL Server\Default Backup.bkf" in the figure).

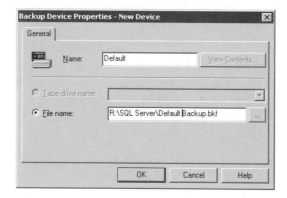

Figure 19-3. *Assigning both a logical and a physical name to the backup file.*

4. Click OK to complete the device definition. Future backups can be directed to the logical device or the physical file.

Backing Up a Database

Even if you haven't yet defined a backup device, you can add a backup device as part of the backup process when you are doing your backup from the SQL Server Enterprise Manager. When you back up using the SQL Server Enterprise Manager, you can use existing backup devices or specify new ones.

To back up a database from SQL Server Enterprise Manager, complete the following steps:

1. Open the SQL Server Enterprise Manager if it isn't already open.

2. Expand the (local) SQL Server Group, expand Management, and then select Backup.

3. Right-click Backup and select Backup A Database to open the SQL Server Backup dialog box shown in Figure 19-4.

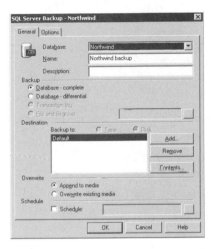

Figure 19-4. *The SQL Server Backup dialog box.*

4. Select the database to back up from the drop-down list.

Note The database tempdb appears in the drop-down list but cannot be backed up.

5. Type a name for the database backup in the Name field.

6. Type a description for the backup in the Description field.

7. Select the type of backup to be performed. The available choices will vary depending on the database being backed up. For most databases, the choices are either Database–Complete or Database–Differential.

8. Select the backup destination. If the destination you want to use is not shown, click Add to add an additional destination to the list.

9. Select Append To Media to append to an existing tape or disk backup. Select Overwrite Existing Media to erase the previous contents of the backup destination and create a new backup.

10. Select the Schedule check box and then click the ellipsis button (..) to create a schedule for the backup using the Edit Schedule dialog box, as shown in Figure 19-5.

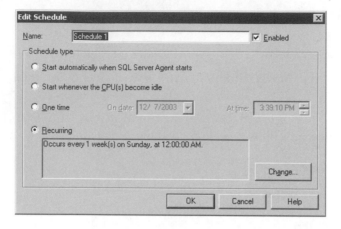

Figure 19-5. *The Edit Schedule dialog box.*

11. Click OK to schedule the backup job if you created a schedule or to start the backup immediately if you didn't.

Viewing the Contents of a Backup Device

Because a backup device might contain more than one backup, it is useful to be able to see what the contents of the device are. To view the contents of a backup device, do the following:

1. Open the SQL Server Enterprise Manager if it isn't already open.

2. Expand the (local) SQL Server Group, expand Management, and then select Backup.

3. Double-click the backup device to open the Backup Device Properties dialog box shown in Figure 19-6.

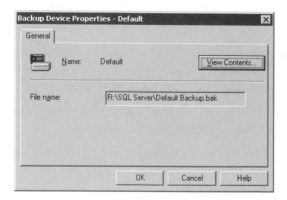

Figure 19-6. *The Backup Device Properties of the Default device, a file system backup.*

4. Click View Contents to open up the View Backup Media Contents dialog box shown in Figure 19-7.

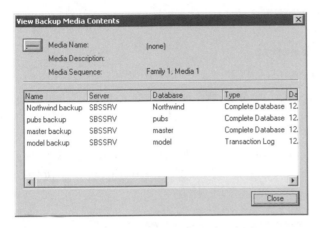

Figure 19-7.   *The contents of the Default backup device on SBSSRV.*

Import and Export Data

You can use the Data Transformation Services (DTS) Import/Export Wizard to make or restore a logical backup of a database and to transfer data between databases. The databases can be SQL Server databases or other databases for which there are drivers.

More Info   There are several other methods that can be used to import or export data from a SQL Server database. For more information about Import and Export methods and SQL Server in general, see the *Microsoft SQL Server 2000 Administrator's Companion* (Microsoft Press) or one of the many other books available on SQL Server 2000.

As shipped, the supported formats for Import and Export are:

- dBase (several versions)
- Microsoft Access
- SQL Server
- Microsoft Excel
- Microsoft Exchange
- Oracle
- Microsoft Visual FoxPro

- Paradox (several versions)
- Text files

Also, any OLE DB or ODBC driver you have can be used with DTS.

Exporting Data from SQL Server

To export data from SQL Server, complete the following steps:

1. Open the Data Transformation Services Import/Export Wizard by clicking Start, All Programs, Microsoft SQL Server, and then Import And Export Data. Click Next.

2. On the Choose A Data Source page, shown in Figure 19-8, select Microsoft OLE DB Provider For SQL Server from the Data Source drop-down list.

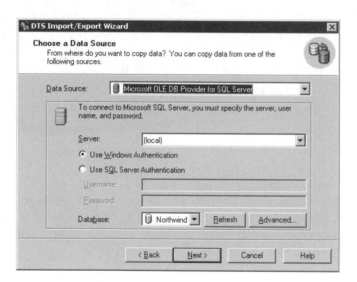

Figure 19-8. *The Choose A Data Source page of the DTS Import/Export Wizard.*

3. Select (local) from the Server drop-down list.

4. Select Use Windows Authentication unless you need to specify specific credentials for the database you are exporting.

5. Select the database you want to export data from using the Database drop-down list. Click Next.

6. On the Choose A Destination page shown in Figure 19-9, select a destination format. The destination options will vary depending on the output format you select. Click Next.

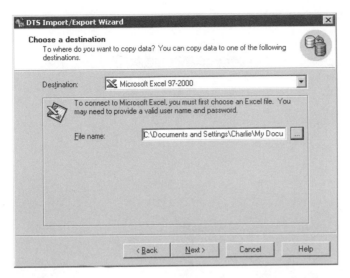

Figure 19-9. *The Choose A Destination page of the DTS Import/Export Wizard.*

7. On the Specify Table Copy Or Query page shown in Figure 19-10, you can choose whether to copy whole tables and views or to use a SQL query to filter the data. Click Next.

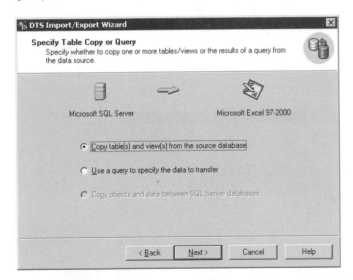

Figure 19-10. *The Specify Table Copy Or Query page of the DTS Import/ Export Wizard.*

8. If you selected Copy Tables And Views From The Source Database, you'll see a list of the available tables and views in the source database. Select the check boxes next to the tables or views you want to export, as shown in Figure 19-11. If you selected a query, you get a

page that lets you enter a SQL query, or you can use the Query Builder to build the query interactively.

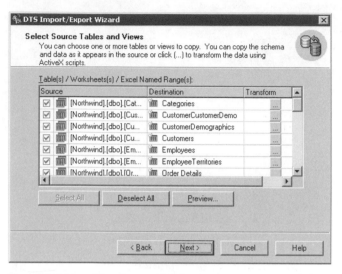

Figure 19-11. *The Source Tables And Views page of the DTS Import/Export Wizard.*

9. Select a row in the list of tables and click Preview to see the data in the source table that will be exported. Click OK to close the View Data dialog box and then click Next in the wizard.

10. On the Save, Schedule, And Replicate Package page shown in Figure 19-12, select the Run Immediately check box to run the export immediately.

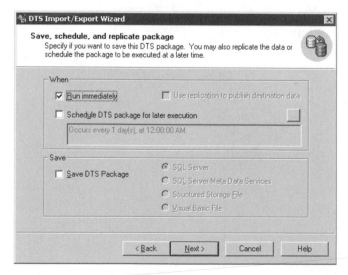

Figure 19-12. *The Save, Schedule, And Replicate Package page of the DTS Import/Export Wizard.*

11. Select the Schedule DTS Package For Later Execution check box if you want to run this export later or on a regular schedule. Click the ellipsis button (..) to adjust the schedule—the default is once a day.

12. Select the Save DTS Package check box and choose a format to save your DTS selections for later reuse. You'll see an additional Save DTS Package dialog box. Click Next.

13. On the Save DTS Package page are settings for saving packages. The settings for storing packages in SQL Server are shown in Figure 19-13. If you choose to save your package in a different storage format, the page will have options appropriate to your choice. If you didn't select either a schedule or a save option, you'll skip past this page entirely. Click Next.

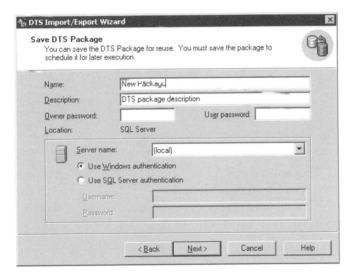

Figure 19-13. *The Save DTS Package page, which appears if you've selected SQL Server as your storage mechanism.*

14. On the final summary and confirmation page, if everything looks right, click Finish and the export will be executed or stored as selected.

Importing Data into SQL Server

To import data into SQL Server, complete the following steps:

1. Open the Data Transformation Services Import/Export Wizard by clicking Start, All Programs, Microsoft SQL Server, and then Import And Export Data. Click Next.

2. On the Choose A Data Source page, select a data source from the Data Source drop-down list. The available options will be different depending on the data source chosen. Figure 19-14 shows the options for an Oracle ODBC source. Click Next.

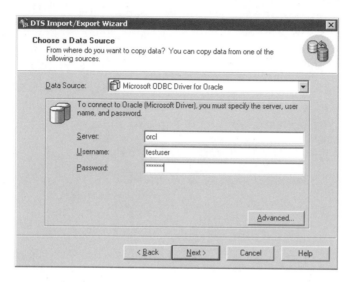

Figure 19-14.   *The Choose A Data Source page with an Oracle ODBC source.*

3. On the Choose A Destination page, select Microsoft OLE DB Provider For SQL Server to import into SQL Server 2000. Set the rest of the options for the SQL Server database connection. You can choose to create a new database, or import into an existing one. Click Next.

4. On the Specify Table Copy Or Query page, you can choose whether to copy whole tables and views or to use a SQL query to filter the data. Click Next.

5. If you selected Copy Tables And Views From The Source Database, you'll see a list of the available tables and views in the source database. Click Preview to see the data in the source table that will be imported. If you selected a query, you get a page that lets you enter a SQL query, or you can use the Query Builder to build the query interactively. Click Next.

6. On the Save, Schedule, And Replicate Package page, shown previously in Figure 19-12, select the Run Immediately check box to run the export immediately.

7. Select the Schedule DTS Package For Later Execution check box if you want to run this export later or on a regular schedule. Use the ellipsis button (..) to adjust the schedule—the default is once a day.

8. Select the Save DTS Package check box and choose a format to save your DTS selections for later reuse. You'll see an additional Save DTS Package page. Click Next.

9. On the Save DTS Package page are the settings for storing packages in SQL Server (shown earlier in Figure 19-13). If you choose to save your package in a different location, the page will have options appropriate to your choice. If you didn't select either a schedule or a save option, you'll skip past this page entirely. Click Next.

10. On the final summary and confirmation page, verify that the information is correct and then click Finish. The export will be executed or stored as selected.

> **Real World**   **The DTS Tool**
>
> The Data Transformation Services (DTS) tool that is included with SQL Server 2000 is really useful even if you have no need to import or export to SQL Server. Because it understands a wide variety of database formats, you can easily use the tool to create and store transformations between different data formats. This gives you a lot of flexibility when dealing with data from a wide variety of sources.

SQL Query Analyzer

The SQL Query Analyzer is a useful tool for both creating quick queries of the database and conducting more in-depth analysis of the best way to structure a particular query to improve execution speed. The SQL Query Analyzer application is shown in Figure 19-15.

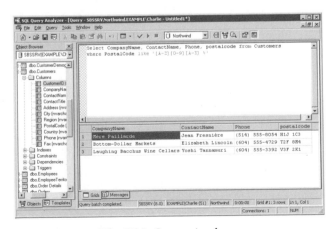

Figure 19-15. *The SQL Query Analyzer.*

The left pane of the SQL Query Analyzer is an Object Browser that lets you browse through the databases that are registered on your server. You can use the browser to find the tables, indexes, procedures, or any other objects in the available databases. A useful tool just for that portion.

The right pane of the object browser will change appearance and content depending on what is being done. Figure 19-15 shows a simple query against the Northwind sample database that ships with SQL Server. Here we've queried the Customers table to find all the Canadian customers, taking advantage of the fact that we know the format of the PostalCode field for a Canadian address. Probably not the most effective way to get there, since the database includes a Country field, but an example of the flexibility of the SQL language.

The upper half of the right pane shows the actual query that was executed, whereas the lower half shows a grid view of the results. You can send the results of your query to a file by selecting Results To File from the Query menu, or analyze the efficiency of the query by selecting Show Execution Plan from the Query menu.

The SQL Query Analyzer has a wealth of additional features that make it an invaluable tool for the database administrator (DBA) or developer who needs to tune an application or database for maximum performance.

Summary

In this chapter, we've taken a brief look at the Microsoft SQL Server 2000 component of the Premium Technologies disc, especially the administrative components used to maintain the database and get data in and out of it.

In the next chapter, we'll examine the tools and techniques for monitoring and troubleshooting your Microsoft Windows Small Business Server 2003 network.

Part VI
Tuning and Troubleshooting

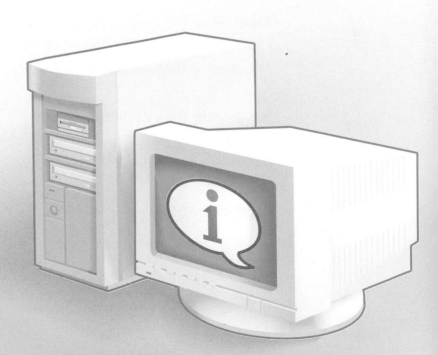

Chapter 20
Monitoring and Fine-Tuning Performance

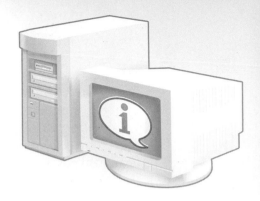

For a network to operate at its best, you must be able to recognize bottlenecks and take action to eliminate them. This chapter covers the system and network monitoring tools in Microsoft Windows Small Business Server that enable you to detect problems and tune your system to its optimum performance level.

More Info Configuring and using the predefined performance and usage reports is covered in Chapter 10, "Shares, Permissions, and Group Policy."

Selecting a Monitoring Method

If you need to observe a system event as it's happening, use a graph in System Monitor. Graphs are helpful for real-time, short-term monitoring of a remote or local computer. Choose an update interval that best captures the data for the type of activity you are observing. Performance logs are better suited for long-term monitoring and record keeping. You can export logged data and use it to generate reports, and you can also view the information as graphs or histograms using System Monitor. Logging in this manner is also more practical when you need to monitor several computers at once.

Health Monitor can track just about everything that System Monitor and performance logs can, plus it includes a preconfigured set of alerts that are only for Windows Small Business Server.

Planning This is a good place to repeat the adage that just because something *can* be done, it doesn't mean it *should* be done. Many counters, logs, and alerts are quite esoteric and of no practical use in a Windows Small Business Server environment. Keep the number of counters and logs you have to manage to a bare minimum. Reduce the number of conditions that generate alerts so that you are using only those conditions that are genuinely critical.

Using System Monitor

System Monitor tracks various processes on a Windows Small Business Server system in real time, returning the results in a graphical display. Use the data from System Monitor to target processes and components that need to be optimized, check the results of your tuning and configuration, and understand trends in workloads and their effect on resource usage.

System Monitor Items

System Monitor uses three types of items to monitor the system:

- **Counter** A component within an object that represents data for a specific aspect of the system or service.

- **Instance** A single occurrence of multiple-performance objects of the same type on a machine. If a particular object has multiple instances, you can track the statistics for each instance by adding a counter for each. You can also add a counter to track all instances at once. An instantaneous counter, such as Process\ Thread Count, is an example of an instance. It displays the most recent count of the number of threads for a particular process. An instance can also be an average of the last two values for a process over a period of time between samples.

- **Object** A collection of counters associated with a resource or service that generates data you can evaluate. Each time an object performs a function, its corresponding counters are updated. A range of objects typically corresponding to major hardware components is built into the operating system. Some programs that you install add other components and their corresponding objects. Table 20-1 lists some of the more common objects and what each type monitors.

Table 20-1.   Objects tracked in System Monitor

Object	What It Monitors
Browser	The Browser service for a domain or workgroup.
Cache	Disk cache usage.
Memory	Memory performance for physical and virtual memory.
Objects	The number of events, mutexes, processes, sections, semaphores, and threads on the computer at the time of data collection.
Paging File	Pagefile usage.
PhysicalDisk	Hard disks with one or more partitions.
Process	All processes running on a machine.
Processor	Each processor on the system.
Server	Bytes, sessions, certain system errors, pool nonpaged usage, and pool paged usage.

Table 20-1.   Objects tracked in System Monitor

Object	What It Monitors
System	Counters that affect all the hardware and software running on the system.
Thread	All threads running in the system.

Running System Monitor

To launch System Monitor, select Performance from the Administrative Tools menu. By default, System Monitor displays the system's current processor utilization as a line graph. Most functions are performed using the System Monitor toolbar (Figure 20-1).

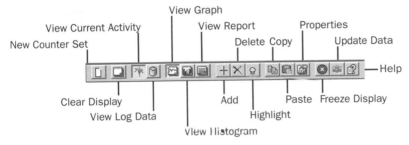

Figure 20-1.   *System Monitor toolbar.*

Adding Counters

You can add counters by clicking the Add button to display the Add Counters dialog box (Figure 20-2). System Monitor compresses the data as necessary so that it fits into the details pane, and you can display dozens of counters at a time, more than you can comfortably view on a single screen.

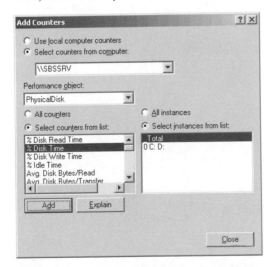

Figure 20-2.   *The Add Counters dialog box.*

Selecting Counters

In the Add Counters dialog box, select either the Use Local Computer Counters option or the Select Counters From Computer option. If you're monitoring the computer on which System Monitor is running, you'll want to select Use Local Computer Counters. If you want to monitor a different computer, select the Select Counters From Computer option, and then choose the name of the computer to be monitored from the list box.

In the Performance Object list, specify an object to monitor. The Processor object is selected by default. For each object, you can choose to monitor all the available counters or only those you specify. To monitor all the available counters for a particular object, select the All Counters option. To monitor only the counters you specify, select the Select Counters From List option. For a description of any counter, select the name of the counter and then click Explain.

> **Tip** When you monitor multiple instances of the same counter, the instance index number assigned to a particular instance might change over time. This happens because the instance starts and stops and in the process is assigned a different instance index number.

Matching Counters to Graph Lines

A color and bar thickness is assigned to each counter within the legend. If you aren't monitoring many counters, you can easily match the color to the counter. However, there are certainly occasions when several counters bunch together on the graph, making it difficult to visually separate them. When that happens, click a counter in the list below the graph and then click Highlight. As you can see in Figure 20-3, the selected line is heavily traced to make it more visible.

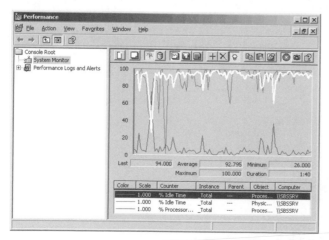

Figure 20-3. *Using the Highlight option to make a graph line more visible.*

Deleting Counters

To stop monitoring one or more counters, you can delete only specific counters or delete all counters. Open System Monitor, select the name of a counter in the legend in the System Monitor details pane, and click the Delete button on the toolbar. To delete all the counters currently being monitored so that you can monitor a new set of counters, click New Counter Set on the toolbar.

Determining How Often to Monitor

How often you monitor a particular data set is important because if the interval is too short, the resulting log is large and unwieldy. If the interval is too long, the event might not be captured. For routine data logs, start out by setting the value in the Sample Data Every box in the Properties dialog box for the log to 15 minutes. To find this option, display the Properties dialog box of the specific counter log. You can adjust this interval to fit the type of data you are monitoring. If you have a slow memory leak, for example, use a longer time interval. Another consideration is the overall length of time you monitor a system. If you are monitoring for fewer than 4 hours, a 15-minute interval is acceptable. If you are monitoring a system for 8 hours or more, don't set a time interval that is shorter than 5 minutes (300 seconds). Monitoring at a frequent rate causes the system to generate a lot of data, producing large log files. It also greatly increases the overhead.

Modifying the Display

Change the way System Monitor displays information by using the System Monitor Properties dialog box (Figure 20-4). Click Properties on the toolbar or right-click in the details pane and choose Properties from the shortcut menu.

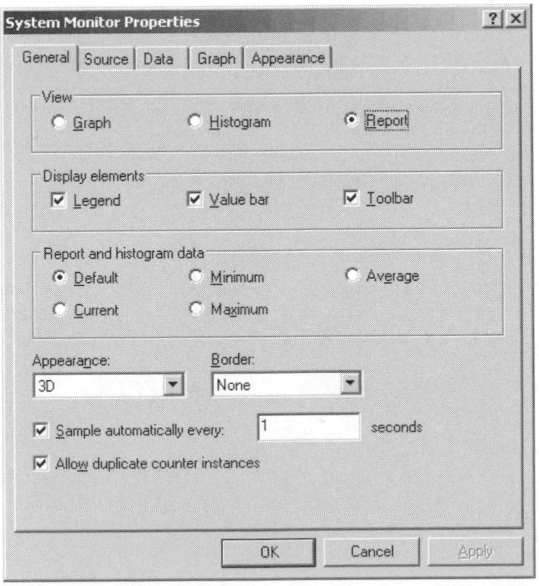

Figure 20-4.   *The System Monitor Properties dialog box.*

Choosing a View

On the General tab, choose to view the data in the form of a graph, a histogram, or a report:

- **Graph view** Presents information in a traditional line graph format. Each counter and instance is displayed in a different color and line thickness. Although the graph view is the most versatile, it's better to use the histogram or report view because the graph view increases monitoring overhead, particularly when a large number of counters are being monitored.

- **Histogram view** Presents information in a bar graph format (Figure 20-5). As in graph view, each of the counters and instances is presented in a different color. You can track up to 100 counters using this view because System Monitor adjusts the bars to fit the display.

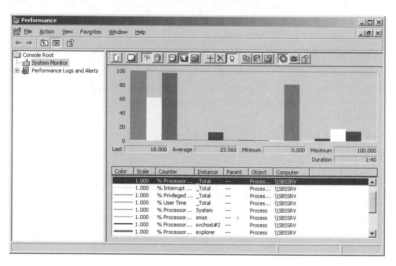

Figure 20-5. *Displaying system information in histogram view.*

- **Report view** Objects are listed in alphabetical order, as are each of the chosen counters for each object. The data itself is displayed numerically. Each object displays the total percentage of processor time in use for the chosen counters. (See Figure 20-6.) This view is best when you need to track a large number of counters.

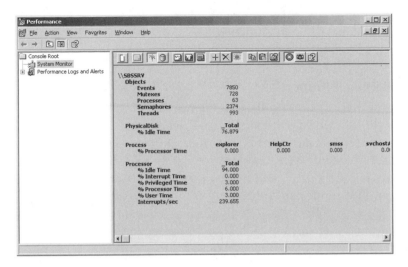

Figure 20-6. *Viewing system information in report view.*

Choosing Display Elements

On the General tab, you can also choose the following display options in the Display Elements area:

- **Legend** At the bottom of the details pane, shows the data scale used for each counter, the counter name, the instance, the parent object (if applicable), the object the counter belongs to, the computer being monitored, and the color used to draw the line for the counter. The legend is available for the graph and histogram views. You must display the legend to see the counter name associated with the data line.

- **Value Bar** Provides a quick way to see the values for a specific counter. Click a counter in the legend or double-click a data line to display the last, average, minimum, and maximum values recorded. The values are calculated from the number of samples and time period displayed in the graph. The duration value is based on the update interval time and is calculated to show the total elapsed time displayed in the graph. This display element is available for the graph and histogram views and is helpful for monitoring a specific value that you want to keep a close watch on.

- **Toolbar** Displays the toolbar across the top of the details pane.

Choosing the Time Interval for Monitoring

You can sample data for all three views at regular intervals. To set the time interval option, click the Properties button on the toolbar, and on the General tab, select the Sample Automatically Every *n* Seconds check box. The default interval is 1 second, but consider specifying a longer interval to reduce the size of log files. Select the update interval that is best for capturing the type of activity you want to view.

Selecting Additional Properties

Add vertical and horizontal grid lines to the graph and histogram views on the Graph tab of the System Monitor Properties dialog box. You can also change the maximum and minimum vertical scale values on the Graph tab; the defaults are 100 for the maximum value and 0 for the minimum value. The highest value you can specify is 999999999, and the lowest value is 0. Both values must be a positive integer. Determine the vertical scale range from the ranges of values for the counters you are monitoring. Change the display colors on the Data tab and the background and font display on the Appearance tab (Figure 20-7).

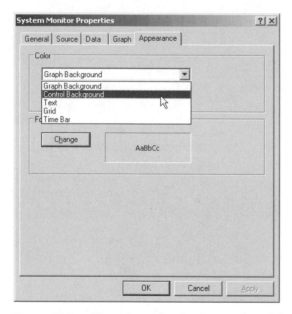

Figure 20-7. *Changing color, background, and font used for System Monitor.*

On the Source tab, select the log file or database to view as part of configuring your monitoring plan.

Monitoring Another Computer

By default, System Monitor displays information about the local system, but you can also configure it to monitor another computer on the network. To do so, click Add Counters, select the Select Counters From Computer option, and, in the text box, type the name of the computer to be monitored. You can choose and delete counters and modify the display as described in the previous sections.

You need administrative permissions on the other computer to monitor that computer through System Monitor. If you don't have administrative permissions, an error message is generated. The counter appears in the display, but no data or graph lines are associated with it. If a particular counter that you want to monitor does not appear in the counter list, it is likely that the service or feature providing the counter has not been installed or enabled on that computer.

Performance Logs and Alerts

Performance Logs and Alerts expands the monitoring capabilities of System Monitor to include features for logging counter and trace data and for generating performance alerts. Logged counter data information can be exported to spreadsheets or databases for analysis and report generation. The data can be stored as a text file (comma- or tab-delimited), a binary file, a binary circular file where the log file is a set size and new data overwrites old data, or a SQL database.

Performance logging runs as a service. As a result, a user doesn't have to be logged on to the monitored computer for data collection to occur. You can manage multiple logging sessions from a single console window and view data as it is collected as well as after collection has stopped. Automatic log generation enables the defining of parameters such as filename, file size, and start and stop times. An alert can be set on a counter to cause a specific action to occur, such as starting a specified program, sending a notification message, or starting a log when the value of a selected counter falls below or exceeds a specified setting.

Counter Logs

A counter log collects data at a predefined interval. Counter logs are helpful for recording data about system services activities and hardware usage from the local machine or a remote machine. You can log data manually on demand or schedule logging to start and stop automatically. The system can also perform continuous logging, depending on the file size and duration limits you set. The logged data can be viewed through the System Monitor display or exported to spreadsheets or databases.

You can view the counters configured in the counter log dynamically through System Monitor by saving log settings such as counters as an HTML page. The resulting page hosts the System Monitor control through an ActiveX control that provides the interface for the monitoring user.

Trace Logs

Rather than measure samples at a predefined interval, as counter logs do, a trace log monitors data continuously and waits for specific events such as page faults to occur. That data is then recorded into a binary trace log file. Developers can use the tools in the Microsoft Platform SDK to translate binary trace logs into human-readable form.

Creating Counter and Trace Logs

To create a counter log or a trace log, complete the following steps:

1. Launch Performance from the Administrative Tools menu, and in the console tree, expand Performance Logs And Alerts.

2. In the console tree, select Counter Logs to create a counter log, or select Trace Logs to create a trace log. Existing logs are listed in the details pane. A red icon indicates a log that is not running or has been stopped; a green icon indicates a log that is running.

3. Right-click in a blank area of the details pane and choose New Log Settings (Figure 20-8).

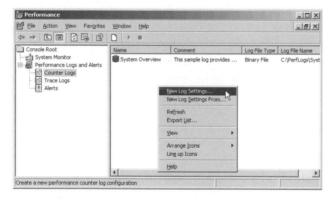

Figure 20-8. *Creating new log settings.*

4. In the Name text box, type the name of the counter or trace log you are creating and click OK. A Properties dialog box for configuring the counter or trace log you are creating is displayed.

5. Configure the counter or trace log to monitor your local or remote machine by choosing the proper counters for the resources to be monitored, selecting log file properties, and choosing the desired scheduling options. The sample data interval for counter logs is set on the General tab of the Properties dialog box for the log.

> **More Info**   For guidelines about setting time intervals, see the "Determining How Often to Monitor" section earlier in this chapter.

Adding Counters to Counter Logs

Counters are added on the General tab of a log's Properties dialog box (Figure 20-9). When you create a counter log file, the Properties dialog box is displayed automatically. If you need to add counters later, you can display the Properties dialog box by right-clicking the name of the log file, choosing Properties from the shortcut menu, clicking Add on the General tab, and then choosing the desired counters. The procedure for selecting counters is identical to that described earlier this chapter in the section titled "Selecting Counters."

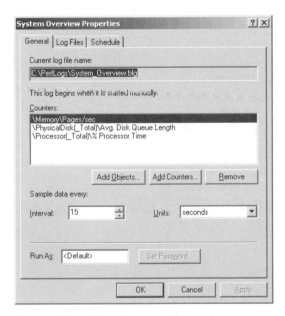

Figure 20-9.   *The General tab of a log's Properties dialog box.*

Saving Log and Alert File Settings

To save the settings for a log or an alert file, right-click the name of the log or alert file in the details pane, and then choose Save Settings As from the shortcut menu. Type the name you want to give to the log or alert file, and save it as an .HTM file. You can use the saved settings for a new log or alert by right-clicking in the details pane, choosing New Log Settings From, and then selecting the .HTM file containing the settings you want to reuse.

Selecting System and Nonsystem Providers for Trace Logs

Events in trace logs are monitored not by counters but by providers. You can choose to log events by system or nonsystem providers. The default system provider, the Windows Kernel Trace Provider, monitors threads, processes, disk input/output, network TCP/IP, page faults, and file details. The default system provider uses the most overhead to monitor events. Only one trace log at a time can be run using the system provider. If you attempt to run more than one, you receive an error message.

To choose providers, right-click the name of the trace log file and choose Properties from the shortcut menu. On the General tab (Figure 20-10), select the Events Logged By System Provider option and then choose the events you want to monitor, or select the Nonsystem Providers option and then add the nonsystem providers of your choice (for example, Active Directory) by clicking Add.

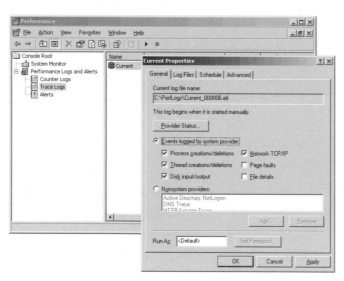

Figure 20-10. *Specifying events logged by the system provider.*

Remember that trace logging of page fault and file details generates a huge amount of data. Microsoft recommends that you limit trace logging using these fault options to a maximum of two hours; otherwise, you might run out of disk space on your machine.

Choosing nonsystem providers to monitor the system incurs less overhead. With nonsystem providers, you can select the data providers of your choice. You cannot run concurrent multiple trace logs using the same nonsystem provider, but you can do so using different nonsystem providers. Some nonsystem providers available in Microsoft Windows Server 2003 are ACPI Driver Trace

Provider; Active Directory: Kerberos; Active Directory: NetLogon; Active Directory: SAM; DNS Trace; Local System Authority (LSA); NTLM Security Protocol; and Exchange Information Store.

Setting File Parameters for Counter and Trace Logs

To set file parameters for counter and trace logs, complete the following steps:

1. Open Performance and expand Performance Logs And Alerts.

2. In the console tree, select Counter Logs to set file parameters for counter logs, or select Trace Logs to set file parameters for trace logs.

3. Double-click the name of the log for which you want to set the file parameters. A dialog box displaying the properties of the log appears.

4. Click the Log Files tab, and set the desired parameters for the log file. (The available parameters are described in the next section.)

Understanding the Log File Parameters

The Log Files tab of the Properties dialog box for a counter or trace log (Figure 20-11) allows the setting of a number of file parameters, such as the file type and whether to end the filename with a set of sequential numbers or a date to keep track of multiple log files. To specify a folder other than the default chosen by Windows (the PerfLogs folder at the root directory), click Configure.

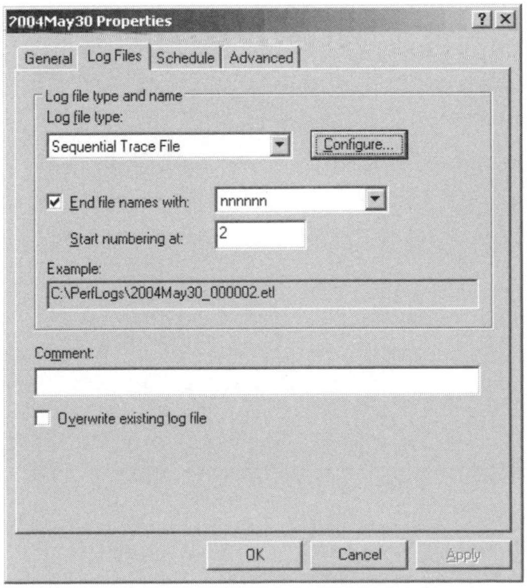

Figure 20-11.   *The Log Files tab of a trace log's Properties dialog box.*

The Configure Log Files dialog box also has a log file size option to allow the log file to become as large as disk quotas or the operating system permits or to limit the size to a specific size. Limit the size of a log file if you want to use one of the circular logging options. In conjunction with limiting the size of a log file, you can use the When The Log File Is Full option on the Schedule tab to run a command if you want a particular action to occur when the log file reaches its limit. You can choose from among five file types for a counter log:

- **Text File - Comma Delimited**   Used to export data to a spreadsheet program. The data is stored as a comma-delimited log file with the file extension .CSV.

- **Text File - Tab Delimited**   Can also be used to export data to a spreadsheet program. The data is stored as a tab-delimited log file with the file extension .TSV.

- **Binary File**   Used for intermittent instances (instances that stop and start after the log has been started). The data is stored as a sequential, binary-format log file with the file extension .BLG.

- **Binary Circular File**   Records data continuously to the same log file where the new records overwrite the previous ones. The data is stored in binary format as a circular file with the file extension .BLG.

- **SQL Database**   Records data into an existing SQL database.

Trace logs can be either of two file types:

- **Circular Trace File**   Records data continuously to the same log file where the new records overwrite the previous ones. The data is stored in a circular file with the file extension .ETL.

- **Sequential Trace File**   Collects data until a user-defined limit is reached. When the limit is reached, the current file is closed and a new one is started. The data is stored as a sequential file using the file extension .ETL.

The default file type for counter logs is Binary File (with the extension .BLG), and the default file type for trace logs is Sequential Trace File (with the extension .ETL).

Using Alerts

An alert notification is sent to the user by means of the Messenger service when a predefined counter value reaches, falls below, or rises above a defined threshold. The Messenger service must be running for alert notifications to be sent to the user.

Creating an Alert

To create an alert, complete the following steps:

1. Open Performance, and expand Performance Logs And Alerts.

2. In the console tree, select Alerts. Existing alerts are listed in the details pane. A red icon indicates an alert that is not running or has been stopped; a green icon indicates an alert that is running.

3. Right-click Alerts and select New Alert Settings from the shortcut menu.

4. In the Name text box, type the name of the alert you are creating and click OK. A Properties dialog box for configuring the alert (in this case named High Level Activity) opens.

5. Click Add on the General tab to open the Add Counters dialog box (Figure 20-12).

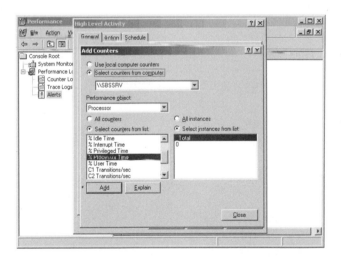

Figure 20-12.   *The Add Counters dialog box for new alert settings.*

6. Configure the alert by specifying whether to monitor the local machine or a remote machine, choosing one or more counters, and setting threshold values for the counters. Click Add to add the alerts, and then click Close to close the Add Counters dialog box.

7. On the Action tab, select an action to perform when an alert is triggered.

8. On the Schedule tab, choose when and how the Alert log starts. (These settings are described in the next section.)

Configuring an Alert

You must choose threshold values for each counter on which you set an alert. This is done on the General tab of the Properties dialog box for the alert. When you create an alert, the Properties dialog box is displayed automatically. If you need to add counters at a later date, you can access the Properties dialog box by right-clicking the name of the alert file, choosing Properties from the shortcut menu, and clicking Add on the General tab.

> **More Info** For information about specifying a computer to monitor and on selecting counters for the alert, see the section titled "Selecting Counters" earlier in this chapter.

Thresholds trigger an alert when the value of the counter falls either above or below a baseline you've chosen. To establish a baseline, determine the acceptable level of system performance when your system is experiencing a typical workload and running all required services. You do this by reviewing logged data graphed by System Monitor or by exporting the data and generating reports for analysis.

On the Action tab of the Properties dialog box (Figure 20-13), you can specify actions that should occur when a threshold is exceeded.

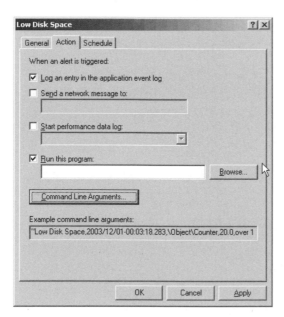

Figure 20-13. *Specifying actions to take when a threshold is crossed.*

Four options are available:

- **Log An Entry In The Application Event Log** Causes the alert to log an entry that is visible to you in Event Viewer.

- **Send A Network Message To**   Triggers the Messenger service to send an alert message to a specified computer.

- **Start Performance Data Log**   Runs an existing counter log.

- **Run This Program**   Specifies a program to run when an alert is triggered. Click the Command Line Arguments button to add command-line arguments that provide additional information. For example, in Figure 20-14, selecting Alert Name, Counter Name, and Limit Value adds the details shown in the Example box.

Figure 20-14.   *Adding arguments to the alert to produce additional information.*

Permissions for Counter Logs, Trace Logs, and Alerts

To create or modify a log or alert, you must have Full Control permission for the registry entry HKEY_LOCAL_MACHINE\SYSTEM\CurrentControlSet\Services \SysmonLog\LogQueries. Administrators are assigned this permission by default, and they can grant this permission to users in Regedit.exe.

To run the Performance Logs and Alerts service, you must have permission to configure or start services on the system. Administrators are assigned this permission by default and can grant this permission to others using Group Policy. (The built-in groups Performance Log Users and Performance Monitor Users are useful for this.) To log data for a remote computer, the Performance Logs and Alerts service must run under an account that has access to that remote system. The service runs in the background after a log or alert is configured and running.

Real World   **Tuning and Testing Strategies**

Before starting System Monitor or Performance Logs and Alerts on the computer you are monitoring, turn off screen savers and stop services that are not essential to monitoring the system. Other best practices include the following:

- Set up Performance Logs and Alerts to monitor and report data on counters at regular intervals, such as every 10 to 15 minutes.

- Make only one change at a time. Bottlenecks can be caused by one component, or they can be the result of a series of faults. Making multiple changes at once can make it impossible to assess the impact each change has on the system.

- Keep a record of changes you make, and repeat the monitoring process after every change. Changes can affect other resources, and keeping records helps to determine the effect of each change and whether additional changes are necessary.

- Compare programs that run over the network against those that run locally. This tells you whether network components might be playing a part in performance problems.

- Pay regular attention to event logs. Some performance problems generate output into Event Viewer.

- When logging data through Performance Logs and Alerts, exclude times that include start-up events. Start-up events tend to skew overall performance results because they show temporarily high values.

Monitoring Memory Usage

Memory usage is usually the first item to look at when experiencing performance problems. If you find that your system is paging frequently, you probably need more memory. Some paging is expected to expand memory, but too much paging is a drain on system performance.

Note   Paging is used to free memory for other uses by moving fixed-size blocks of data and code from RAM to your disk in units called *pages*.

Before monitoring memory usage, perform a few checks. For example, verify that your system has the recommended amount of memory for running the operating system as well as other applications and services. If you don't know what the memory requirements are for a process, you can discover its working set within System Monitor. Shut the process down and observe the effect on paging activity. The amount of memory that is freed when you terminate a process is the amount of memory the process was using.

Note A *working set* is the portion of physical memory allocated to each program running on the computer.

Recommended Counters

To check for possible memory leaks or bottlenecks, monitor these counters:

- **Memory\ Pages/Sec** Displays the number of pages written to or read from disk to resolve hard page faults. A *hard page fault* occurs when a process requires code or data that must be retrieved from disk rather than from its working set or elsewhere in physical memory. If this value is above 20 per pagefile, you need to research paging activity and make adjustments as necessary. A high value for this counter might be more indicative of a paging problem than a memory problem.

- **Memory\ Committed Bytes** Displays the number of committed bytes of virtual memory on your system and is an instantaneous counter. Monitor this counter, along with Memory\ Available Bytes, over a period of time if you suspect a memory leak.

- **Memory\ Pool Nonpaged Bytes** Displays the number of bytes allocated to the nonpaged pool for objects that cannot be written to disk but must instead remain in physical memory as long as they are allocated. If this value is high, you need additional memory on your system. Use this counter in conjunction with Memory\ Pool Nonpaged Allocs if you suspect that a kernel-mode process is the cause of a memory leak.

- **Memory\ Pool Nonpaged Allocs** Shows the number of calls to allocated space in the nonpaged pool. Use this counter in conjunction with Memory\ Pool Nonpaged Bytes to determine whether you have a memory leak.

- **Server\ Bytes Total/Sec** Monitors the number of bytes the machine has received from and sent to the network. The value is indicative of how busy the server is. You need to add memory if you have a sustained, dramatic increase in this value.

- **Server\ Pool Paged Bytes** Monitors the number of bytes of pageable computer memory currently in use by the system. Use this information to determine values for the MaxPagedMemoryUsage entry in the Windows registry.

- **Server\ Pool Nonpaged Bytes**   Monitors the number of bytes of non-pageable computer memory in use by the system. Use this information to determine the values for the MaxNonpagedMemoryUsage entry in the Windows registry.

To monitor for a low memory condition, use these counters:

- **Memory\ Available Bytes**   When free bytes fall into short supply (4 MB or fewer), the shortage is replenished by taking memory from the working sets of less active programs. As a result, you see an increase in the working set value for one program and a steady decrease in the values of other programs, causing an increase in paging that causes performance to suffer. You'll need to add memory to solve the problem.

- **Memory\ Cache Bytes**   Monitors the number of bytes being used by the file system cache. Use this counter in conjunction with Memory\ Available Bytes.

- **PhysicalDisk\ % Disk Time and PhysicalDisk\ Avg. Disk Queue Length**   Indicates a memory shortage when used in conjunction with Memory\ Page Read/Sec. If an increase in queue length is not accompanied by a decrease in the Memory\ Page Read/Sec value, a shortage does exist.

To check for excessive paging, monitor these counters:

- **Paging File\ % Usage (all instances)**   Paging files are shared by every process and are used to store pages of memory on your system. If you suspect that paging is to blame for your bottleneck, it is helpful to review this value, along with Memory\ Available Bytes and Memory\ Pages/Sec. The acceptable threshold for this value is 99 percent. Enlarge Pagefile.sys if the value increases to 100 percent.

- **Paging File\ % Usage Peak**   If the value for this counter approaches the maximum paging file setting, the size of Pagefile.sys needs to be increased.

- **PhysicalDisk\ Avg. Disk Sec/Transfer and Memory\ Pages/Sec**   The PhysicalDisk\ Avg. Disk Sec/Transfer counter displays the average disk transfer in seconds. The Memory\ Pages/Sec counter displays the number of pages written to or read from the disk when a process requires information that is no longer in its working set and must be retrieved from disk. To determine whether the system is paging excessively, multiply the values of these two counters. If the result exceeds 0.1, paging is taking up more than 10 percent of disk access time. If this condition persists over a period of time, you need additional memory.

Under the Hood   Tips for Memory Troubleshooting

If you are experiencing problems with memory, try checking these areas:

- **Paging file**   Verify that the paging file is the correct size. You can also split the paging file between multiple physically separate disks (not multiple volumes on the same physical disk) of similar speeds to increase access time.

  When the paging file reaches the maximum limit assigned to it, a warning is displayed and the limit is increased. Programs might become unstable while the limit is increased, and the system might crash if there isn't enough disk space for additional virtual memory.

- **Physical memory**   Increase the physical memory above the required minimum.

- **Memory settings**   Confirm that memory settings are configured properly.

- **Memory-intensive programs**   If possible, run memory-intensive programs when your system workload is lightest or on another server.

Monitoring Processor Activity

High processor values can mean either that your machine is handling the workload in a very efficient manner or that it is struggling to keep up. When a bottleneck occurs because a process's threads need more processor cycles than are available, long processor queues build up, causing the system response to suffer. The two common causes of processor bottleneck are excess demand placed on the processor by CPU-bound programs and excess interrupts generated by drivers or subsystem components, such as disk or network components.

Minimum Recommended Counters

The minimum recommended counters for monitoring the server's processor component for possible bottlenecks are the following.

- **System\ Processor Queue Length (all instances)**   A sustained queue length of more than 10 items per processor indicates a bottleneck.

- **Server Work Queues\ Queue Length**   A queue length of greater than four over a sustained period of time indicates possible processor congestion.

- **Processor\ Interrupts/Sec** Use this counter to determine whether interrupt activity is causing a bottleneck. A dramatic increase in this counter value without a corresponding increase in system activity indicates a hardware problem. To resolve this problem, you need to find the network adapter or other device that is the source of the interrupts. Refer to the manufacturer's specifications for the acceptable processor threshold; use 1000 interrupts per second as a starting point.

- **Processor\ % Interrupt Time** Displays the percentage of time the processor spends receiving and servicing hardware interrupts during the sample interval. This value provides an indirect indication of the activities of devices that generate interrupts, such as disk drives, network adapters, and other peripheral devices. These devices interrupt the processor when they require attention or complete a task. Look for a dramatic increase in the value without a corresponding increase in system activity.

To monitor possible usage problems, use these counters:

- **Processor\ % Processor Time (all instances)** Use this counter to discover a process that is using more than 85 percent of processor time. You might need to install an additional processor or upgrade to a faster one.

- **Processor\ % User Time** Monitors the percentage of nonidle processor time that is spent in user mode. A high rate could indicate a need to upgrade or install additional processors. Use this counter in conjunction with Processor\ % Processor Time (all instances).

- **Processor\ % Privileged Time** Monitors the percentage of nonidle processor time designated for hardware-manipulating drivers and operating system components. A high rate might be attributed to a large number of interrupts being generated by a device that is failing. Use this counter in conjunction with Processor\ % Processor Time (all instances).

Under the Hood Tips for Processor Monitoring

Try the following to resolve problems with the processor:

- **Upgrade the processor** Upgrade to a faster processor, replace a failing one, or add another processor to the machine, especially if you are running multithreaded programs.

- **Adjust the workload of the system** Distribute programs more efficiently among servers, or schedule programs to run at off-peak hours.

- **Manage processor affinity on multiprocessor computers**   Managing the processor affinity with respect to interrupts and process threads can improve performance because it reduces the number of processor cache flushes during thread movement from one processor to another.

You set affinity for a particular process or program when you assign it to a single processor to improve its performance, at the expense of the other processors. Be warned that when you dedicate a process or program to a processor, your other program threads might not be permitted to migrate to the least busy processor. You can set affinity in Task Manager, and it is available only on multiprocessor systems.

Monitoring Disk Activity

Monitoring disk usage helps to balance the load of servers. When monitoring disk performance, log the performance data to another disk or computer to prevent it from skewing the data for the disk you are testing.

> **Note**   Disk counters are permanently enabled in Windows Small Business Server and Microsoft Windows XP. To enable disk counters for Microsoft Windows 2000 or Windows NT, use the Diskperf command. (Type **diskperf -?** at a command prompt for additional information.)

Minimum Recommended Counters

The following list shows the minimum recommended counters for monitoring the server's disk performance for possible bottlenecks:

- **PhysicalDisk\ Current Disk Queue Length (all instances)**   Monitors the number of system requests that are waiting for disk access. This number should remain steady at no more than 1.5 to 2 times the number of spindles that make up the physical disk. Most disks have one spindle. The exception is Redundant Array of Independent Disks (RAID) devices, which usually have more than one spindle. You need to observe this value over several intervals because it is an instantaneous counter.

- **PhysicalDisk\ % Disk Time**   Indicates how busy your server's disk drives are by displaying the percentage of time that a drive is active. If the value of this counter rises to more than 90 percent or if you are using a RAID device, check the PhysicalDisk\ Current Disk Queue Length (all instances) counter to see how many disk requests are queued for disk access. RAID devices can cause the PhysicalDisk\ % Disk Time value to exceed 100 percent and thus give an incorrect reading.

- **PhysicalDisk\ Avg. Disk Sec/Transfer**   Monitors the amount of time a disk takes to fulfill a request. A high value might indicate that the disk controller is continually trying to access the disk as a result of failures. For most systems, a value of 0.3 seconds or higher indicates a high average disk transfer time.

To monitor possible usage problems, use these counters:

- **PhysicalDisk\ Avg. Disk Bytes/Transfer**   Monitors the average number of bytes that are transferred from or to a disk during read or write operations. A value less than 20 KB indicates that an application is accessing the disk drive inefficiently.

- **PhysicalDisk\ Disk Reads/Sec and Disk Writes/Sec**   If these counters show that actual usage is near the specified transfer rate of the physical disks, consider reducing the server's workload or upgrading to a RAID setup.

Under the Hood   Tuning and Upgrading Tips for Disks

If you are experiencing problems with disk performance, try the following solutions:

- Verify that you have installed the latest driver software for your host adapters.

- Install additional disks, or upgrade your hard disk to a faster disk. Update the bus and the disk controller at the same time.

- On servers, create striped volumes on several physical disks to increase throughput.

- Distribute applications among your servers to help balance the workload.

- Optimize disk space by running Disk Defragmenter.

- To help in balancing the server workload, isolate tasks that use disk I/O heavily to separate disk controllers or physical disks.

See Chapter 7, "Disk Management," for more information about disk management and optimization.

Using Health Monitor

Health Monitor is the easiest tool for checking current conditions on the server. To launch this tool, select Health Monitor from the Administrative Tools menu. In the console tree, expand Health Monitor and All Monitored Computers to the name of your server. Under the server name, expand Small Business Server Alerts and then Core Server Alerts (Figure 20-15).

> **Note**   For the Small Business Server Alerts to appear in Health Monitor, you must first run the Monitoring Configuration Wizard. To start the Monitoring Configuration Wizard, open Server Management, select Monitoring And Reporting in the console tree, and then click Set Up Monitoring Reports And Alerts in the details pane. For more information about monitoring reports and alerts, see Chapter 10.

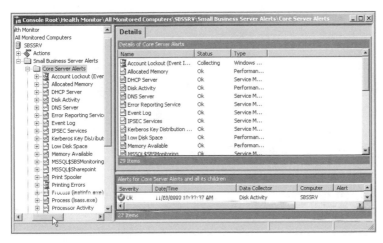

Figure 20-15.   *The Core Server Alerts in Health Monitor.*

Select an alert in the list to display details about it in the right panes. On the Thresholds tab (Figure 20-16), the name and status of the alert rule are displayed. In the Alerts pane (lower pane) are the alerts that have been generated by the rule.

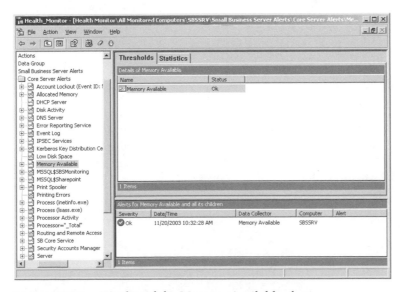

Figure 20-16.   *Display of the Memory Available alert.*

To see the actual settings for the alert, right-click the name in the details pane and select Properties from the shortcut menu. As you can see in Figure 20-17, the status for Memory Available changes to Critical if the average available memory is less than 4 MB for 10 minutes (10 samplings).

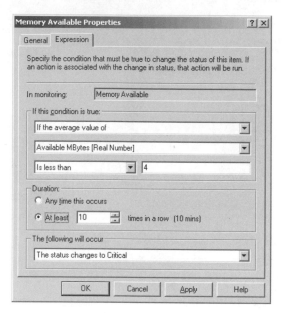

Figure 20-17. *Settings to generate an alert.*

Under Small Business Server Alerts in the console tree, there are also folders for Exchange Server Alerts and Fax Server Alerts. In general, the preconfigured settings are optimal for all the Alerts, but you can modify the settings or add another threshold to the existing one.

Modifying an Existing Threshold

To change the conditions that trigger an alert, select the alert in the console tree. Right-click the threshold and select Properties from the shortcut menu, as shown in Figure 20-18. Make changes on the Expressions tab and click OK when you finish.

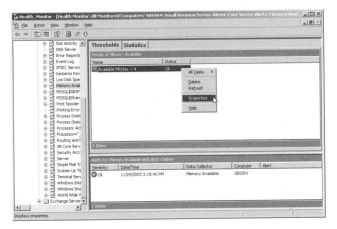

Figure 20-18.   *Opening an alert threshold Properties page.*

Adding a Threshold

To add a threshold that triggers an alert, right-click the alert in the Health Monitor console tree and select New and then Threshold from the shortcut menu. Click the Expression tab and make your settings.

If you select an average value condition, the status of the threshold always shows as Collecting.

Configuring Actions

When an alert is generated because a threshold is crossed, the response is an action. Actions can take the form of an e-mail sent to specified recipients, a specific Windows event recorded to an event log, and several other forms. Once you configure an action, you can select it when setting up the Action tab of a data collector's Properties. (See the section titled "Creating a Data Collector" later in this chapter.)

Command-Line Action

A command-line action runs a program and parameters in response to a threshold being crossed.

To create a command-line action, complete the following steps:

1. In the console tree, right-click Actions, select New, and then select Command Line Action to open the Properties dialog box.

2. On the Details tab, click the Browse button next to the File Name box. In the Browse For File dialog box, locate the program you want to run.

3. To specify a directory the program should run in, browse for a folder by clicking the Browse button next to the Working Directory box.

4. In the Command Line box, type the parameters for the program. Or click the > button and select one of the strings (Figure 20-19).

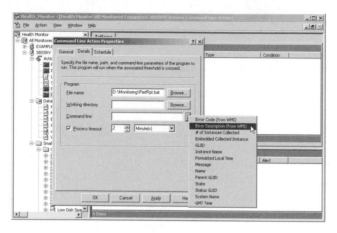

Figure 20-19. *Setting command-line options.*

5. Set a Process Timeout, which refers to the amount of time to allow the program to run before being automatically terminated.

6. Select the Schedule tab to set days and times the action can be taken. (The default is to run all the time.) On the General tab, you can give the action a descriptive name and also type in comments, a description, or other information.

7. Click OK when finished.

E-Mail Action

An e-mail action sends e-mail to specified recipients in response to a threshold being crossed.

To create an e-mail action, complete the following steps:

1. Right-click Actions in the console tree, select New, and then select E-Mail Action to open the Properties dialog box.

2. On the Details tab, specify the SMTP mail server and the recipients.

3. Click the > button next to the Subject field and select the message parameters to be shown in the e-mail's subject line. Or type in your own subject.

4. Click the > button next to the Message field to specify the variables included in the message, or modify the message by typing directly in the Message text field.

5. Select the Schedule tab to set days and times the action can be taken. (The default is to run all the time.) On the General tab, you can give the action a descriptive name and also type in comments, a description, or other information.

6. Click OK when finished.

Text Log Action

A text log action writes to a specified log in response to a threshold being crossed.

To create a text log action, complete the following steps:

1. In the console tree of Health Monitor, right-click Actions, select New, and then select Text Log Action to open the Properties dialog box.

2. Click the Browse button for the File box. In the Browse For File dialog box, find the text log file you want to use.

3. Specify the maximum size for the log file.

4. Click the > button next to the Text box to specify the variables included in the text to be logged, or modify the text by typing directly in the text field.

5. Select the Schedule tab to set days and times the action can be taken. (The default is to run all the time.) On the General tab, you can give the action a descriptive name and also type in comments, a description, or other information.

6. Click OK when finished.

Windows Event Log Action

A Windows event log action launches a specified Windows event in response to a threshold being crossed.

To create a Windows event action, complete the following steps:

1. Right-click Actions in the console tree, select New, and then select Windows Event Log Action to open the Properties dialog box.

2. On the Details tab, select the Event type:

   - **Information**   Report on a successful event such as when a service starts.

   - **Warning**   Event that is not in itself important but suggests future problems.

   - **Error**   A problem that must be heeded. Signifies a failure such as loss of data or a loss of function. For example, if a printer driver fails to load successfully, an Error is reported.

3. Click the > button next to the Text box to select insertion strings or modify the text.

4. Select the Schedule tab to set days and times the action can be taken. (The default is to run all the time.) On the General tab, you can give the action a descriptive name and also type in comments, a description, or other information.

5. Click OK when finished.

Script Action

A script action runs a specified script in response to a threshold being crossed.

To create a script action, complete the following steps:

1. Right-click Actions in the console tree, select New, and then select Script Action to open the Properties dialog box.

2. Select the script type. Type the Path for the script or click the Browse button and navigate to the script file.

3. After you locate the file, you can click the Edit button to edit the script text.

4. Select a process timeout.

5. Select the Schedule tab to set days and times the action can be taken. (The default is to run all the time.) On the General tab, you can give the action a descriptive name and also type in comments, a description, or other information.

6. Click OK when finished.

Using Data Collectors

Data collectors are objects that collect and hold information about counters, events, states, and instances. When you create data collectors, you specify when the data is collected and from which computer it is collected.

Creating a Data Collector

Data collectors are gathered in data groups under the name of the computer from which data is being collected. To create a new data group, right-click the computer name in the Health Monitor console tree, select New, and then Data Group. To add a collector to an existing data group, right-click the group in the Health Monitor console tree. Next, select New, Data Collector, and then select the type of data collector (Figure 20-20).

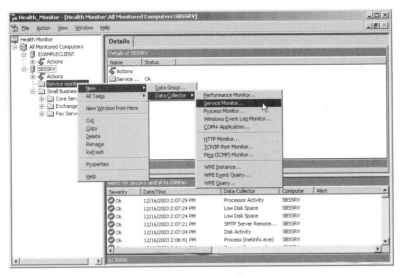

Figure 20-20. *Selecting a type of data collector to create.*

The available data collectors are:

- Performance Monitor
- Service Monitor
- Process Monitor
- Windows Event Log Monitor
- COM+ Application Monitor
- HTTP Monitor
- TCP/IP Port Monitor
- Ping (ICMP) Monitor
- WMI Instance
- WMI Event Query
- WMI Data Query

If you use Health Monitor, you're likely to use only the first four, possibly the next three, and the last three not at all. Not that the various monitors can't be helpful, but most of them are surplus to requirements in the context of Windows Small Business Server.

After you select a data collector, the Properties dialog box for the collector opens. Supply the information required on the Details tab, which varies according to the data collector chosen. The following sections describe the options for the most commonly used data collectors.

In addition to the Details tab, all Properties dialog boxes include a tab to con-figure the message sent with a report and a Schedule tab to select collection days, times, and interval. On the General tab, you can rename the data collector from its default name and also type in comments, a description, or other infor-mation. The Actions tab specifies the actions for the system to take when the status of the data collector changes.

Performance Monitor

On the Details tab of a Performance Monitor data collector, you can specify the object to monitor.

- **Object** Click the Browse button next to the Object field. In the Browse For Objects On *Computer_Name* dialog box (Figure 20-21), select the object to monitor and click OK.

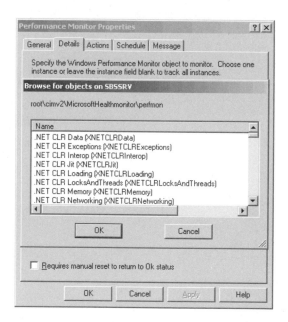

Figure 20-21. *Selecting an object to monitor.*

- **Counter** Select one or more counters to monitor.
- **Instance** Click Browse to select an instance or leave blank to monitor all instances.

By default, one threshold is set:

- Change the state to Critical if the error code is not equal to zero. A nonzero return points toward a data collection error.

To manually configure thresholds, select the data collector in the console tree, right-click the threshold in the details pane, and then select Properties from the shortcut menu. Click the Expression tab and set the conditions that trigger a change in state alert. To add a new threshold, right-click the data collector in the console tree, select New, and then click Threshold.

Real World   **Requires Manual Reset Option**

A data collector that exceeds its configured threshold automatically resets to an OK state when the collected information shows that the values have fallen to *below* the threshold. The logic behind this default behavior is that Health Monitor is intended to display the most current status of the objects being monitored. And most of the time, that's what you use Health Monitor for.

However, there are times when this default behavior is not what you want—for example, when you're having intermittent problems that are proving hard to substantiate, or you want to be sure that when the state of a given object changes, the change is reflected in the console tree.

For those objects, select the option for Requires Manual Reset To Return To OK Status on the Details tab of the data collector's Properties dialog box.

To perform a manual reset, right-click the data collector in the console tree and select All Tasks, and then select Reset & Check Now.

Service Monitor

On the Details tab of a Service Monitor data collector, you can specify the service to monitor.

- **Service**   Click the Browse button next to the Service field. In the Browse For Services On *Computer_Name* dialog box, select the service to be monitored and click OK.

- **Properties**   Select the properties you want to monitor.

By default, services have two thresholds already set:

- Change the state to Critical if error code is not equal to zero. A nonzero return signifies a data collection error.

- Change the state to Critical if the service is not started.

You can right-click either of the thresholds in the details pane and select Properties to make changes. Add a threshold by right-clicking the data collector in the console tree, selecting New, and then clicking Threshold.

Process Monitor

On the Details tab of a Process Monitor data collector, you can specify the process to monitor. Use Process Monitor to monitor applications and processes that are not Windows services. You can monitor only one process at a time.

- **Process** Click the Browse button next to the Process field. Select the Process to be monitored and click OK.

- **Properties** Select the properties to be monitored.

By default, a single threshold is set:

- Change the state to Critical if error code is not equal to zero. A nonzero return points toward a data collection error.

You can right-click the threshold in the details pane and select Properties to make changes. Add a threshold by right-clicking the data collector in the console tree, selecting New, and then clicking Threshold.

Windows Event Log Monitor

On the Details tab of a Windows Event Log Monitor data collector, you can specify the Windows events to monitor.

- **Types** The types of events to monitor.

  - **Information** Report on a successful event such as when a service starts.

  - **Warning** Event that is not in itself important but suggests future problems.

  - **Error** A problem that must be heeded. Signifies a failure such as loss of data or a loss of function. For example, if a printer driver fails to load successfully, an error is reported.

  - **Success Audit** An audited security access event that is successful. For example, a user successfully logs on to the network.

  - **Failure Audit** An audited security access try that is unsuccessful. For example, a user's failed attempt to logon generates a Failure audit event.

- **Log file** Select the log file to use.

  - **Application** Records events reported by applications.

  - **Security** Records changes to the security settings and reports on possible security breaches.

  - **System** Records events reported by Windows system components. For example, a service fails to start.

- **Source, Category, Event ID, User**   To monitor all sources, categories, event IDs, and users, clear these check boxes. To monitor specifics, select the option and type the event source, event category, event ID, or particular user.

By default, two thresholds are set:

- Change the state to Critical if error code is not equal to zero. A non-zero return points toward a data collection error.

- Change the state to Critical if the number of instances collected is greater than zero.

You can right-click either of the thresholds in the details pane and select Properties to make changes. Add a threshold by right-clicking the data collector in the console tree and selecting New and then Threshold.

Other Monitors

Other monitors are available in addition to those just described. For information about how they're used, right-click Data Group in the console tree and select Help from the shortcut menu. Click the Index tab, type **data collection,** and then click the Display button.

Summary

In this chapter, you learned about the many ways to monitor virtually everything that happens on your network. Most of these monitors won't be used in the typical Windows Small Business Server environment, but making an acquaintance with the more accessible methods is time well spent. Chapter 21, "Disaster Planning and Fault Tolerance," covers planning for the inevitable day when disaster—of one form or another—strikes, with a special emphasis on the unique needs of small businesses.

Chapter 21
Disaster Planning and Fault Tolerance

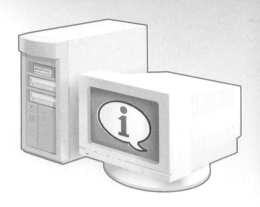

Smart SCUBA divers dive with a "buddy" and carry an alternate air source, even though they've trained extensively and checked their equipment thoroughly. Schools and businesses have fire drills even though the vast majority of buildings never burn down. Similarly, system administrators sincerely hope they'll never need the verified backups and Automated System Recovery disks they have spent so much time creating. Nevertheless, we keep them because there are only two types of networks: those that have experienced disaster and those that haven't—yet.

Disaster can take many forms, from the self-inflicted pain of a user or administrator doing something really, really unwise, to the uncontrollable, unpreventable results of a natural disaster such as a flood or an earthquake. In any case, your business will depend on how well you were prepared for the disaster and how well you and your team responded to it and recovered from it.

This chapter covers emergency preparedness. It discusses creating a disaster recovery plan, with standardized procedures to follow in the event of a catastrophe. It also describes how to prepare for a disaster, including how to make an Automated System Recovery disk, how to make a boot disk, how to install the Recovery Console, how to specify recovery options in Microsoft Windows Server 2003, and how to create an external recovery drive.

Planning for Disaster

Some people seem to operate on the assumption that if they don't think about a disaster, one won't happen. This is similar to the idea that if you don't write a will, you'll never die—and just about as realistic. No business owner or system administrator should feel comfortable about their degree of preparedness without a clear disaster recovery plan that has been thoroughly tested. Even then, you should continually look for ways to improve the plan. You also need to understand the limitations of any disaster recovery plan: none of them are perfect, and even the best disaster recovery plan needs to be constantly examined and adjusted or it quickly gets out of date.

Planning for disaster or emergencies is not a single step, but an iterative, ongoing process. Systems are not mountains, but rivers, constantly moving and changing, and your disaster recovery plan needs to change as your environment changes. To put together a good disaster recovery plan—one you can bet your business on—you need to follow these steps:

1. Identify the risks.
2. Identify the resources.
3. Develop the responses.
4. Test the responses.
5. Iterate.

Identifying the Risks

The first step in creating a disaster recovery plan is to identify the risks to your business and the costs associated with those risks. The risks vary from the simple deletion of a critical file to the total destruction of your place of business and its computers. To properly prepare for a disaster, you need to perform a realistic assessment of the risks, the potential costs and consequences of each disaster scenario, the likelihood of any given disaster scenario, and the resources available to address the risks. Risks that seemed vanishingly remote a few years ago are now part of our everyday life.

Identifying risks is not a job for only one person. As with all the tasks associated with a disaster recovery plan, all concerned parties must participate. There are two important reasons for this: you want to make sure that you have commitment and buy-in from the parties concerned, and you also want to make sure you don't miss anything important.

No matter how carefully and thoroughly you try to identify the risks, you'll miss at least one. You should always account for that missing risk by including an "unknown risk" item in your list. Treat it just like any other risk: identify the resources available to address it and develop countermeasures to take should it occur. The difference with this risk, of course, is that your resources and countermeasures are somewhat more generic, and you can't really test your response to the risk, because you don't yet know what it is.

Start by trying to list all the possible ways that your system could fail. Solicit help from everyone with a stake in the process. The more people involved in the brainstorming, the more ideas you'll get and the more prevention and recovery procedures you can develop and practice. Be careful at this stage in the process to not dismiss *any* idea or concern as trivial, unimportant, or unlikely.

Next, look at all the ways that some external event could affect your system. The team of people responsible for identifying possible external problems is probably similar to a team looking at internal failures, but with some important differences. For example, if your business is housed in a large commercial office building, you'll want to involve that building's security and facilities groups even though they aren't employees of your business. They will not only have important input into the possible threats to the business, but also information on the resources and preventative measures already in place.

Once you've identified as many possible risks as you can, you then need to understand and quantify just how likely a particular risk is. If you're located in a flood plain, for example, you're much more likely to think flood insurance is a good investment.

Identifying the Resources

Once you've identified the risks to your network, you need to identify what the resources are to address those risks. These resources can be internal or external, people or systems, hardware or software.

When you're identifying the resources available to deal with a specific risk, be as complete as you can, but also be specific. Identifying everyone in the Engineering group as a resource to solve a crashed server might look good, but realistically only one or two key people are likely to actually rebuild the server. Make sure you identify those key people for each risk, as well as what more general secondary resources they have to call on. So, for example, the primary resources available to recover a crashed server might consist of your hardware vendor to recover the failed hardware and your own IT person or primary system consultant to restore the software and database. General secondary resources could include Microsoft Premier Support.

An important step in identifying resources in your disaster recovery plan is to specify both the first-line responsibility *and* the back-end or supervisory responsibility. Make sure everyone knows who to go to when the problem is more than they can handle or when they need additional resources. Also, clearly define when they should do that. The best disaster recovery plans include clear, unambiguous escalation policies. This takes the burden off individuals to decide when and whom to notify and makes it simply part of the procedure.

Developing the Responses

An old but relevant adage comes to mind when discussing disaster recovery scenarios: when you're up to your elbows in alligators, it's difficult to remember that your original objective was to drain the swamp. This is another way of saying that people lose track of what's important when they are overloaded by too many problems that require immediate attention. To ensure that your swamp is drained and your network gets back online, you need to take those carefully researched risks and resources and develop a disaster recovery plan. There are two important parts of any good disaster recovery plan:

- Standard operating procedures (SOPs)
- Standard escalation procedures (SEPs)

Making sure these procedures are in place and clearly understood by all *before* a disaster strikes puts you in a far better position to recover gracefully and with a minimum of lost productivity and data.

Standard Operating Procedures

Emergencies bring out both the best and worst in people. If you're prepared for the emergency, you can be one of those who come out smelling like a rose, but if you're not prepared and let yourself get flustered or lose track of what you're trying to accomplish, you can make the whole situation worse than it needs to be.

Although no one is ever as prepared for a system emergency as they'd like to be, careful planning and preparation can give you an edge in recovering expeditiously and with a minimal loss of data. It is much easier to deal with the situation calmly when you know you've prepared for this problem and you have a well-organized, *tested* standard operating procedure (SOP) to follow.

Because the very nature of emergencies is that you can't predict exactly which one is going to strike, you need to plan and prepare for as many possibilities as you can. The time to decide how to recover from a disaster is *before* the disaster happens, not in the middle of it when users are screaming and bosses are standing around looking serious and concerned.

Your risk assessment phase involved identifying as many possible disaster scenarios as you could, and in your resource assessment phase you identified the resources that are available and responsible for each of those risks. Now you need to write up SOPs for recovering the system from each of the scenarios. Even the most level-headed system administrator can get flustered when the system has crashed, users are calling every 10 seconds to see what the problem is, the boss is asking every 5 minutes when you'll have it fixed, and your server won't boot. And that's the easy case compared to the mess that can be caused by an external disaster.

Reduce your stress and prevent mistakes by planning for disasters before they occur. Practice recovering from each of your disaster scenarios. Write down each of the steps, and work through questionable or unclear areas until you can identify exactly what it takes to recover from the problem. This is like a fire drill, and you should do it for the same reasons—not because a fire is inevitable, but because fires do happen, and the statistics demonstrate irrefutably that those who prepare for a fire and practice what to do in a fire are far more likely to survive it.

Your job as a system administrator is to prepare for disasters and practice what to do in those disasters, not because you expect the disaster, but because if you do have one, you want to be the hero, not the goat. After all, it isn't often that the system administrator or IT consultant gets to be a hero, so be ready when your time comes.

The first step in developing any SOP is to outline the overall steps you want to accomplish. Keep it general at this point—you're looking for the big picture here. Again, you want everyone to be involved in the process. What you're really trying to do is make sure you don't forget any critical steps, and that's much easier when you get the overall plan down first. There will be plenty of opportunity later to cover the specific details.

Once you have a broad, high-level outline for a given procedure, the people you identified as the actual resources during the resource assessment phase should start to fill in the blanks of the outline. You don't need every detail at this point, but you should get down to at least a level below the original outline. This will help you identify missing resources that are important to a timely resolution of the problem. Again, don't get too bogged down in the details at this point. You're not actually writing the SOP, just trying to make sure that you've identified all of its pieces.

When you feel confident that the outline is ready, get the larger group back together again. Go over the procedure and smooth out the rough edges, refining the outline and *listening* to make sure you haven't missed anything critical. When everyone agrees that the outline is complete, you're ready to add the final details to it.

The people who are responsible for each procedure should now work through all the details of the disaster recovery plan and document the steps thoroughly. They should keep in mind that the people who actually perform the recovery might not be who they expect. It's great to have an SOP for recovering from a failed router, but if the only person who understands the procedure is the IT person, and she's on vacation in Bora Bora that week, your disaster recovery plan has a big hole in it.

When you create the documentation, write down *everything*. What seems obvious to you now, while you're devising the procedure, will not seem at all obvious in six months or a year when you suddenly have to follow it under stress.

Real World **Multiple Copies, Multiple Locations**

It's tempting to centralize your SOPs into a single, easily accessible database. You should do that, making sure everyone understands how to use it. But you'll also want to have alternative locations and formats for your procedures. Not only do you *not* want to keep the only copy in a single database, you also don't want to have only an electronic version—how accessible is the SOP for recovering a failed server going to be when the server has failed? Always maintain hard-copy versions as well. The one thing you don't want to do is create a single point of failure in your disaster recovery plan!

Every good server room should have a large binder, prominently visible and clearly identified, that contains all the SOPs. Each responsible person should also have one or more copies of at least the procedures he or she is either a resource for or likely to become a resource for. We like to keep copies of all our procedures in several places so that we can get at them no matter what the source of the emergency or where we happen to be when one of our pagers goes off.

Once you have created the SOPs, your job has only begun. You need to keep them up to date and make sure that they don't become stale. It's no good having an SOP to recover your ISDN connection to the Internet when you ripped the ISDN line out a year ago and put in a DSL line with three times the bandwidth at half the cost.

You also need to make sure that all your copies of an SOP are updated. Electronic ones should probably be stored in a database or in a folder on the Windows Small Business Server that is available off-line. However, hard-copy documents are notoriously tricky to maintain. A good method is to make yet another SOP that details who updates what SOPs, how often, and who gets fresh copies whenever a change is made. Then put a version control system into place and make sure everyone understands his or her role in the process. Build rewards into the system for timely and consistent updating of SOPs—if 10 or 20 percent of someone's bonus is dependent on keeping those SOPs up to date and distributed, you can be sure they'll be current at least as often as the review process.

Standard Escalation Procedures

No matter how carefully you've identified potential risks, and how detailed your procedures to recover from them are, you're still likely to have situations you didn't anticipate. An important part of any disaster recovery plan is a standardized escalation procedure. Not only should each individual SOP have its own procedure-specific SEP, but you should also have an overall escalation procedure that covers everything you haven't thought of—because it's certain you haven't thought of everything.

An escalation procedure has two functions—resource escalation and notification escalation. Both have the same purpose: to make sure that everyone who needs to know about the problem is up to date and involved as appropriate, and to keep the overall noise level down so that the work of resolving the problem can go forward as quickly as possible. The *resource escalation procedure* details the resources that are available to the people who are trying to recover from the current disaster so that these people don't have to try to guess who (or what) the appropriate resource might be when they run into something they can't handle or something doesn't go as it is supposed to. This procedure helps them stay calm and focused. They know that if they run into a problem, they aren't on their own, and they know exactly who to call when they do need help.

The *notification escalation procedure* details who is to be notified of serious problems. Even more important, it should provide specifics regarding *when* notification is to be made. If a particular print queue crashes but comes right back up, you might want to send a general message only to the users of that particular printer letting them know what happened. However, if your e-mail has been down for more than half an hour, a lot of folks are going to be concerned. The SEP for e-mail should detail who needs to be notified when the server is unavailable for longer than some specified time, and it should probably detail what happens and who gets notified when it's still down some significant amount of time after that.

This notification has two purposes: to make sure that the necessary resources are made available as required, and to keep everyone informed and aware of the situation. If you let people know that you've had a server hardware failure and that the vendor has been called and will be on site within an hour, you'll cut down the number of phone calls exponentially, freeing you to do whatever you need to do to ensure that you're ready when the vendor arrives.

Testing the Responses

A disaster recovery plan is nice to have, but it really isn't worth a whole lot until it has actually been tested. Needless to say, the time to test the plan is at your convenience and under controlled conditions, rather than in the midst of an actual disaster. It's a nuisance to discover that your detailed disaster recovery plan has a fatal flaw in it when you're testing it under controlled conditions. It's a bit more than a nuisance to discover it when every second counts.

You won't be able to test everything in your disaster recovery plans. Even most large organizations don't have the resources to create fully realistic simulated natural disasters and test their response to each of them under controlled conditions, and even fewer small businesses have those kinds of resources. Nevertheless, there are things you can do to test your response plans. The details of how you test them depend on your environment, but they should include as realistic a test as feasible and should, as much as possible, cover all aspects of the response plan. The other reason to test the disaster recovery plan is that it provides a valuable training ground. If you've identified primary and backup resources, as you should, chances are that the people you've identified as backup resources are not as skilled or knowledgeable in a particular area as the primary resource. Testing the procedures gives you a chance to train the backup resources at the same time.

You should also consider using the testing to cross-train people who are not necessarily in the primary response group. Not only will they get valuable training, but you'll also create a knowledgeable pool of people who might not be directly needed when the procedure has to be used for real, but who can act as key communicators with the rest of the community.

Iterating

When you finish a particular disaster recovery plan, you might think your job is done, but in fact it has just begun. Standardizing a process is actually just the first step. You need to continually look for ways to improve it.

You should make a regular, scheduled practice of pulling out your disaster recovery plan with those responsible and making sure it's up to date. Use the occasion to actually look at it and see how you can improve on it. Take the opportunity to examine your environment. What's changed since you last looked at the plan? What equipment has been retired, and what has been added? What software is different? Are all the people on your notification and escalation lists still working at the company in the same roles? Are the phone numbers, including home phone numbers, up to date?

Another important way to iterate your disaster recovery plan is to use every disaster as a learning experience. Once the disaster or emergency is over, get everyone together *as soon as possible* to talk about what happened. Find out what they think worked and what didn't in the plan. Actively solicit suggestions for how the process could be improved. Then make the changes and test them. You'll not only improve your responsiveness to this particular type of disaster, but you'll improve your overall responsiveness by getting people involved in the process and enabling them to be part of the solution.

Preparing for a Disaster

As Ben Franklin was known to say, "Failure to prepare is preparing to fail." This is truer than ever with modern operating systems, and although Windows Small Business Server 2003 includes a number of exceptionally useful recovery modes and tools, you still need to prepare for potential problems. Some of these techniques are covered in detail in other chapters and are discussed here only briefly, whereas others are covered here at length.

Setting Up a Fault-Tolerant System

A fault-tolerant system is one that is prepared to continue operating in the event of key component failures. This technique is very useful for servers running critical applications. Here are a few of the many ways to ensure fault tolerance in a system:

- Use one or more RAID arrays for system and data storage, protecting you from hard disk failure. If a hard disk in the array fails, only that disk needs to be replaced—and no data is lost. See Chapter 7, "Disk Management," for information about using Windows Small Business Server 2003 to implement software RAID.

- Use multiple SCSI adapters to provide redundancy if a SCSI controller fails.

- Use an uninterruptible power supply (UPS) to allow the server to shut down gracefully in the event of a power failure.

- Use multiple network cards to provide redundancy in case a network card fails.

- Use multiples of everything that is likely to fail, including power supplies.

Backing Up the System

Back up the system and system state regularly using a good Windows Small Business Server 2003 backup program. If a hard disk fails and must be replaced and you're not using some sort of RAID array, the data and system can be restored from backup. See Chapter 13, "Backing Up and Restoring Data," for details about using the Windows Small Business Server 2003 backup program.

Creating Automated System Recovery Disks

Whereas earlier versions of Windows Small Business Server created an emergency repair disk (ERD) to help rescue the system in the event of a disaster, Windows Small Business Server 2003 creates an Automated System Recovery (ASR) disk. The ASR disk contains important information that can be used to fix system files, the boot sector, and the startup environment. The ASR disk is easy to make, and it is *very* useful in the event of a disaster.

> **Tip** In Windows Small Business Server 2003, you might have noticed that you didn't get prompted to create an ERD during installation, as you did during the setup of earlier versions. In fact, the entire procedure has changed. Now, instead of an ERD, you run the Backup program in Windows Small Business Server 2003 to create an ASR disk and backup. To make a fresh ASR disk, you need a floppy disk that you don't mind being formatted and a fresh tape for your tape drive. Always use a freshly formatted floppy disk to create an ASR disk. It's also a good idea to have a backup of your ASR disk, so always keep at least one generation back. We also like to keep an original ASR disk created immediately after the installation process as a kind of ultimate fall-back position.

To make an ASR disk, complete the following steps:

1. Open the Windows Small Business Server Backup program. From the Start menu, point to All Programs, Accessories, System Tools, and then click Backup.

2. Switch to the Advanced Mode (Figure 21-1) if you get a wizard prompt.

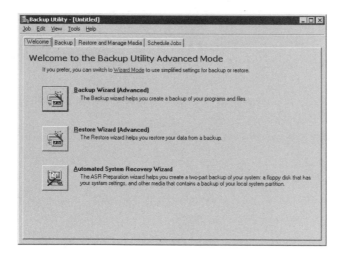

Figure 21-1. *The Advanced mode of the Windows Small Business Server Backup utility.*

3. Click Automated System Recovery Wizard to open the Automated System Recovery Preparation Wizard. Click Next.

4. On the Backup Destination page shown in Figure 21-2, select the backup type and destination you'll be using. Click Next.

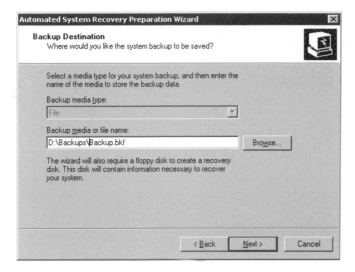

Figure 21-2.   *The Backup Destination page of the Automated System Recovery Preparation Wizard.*

5. Click Finish to complete the wizard. The backup starts automatically when you exit the wizard, as shown in Figure 21-3.

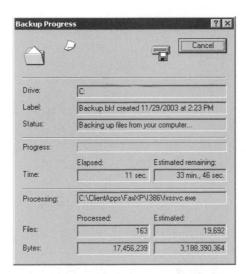

Figure 21-3.   *The Backup Progress window during Automated System Recovery Preparation.*

6. Once the backup has completed, you'll be prompted to insert a blank floppy disk to create the ASR disk, as shown Figure 21-4.

Figure 21-4. *The Create Automated System Recovery Disk prompt.*

7. Insert a blank floppy disk in drive A, and click OK.

8. Backup writes the necessary files to the floppy disk and confirms that the process has been successful, as shown in Figure 21-5. Label the disk and the backup media used as requested and store them in a safe place.

Figure 21-5. *Always carefully label each ASR disk exactly as requested.*

Note The ASR disk is not bootable; it must be used in conjunction with the Windows Small Business Server 2003 installation media. Also, each ASR is viable only with the specific backup it was created as part of, so make sure you label the ASR carefully.

Under the Hood **Using the ASR Set Effectively**

What, exactly, is on the ASR disk? Well, certainly not all the stuff that used to be there in Microsoft Windows NT. Instead of trying to fit all of the files necessary to recover your system onto a single floppy disk, a task that had become more than a little problematic, Windows Small Business Server now copies only three files to the floppy:

- **Setup.log** Points to the location of system files on your server

- **Asr.sif** Contains information on disk, partitions and volumes on the system, and the location of the backup media used

- **Asrpnp.sif** Contains information on the various plug-and-play devices on the system

With this change to the ASR disk, it's easy to maintain multiple generations of repair information, because each ASR disk points to a specific system backup. You should always keep the ASR disk with the specific backup that it was made with.

Whenever you make a major change to your system, it's a good idea to make a fresh ASR set *before* you make the change. This gives you a fallback position if something goes wrong. If something doesn't work right, you can quickly restore the previous configuration. After you confirm that the new configuration is stable and working, then and only then should you update your ASR set for that server.

What constitutes a major change? Adding, removing, or otherwise modifying the hard disks or their partitions, formats, configurations, and so on, for one. Any time you make a change to the hard disk configuration, you'll definitely want to make a fresh ASR set just before you make the change. Another major change would be the addition of a new component to the server, such as adding the components of the Premium Technologies Disk - Microsoft ISA Server or Microsoft SQL Server. Any changes made from Control Panel are candidates for redoing the ASR set as well.

Creating a Boot Disk

With Windows Small Business Server 2003, you can still create a useful boot disk that can help with recovery in the event something corrupts a critical file on your hard disk. Although this is less important these days, because you can add the Recovery Console to your boot menu or run it from the Windows Small Business Server 2003 installation CD-ROM, we're the cautious type; we like to have available every possible way to recover. Although a Windows Small Business Server 2003 boot disk doesn't get you to a command prompt, as a Microsoft Windows 95 or Microsoft Windows 98 boot disk does, it does permit you to boot the system under the following circumstances (provided that your actual Windows Small Business Server installation isn't damaged in any other way):

- Corrupted boot sector
- Corrupted master boot record (MBR)
- Virus infections of the MBR
- Missing or corrupt Ntldr or Ntdetect.com files

The boot disk can also be used to boot from the shadow drive of a broken mirror set, although you might need to edit the Boot.ini file on the boot disk.

Under the Hood   Why MS-DOS Boot Disks Won't Help

More than one person new to Windows Small Business Server 2003 has accidentally deleted or corrupted a key file required to boot the system and tried to recover by digging out an old MS-DOS or Windows boot floppy disk. Alas, it doesn't work.

The files you need to get your hard disk back to booting condition aren't even on an MS-DOS floppy disk. When you install Windows Small Business Server 2003, the software modifies the system's boot sector to look for and run a file called Ntldr. When you format a floppy disk under MS-DOS, even when you make it a system disk, this file doesn't get created, because MS-DOS doesn't know anything about Windows Small Business Server 2003 and doesn't know anything about NTFS file systems, either.

As such, a boot disk is occasionally useful, and because it's easy to make and floppy disks grow on trees (although these trees are rarely seen outside of the Microsoft campus), you might as well make one. Follow these steps to create a boot disk:

1. Insert a blank floppy disk into your floppy drive.

2. At a command prompt, type the command **format a: /u** and follow the instructions that appear.

3. Copy the Ntdetect.com and Ntldr files from the \i386 folder on the first Windows Small Business Server 2003 CD-ROM to the floppy disk.

4. Create a Boot.ini file, or copy the file from the boot drive to the floppy disk.

Under the Hood **ARC Naming Conventions**

Understanding how the hard disks and partitions are named on your system is not a trivial task, unfortunately. To provide a uniform naming convention across multiple platforms, Microsoft uses a fairly arcane designation for all the disks and partitions on your computer. Called ARC—short for Advanced RISC Computing—this is a generic naming convention that can be used in the same way for both Intel-based and RISC-based computers.

The convention describes the adapter type and number, the disk number, the rdisk number, and finally the partition number. The format is as follows:

```
<adaptertype>(x)disk(y)rdisk(z)partition(n)
```

where *<adaptertype>* can be SCSI, multi, or signature. Use multi for all non-SCSI adapters and for SCSI adapters that use a BIOS—as most adapters used with Intel-based processors do. The (x) is the adapter number, starting at 0. If *<adaptertype>* is signature, (x) is an 8-character drive signature.

The value for (y) is the SCSI ID of the disk for SCSI adapters. For multi, this is always 0. The number for (z) is 0 for SCSI, and is the ordinal number of the disk for multi, starting with 0. Finally, the partition number (n) is the number of the partition on the target disk. Here the partitions start at 1, with 0 reserved for unused space.

Installing the Recovery Console

One of the most useful recovery features in Windows Small Business Server 2003 is the Recovery Console. This is basically an enhanced, NTFS-enabled, secure command prompt that can be used to copy files, start and stop services, and perform other recovery actions when you can't boot the system using Windows Small Business Server 2003's safe mode. The Recovery Console is always available for use through the first Windows Small Business Server 2003 CD-ROM; however, you can also install it as an option on the Boot menu for use in those instances when you can't boot using safe mode. You'll still need to use the boot disk if you can't get to the Boot menu or the Recovery Console is damaged.

To install the Recovery Console, complete the following steps:

1. Insert the first Windows Small Business Server 2003 CD-ROM.

2. Close the autorun dialog box if one appears.

3. At a command prompt or in the Run dialog box, type the command **d:\i386\winnt32/cmdcons**, replacing *d* with the drive letter of the Windows Small Business Server 2003 CD-ROM or network share.

4. Click Yes to install the Recovery Console, as shown in Figure 21-6.

Figure 21-6.   *The Windows Setup window, installing the Recovery Console.*

5. If a Getting Updated Setup Files page appears, select an appropriate option and click Next. The Copying Installation Files page appears and copies the necessary files from the CD.

6. A message box appears indicating that Recovery Console was successfully installed. Click OK. The next time you reboot, one of the boot options will be Microsoft Windows Recovery Console.

Specifying Recovery Options

You can specify how you want Windows Small Business Server 2003 to deal with system crashes by changing a few options in the System tool in Control Panel. To do so, complete the following steps:

1. Open the System tool from Control Panel, and click the Advanced tab.

2. Click Settings in the Startup And Recovery box to display the Startup And Recovery dialog box, shown in Figure 21-7.

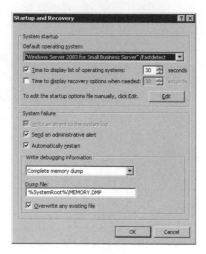

Figure 21-7. *The Startup And Recovery dialog box.*

3. If you have multiple operating systems on the machine, from the Default Operating System list box, select the operating system you want to have boot by default.

4. If you want to boot the default operating system automatically, without waiting, clear the Time To Display List Of Operating Systems check box. Otherwise, specify how long you want to display a list of options in the box provided.

5. If you want recovery options automatically displayed in the event of problems, select the Time To Display Recovery Options When Needed check box, and set the time for it.

6. Select the Write An Event To The System Log check box, if available, to record an entry in the event log when the system experiences a crash.

7. Select the Send An Administrative Alert check box to send an alert to administrators over the network when the system crashes.

8. Select the Automatically Restart option to instruct Windows Small Business Server to reboot the system in the event of a crash. Otherwise the system remains at a blue screen until an administrator manually reboots it.

9. From the Write Debugging Information list box, select how much debugging information you want to record. Note that if you have a

large amount of RAM, you need the same amount of free disk space if you want to use the Complete Memory Dump option.

10. Enter the file name for the dump file in the Dump File text box, and select the Overwrite Any Existing File check box to maintain only a single dump file.

Creating and Using a Recovery Drive

An excellent way to recycle an old, small SCSI drive that's not good for much else is to use it as an external recovery drive. This drive needs to be only about 2 GB or so, smaller than you could even buy today. Using a recovery drive in this way offers a somewhat cheaper alternative to mirroring the drive.

To create the recovery drive, perform a minimal install of Windows Server 2003 on the drive, configuring your swap file to be on that drive. Do not install all of Windows Small Business Server, but stop after the initial operating system installation, before additional CDs are requested. Create a bootable Windows Small Business Server 2003 floppy disk, following the procedure outlined earlier in the section entitled "Creating a Boot Disk," and edit the Boot.ini file on it to point to the SCSI address of the recovery drive.

If you have a completely failed system drive, for example, you can simply cable the recovery drive to the server and boot from the boot disk that points to the recovery drive. You won't have any of Windows Small Business Server's features on the drive, such as Exchange or all the wizards, but you will have enough of an operating system to run the Backup utility to restore your server from tape. And it will take a *lot* less time than reinstalling from scratch.

Summary

Assume that disaster will eventually occur, and plan accordingly. Create standardized recovery procedures and keep them up to date. When there's a lot of turmoil, as always happens in the case of a major failure, people forget important steps and can make poor decisions. Standardized procedures provide a course of action without the need for on-the-spot decisions.

Part VII
Appendixes

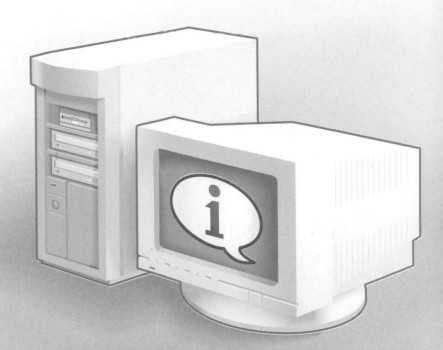

Appendix A
Partially Automating Installation

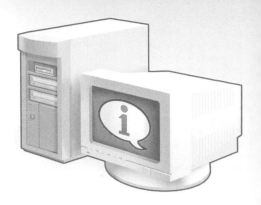

Those who install Microsoft Windows Small Business Server 2003 often can save a good deal of time by automating Setup. There are two significant ways to automate Windows Small Business Server 2003 Setup: using answer files, and using the System Preparation Tool (Sysprep) in conjunction with a disk imaging program to make a copy of Windows Small Business Server 2003 halfway through Setup.

> **Note** You can automate only the installation of the underlying operating system—you can't automate the Microsoft Windows Small Business Server Setup Wizard, which is run in the second major phase of Windows Small Business Server Setup. (See Chapter 4, "Installing Windows Small Business Server 2003.")

Automating CD-Based Installations

During a normal installation of Windows Small Business Server, Setup stops a number of times to prompt the user for information. This process can be automated by using an *answer file*, which is a text file with answers to the questions Setup asks. You can create answer files manually using any text editor, or by using the handy Setup Manager tool, as described in the following steps:

1. From any Windows computer, insert Windows Small Business Server 2003 CD 1, or download updated Support Tools from the Microsoft Web site. Support Tools are usually upgraded with each Service Pack. Navigate to the \Support\Tools folder and extract the contents of the Deploy.cab file to a location on the hard drive.

2. Launch the Setupmgr.exe file from the location on the hard drive to which you copied the contents of the Deploy.cab file. The Setup Manager Wizard appears.

3. Click Next to begin using the wizard.

4. On the New Or Existing Answer File page, choose Create New and then click Next.

5. On the Type Of Setup page, choose Unattended Setup and then click Next.

6. On the Product page (Figure A-1), choose Windows Server 2003, Standard Edition, and then click Next.

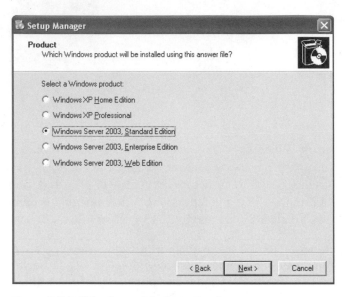

Figure A-1. *The Setup Manager Product page.*

7. On the User Interaction page, choose the level of interaction that will be available during Setup (Figure A-2), and then click Next.

More Info For more information about determining user interaction during Setup, see the Real World sidebar "Choosing an Interaction Level" later in this appendix.

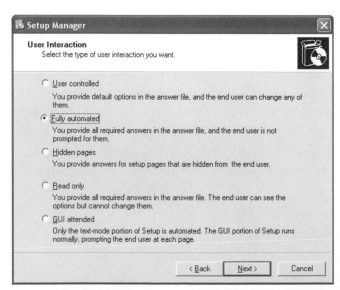

Figure A-2. *The Setup Manager User Interaction page.*

8. On the Distribution Share page, select Set Up From A CD and then click Next.

> **More Info** Windows Small Business Server 2003 can be installed from a network distribution share, but this requires the client to have network connectivity before running Setup, which often is impractical for Windows Small Business Server 2003 installations. For information about distribution shares, refer to *Microsoft Windows Server 2003 Administrator's Companion* (Microsoft Press).

9. If you chose to fully automate the first phase of Windows Small Business Server Setup, on the License Agreement page, accept the terms of the End User License Agreement (EULA), and then click Next. OEMs aren't permitted to use this step, and must use the OEM Preinstallation Kit (OPK) instead of Setup Manager.

10. On the Name And Organization page, supply the name and organization you want to use, and then click Next. A name and organization are required for a fully automated answer file.

11. On the Display Settings page, select the display settings for the computer, as shown in Figure A-3, and then click Next.

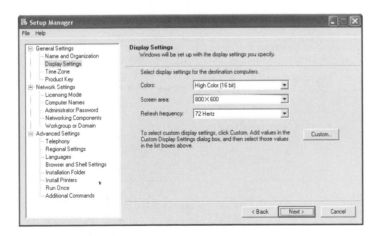

Figure A-3. *Specifying display settings.*

> **Caution** Although the Windows default display, which is 640 × 480, 60 Hz, and 16 colors, is dated, use extreme caution here. A usable setting that is mostly safe is 800 × 600, 72 Hz, and High Color (16-bit). If the screen area (*resolution*), colors, or refresh frequency is too high for the monitor plugged into the computer, the monitor could be damaged; at the very least you'll be forced to reboot using the Safe Mode or Enable VGA Mode boot options and adjust the display settings to something safer.

12. On the Time Zone page, specify the time zone in which the servers will be placed and then click Next.

13. On the Product Key page, type the product key and then click Next. You'll have to edit the answer file for each installation to update the product key, unless you have a Volume License version of Windows Small Business Server 2003.

14. On the Licensing Mode page, click Next to accept licensing Per Server with 5 CALs. (Windows Small Business Server 2003 licensing is configured after Setup, as discussed in Chapter 4.)

15. On the Computer Names page, create a list of computer names to use for the systems on which you will be installing Windows Small Business Server, as shown in Figure A-4. Type a computer name in the Computer Name text box, and then click Add. Setup Manager takes the names (if you have two or more) and creates a Uniqueness Database File (.UDF) that Setup then queries for computer names, using each name only once. Click Next to continue.

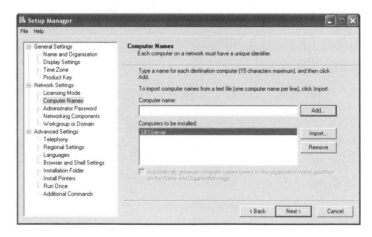

Figure A-4. *The Setup Manager Computer Names page.*

16. On the Administrator Password page, you can specify an administrator account password for the systems and other settings. If you choose to specify a password now, select the Encrypt The Administrator Password In The Answer File check box, as shown in Figure A-5. If you don't select this check box, the password is stored in plain text for anyone with Microsoft Notepad to read. Click Next to continue.

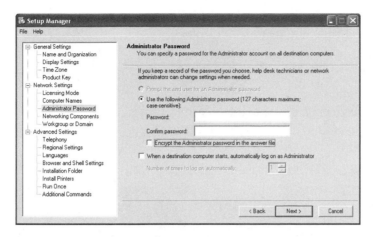

Figure A-5. *Setting the Administrator password.*

17. Click Next on the Networking Components page, and then click Next again on the Workgroup Or Domain page. (Typical settings will be used for Networking Components and the computer will belong to a Workgroup.)

18. Use the rest of the pages to customize other settings such as Telephone, Regional, and Internet Explorer settings. On the Additional Commands page, click Finish.

19. In the Setup Manager dialog box, type the folder path in which you want to store the answer file, and name the answer file **Winnt.sif** (or **Unattend.txt** if you want to use the answer file with a distribution folder). Click OK and then click Cancel to exit Setup Manager.

20. Copy the Winnt.sif and Winnt.udb files to a floppy disk. (The Winnt.udb file exists only if you enter more than one computer name.) To use the disk, insert it immediately after the computer boots from the Windows Small Business Server 2003 CD-ROM, before Setup prompts you to press F2 to start the Automated System Recovery process.

More Info   For detailed information about the parameters in the answer file, see the Microsoft Windows Corporate Deployment Tools User's Guide help file, Deploy.chm, which is located in the \Support\Tools\Deploy.cab file on Windows Small Business Server 2003 CD 1.

Real World   Choosing an Interaction Level

The level of user interaction determines how much the person running the installation needs to attend to the process. Here's a more detailed explanation of the interaction levels:

- **User Controlled**   Uses the information in the answer file as default answers during the Windows installation. The user still has to confirm the defaults or make changes as the installation progresses.

- **Fully Automated**   Completely automates Setup by using the answer file. This option is best for quickly setting up multiple systems with identical configurations. If any settings don't work properly (such as might happen when the product key is wrong), Setup will prompt for the correct information.

- **Hidden Pages**   Automates the parts of Setup for which you provide information, and prompts the user to supply any information not included in the answer file. The user sees only the parts of Setup that aren't covered in the answer file. Use this option to standardize some aspects of installation but not others (such as the product key, the computer name, and user information).

- **Read Only**   Hides the parts of Setup for which you provide information, just like the Hidden Pages option. However, if a window with only partial answers is supplied in the answer file (and therefore not hidden from the user), the user can complete only the unanswered portion of the window. Settings provided by the answer file can't be changed during installation.

- **GUI Attended**   Automates the text-based portion of Setup. The person running Setup supplies answers for the Windows Setup Wizard. Use this level when you want to automate the text-based portion of Setup and allow the person running the installation to provide the settings during the graphical user interface (GUI) portion.

Using the System Preparation Tool to Image Windows Server 2003

Running the first phase of Windows Small Business Server 2003 Setup using a fully automated answer file usually takes 45–60 minutes, excluding the Microsoft Windows Small Business Server Setup Wizard (which can't be automated).

You can achieve the same results in about 5 or 10 minutes using the System Preparation Tool (Sysprep) in conjunction with a hard-drive imaging program.

However, this process has a few restrictions that make it useful only to consultants and OEMs who frequently install Windows Small Business Server 2003 on identical or nearly identical hardware. First of all, you must use a third-party drive imaging tool such as PowerQuest DriveImage or Symantec Ghost. Second, the computers must have identical mass storage controllers (SCSI controller or IDE chipset), and share the same HAL—no mixing ACPI systems with non-ACPI systems or uniprocessor systems with multiprocessor systems. Third, the system must be imaged before running the Microsoft Windows Small Business Server Setup Wizard (the second major phase of Setup).

More Info   For information about the Microsoft Windows Small Business Server Setup Wizard, see Chapter 4.

As such, you should thoroughly investigate these tools and experiment with them in a test environment before attempting to use this procedure in your business. The following steps summarize how to image and deploy a partially installed Windows Small Business Server 2003 computer (the process also works for Windows Server 2003).

1. Install Windows Small Business Server 2003 on the reference system, but do not run the Microsoft Windows Small Business Server Setup Wizard. (If you're an OEM, contact Microsoft for information about imaging computers after running the Microsoft Windows Small Business Server Setup Wizard.)

2. Create a folder named Sysprep in the root directory of the system partition (for example, C:\Sysprep).

3. Extract Sysprep.exe and Setupcl.exe from the \Support\Tools\Deploy.cab file on the Windows Small Business Server 2003 CD 1 to the newly created \Sysprep folder.

4. Empty the Recycle Bin, delete any temporary files (including Temporary Internet files and cookies), and if the computer is a member of a domain, remove it from the domain.

5. Defragment the hard disk, check for viruses, and scan for hard-drive errors.

6. Clear the Event View log files and clear the Administrator account password so that there is no password (otherwise, all machines will use the same password).

7. Right-click the Start button, choose Properties, click Customize, and then click Clear List to reset the Recently Used Programs listing. Then click the Advanced tab and click Clear List to reset the Recent Documents list.

8. Run Sysprep.exe. A message box appears indicating that Sysprep can modify security settings and that after you run Sysprep, Windows will automatically shut down. Click OK. The Sysprep tool appears, as shown in Figure A-6.

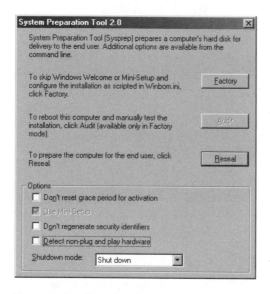

Figure A-6. *Running Sysprep.*

9. To force a full hardware detection that can take up to 20 minutes to complete during the Mini-Setup Wizard (Step 14), select Detect Non-Plug And Play Hardware.

10. Click Reseal, and then click OK in the message box to remove all identity information from the computer. The computer is automatically shut down.

11. Use a drive imaging program to create an image of the hard-drive partition, and save it to a network share, CD, DVD, or external hard drive.

12. On a new computer, use your drive imaging boot disk (created with the drive imaging program) to boot the computer on which you want to deploy Windows Small Business Server 2003.

13. Connect to the network share, CD, DVD, or hard drive on which the image file is located and restore it onto the new computer's hard drive.

14. Restart the computer. A Mini-Setup Wizard runs (which is nothing more than an abbreviated version of Setup), personalizing the software, detecting any additional Plug and Play (PnP) devices, and hiding any missing devices. The system is now fully functional.

Tip   You can also provide an answer file to modify system configurations without recreating the disk image. To do this, use Setup Manager to create a Sysprep answer file (choose Sysprep Setup on the Type Of Setup page), save it to a floppy disk as Sysprep.inf, and insert the disk right after booting the new computer, before the Mini-Setup Wizard opens.

Appendix B
Installing ISA Server 2000 and SQL Server 2000

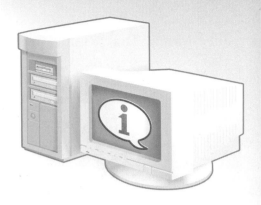

ISA Server 2000 and SQL Server 2000 are included with Microsoft Windows Small Business Server 2003, Premium Edition, but aren't installed along with the rest of the operating system. To install these programs, use the Premium Technologies CD, as described in this appendix. Microsoft Office FrontPage 2003 is also included with Windows Small Business Server 2003, Premium Edition, but is self-explanatory to install, so we don't discuss it here.

Installing ISA Server 2000

To install ISA Server 2000, make sure that the server is disconnected from the Internet or is behind a firewall, and then complete the following steps:

1. Insert the Windows Small Business Server 2003 Premium Technologies CD. The Microsoft Windows Small Business Server 2003 Premium Technologies Setup window appears.

2. Click Install Microsoft Internet Security And Acceleration Server 2000. The Microsoft Internet Security And Acceleration Server Standard Edition Setup appears.

3. Click Continue on the first page and then click OK when the Product ID is displayed. The license agreement is displayed.

4. Read the standard Microsoft license agreement, and then click I Agree to continue.

5. On the installation type page, click the button associated with the type of installation you want to perform. Choose Typical Installation to install the most commonly used options, Custom Installation to specify exactly which options to install, or Full Installation to install all options.

6. If you chose to perform a custom installation, click Change Folder to optionally change the installation location. Roughly 15 MB of disk space is used at this location. (The ISA Server cache can be stored elsewhere.)

7. On the mode page, choose which mode of ISA Server to use (Figure B-1).

   • Firewall Mode for security purposes only

   • Cache Mode for Internet acceleration purposes only

   • Integrated Mode to provide both security and acceleration services (the best mode for most networks)

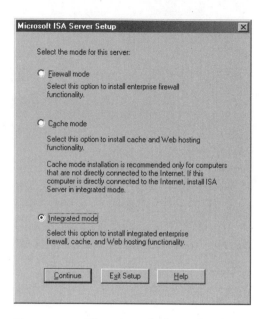

Figure B-1. *Choosing which mode of ISA Server to use.*

Tip You can enable or disable ISA Server's firewall and caching services any time after installation by selecting Microsoft ISA Server in Add/Remove Programs, clicking Change, and then choosing Reinstall. Select a new mode and away you go. Make sure to back up the ISA Server configuration first.

8. Click Continue. Setup stops Microsoft Internet Information Services (IIS). Click OK to continue.

9. On the cache page, set the size and location of the local Web cache as shown in Figure B-2. Hard disk space is inexpensive, so set aside a large chunk of disk space for the cache; 2–10 GB is a good amount for most companies.

Tip You can place the cache on any NTFS drive, but for the best performance, place it on the fastest hard drive or spread it across several physical disks. (Spreading across partitions on the same physical disk offers no performance improvements.)

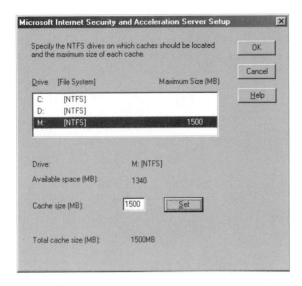

Figure B-2. *Specifying on which drives to store the Web cache.*

10. On the internal network address space page, click Construct Table.

11. In the Local Address Table dialog box (Figure B-3), verify that the network card connected to the internal network is selected. (Do not select the adapter connected to the Internet or perimeter network.) If the server is connected directly to the Internet (it isn't behind a firewall or router that uses NAT), select the Add The Following Private Ranges check box; otherwise, leave it cleared. Click OK when you're done constructing the local address table (LAT).

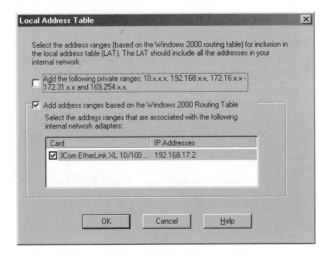

Figure B-3. *The Local Address Table dialog box.*

Note The local address table (LAT) identifies which addresses are on the local network, and it is thus accessible through the network adapter connected to the internal network. Addresses not located in the LAT are accessed using the network adapter connected to the external network (the Internet).

12. A Setup Message appears, warning you that the automatically constructed LAT might include external addresses. Click OK.

13. You see the automatically configured LAT as ISA Server is about to construct it. When the table is correct, click OK to install ISA Server.

14. When the Launch ISA Management Tool dialog box appears, clear the Start The ISA Server Getting Started Wizard check box and then click OK to finish Setup. Click OK again. The Configure E-Mail and Internet Connection Wizard appears.

15. Reconnect the computer to the Internet and enable the network adapter connected to the Internet or perimeter network. Use the Configure E-Mail and Internet Connection Wizard to configure Windows Small Business Server and ISA Server 2000 for Internet connectivity, as discussed in Chapter 6, "Completing the To Do List and Other Post-Installation Tasks."

Installing a New SQL Server 2000 Instance

Use the following steps to install a new instance of SQL Server 2000 and install SQL Server 2000 Service Pack 3a:

Note The version of SQL Server 2000 included on the Premium Technologies CD is an updated version that addresses the Slammer worm. To ensure SQL Server is not exposed to other potential vulnerabilities before Service Pack 3a is installed, make sure that the server is disconnected from the Internet or is behind a firewall.

1. Insert the Windows Small Business Server 2003 Premium Technologies CD. The Microsoft Windows Small Business Server 2003 Premium Technologies Setup window appears.

2. Click Install Microsoft SQL Server 2000. A dialog box appears warning that SQL Server 2000 SP2 and earlier are unsupported. Click Continue and then click Next on the first page of the Microsoft SQL Server Installation Wizard.

3. On the Computer Name page, click Next to install SQL Server on the local computer (the only supported configuration in Windows Small Business Server 2003).

Tip   If you have trouble getting past the Computer Name page because Setup insists that a previous installation didn't complete, reboot the server and log on locally (not using Remote Desktop).

4. On the Installation Selection page (Figure B-4), choose Create A New Instance Of SQL Server, Or Install Client Tools and then click Next.

Note   You can install or upgrade only a single instance at a time—to install or upgrade another instance, rerun the Microsoft SQL Server Installation Wizard.

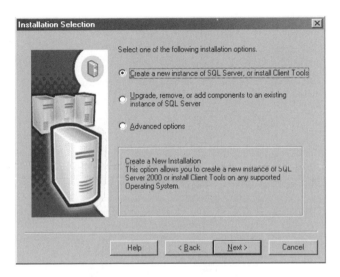

Figure B-4.   *The Installation Selection page.*

5. On the User Information page, type your name and company and then click Next.

6. On the Software License Agreement page, read the End-User License Agreement (EULA) and then click Yes.

7. On the Product Key page, type the CD key from the Windows Small Business Server 2003 packaging and then click Next. (This page appears only when installing the first instance.)

8. On the Installation Definition page, choose Server And Client Tools and then click Next.

9. On the Instance Name page, select the Default check box and then click Next.

10. On the Setup Type page (Figure B-5), choose either Typical or Minimum (or Custom if you want to tweak the installation options), specify where to place the SQL Server files, and then click Next.

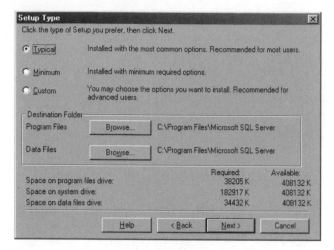

Figure B-5. *The Setup Type page.*

11. On the Services Accounts page (Figure B-6), specify the user account to use for the SQL Server service and then click Next.

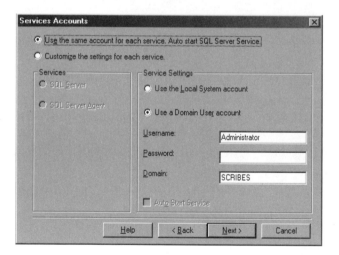

Figure B-6. *The Services Accounts page.*

Security Alert For maximum security, use an administrator account created specifically for use by SQL Server. If password policies are in place on the network, remember to reset the password on this account and change the password in SQL Server when the password expires.

12. On the Authentication Mode page, choose Windows Authentication Mode. The authentication mode can be changed after SQL Server is installed.

13. On the Start Copying Files page, click Next to install SQL Server.

14. After installation completes, click Finish.

15. Double-click Setup.exe on the Windows Small Business Server 2003 Premium Technologies CD. The Microsoft Windows Small Business Server 2003 Premium Technologies Setup window appears again.

16. Click Install SQL Server 2000 Service Pack 3a. When the Welcome page of the Microsoft SQL Server 2000 Service Pack 3a Wizard appears, click Next.

Planning   You *must* install Service Pack 3a (or newer) on every SQL Server instance that you install or upgrade. For example, if you install a default instance of SQL Server to store business data and you upgrade the Share-Point database to SQL Server, install Service Pack 3a twice: once to the default instance and once to the SharePoint instance.

---

17. Read the standard Microsoft license agreement, and then click Yes to continue.

18. On the Instance Name page, select the Default check box and then click Next.

19. On the Connect To Server page, select The Windows Account Information I Use To Log On To My Computer With (Windows Authentication) option and then click Next.

20. On the SA Password Warning page, type a secure password for the System Administrator (SA) login and then click OK.

Security Alert   The System Administrator login is present for backwards compatibility with earlier versions of SQL Server and is disabled while Windows authentication mode is used. However, if an administrator reconfigures SQL Server for mixed mode authentication, SQL Server enables the SA login, which has a blank password by default (essentially rolling out the red carpet for hackers). Because of this potential vulnerability, always set a strong SA password, even if you never plan on switching authentication modes.

---

21. On the Backward Compatibility Checklist page, make sure the check box is cleared to disable cross-database ownership chaining, thereby improving security. Click Continue.

22. On the Error Reporting page, optionally select the Automatically Send Fatal Error Reports To Microsoft check box to send error information to Microsoft and then click OK.

23. On the Start Copying Files page, click Next to install SQL Server 2000 Service Pack 3a.

24. After installation completes, a dialog box appears telling you to back up the SQL databases. Click OK.

25. On the Setup Complete page, click Finish.

26. Open Services from the Administrative Tools folder on the Start menu and verify that the MSSQLSERVER service is started. If the service isn't started, select it and click the Start Service toolbar button.

Upgrading SharePoint to Use SQL Server

Use the following steps to upgrade the SharePoint Microsoft SQL Server Desktop Engine (MSDE) to a full-fledged SQL Server instance and install SQL Server 2000 Service Pack 3a.

1. Open Services from the Administrative Tools folder on the Start menu and verify that the MSSQL$SHAREPOINT service is stopped. If the service isn't stopped, select it and click the Stop Service toolbar button.

2. Insert the Windows Small Business Server 2003 Premium Technologies CD. The Microsoft Windows Small Business Server 2003 Premium Technologies Setup window appears.

3. Click Install Microsoft SQL Server 2000. A dialog box appears warning that SQL Server 2000 SP2 and earlier are unsupported. Click Continue and then click Next on the first page of the Microsoft SQL Server Installation Wizard.

4. On the Computer Name page, click Next to install SQL Server on the local computer (the only supported configuration in Windows Small Business Server 2003).

Tip If you have trouble getting past the Computer Name page because Setup insists that a previous installation didn't complete, reboot the server and log on locally (not using Remote Desktop).

5. On the Installation Selection page, choose Upgrade, Remove Or Add Components To An Existing Instance Of SQL Server and then click Next.

Note You can only install or upgrade a single instance at a time. To install or upgrade another instance, you need to rerun the Microsoft SQL Server Installation Wizard.

6. If the Product Key page appears, type the CD key from the Windows Small Business Server 2003 packaging and then click Next. (This page appears only when installing or upgrading the first instance.)

7. On the Instance Name page (Figure B-7), clear the Default check box, select SHAREPOINT from the Instance Name box (don't upgrade the SBSMONITORING instance), and then click Next.

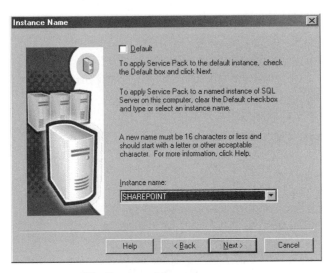

Figure B-7. *The Instance Name page.*

8. On the Existing Installation page, select Upgrade Your Existing Installation and then click Next.

9. On the Upgrade page, select the Yes Upgrade My Programs check box and then click Next. If a dialog box appears asking whether you want to install additional components, click Yes.

10. On the Select Components page, make sure that Full-Text Search, Management Tools, and Books Online are selected, and then click Next.

11. On the Start Copying Files page, click Next to upgrade SharePoint to use SQL Server.

Note   If the installation appears to hang and displays the message "Setup is preparing to copy files" for an extended length of time, it might be because the MSSQL$SHAREPOINT service is running. Stop the service, and the installation should continue.

12. After installation completes, click Finish.

13. Double-click Setup.exe on the Windows Small Business Server 2003 Premium Technologies CD. The Microsoft Windows Small Business Server 2003 Premium Technologies Setup window appears again.

14. Click Install SQL Server 2000 Service Pack 3a. When the Welcome page of the Microsoft SQL Server 2000 Service Pack 3a Wizard appears, click Next.

Note   You *must* install Service Pack 3a on every SQL Server instance that you install or upgrade. For example, if you install a default instance of SQL Server to store business data and you upgrade the SharePoint database to SQL Server, install Service Pack 3a twice: once to the default instance and once to the SharePoint instance.

15. Read the standard Microsoft license agreement, and then click Yes to continue.

16. On the Instance Name page, clear the Default check box and then select SHAREPOINT from the Instance Name box. Click Next to continue.

17. On the Connect To Server page, select The Windows Account Information I Use To Log On To My Computer With (Windows Authentication) option and then click Next.

18. If the SA Password Warning page appears, type a secure password for the System Administrator (SA), and then click OK.

Security Alert The System Administrator login is present for backwards compatibility with earlier versions of SQL Server and is disabled while Windows authentication mode is used. However, if an administrator reconfigures SQL Server for mixed mode authentication, SQL Server enables the SA login, which has a blank password by default (essentially rolling out the red carpet for hackers). Because of this potential vulnerability, always set a strong SA password, even if you never plan on switching authentication modes.

19. On the Backward Compatibility Checklist page, make sure the check box is cleared to disable cross-database ownership chaining, thereby improving security. Click Continue.

20. On the Error Reporting page, optionally select the Automatically Send Fatal Error Reports To Microsoft check box to send error information to Microsoft, and then click OK.

21. On the Start Copying Files page, click Next to install SQL Server 2000 Service Pack 3a.

22. After installation completes, a dialog box appears telling you to back up the SQL databases. Click OK, and then click Finish on the Setup Complete page.

23. Open Services from the Administrative Tools folder on the Start menu and verify that the MSSQL$SHAREPOINT services is started. If the service isn't started, select it and click the Start Service toolbar button.

24. Click Start, and then choose All Programs, Microsoft SQL Server, and Enterprise Manager. The SQL Server Enterprise Manager console appears.

25. Expand the Microsoft SQL Servers container, right-click SQL Server Group, and then choose New SQL Server Registration from the shortcut menu. When the Register SQL Server Wizard appears, click Next.

26. On the Select A SQL Server page shown in Figure B-8, type *SBSSRV\SHAREPOINT* in the Available Servers box and then click Add (assuming the name of the Windows Small Business Server computer is SBSSRV). Click Next to continue.

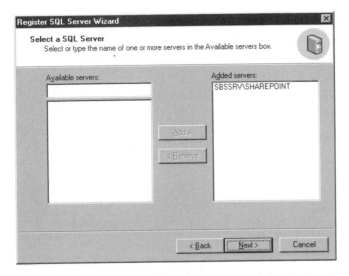

Figure B-8.   *The Select A SQL Server page of the Register SQL Server Wizard.*

27. On the Select An Authentication Mode page, choose The Windows Account Information I Use To Log On To My Computer With (Windows Authentication) option and then click Next.

28. On the Select SQL Server Group page, choose the Add The SQL Server(s) To An Existing SQL Group option and then click Next. Click Finish when you're done.

29. Click Close in the Register SQL Server Messages dialog box. If registration is successful, SHAREPOINT will appear in the SQL Server Group as shown in Figure B-9.

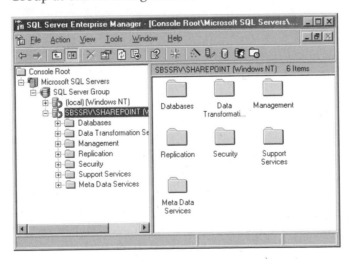

Figure B-9.   *SHAREPOINT added to the SQL Server Enterprise Manager console.*

Glossary

Numbers and Special Characters

802.11   Refers to a family of specifications for wireless networking.

802.11a   An extension to 802.11 that applies to wireless LANs and provides up to 54 Mbps in the 5 GHz band.

802.11b   (also called Wi-Fi) An extension to 802.11 that applies to wireless LANs and provides 11 Mbps transmission (with a fallback to 5.5, 2 and 1 Mbps) in the 2.4 GHz band. 802.11b is a 1999 ratification to the original 802.11 standard, allowing wireless functionality comparable to Ethernet.

A

Access control entry (ACE)   An entry in an access control list (ACL) that defines the level of access for a user or group.

Access control list (ACL)   A set of data associated with a file, directory, or other resource that defines the permissions users or groups have for accessing it. In Active Directory, the ACL is a list of access control entries (ACEs) stored with the object it protects. In Microsoft Windows Server 2003, Windows 2000, and Windows NT, an ACL is included in a data structure called a security descriptor.

Access point   Hardware device or software that acts as a communication hub for users of a wireless device to connect to a wired LAN.

Account lockout   A security feature that disables a user account if failed logons exceed a specified number in a specified period of time. Locked accounts can't log on and must be unlocked by an administrator.

Active Directory   Beginning in Microsoft Windows 2000 Server and continuing in Windows Server 2003, Active Directory replaces the Windows NT collection of directory functions with an integrated implementation that includes DNS, DHCP, LDAP, and Kerberos.

ActiveX   A loosely defined set of technologies that allows software components to interact with each other in a networked environment.

ActiveX component   Reusable software component that adheres to the ActiveX specification and can operate in an ActiveX-compliant environment.

Address   A precise location where a piece of information is stored in memory or on disk. Also, the unique identifier for a node on a network. On the Internet, the code by which an individual user is identified. The format is *username@hostname*, where *username* is your user name, logon name, or account number; and *hostname* is the name of the computer or Internet provider you use. The host name might be a few words strung together with periods.

Address Resolution Protocol (ARP) A TCP/IP and AppleTalk protocol that provides IP-address-to-MAC (media access control) address resolution for IP packets.

Administrative credentials Logon information used to verify the identity of a member of the administrators group.

Advanced Configuration Power Interface (ACPI) An industry specification defining power management on a range of computer devices. ACPI compliance is necessary for devices to take advantage of Plug and Play and power management capabilities.

Allocation unit The smallest unit of managed space on a hard disk or logical volume. Also called a cluster.

Anonymous FTP A way to use the FTP program to log on to another computer to copy files when you don't have an account on that computer. When you log on, type **anonymous** as the user name and your address as the password. This gives you access to publicly available files. See *File Transfer Protocol (FTP)*.

AppleTalk Local area network architecture built into Macintosh computers to connect them with printers and other devices. A network with a Windows Server 2003 server and Macintosh clients can function as an AppleTalk network with the use of AppleTalk network integration (formerly Services for Macintosh).

Associate To connect files having a particular extension to a specific program. When you double-click a file with the extension, the associated program is launched and the file you clicked is opened. In the Windows operating system, associated file extensions are usually called registered file types.

Asynchronous Transfer Mode (ATM) A network technology based on sending data in cells or packets of a fixed size. It is asynchronous in that the transmission of cells containing information from a particular user isn't necessarily periodic.

Attribute A characteristic. In Windows file management, it is information that shows whether a file is read-only, hidden, compressed, encrypted, ready to be backed up (archived), or should be indexed.

Audit policy Defines the type of security events to be logged. It can be defined on a server or an individual computer.

Authentication Verification of the identity of a user or computer process. In Windows Server 2003, Windows 2000, and Windows NT, authentication involves comparing the user's security identifier (SID) and password to a list of authorized users on a domain.

B

Bandwidth On a network, the transmission capacity of a communications channel stated in megabits per second (Mbps). For example, Ethernet has a bandwidth of 10 Mbps. Fast Ethernet has a bandwidth of 100 Mbps.

Binding A software connection between a network card and a network transport protocol (such as TCP/IP).

BOOTP Boot Protocol. Used on TCP/IP networks to enable a diskless workstation to learn its own IP address, the location of a BOOTP server on the network, and the location of a file to be loaded into memory to boot the machine. This allows a computer to boot without a hard disk or a floppy disk.

Bottleneck A condition in which one resource is preventing another resource from functioning at its best. For example, when one application monopolizes the system processor to the exclusion of all other operations, there is a bottleneck at the processor.

Broadband A type of data communications channel in which the medium (such as a wire or fiber-optic cable) carries multiple messages at a time.

Broadcasting To simultaneously send a message to everyone on a network. See *multicasting*.

Browser service The service that maintains a current list of computers and provides the list to applications when needed. When a user attempts to connect to a resource in the domain, the Browser service is contacted to provide a list of available resources.

C

Certificate A credential used to prove the origin, authenticity, and purpose of a public key to the entity that holds the corresponding private key.

Certificate authority (CA) The service that accepts and fulfills certificate requests and revocation requests and that can also manage the policy-directed registration process a user completes to get a certificate.

Certificate revocation list (CRL) A digitally signed list (published by a certificate authority) of certificates that are no longer valid.

Child domain Domains located directly beneath another domain name (parent domain). For example, *engineering.scribes.com* is a child domain of *scribes.com*, the parent domain. Also called a subdomain.

Child object An object based on another object or inside another object. For example, a file is a child object inside a folder, which is the parent object.

Counter A component within an object that represents data for a specific aspect of the system or service.

Counter log A recorder of data at predefined intervals.

D

Directory service A means of storing directory data and making it available to network users and administrators. For example, Active Directory stores information about user accounts, such as names, passwords, and phone numbers, and enables other authorized users on the same network to access this information.

Disk quota A limitation, set by an administrator, on the amount of disk space available to a user.

Distinguished name (DN) In the context of Active Directory, "distinguished" means the qualities that make the name distinct. The distinguished name identifies the domain that holds the object, as well as the complete path through the container hierarchy used to locate the object.

Distributed file system (DFS) A file management system in which files can be located on separate computers but are presented to users as a single directory tree.

DNS name servers Servers that contain information about part of the Domain Name System (DNS) database. These servers make computer names available to queries for name resolution across the Internet. Also called domain name servers.

Domain A group of computers that share a security policy and a user account database.

Domain controller A server in a domain that accepts account logons and initiates their authentication. In an Active Directory domain, a domain controller controls access to network resources and participates in replication.

Domain local group A local group used on ACLs only in its own domain. A domain local group can contain users and global groups from any domain in the forest, universal groups, and other domain local groups in its own domain.

Domain name In Active Directory, the name given to a collection of networked computers that share a common directory. On the Internet, the unique text name that identifies a specific host. A machine can have more than one domain name, but a given domain name points to only one machine. Domain names are resolved to IP addresses by DNS name servers.

Domain Name System (DNS) A service on TCP/IP networks (the Internet included) that translates domain names into IP addresses. This allows users to employ friendly names like Finance-Server or Ourbusiness.com when querying a remote system, instead of using an IP address such as 198.45.233.59.

Dynamic Data Exchange (DDE) Communication between processes implemented in the Windows family of operating systems. When programs that support DDE are running at the same time, they can exchange data by means of conversations. Conversations are two-way connections between two applications that transmit data alternately.

Dynamic Host Configuration Protocol (DHCP) A TCP/IP protocol used to automatically assign IP addresses and configure TCP/IP for network clients.

Dynamic-link library (DLL) A program module that contains executable code and data that can be used by various programs. A program uses the DLL only when the program is active, and the DLL is unloaded when the program closes.

E

Environment variable A string of environment information, such as a drive, path, or filename, associated with a symbolic name. The System option in

Control Panel or the Set command from the command prompt can be used to define environment variables.

Ethernet   A local area network protocol. Ethernet supports data transfer rates of 10 Mbps and uses a bus topology and thick or thin coaxial, fiber-optic, or twisted-pair cabling. A newer version of Ethernet called Fast Ethernet supports data transfer rates of 100 Mbps, and an even newer version, Gigabit Ethernet, supports data transfer rates of 1000 Mbps.

Extended partition   A nonbootable portion of a hard disk that can be subdivided into logical drives. There can be only a single extended partition per hard disk.

Extensible Authentication Protocol (EAP)   An extension to the Point-to-Point Protocol (PPP) that allows the use of arbitrary authentication methods for validating a PPP connection.

Extensible Markup Language (XML)   A text format derived from the Standard General Markup Language (SGML). It allows the flexible development of user-defined document types and provides a non-proprietary, persistent, and verifiable file format for the storage and transmission of text and data both on and off the Web.

F

Failover   An operation that automatically switches to a standby database, server, or network when the primary system fails or is temporarily shut down for servicing. In server clusters, the process of taking resources off one node in a prescribed order and restoring them on another node.

Fault tolerance   The ability of a system to ensure data integrity when an unexpected hardware or software failure occurs. Many fault-tolerant computer systems mirror all operations—that is, all operations are done on two or more duplicate systems, so if one fails the other can take over.

File Transfer Protocol (FTP)   A method of transferring one or more files from one computer to another over a network or telephone line. Because FTP has been implemented on a variety of systems, it's a simple way to transfer information between usually incongruent systems such as a PC and a minicomputer.

Firewall   A protective filter for messages and logons. An organization connected directly to the Internet uses a firewall to prevent unauthorized access to its network. See *proxy server*.

Folder redirection   An option in Group Policy to place users' special folders, such as My Documents, on a network server.

Fully qualified domain name (FQDN)   A domain name that includes the names of all network domains leading back to the root to clearly indicate a location in the domain namespace tree. Examples of an FQDN are sbssrv.example.local or sales.europe.microsoft.com

G

Global group   A group that can be used in its own domain and in trusting domains. However, it can contain user accounts and other global groups only from its own domain.

Globally unique identifier (GUID)   Part of the identifying mechanism generated by Active Directory for each object in the directory. If a user or computer object is renamed or moved to a different name, the security identifier (SID), relative distinguished name (RDN), and distinguished name (DN) will change, but the GUID will remain the same.

Group Policy   Setting of rules for computers and users. Group Policy stores policies for file deployment, application deployment, logon/logoff scripts, startup/shutdown scripts, domain security, Internet Protocol security (IPSec), and so on.

Group Policy Object (GPO)   A collection of policies stored in two locations: a Group Policy container (GPC) and a Group Policy template (GPT). The GPC is an Active Directory object that stores version information, status information, and other policy information (for example, application objects). The GPT is used for file-based data and stores software policy, script, and deployment information. The GPT is located in the system volume folder of the domain controller.

H

Host   Any device on the network that uses TCP/IP. A host is also a computer on the Internet you might be able to log on to. You can use FTP to get files from a host computer and use other protocols (such as Telnet) to make use of the host computer.

Hosts file   A local ASCII text file that maps host names to IP addresses. Each line represents one host, starting with the IP address, one or more spaces, and then the host's name.

Hypertext   A system of writing and displaying text that enables the text to be linked in multiple ways, available at several levels of detail. Hypertext documents can also contain links to related documents, such as those referred to in footnotes.

Hypertext Markup Language (HTML)   A system used for writing pages for the World Wide Web. HTML allows text to include codes that define fonts, layout, embedded graphics, and hypertext links.

Hypertext Transfer Protocol (HTTP)   The method by which Web pages are transferred over a network.

I

Integrated Services Digital Network (ISDN)   An international communications standard for sending voice, video, and data over regular or digital telephone wires. ISDN supports data transfer rates of 64 Kbps (64,000 bits per second).

Internet Authentication Service (IAS)   The Microsoft implementation of Remote Authentication Dial-In User Service (RADIUS), an authentication and accounting system used by many Internet Service Providers (ISPs). When a user connects to an ISP using a user name and password, the information is passed to a RADIUS server, which checks that the information is correct, and then authorizes access to the ISP system.

Internet Control Message Protocol (ICMP) A protocol used to report problems encountered with the delivery of data, such as unreachable hosts or unavailable ports. ICMP is also used to send a request packet to determine whether a host is available. The receiving host sends back a packet if it is available and functioning. See *ping*.

Internet Protocol (IP) The inter-network layer protocol used as a basis of the Internet. IP enables information to be routed from one network to another in packets and then reassembled when they reach their destination.

Internet Protocol security (IPSec) An Internet Engineering Task Force (IETF) standard for creating Virtual Private Networks (VPNs).

IP number or IP address In IPv4, a four-part number separated by periods (for example, 165.113.245.2) that uniquely identifies a machine on the Internet. Every machine on the Internet has a unique IP number.

K

Kerberos An identity-based security system that authenticates users at logon. It works by assigning a unique key, called a ticket, to each user who logs on to the network. The ticket is then embedded in messages to identify the sender of the message. The Kerberos security protocol is the primary authentication mechanism in Windows Server 2003 and Windows 2000 Server.

L

Layer 2 Tunneling Protocol (L2TP) An extension to the PPP (Point-to-Point Protocol) allowing ISPs to operate Virtual Private Networks (VPNs).

Lightweight Directory Access Protocol (LDAP) A protocol used to access a directory service. LDAP is a simplified version of the Directory Access Protocol (DAP), which is used to gain access to X.500 directories. LDAP is the primary access protocol for Active Directory.

LISTSERV A family of programs that manage Internet mailing lists by distributing messages posted to the list, and adding and deleting members automatically.

Lmhosts An ASCII text file like Hosts but used to associate IP addresses to host names inside a network.

Local area network (LAN) A group of connected computers, usually located close to one another (such as in the same building or the same floor of the building) so that data can be passed among them.

Log A record of transactions or activities on a computer. See also *counter log, trace log*.

Log on The act of entering into a computer system; for example, "Log on to the network and read your e-mail."

Logon The account name used to gain access to a computer system. Unlike a password, the logon name isn't a secret.

Logon or logoff script Typically a batch file set to run when a user logs on or logs off a system. A logon script is used to configure a user's initial environment. A logoff script is used to return a system to some predetermined condition. Either script can be assigned to multiple users individually or through Group Policy.

M

Master boot record (MBR)   The first sector on a hard disk where the computer gets its startup information. The MBR contains the partition table for the computer and a small program called the master boot code.

Media access control (MAC) address   A unique 48-bit number assigned to network interface cards by the manufacturer. MAC addresses are used for mapping in TCP/IP network communication.

Media pool   A logical collection of removable media sharing the same management policies.

Member server   A server that is part of a domain but is *not* a domain controller. Member servers can be dedicated to managing files or printer services or other functions. A member server doesn't verify logons or maintain a security database.

Mirror   1. Two partitions on two hard disks configured so that each will contain identical data to the other. If one disk fails, the other contains the data, and processing can continue. 2. Web site that is a replica of an already existing site, used to reduce network traffic or improve the availability of the original site.

Mount   To make a physical disk or tape accessible to a computer's file system.

Multicasting   Simultaneously sending a message to more than one destination on a network. Multicasting is distinguished from broadcasting in that multicasting sends to only selected recipients.

Multilink dialing   Combining two or more physical communication links into a single logical link to increase available bandwidth.

Multithreading   The simultaneous processing of several threads inside the same program. Because several threads can be processed in parallel, one thread doesn't have to finish before another one can start. See *thread*.

N

Name resolution   The process of mapping a name to its corresponding address.

Namespace   A name or group of names defined according to a naming convention; any bounded area in which a given name can be resolved. Active Directory is primarily a namespace, as is any directory service. The Internet uses a hierarchical namespace that partitions names into categories known as top-level domains, such as .com, .edu, and .gov.

NetBIOS Enhanced User Interface (NetBEUI)   A small and fast protocol that requires little memory but can be routed only by using token ring routing. Remote locations linked by routers can't use NetBEUI to communicate.

Net Logon service A service that accepts logon requests from any client and provides authentication from the Security Accounts Manager (SAM) database of accounts.

Network Two or more computers connected for the purpose of sharing resources.

Network Access Server (NAS) A server that accepts Point-to-Point Protocol connections and places them on the network served by NAS.

Network Address Translation (NAT) Enables a local-area network (LAN) to use one set of IP addresses for internal traffic and a second set of addresses for external traffic.

Network News Transfer Protocol (NNTP) A protocol defined for distribution, inquiry, retrieval, and posting of news articles on the Internet.

Newsgroup On the Internet, a distributed bulletin board system about a particular topic. USENET News (also known as Netnews) is a system that distributes thousands of newsgroups to all parts of the Internet.

Node A location in a tree structure with links to one or more items below it. On a LAN, a device that can communicate with other devices on the network. In clustering, a computer that is a member of a cluster.

NTFS file system The native file system for Windows Server 2003, Windows 2000, and Windows NT. Supports long filenames, a variety of permissions for sharing files, and a transaction log that allows the completion of any incomplete file-related tasks if the operating system is interrupted.

O

Object A particular set of attributes that represents something concrete, such as a user, a printer, or an application. The attributes hold data describing the thing that is identified by the object. Attributes of a user might include the user's given name, surname, and e-mail address. The classification of the object defines which types of attributes are used. For example, the objects classified as users might allow the use of attribute types like common name, telephone number, and e-mail address, whereas the object class of organization allows for attribute types like organization name and business category. An attribute can take one or more values, depending on its type.

Object identifier (OID) A globally unique identifier (GUID), which is assigned by the Directory System Agent (DSA) when the object is created. The GUID is stored in an attribute, the object GUID, which is part of every object. The object GUID attribute can't be modified or deleted. When storing a reference to an Active Directory object in an external store (for example, a database), you should use the object GUID because, unlike a name, it won't change.

Organizational unit (OU) A container object in Active Directory used to separate computers, users, and other resources into logical units. An organizational unit is the smallest entity to which Group Policy can be linked. It is also the smallest scope to which administration authority can be delegated.

P

Packet   The basic unit of information sent over a network. Each packet contains the destination address, the sender's address, error-control information, and data. The size and format of a packet depend on the protocol being used.

Page   A document, or collection of information, available over the World Wide Web. A page can contain text, graphics, video, and sound files. Also, a portion of memory that the virtual memory manager can swap to and from a hard disk.

Paging   A virtual memory operation in which pages are transferred from memory to disk when memory becomes full. When a thread accesses a page that's not in memory, a page fault occurs and the memory manager uses page tables to find the page on disk and then loads the page into memory.

Partition   A portion of a memory device that behaves as if it were a physically separate unit.

Ping   A network management utility that checks to see whether another computer is available and functioning. It sends a short message to which the other computer automatically responds. If the other computer doesn't respond to the ping, you usually can't establish communications.

Point of presence (POP)   A physical site in a geographic area where a network access provider, such as a telecommunications company, has equipment to which users connect. The local telephone company's central office in a particular area is also sometimes referred to as their POP for that area.

Point-to-Point Tunneling Protocol (PPTP)   A protocol that provides router-to-router and host-to-network connections over a telephone line (or a network link that acts like a telephone line). See *Serial Line Internet Protocol (SLIP)*.

Post Office Protocol (POP)   A protocol by which a mail server on the Internet lets you access your e-mail and download it to a PC or Macintosh. Most people refer to this protocol with its version number (POP2, POP3, and so on) to avoid confusing it with points of presence (POPs).

Primary partition   A portion of the hard disk that's been marked as a potentially bootable logical drive by an operating system. MS-DOS can support only a single primary partition. Master boot record disks can support four primary partitions. Computers with the Intel Itanium processor use a GUID partition table that supports up to 128 primary partitions.

Profile   Loaded by the system when a user logs on, the profile defines a user's environment, including network settings, printer connections, desktop settings, and program items.

Protected Extensible Authentication Protocol (PEAP)   A protocol developed jointly by Microsoft, RSA Security, and Cisco for transmitting authentication data, including passwords, over 802.11 wireless networks.

Protocol   A set of rules for transferring data between two devices.

Proxy server   A server that receives Web requests from clients, retrieves Web pages, and forwards them to clients. Proxy servers can dramatically improve performance for groups of users by caching retrieved pages. Proxy servers also provide security by shielding the IP addresses of internal clients.

Public-key cryptography   A method of secure transmission in which two different keys are used—a public key for encrypting data and a private key for decrypting data.

Q

Quality of Service (QoS)   A set of standards for assuring the quality of data transmission on a network.

R

Redundant array of independent disks (RAID)   A range of disk management and striping techniques to implement fault tolerance.

Relative distinguished name (RDN) Active Directory uses the concept of a relative distinguished name (RDN), which is the part of the distinguished name that is an attribute of the object itself.

Relative identifier (RID)   The part of the security identifier (SID) that is unique to each object.

Remote Access Service (RAS)   Allows users to connect from remote locations and access their networks for file and printer sharing and e-mail. The computer initiating the connection is the RAS client; the answering computer is the RAS host.

Remote Authentication Dial-In User Service (RADIUS)   A security authentication system used by many Internet service providers (ISPs). A user connects to the ISP and enters a user name and password. This information is verified by a RADIUS server, which then authorizes access to the ISP system.

Remote Installation Services (RIS) Allows clients to boot from a network server and use special preboot diagnostic tools installed on the server, or to automatically install client software.

Replication   On network computers, enables the contents of a directory, designated as an export directory, to be copied to other directories, called import directories.

Requests for comments (RFCs)   An evolving collection of material that details the functions within the TCP/IP family of protocols. Some RFCs are official documents of the Internet Engineering Task Force (IETF), defining the standards of TCP/IP and the Internet, whereas others are simply proposals trying to become standards, and others fall somewhere in between. Some are tutorial in nature, whereas others are quite technical.

Router   A special-purpose device, computer, or software package that handles the connection between two or more networks. Routers look at the destination addresses of the packets passing through them and decide which route to use to send them.

S

Scope   In DHCP, the range of IP addresses available to be leased to DHCP clients by the DHCP service. In groups, scope describes where in the network permissions can be assigned to the group.

Security Accounts Manager (SAM)
Manager of user account information including group membership. A service used at logon.

Security Identifier (SID)   A unique number assigned to every computer, group, and user account on a Windows Server 2003, Windows 2000, or Windows NT network. Internal processes in the operating system refer to an account's SID, rather than to a name. A deleted SID is never reused.

Serial Line Internet Protocol (SLIP)   A protocol used to run IP over serial lines or telephone lines using modems. Rapidly being replaced by Point-to-Point Tunneling Protocol (PPTP). SLIP is part of Windows remote access for compatibility with other remote access software.

Server   A computer that provides a service to other computers on a network. A file server, for example, provides files to client machines.

Shadow copies   Point-in-time copies of files on network shares. With shadow copies of shared folders,

you can view the contents of network folders as they existed at specific times in the past.

Simple Mail Transport Protocol (SMTP)
A TCP/IP protocol for sending e-mail messages between servers.

Simple Object Access Protocol (SOAP)
An XML/HTTP–based protocol that provides a way for applications to communicate with each other over the Internet, independent of platform.

Smart card   A credit card–sized device that securely stores user credentials and other personal information such as passwords, certificates, and public and private keys.

Socket   An end point to a connection. Two sockets form a complete path for a bidirectional pipe for incoming and outgoing data between networked computers. The Windows Sockets API is a networking API for programmers writing for the Windows family of products.

Subnet   The portion of a TCP/IP network in which all devices share a common prefix. For example, all devices with an IP address that starts with 198 are on the same subnet. IP networks are divided using a subnet mask.

Superscope   A collection of scopes grouped into a single administrative whole. Grouping scopes together into a superscope makes it possible to have more than one logical subnet on a physical subnet.

SystemRoot   The path and folder where the Windows system files are located. The variable %SystemRoot% can be used in paths to replace the actual location. To identify the SystemRoot folder on a computer, type **%SystemRoot%** at a command prompt.

T

Telnet The protocol and program used to log on from one Internet site to another. The Telnet protocol/program gets you to the logon prompt of another host.

Terminal A device that allows you to send commands to another computer. At a minimum, this usually means a keyboard, a display screen, and network connectivity. You usually use terminal software in a personal computer—the software pretends to be, or emulates, a physical terminal and allows you to type commands to another computer.

Thread An executable entity that belongs to one (and only one) process. In a multitasking environment, a single program can contain several threads, all running at the same time.

Threshold A configured baseline. When a counter falls above or below the baseline, an action is triggered.

Token ring A type of computer network in which the computers are connected in a ring. A token, which is a special bit pattern, travels around the ring. To communicate to another computer, a computer catches the token and attaches a message to it, and the token continues around the network, dropping off the message at the designated location.

Trace log Record of data monitoring for a specific event, such as page faults.

Transmission Control Protocol/Internet Protocol (TCP/IP) A set of protocols that networks on the Internet use to communicate with one another.

Transport Layer Security (TLS) Protocol assuring privacy and data reliability between client/server applications communicating over the Internet.

Tree A tree in Active Directory is just an extension of the idea of a directory tree. It's a hierarchy of objects and containers that demonstrates how objects are connected, or the path from one object to another. End points on the tree are usually objects.

U

Uniform Resource Locator (URL) The standard way to give the address of any resource that is part of the World Wide Web. For example, *http://www .microsoft.com/info/cpyright.htm*. The most common way to use a URL is to enter it into a Web browser program.

Universal Naming Convention (UNC) A PC format for indicating the location of resources on a network. UNC uses the following format: *ServerName* *ShareName\ResourcePath*. To identify the Ample.txt file in the Sample folder in the Docs share on the server named Example, the UNC would be \\Example \Docs\Sample \Ample.txt.

User account A user's access to a network. Each user account has a unique user name and security ID (SID).

User profiles Information about user accounts. See *profile*.

V

Virtual Private Network (VPN) A network constructed by using public wires to connect nodes. VPNs use encryption and other security mechanisms to make sure only authorized users can access the network and that the data cannot be intercepted.

Voice over Internet Protocol (VoIP) A method for using the Internet as a transmission medium for telephone calls.

W

Well connected Sufficiently fast and reliable for the needs of Active Directory clients and servers. The definition of "sufficiently fast and reliable" for a particular network depends on the work being done on the specific network.

Wide area network (WAN) Any Internet or network that covers an area larger than a single building or campus.

Windows Internet Name Service (WINS) A name resolution service that converts computer names to IP addresses in a routed environment.

Windows Sockets (Winsock) Winsock is a standard way for Windows-based programs to work with TCP/IP. You can use Winsock if you use SLIP to connect to the Internet.

Workstation In Windows NT, a computer running the Windows NT Workstation operating system. In a wider context, used to describe any powerful computer optimized for graphics or computer-aided design (CAD) or any of a number of other functions requiring high performance.

X

X.500 A standard for a directory service established by the International Telecommunications Union (ITU). The same standard is also published by the International Standards Organization/International Electrotechnical Commission (ISO/IEC). The X.500 standard defines the information model used in the directory service. All information in the directory is stored in entries, each of which belongs to at least one object class. The actual information in an entry is determined by attributes that are contained in that entry.

Z

Zone A part of the DNS namespace that consists of a single domain or a domain and subdomains managed as a single, separate entity.

Index

Numerics

D

Z

Charlie Russel and **Sharon Crawford** are coauthors of numerous books on operating systems. Their titles include *Microsoft Windows 2000 Server Administrator's Companion*, *Microsoft Windows Server 2003 Administrator's Companion*, *UNIX and Linux Answers*, and *Upgrading to Windows 98*.

Charlie Russel is an information technology consultant, specializing in combined Windows and UNIX/Linux networks. He's also the coauthor, with Robert Cordingley, of the Oracle DBA Quick Reference series. A Microsoft MVP, Charlie regularly writes about Windows XP Professional for the Microsoft Windows XP Expert Zone (*http://www.microsoft.com/windowsxp /expertzone*) and is the author of many case studies and white papers on Microsoft Services for UNIX.

Sharon Crawford is a veteran, even grizzled, writer of computer books and a Microsoft MVP. In addition to the books with Charlie, Sharon recently co-authored (with Jason Gerend) *Faster Smarter Microsoft Windows 98*. Sharon writes a regular column on using Windows XP at home for the Microsoft Windows XP Expert Zone at *http://www.microsoft.com/windowsxp/expertzone*.

Jason Gerend has coauthored numerous computer books. He conspired with Sharon and Charlie to write *Microsoft Windows 2003 Server Administrator's Companion* and with Sharon to write *Windows 2000 Pro: The Missing Manual*. Jason coauthored (with Sharon) *Faster Smarter Microsoft Windows 98*. A Microsoft MVP and a Microsoft Certified Systems Engineer (MCSE), Jason enjoys mountain climbing, backcountry snowboarding and installing operating systems. He's been fooling around with PCs since the days of MS-DOS 2.0, loved OS/2 2.1 and BeOS, and has been a freelance computer consultant and Webmaster since 1995.

The manuscript for this book was prepared and submitted to Microsoft Press in electronic form. Pages were composed by Microsoft Press using Adobe FrameMaker for Windows, with text in Sabon and display type in ITC Franklin Gothic. Composed pages were delivered to the printer as electronic pre-press files.

Cover designer: Patricia Bradbury

Interior Graphic Designer: James D. Kramer

Principal Compositor: Carl Diltz

Interior Graphic Artist: Joel Panchot

Principal Proofreader: John Hammett

Indexer: Seth Maislin

Microsoft Press Support Information

Every effort has been made to ensure the accuracy of this book. Microsoft Press provides corrections for books through the Microsoft Press Technical Support Web site at *http://www.microsoft.com/learning/support*.

If you have comments, questions, or ideas regarding the book and the CD-ROM, please send them to Microsoft Press via e-mail to:

mspinput@microsoft.com

Or via postal mail to:

Microsoft Press
Attn: Editor, *Microsoft Windows Small Business Server 2003 Administrator's Companion*
One Microsoft Way
Redmond, WA 98052-6399

Please note that product support is not offered through the above address. For more information about Microsoft software support options, connect to *http://www.microsoft.com/support*.

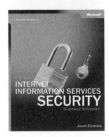

In-depth, daily administration guides
for Microsoft Windows Server 2003

Microsoft® Windows® Server 2003 Administrator's Companion
ISBN 0-7356-1367-2

The in-depth, daily operations guide to planning, deployment, and maintenance. Here's the ideal one-volume guide for the IT professional who administers Windows Server 2003. This ADMINISTRATOR'S COMPANION offers up-to-date information on core system-administration topics for Windows, including Active Directory® services, security, disaster planning and recovery, interoperability with NetWare and UNIX, plus all-new sections about Microsoft Internet Security and Acceleration (ISA) Server and scripting. Featuring easy-to-use procedures and handy workarounds, this book provides ready answers for on-the-job results.

Microsoft Windows Server 2003 Security Administrator's Companion
ISBN 0-7356-1574-8

The in-depth, daily operations guide to enhancing security with the network operating system. With this authoritative ADMINISTRATOR'S COMPANION—written by an expert on the Windows Server 2003 security team—you'll learn how to use the powerful security features in the latest network server operating system. The guide describes best practices and technical details for enhancing security with Windows Server 2003, using the holistic approach that IT professionals need to grasp to help secure their systems. The authors cover concepts such as physical security issues, internal security policies, and public and shared key cryptography, and then drill down into the specifics of key security features of Windows Server 2003.

To learn more about the full line of Microsoft Press® products for IT professionals, please visit:

microsoft.com/mspress/IT

The practical, portable guides to
Microsoft Windows Server 2003

Microsoft® Windows® Server 2003 Admin Pocket Consultant
ISBN 0-7356-1354-0

The practical, portable guide to Windows Server 2003. Here's the practical, pocket-sized reference for IT professionals who support Windows Server 2003. Designed for quick referencing, it covers all the essentials for performing everyday system-administration tasks. Topics covered include managing workstations and servers, using Active Directory® services, creating and administering user and group accounts, managing files and directories, data security and auditing, data back-up and recovery, administration with TCP/IP, WINS, and DNS, and more.

Microsoft IIS 6.0 Administrator's Pocket Consultant
ISBN 0-7356-1560-8

The practical, portable guide to IIS 6.0. Here's the eminently practical, pocket-sized reference for IT and Web professionals who work with Internet Information Services (IIS) 6.0. Designed for quick referencing and compulsively readable, this portable guide covers all the basics needed for everyday tasks. Topics include Web administration fundamentals, Web server administration, essential services administration, and performance, optimization, and maintenance. It's the fast-answers guide that helps users consistently save time and energy as they administer IIS 6.0.

To learn more about the full line of Microsoft Press® products for IT professionals, please visit:

microsoft.com/mspress/IT

Get a **Free**
e-mail newsletter, updates,
special offers, links to related books,
and more when you

register online!

Register your Microsoft Press® title on our Web site and you'll get a FREE subscription to our e-mail newsletter, *Microsoft Press Book Connections.* You'll find out about newly released and upcoming books and learning tools, online events, software downloads, special offers and coupons for Microsoft Press customers, and information about major Microsoft® product releases. You can also read useful additional information about all the titles we publish, such as detailed book descriptions, tables of contents and indexes, sample chapters, links to related books and book series, author biographies, and reviews by other customers.

Registration is easy. Just visit this Web page and fill in your information:

http://www.microsoft.com/mspress/register

Microsoft®

System Requirements

This book is designed to be used with either of the following software editions.

- Windows Small Business Server 2003, Standard Edition
- Windows Small Business Server 2003, Premium Edition

For information on Windows Small Business Server 2003, visit *http://www.microsoft.com/windowsserver2003/sbs/*.

The following are the minimum system requirements to run the companion CD provided with this book:

- Microsoft Windows 98 or higher
- CD-ROM drive
- Internet connection
- Display monitor capable of 800 × 600 resolution or higher
- Microsoft Mouse or compatible pointing device
- Adobe Reader for viewing the eBook (Adobe Reader is available as a download at *http://www.adobe.com.*)